Shared Capitalism at Work

A National Bureau of Economic Research Conference Report

Shared Capitalism at Work
Employee Ownership, Profit and Gain Sharing, and Broad-Based Stock Options

Edited by **Douglas L. Kruse, Richard B. Freeman, and Joseph R. Blasi**

The University of Chicago Press

Chicago and London

Douglas L. Kruse is professor of human resource management and labor studies and employment relations at the Rutgers School of Management and Labor Relations, and a research associate of the National Bureau of Economic Research. Richard B. Freeman holds the Herbert Ascherman Chair in Economics at Harvard University and is a research associate of the National Bureau of Economic Research. Joseph R. Blasi is professor of human resource management and labor studies and employment relations at the Rutgers School of Management and Labor Relations, and a research associate of the National Bureau of Economic Research.

The University of Chicago Press, Chicago 60637
The University of Chicago Press, Ltd., London

Printed in the United States of America

19 18 17 16 15 14 13 12 11 10   1 2 3 4 5
ISBN-13: 978-0-226-05695-1 (cloth)
ISBN-10: 0-226-05695-3 (cloth)

Library of Congress Cataloging-in-Publication Data

Shared capitalism at work : employee ownership, profit and gain sharing, and broad-based stock options / edited by Douglas L. Kruse, Richard B. Freeman, and Joseph R. Blasi.
p. cm.— (National Bureau of Economic Research conference report)
Includes bibliographical references and index.
ISBN-13: 978-0-226-05695-1 (alk. paper)
ISBN-10: 226-05695-3 (alk. paper)
1. Employee ownership—Congresses. 2. Employee stock options—Congresses. 3. Management—Employee participation—Congresses. I. Kruse, Douglas. II. Freeman, Richard B. (Richard Barry), 1943–III. Blasi, Joseph R. IV. Series: National Bureau of Economic Research conference report.
HD5650.S468 2010
338.6'9—dc22

2009034189

♾ The paper used in this publication meets the minimum requirements of the American National Standard for Information Sciences—Permanence of Paper for Printed Library Materials, ANSI Z39.48-1992.

Relation of the Directors to the Work and Publications of the National Bureau of Economic Research

1. The object of the NBER is to ascertain and present to the economics profession, and to the public more generally, important economic facts and their interpretation in a scientific manner without policy recommendations. The Board of Directors is charged with the responsibility of ensuring that the work of the NBER is carried on in strict conformity with this object.

2. The President shall establish an internal review process to ensure that book manuscripts proposed for publication DO NOT contain policy recommendations. This shall apply both to the proceedings of conferences and to manuscripts by a single author or by one or more coauthors but shall not apply to authors of comments at NBER conferences who are not NBER affiliates.

3. No book manuscript reporting research shall be published by the NBER until the President has sent to each member of the Board a notice that a manuscript is recommended for publication and that in the President's opinion it is suitable for publication in accordance with the above principles of the NBER. Such notification will include a table of contents and an abstract or summary of the manuscript's content, a list of contributors if applicable, and a response form for use by Directors who desire a copy of the manuscript for review. Each manuscript shall contain a summary drawing attention to the nature and treatment of the problem studied and the main conclusions reached.

4. No volume shall be published until forty-five days have elapsed from the above notification of intention to publish it. During this period a copy shall be sent to any Director requesting it, and if any Director objects to publication on the grounds that the manuscript contains policy recommendations, the objection will be presented to the author(s) or editor(s). In case of dispute, all members of the Board shall be notified, and the President shall appoint an ad hoc committee of the Board to decide the matter; thirty days additional shall be granted for this purpose.

5. The President shall present annually to the Board a report describing the internal manuscript review process, any objections made by Directors before publication or by anyone after publication, any disputes about such matters, and how they were handled.

6. Publications of the NBER issued for informational purposes concerning the work of the Bureau, or issued to inform the public of the activities at the Bureau, including but not limited to the NBER Digest and Reporter, shall be consistent with the object stated in paragraph 1. They shall contain a specific disclaimer noting that they have not passed through the review procedures required in this resolution. The Executive Committee of the Board is charged with the review of all such publications from time to time.

7. NBER working papers and manuscripts distributed on the Bureau's web site are not deemed to be publications for the purpose of this resolution, but they shall be consistent with the object stated in paragraph 1. Working papers shall contain a specific disclaimer noting that they have not passed through the review procedures required in this resolution. The NBER's web site shall contain a similar disclaimer. The President shall establish an internal review process to ensure that the working papers and the web site do not contain policy recommendations, and shall report annually to the Board on this process and any concerns raised in connection with it.

8. Unless otherwise determined by the Board or exempted by the terms of paragraphs 6 and 7, a copy of this resolution shall be printed in each NBER publication as described in paragraph 2 above.

Contents

Acknowledgments

This book presents the papers from the National Bureau for Economic Research Shared Capitalism Conference on October 6–7th, 2006, sponsored by the Russell Sage Foundation and the Rockefeller Foundation and hosted at the Manhattan offices of Sage. The project received support over an eight-year period from 2000 to 2007 from several foundations.

We would like to thank the following for their assistance: Eric Wanner of the Russell Sage Foundation, and the staff of the Rockefeller Foundation, the primary funders of the project; Katherine McFate of the Ford Foundation who helped develop the project when she was at Rockefeller; the Employee Ownership Foundation; the ESOP Association; the Foundation for Enterprise Development; the National Center for Employee Ownership (NCEO); and the Profit Sharing/401k Council of America, who provided supplemental funding for the General Social Survey (GSS) survey supplement and helped identify a few survey participants.

We especially appreciate the executives and workers of the companies who contributed their time to the survey effort and provided comments at the final conference. They gave us insights into shared capitalism that help frame the analysis and interpretation of the statistics. Because we promised all the firms confidentiality we cannot give the names of the executives and workers but without your assistance we would have never been able to do this study and would surely have misinterpreted some of the statistics.

We also received assistance from Christopher Mackin of Ownership Associates in Cambridge, Massachusetts, who helped us conceive the project, served as coprincipal investigator, worked with a team on surveys, and organized a preparatory conference in Washington, DC; and Andrei Shleifer (Harvard) who spoke at this conference that convinced us to undertake the project; Martin Feldstein, who encouraged the project as part of the

NBER micro analysis of firms. Additionally, we received assistance from Alex Bryson (Policy Studies Institute, London), John Budd (University of Minnesota), Bob Buchele (Smith), Ed Carberry (Rotterdam School of Management), Arin Dube (UC Berkeley), Erika Harden (Rutgers University), Rhokeun Park (Kwangwoon University), Loren Rodgers (NCEO), and Adria Scharf (formerly of the University of Washington), who collaborated on different chapters.

The following academics generously contributed valuable comments at our final conference: John Addison (University of South Carolina), David G. Blanchflower (Dartmouth), Peter Cappelli (Wharton School at Penn), Casey Ichniowski (Columbia), Erik Kaarsemaker (University of York), Michael Handel (Northeastern University), Katherine Klein (Wharton School at Penn), Brigitte C. Madrian (Kennedy School at Harvard), Eric Maskin (Institute for Advanced Study), Canice Prendergast (University of Chicago), and William Rodgers III (Bloustein School at Rutgers). We thank Daniel Kahneman (Princeton), who gave the conference's keynote talk and provided some insights for the paper on risk. We appreciate the work of Harry M. Markowitz, who collaborated on the risk chapter after the conference.

We had considerable assistance from other scholars and colleagues in the actual work: Ron Bernstein (formerly of the Beyster Institute, UCSD), David Binns (formerly of the Beyster Institute, UCSD), Bob Buchele, Ed Carberry, Arin Dube, Nien-he Hsieh (Wharton School at Penn), Chris Mackin, Loren Rodgers (NCEO), and Adria Scharf (formerly at the University of Washington), who helped with survey design and helped carry out some surveys; Jean Roth of NBER, who developed the online survey at a time when there were no commercial products that met our needs; Refen Koh, who masterfully coordinated the scanning of the forty thousand surveys and the preparation of the final data set; Patricia Berhau and Michele Pinheiro, who helped with survey checking; Tom Johnson of Princeton Imaging (www.princetonimaging.com), who scanned the surveys; Tom Smith of the National Opinion Research Center of the University of Chicago, who advised us on the design of the compensation supplement to the GSS in 2002 and 2006 and identified the survey technology for the NBER project; and Carl Beck of NBER, who helped organize the final conference.

We are grateful to Dean Barbara Lee and Dean David Finegold and the entire School of Management and Labor Relations, which hosted the project at Rutgers; J. Robert Beyster and Mary Ann Beyster of the Foundation for Enterprise Development, who supported coauthors Blasi and Kruse as Beyster Faculty Fellows during the revision of the manuscripts; the School of Historical Studies of the Institute for Advanced Study, for supporting Blasi during a sabbatical year in which he worked on the economic history research for the book; and the faculty of the School of Social Science at the Institute; Helena Fitz-Patrick of NBER; David Pervin, who is senior editor at the University of Chicago Press; editorial assistant Ed Scott; the anonymous reviewers, for assistance in developing and publishing this book; and Jennifer Amadeo-Holl of the Labor Studies Research Program of NBER, who played an irreplaceable role in helping us administer the project at every turn and whose efficiency, grace, and good cheer kept us all going.

The completion of the work on this book would simply not have been possible without the support of this great number of institutions and, more important, individuals.

Finally, Kruse thanks his wife Lisa. Freeman thanks Alida Castillo-Freeman for helping with some of the statistical analysis, and Blasi thanks his wife Nancy, his son Teddy, and his parents and sister for their support.

Introduction

Richard B. Freeman, Joseph R. Blasi, and
Douglas L. Kruse

Almost half of American private-sector employees participate in "shared capitalism"—employment relations where the pay or wealth of workers is directly tied to workplace or firm performance. In many of these firms employees also participate in employee involvement committees or workplace teams that help management make decisions regarding the economic activities of the firm. Employees in other countries have similar types of pay and work arrangements but the US is arguably the world leader in shared compensation and decision-making arrangements (Freeman 2008).

This book presents papers from the National Bureau of Economic Research (NBER)'s Shared Capitalism Research Project that investigated the shared capitalist part of the US economy.[1] To determine how shared capitalist arrangements work and how they affect workplace outcomes we developed two new data sets and analyzed some existing data sets. Our main data innovation was a survey of over 40,000 employees in fourteen compa-

Richard B. Freeman holds the Herbert Ascherman Chair in Economics at Harvard University and is a research associate of the National Bureau of Economic Research. Joseph R. Blasi is a professor of human resource management and labor studies and employment relations at the Rutgers School of Management and Labor Relations, and a research associate of the National Bureau of Economic Research. Douglas L. Kruse is a professor of human resource management and labor studies and employment relations at the Rutgers School of Management and Labor Relations, and a research associate of the National Bureau of Economic Research.

1. On the development of shared capitalism in different sectors of the US economy with related research, see Blasi (1987) on ESOPs, Blasi (1988) on employee ownership in privately-held firms, Blasi and Kruse (1991) on employee ownership in publicly traded corporations, Kruse (1993) on profit sharing, and Blasi, Kruse, and Bernstein (2003) on the high technology sector with special emphasis on stock options and the 100 largest firms that created the Internet.

nies and 323 worksites that have a variety of shared capitalism programs. While our sample of companies is small for a quantitative study, it is large for a qualitative case study, and while the firms are a nonrepresentative sample of those engaged in shared capitalist activities, they mirror how shared capitalism is implemented in most mainstream US corporations. About 90 percent of the workers surveyed are in five Fortune 500 multinational companies where the employee stock ownership accounts for a minority stake of the firm's equity, where workers elect no board representatives, and where the employee stock ownership is combined with cash profit sharing, gain sharing, or broad-based stock options. About 10 percent of the workers surveyed are in nine medium sized ESOP (Employee Stock Ownership Plan) firms with under 1,000 workers that are in most cases 100 percent employee-owned but where nonmanagement employees at times have some board representatives but not a majority of any of the boards.

We asked workers about their experiences with their firms' programs and other aspects of their jobs. We also placed questions about shared capitalism on the nationally representative General Social Survey (GSS) in 2002 and 2006.[2] Since standard labor force surveys do not ask workers a comprehensive set of questions about shared capitalist forms of pay, the GSS provides the best available estimates of the extent of shared capitalism among US workers.

Our analyses show that shared capitalism modes of compensation are spread broadly throughout the US economy and that shared capitalism is linked to worker behavior likely to raise productivity and profits, such as reduced turnover and greater willingness to work hard. We also find that shared capitalism is linked to outcomes that benefit workers, such as better pay, job security, and perceived positive relations with the employer. Workers with more intensive shared capitalist programs report that co-workers are more interested in the firm's performance and are more cooperative than workers in firms with less intensive programs.

But while shared capitalism appears beneficial for workers and firms on average, our analyses also show that it is not a magic potion that cures all economic ills. There is considerable variation in its effects across firms. The positive effects are contingent on an array of human resource policies and workplace practices that give workers freedom from close supervision and create good labor-management relations.

Many economists and others are uneasy about shared capitalist arrange-

2. The General Social Survey is conducted by the National Opinion Research Center of the University of Chicago and supported by the National Science Foundation, among other funders. It is widely viewed as one of the most valuable surveys for research purposes in the United States. The Shared Capitalism segment appears in the 2002 and 2006 survey and is being planned for the 2010 survey. All the data are publicly available from the General Social Survey or repository libraries at various universities.

ments. One reason for their concern is the free rider problem that arises whenever someone gains only part of the reward from their activity. Why should an individual give full effort in an N person firm if he or she gains only 1/Nth of the payoff from that effort? It makes rational "prisoners' dilemma" sense to shirk and reap rewards from the effort of others. By the free rider argument, shared capitalism should not succeed in motivating workers to do better. Another reason for concern is that shared capitalism increases economic risk by linking individuals' employment and wealth/income to the performance of their employer. When Enron went belly-up its workers lost not only their jobs but their retirement and other savings held in company shares. Similarly, when United Airlines went bankrupt, the airline pilots and machinists who had received majority ownership were losers in the capital market as well as in the labor market. By inducing workers to invest in their firm, shared capitalism can run counter to the investment precept that one should not put "all the eggs in one basket," though there are ways to limit the risk through diversification of portfolios.

Our analysis offers some answers to these concerns. On the free rider issue, we examine the hypothesis that workers' co-monitoring of fellow employees in shared capitalist firms is an important deterrent to free riding. Using a novel set of questions on workers' ability to observe co-worker activity and their response to shirking, we find that the vast majority of workers have a good idea of what fellow workers are doing (a prerequisite for co-monitoring); that workers paid shared capitalist compensation are more likely than other workers to act against "shirking" by fellow workers; and that worker co-monitoring or anti-shirking behavior is associated with higher worker effort and better workplace performance. Shared capitalist firms seemingly create a cooperative workplace culture that combats the free rider problem inherent in any group incentive pay scheme.

With respect to risk, we found that many workers are highly risk-averse but that even many highly risk-averse workers prefer to receive some of their pay through shared capitalist arrangements. Given plausible risk aversion parameters and the thickness of asset markets, we estimate that by diversifying their portfolios, workers can hold a moderate amount of wealth in their employer without suffering significant losses of utility due to risk. The average amount of share ownership in our data is on the order of the estimated tolerable level of risk, though there are workers who hold too much of their wealth in their firm. Less risky cash profit sharing or stock options can also be combined with reasonable levels of share ownership in order to moderate risk.

The findings in the book show that shared capitalism is an important part of the US economic model. Its magnitude and success merits increased attention from businesses, unions, policymakers, and social scientists, and from economic science more broadly.

What Exactly is Shared Capitalism?

We use the term "shared capitalism" to refer to a diverse set of compensation practices through which worker pay or wealth depends on the performance of the firm or work group.

Employee ownership. The extent of employee ownership varies from workers having complete ownership of the firm to owning a majority stake or a nonnegligible minority stake, usually through a trust or other legal entity that votes the shares as a group. In the US one major form for employee ownership is the Employee Stock Ownership Plan (ESOP), which federal legislation established to allow companies to contribute money to a trust to buy worker shares or to borrow money to fund worker ownership and then repay in installments from company revenues. Under this approach, workers gain an ownership stake without investing their own money to buy the stock. The ESOPs where workers make wage or benefit concessions, while often the subject of major media coverage, actually represent the exception, not the rule, in this sphere. Partnerships are another major form of employee ownership.

Individual employee stock ownership. This refers to situations in which workers buy shares in the firm and vote those shares privately. American workers can purchase stock through their company 401k plan, a retirement plan in which they make pretax contributions from their pay. Sometimes firms match employee contributions to 401k plans with company stock. Workers can also buy shares of their firm on the stock market. Sometimes firms subsidize part of employee purchases of shares outside of retirement plans through Employee Stock Purchase Plans, which typically offer stock at a 10 to 15 percent discount to market. The United Kingdom tax code privileges this form of employee ownership.

Profit sharing pays workers specified shares of profits when the firm makes money. The payments can be cash bonuses on a yearly or more frequent basis or can take the form of placing the workers' share of profits in a retirement plan (called "deferred profit-sharing"). Some firms pay profit-sharing bonuses in company stock, so what is received as a profit share becomes employee ownership. Some profit-sharing plans are formal, laying out a formula linking profits to worker payments (sometimes after a certain threshold is met, and sometimes with an additional discretionary component), and other profit-sharing plans are fully discretionary, in which companies decide at the end of each year how much should be given to workers. In this book we use a broad definition, counting as profit sharing all bonus plans in which the payments depend in some way on company performance.

Gain sharing offers workers payments based on the performance of their work units rather than of the whole enterprise. These systems often measure performance in productivity or cost saving at a particular work site. One group of workers can benefit from their effort even if the firm does poorly or if other groups of workers are not meeting their targets. Nonprofit enterprises, including government agencies, can do gain sharing while they cannot readily engage in profit sharing.

Stock options are a hybrid between profit sharing and employee ownership. A stock option gives the employee the right to buy stock at a set price anytime during a specified period following the granting of the option. The employee gets the upside gain of a rise in the share price without the downside risk of losing part of their investment. Unlike company stock, stock options are not purchased with employee savings unless they are used for wage substitution. High technology companies began granting stock options to a broad base of employees in the 1960s and 1970s (see, for example, Beyster and Economy [2007]). Start-ups without the resources to match the pay packages of large firms found that they could attract young, highly educated workers through granting shares or options. In the 1990s to 2000s some managers abused stock options for themselves by "backdating" the option to a period when shares were lower, which runs counter to the professed intent of options—to give managers incentives to make decisions that increase the long-run value of the firm and thus its share price. When stock prices fell greatly other managers rewrote options at lower stock prices, which encouraged excessive risk-taking as it reduced the loss to management of poor performance.

By "shared capitalism" we do not include all performance-based pay, or all pay at risk. There are a variety of pay systems based on individual performance (e.g., piece rates, commissions), and some forms of pay may simply be risk-sharing tied to external indicators (e.g., stock market indexes). We restrict the term "shared capitalism" to plans that tie worker pay or wealth to the performance of their own workplace, whether at the level of the work group, establishment, or company.

There are substantive differences among these forms of sharing the rewards and risks of business. Employee ownership can in theory give workers the power to make decisions that shareholders have in capital-owned firms. Beginning with Benjamin Ward (1958) and Evsey Domar (1966), economists have modeled how worker-owned enterprises might operate compared with other firms. Those models predict that the employee-owned firm will hire fewer workers and respond differently to changes in prices of output than traditional firms, at least in a short or medium time period. If firms can freely enter an industry, these very unique models predict that worker-owned and capital-owned firms will reach the same equilibrium output and employment. Individual share ownership does not have clear consequences for the way the firm operates since individual workers almost never own enough shares to influence management decisions.

None of the fourteen firms in our study are "worker-owned" in the strict sense of this theoretical literature. None have nonmanagement employees representing a majority of their boards, including those that are 100 percent employee-owned. All of them have hierarchical management teams. Management was chosen by boards with the input of outside investors and financial institutions or advisors, not by the workers themselves. Workers participate in the firm's life mostly at the level of their jobs and departments.[3] Shared capitalism as it has developed in the United States and elsewhere differs greatly from the simple economic models that have made some economists uneasy about the way these businesses operate.

Profit sharing and gain sharing give workers rewards for success without the ownership authority to make management decisions. This difference underlies Martin Weitzman's (1984) model of the share economy, in which profit sharing makes the cost of labor completely flexible and gives firms the incentive to hire as many workers as are willing to take jobs. Heuristically, a firm that pays workers a fixed share of profits views workers as comparable to salespersons paid commissions. Since employing more sales workers should increase total sales, profit-sharing firms should want to hire as many persons as will accept jobs. Sales and profits will rise even as the increased number of sales workers drives down sales per employee and the earnings of workers. Firms will also have the incentive to hang onto workers if the demand for the firm's output goes down, leading to Weitzman's prediction that an economy of profit-sharing firms will have lower levels of unemployment and greater macroeconomic stability.[4]

What unifies ownership, profit sharing, gain sharing, and stock options as "shared capitalism" is that in each case workers' compensation depends on the performance of their firm or work group. It is group incentive pay rather than individual incentive pay. By defining shared capitalism in this way, we exclude another prominent form of worker ownership of capital—pension fund ownership of shares (Drucker 1976).

3. A random sample of ESOP (Employee Stock Ownership Plan) firms that tend to have high concentrations of employee ownership, and from which nearly all majority employee-owned and 100 percent employee-owned firms come, found that the ESOP Trustee (often a bank trustee) votes the shares, not the individual workers. In only 14 percent of the cases do the employee owners instruct the trustee of the Employee Stock Ownership Trust how to vote their shares in board elections (National Center for Employee Ownership [NCEO] 2007, 87). Our interviews with the major national associations of these firms could not elicit one example of an ESOP firm where nonmanagement employees made up a majority of a firm's board of directors. The corporate governance patterns of majority and 100 percent employee-owned firms in the United States appear to have converged with the general pattern: single slates of directors put forward by management that are ratified by shareholders or their "trustees" with virtually no examples of corporate governance insurgency on the part of worker owners. In fact, among publicly-traded firms in the United States it is hard to find more than a few cases where nonmanagement worker owners have even one or two board representatives.

4. Weitzman's predictions have received some support in examinations of firm behavior, but the theory is complex to test at this level (requiring good information on average profit share as a percent of pay, the extent of substitution with fixed pay, the size of the demand shocks faced by firms, and whether a positive demand shock is following a previous negative shock or represents new growth) (Kruse 1993, 1998). The theory would be more appropriately tested by the (unlikely) comparison of an economy of profit-sharing firms to an economy of non-profit-sharing firms.

Shared capitalism is often linked to shared decision making. Employee-owned stock comes with at least limited voting rights, but beyond these legal rights employees are often given increased involvement in different types of workplace decision making. There is a strong logic to this: while shared capitalism provides the *incentive* to improve performance, increased involvement in decision making can provide the *means* to do so. Providing shared capitalism without at least some involvement in decision making may have little or no effect on performance, and may in fact have bad effects if employees see the shared capitalism simply as a device to shift income risk onto them. Likewise, many firms use employee involvement in decisions to help improve a variety of outcomes, but if workers are not financially benefiting from the results of their decisions through some type of shared capitalism then any higher productivity may be difficult to sustain. The empirical overlap and possible complementarities between shared capitalism plans and employee involvement in decision making is a major theme that will be discussed at a number of points in this book.

Why Shared Capitalism is Attractive

Some economists, Alfred Marshall, John Bates Clark, and James Meade, among others, have looked favorably on shared capitalist arrangements. So too have many business leaders and governments.[5] The United States and many other countries give tax incentives to promote worker ownership. The EU directed attention to profit sharing and employee ownership in its 1991 Promotion of Employee Ownership and Profit Sharing report (the "Pepper Report"). It called on member states to promote participation by employed persons in profits and enterprise performance. France requires that some firms pay part of wages in profit shares. What makes shared capitalism attractive to economists, business, labor, and governments is the belief that when workers have a stake in the financial performance of the firm, they will create better outcomes than if the workers were just "paid hands."

The outcome that receives the most attention is *productivity*. Tying workers' pay to workplace performance is expected to induce workers to increase effort, commitment, and willingness to share information, and to decrease turnover and absenteeism, particularly in teamwork settings where cooperation and information sharing among employees is important. The resultant growth of productivity and profits creates the potential for the proverbial "win-win" situation, with workers and the firm sharing the benefits of

5. Fear of communism and unionism led John D. Rockefeller of Standard Oil and other corporate leaders to form a Special Conference Committee that later became The Conference Board, whose agenda included profit sharing and employee stock ownership, though perhaps more to gain the loyalty of workers, than in the belief that these systems would improve company performance. In its early days, Princeton University's Industrial Relations Section studied this phenomenon (see Foerster and Dietel 1927).

the increased production. Most quantitative studies of shared capitalism estimate its impact on productivity by matching information on company stock and profit plans to publicly available measures of performance. They find the expected positive relationship between shared capitalism and performance.[6] But studies show considerable variation in the effects of shared capitalist arrangements on outcomes, with many workplaces having little or no improvement in output or labor productivity. The average effect is positive because shared capitalism is rarely associated with low or declining productivity.

The use of stock options and share ownership in high tech start-ups in Silicon Valley and elsewhere directs attention at the putative impact of shared capitalism on another key aspect of firm performance—its *innovativeness.* Employees whose pay or wealth is tied to the firm's performance are more likely to suggest ideas for innovative products or production technologies, and to help implement these ideas.

In one of the earliest analyses of employee ownership, John Bates Clark argued that, "All the workmen with their employers constitute, collectively, a good entrepreneur" (1886, 183–84), but he was just beginning to review supporting evidence for this claim.[7] Similarly, to the extent that shared capitalism distributes decision making and the rewards from good performance among a larger group of employees than conventional firms, shared capitalist firms could be less prone to the malfeasance in corporate governance that marred corporate America in the 1990s to 2000s. More workers will know how the firm is truly doing and management will have a smaller incentive to cook the books on its behalf since it is sharing ownership with workers as well as with nonemployee shareholders. To the extent that profit sharing helps stabilize employment or that employee ownership gives employees a means to resist job-destroying takeovers or downsizing, it also has the potential to ameliorate fluctuations in employment.

What about the effect of shared capitalism on workers? Many analysts and

6. See reviews in Weitzman and Kruse (1990); Bullock and Tubbs (1990); Kruse (1993); OECD (1995); Doucialiagos (1995); Welbourne and Mejia (1995); Kruse and Blasi (1997); Blasi, Kruse, and Bernstein (2003); Kaarsemaker (2006a, 2006b), and Freeman (2007), plus additional recent studies cited in chapter 4.

7. Taking the opposite side, the first President of the American Economic Association, General Francis Amasa Walker, who later became head of MIT, expected worker shares in performance would increase worker effort, but thought it could possibly fail because of the "lack of an entrepreneur" (1876). Walker was referring to companies that were mainly owned by their workers without professional management and not to established capitalist firms with significant employee ownership, of the type found in the United States today. John Bates Clark saw a role for employee ownership and profit sharing in firms but did not rule out it also having outside investors. Bates was associated with a working group at Johns Hopkins University that began to collect information on employee ownership and profit sharing in various regions of the United States (Adams 1888) and publish it in the journal of the new American Economic Association (see, for example, Bemis [1886].) Soon after, established firms with professional managers, for example, Procter & Gamble in 1887, began to use profit sharing and employee stock ownership more widely.

observers believe that shared capitalism improves employee well-being. It gives workers greater participation on their jobs, is associated with increased skills, and improves labor-management cooperation and job satisfaction. By giving workers across the economic spectrum a share of profits and company stock, moreover, shared capitalism could perhaps play a role in mitigating the rising inequality in income and wealth that has characterized the United States since the 1970s and 1980s. The reason is that capital income has risen more than wages, with labor's share of national income falling in the 2000s, so that those with a share of business profits or appreciation in the value of equities or real estate have done better than wage earners.[8] If the boards of directors of companies with some employee ownership see a business purpose for sharing profits and ownership more widely, employee ownership may also help control runaway CEO pay.

Finally, many advocates of shared capitalism view it as a logical extension of political democracy. Albert Gallatin, Jefferson's Secretary of Treasury and one of the signers of the Declaration of Independence, promoted profit sharing for that reason.[9] Investment banker and political economist Louis Kelso contributed one of the earliest analyses along these lines (Kelso and Adler 1958) and developed the ESOP with Senator Russell J. Long. The National Center for Employee Ownership broadened this analysis to focus on the implications of a variety of equity plans for company objectives and performance (see Rosen, Case, and Staubus [2005]). Senator Russell J. Long favored incentives for ESOPs in federal law to broaden the wealth distribution and to give more Americans direct stakes in the economic system. Political scientists argue that democratic workplace structures produce skills that workers can carry to social and political activities outside the workplace.[10]

But there are potential weaknesses to shared capitalist arrangements. The skills needed to manage a firm with significant employee ownership and profit sharing are likely to differ from the skills needed to manage a standard firm, which may limit the ability of those enterprises to recruit top managers,

8. The overall return to capital, reflecting profits and company stock values, has risen since the 1970s while inflation-adjusted wages for middle- and low-income workers have stagnated (Mishel, Bernstein, and Allegretto 2007, 81, 85, 119, 121).

9. Gallatin wrote that the "democratic principle upon which this Nation was founded should not be restricted to the political processes but should be applied to the industrial operation" (quoted in US Senate 1939, 72).

10. Pateman (1970); Mason (1982); and Dahl (1985). See Dow (2003, 23–44) for a review and discussion of these and other perspectives. Three states have centers that work with mostly local groups of companies with meaningful employee ownership, such as the Ohio Employee Ownership Center (see Logue 2002), the Beyster Institute at the University of California at San Diego, and the Vermont Employee Ownership Center. Several nonprofit think tanks have continued to develop political economic analyses and agendas on shared capitalism among them, the Kelso Institute, directed by Patricia H. Kelso; the Carey Center for Democratic Capitalism, organized by Ray Carey (2004); and the Center for Economic and Social Justice, founded by Norman Kurland (2004). A small US Federation for Worker Coops also exists.

although this issue has not been studied. Firms that choose shared capitalist structures to gain the tax breaks associated with forms such as ESOPs may fail to get the economic gains that accrue to firms that introduced them for business reasons. Some on the left have criticized shared capitalism as simply a management trick to speed up work and effort or transfer more risk to workers.

A balanced assessment of shared capitalism must take account of its drawbacks as well as its virtues. For example, while it could expand capital income for the middle class, how would the issue of risk be addressed? To be helpful to participants, moreover, any analysis should also consider possible ways to limit the drawbacks and strengthen the virtues.

The NBER Project

At the heart of this book are the two new surveys of workers referenced earlier. These surveys are fully described at the end of this introduction, but here we give a brief overview. The NBER company survey administered 80 to 100 questions to workers in fourteen firms and 323 work sites who had some shared capitalism modes of compensation.[11] All of the firms have some sort of broad-based employee ownership plan, but the plan types vary: eight have standard ESOPs, one has a 401(k) ESOP, four have Employee Stock Purchase Plans (ESPPs), and three have 401(k)'s with company stock. Eleven of the firms have broad-based profit-sharing plans, while five have broad-based stock option plans. One has a 401(k) plan that prohibits investments in company stock as too risky, using options and profit sharing instead. Our survey garnered 41,206 employee responses, which makes this the largest single data set on workers in shared capitalist firms. Most of the workers (31,994) were based in the United States. The other countries are represented because three US multinationals participated in the study and encouraged their workers around the world to take the survey. In many of these countries, the workers have access to shared capitalism comparable to that of the US workers. The companies vary in industry group and size. Eight are manufacturers, seven with a workforce ranging from 250 to 5,000, and one large multinational manufacturer with approximately 40,000 to 75,000 employees.[12] There are two high technology firms, one with a workforce on the order of 25,000 to 50,000 and one with a workforce of close to 1,000 employees. There is one large national financial services firm with a workforce of 10,000 to 20,000. There are three service firms with workforces of approximately 500, 2,000, and 11,000 employees. Three of the firms are in the Fortune 500.

11. We included special questions of concern to each participating company and provided them analysis of those questions gratis.

12. We give ranges so as not to risk someone identifying the firms.

Initially, we sought to survey paired comparison competitor companies for each company in our data set, but we found that this was a fruitless endeavor. Many firms similar to those in our sample have some shared capitalist compensation programs as well—profit sharing instead of employee ownership or gain sharing instead of profit sharing. Managers in firms that had no programs did not find attractive the idea of being controls for a competitor. In any case, the shared capitalist arrangements differed enough among our fourteen firms and among workers and establishments within those firms to allow us to analyze the effects of these modes of compensation and other management labor practices on outcomes.

The principle drawback of the NBER firm survey is that it is a self-selected nonrandom sample of US establishments. To the extent that our questions relate to issues that face all firms and reflect basic human nature, there are reasons to expect any findings to generalize to a broader population. The empirical study of management and firm behavior and much of psychology is replete with in-depth and useful analysis of nonrandom samples, often of just a single firm or person. Still, we sought a way to address the selectivity problem. Our solution was to apply to the board of the General Social Survey at the National Opinion Research Center at the University of Chicago in order to place a special module on shared capitalism on the nationally representative General Social Survey (GSS) in 2002 and 2006, with a sample of 1,145 employees in for-profit companies in 2002, and 1,081 employees in 2006. We placed questions on the GSS about the incidence of shared capitalism and replicated several key questions from the NBER company survey, such as whether workers observed how fellow employees performed and how they reacted to someone not working as hard as they should. Thus, the GSS provides a validation check on some results in the company survey. It also provides information on the "control" group of workers without shared capitalist arrangements that we could not obtain from our firm surveys.

The Main Findings

As an introduction to what the reader will find in the remaining chapters of this book, in the following we summarize the main findings in the form of six cross cutting "take away messages." Exhibit 1 lists each of the messages and gives some related information on the underlying findings. To see how the researchers obtained the findings and to assess the strengths and weaknesses of the analyses that developed them, we direct the reader to the chapters themselves.

1. Shared Capitalism is a Significant Part of the US Economic Model

For many years most economists viewed shared capitalism as a niche part of the capitalist system. Worker-owned firms, firms with significant minority

Exhibit 1	Six "take-away" findings on shared capitalism

1. Shared capitalism is a significant part of the US economic model.
   Almost half of workers have some form of shared capitalist pay.
   It has grown rapidly in the 1980s–2000s.
   Shared capitalism is also significant in the United Kingdom and is growing in other advanced countries.
   Shared capitalism can increase wealth for workers at lower and middle income levels.
2. Worker co-monitoring helps shared capitalist firms overcome incentives to free ride.
   Most workers can observe work activity of co-workers.
   Many take action against shirkers.
   Shared capitalist compensation increases the likelihood of acting against shirkers.
   Combining shared compensation and advanced personnel and labor policies has an even larger effect on worker efforts to discourage shirking.
3. The risk of shared capitalist investments in one's employer is manageable.
   Portfolio theory suggests employee ownership can be part of an efficient portfolio as long as the overall portfolio is properly diversified.
   Some workers have invested excessively in shares of their own firm, contrary to the precepts of diversification, but most workers have modest amounts of employee ownership within the ranges suggested by portfolio theory.
   Less risky forms of shared capitalism such as cash profit sharing and stock options where workers are paid market wages, or company stock is not financed by worker savings, can be prudently combined with riskier forms where workers purchase stock.
4. Shared capitalism improves the performance of firms.
   It is associated with greater attachment, loyalty, and willingness to work hard; lower chances of turnover; worker reports that co-workers work hard and are involved in company issues; and worker suggestions for innovations.
   Shared capitalism is most effective when combined with employee involvement and decision-making and with other advanced personnel and labor policies.
5. Shared capitalism improves worker well-being.
   It is associated with greater participation in decision-making; higher pay, benefits, and wealth; greater job security, satisfaction with influence at the workplace, trust in the firm, and assessment of management; and better labor management relations practices.
   Shared capitalism is most effective when combined with employee involvement and decision-making and with other advanced personnel and labor policies.
6. Shared capitalism complements other labor policies and practices.
   Firms with shared capitalist compensation are more likely to have other worker-friendly labor policies and practices
   Combinations of shared capitalist pay and other policies, such as devolving decision-making to employees, wages at or above the market rate, and lower supervisory monitoring, produce the largest benefits for workers and firms.

employee ownership stakes, or profit sharing might attract the interest of a small band of aficionados but most of the profession viewed the topic as too narrow and small to be worth broad scholarly attention. Many expressed suspicion about the seeming positive effects of shared capitalism on economic performance. One comment we often received was, "If this stuff is as good as some of the research indicates how come all firms don't choose employee ownership/profit sharing or grant stock options to all workers?"

Another line of critical commentary argued that shared capitalism missed the boat because what really matters in most businesses is top management: "If you want to know why firms succeed, study the superstar CEOs, not regular employees. The CEOs are paid huge sums because they are the key to enterprise performance."[13]

The evidence on the extent and impacts of shared capitalist arrangements presented in this volume refutes such dismissive views. As noted in the opening paragraph, almost half of US employees participate in some form of shared capitalism. The 2006 GSS estimates that 47 percent of workers are covered by at least one such form, with 38 percent having profit sharing, 27 percent having gain sharing, 18 percent owning their company's stock, 9 percent holding company stock options, and 5 percent receiving company stock options in any year. Based on these figures, shared capitalism covered 53.4 million American workers.

There is also a substantial amount of overlap among shared capitalism plans. Over three-fourths of workers who own company stock also have profit sharing or stock options, and workers with profit sharing often have other programs as well. These patterns suggest that some firms combine the longer-term incentives associated with employee stock ownership or deferred profit sharing in retirement accounts with shorter-term incentives of cash profit or gain sharing bonuses and stock options, presumably to maximize worker commitment and effort over different time horizons and also to combine more and less risky shared capitalist practices.

The data also show that shared capitalist arrangements cover much of the economy, though they are more prevalent in some sectors than others. For example, employee ownership ranges from 10 percent of employees in noncomputer services to 43 percent of employees in computer services. However, contrary to some notions that it is more adaptive to service companies, employee ownership and stock options have a moderately high incidence in manufacturing. It is more common in larger establishments, in jobs where it is easier to see how other workers perform, and in jobs with teamwork, low levels of supervision, employee involvement, employer-sponsored training, and job security. Union members are less likely than nonunion members to be part of profit-sharing and gain-sharing plans, but are more likely to hold company stock and stock options (Kruse, Blasi, and Park, chapter 1).

Shared capitalism was not always such a large part of the US economic system. In 1886 John Bates Clark wrote that the test of the economic efficacy of what was then called cooperation was how the firms grew relative to other types of enterprises. For decades, shared capitalist modes of compensation

13. Identifying superstar business leaders is difficult and finding out what they do and whether the huge amounts they make reflect their marginal product is even more difficult. One effort to identify the stars on the basis of business awards and to examine their activities finds that after the CEO gets fame as a superstar, performance falls and shareholders lose. See Malmendier and Tate (2008).

and work as a whole did not expand their share of the market, justifying the dismissal of these institutions as interesting but unimportant aberrations. However, important exceptions appeared throughout American history: Pillsbury dominated flour production in the 1800s with a very public emphasis on profit sharing and Procter & Gamble dominated soap and related cleaning products in the late 1800s and 1900s with a very public emphasis on profit sharing and later employee ownership (on Pillsbury, see Blasi and Kruse [2008]). But from the 1970s to the present, shared capitalist modes of compensation have grown rapidly. Data from diverse administrative sources shows that shared capitalism increased its reach in the economy in the latter part of the twentieth century (Dube and Freeman, chapter 5, figure 5.1). While some of this growth—of ESOPs, in particular[14]—depends on tax advantages given to that form, firms introduced other modes of shared capitalism without any such support. Shared capitalism has also increased its importance in the United Kingdom (Bryson and Freeman, chapter 6) and in many other advanced countries, though it seems most successful at spreading in the United States. Shared capitalism has met Clark's market test.

2. Worker Co-Monitoring Helps Overcome Free Riding

The notion that workers will co-monitor themselves when their pay depends on the performance of the work group and act to reduce free riding behavior has long been in the air in discussion of employee ownership and profit sharing.[15] If worker A's pay depends on how worker B performs, then A might be expected to intervene when B is not working up to speed. What was missing was evidence that co-monitoring is extensive and that it helps overcome free-riding and in so doing contributes to the performance of shared capitalist enterprises.

The co-monitoring modules in the NBER fourteen firm survey and in the GSS survey fill some of this lacuna in knowledge (Freeman, Kruse, and Blasi, chapter 2). Asked how well they could observe what co-workers were doing at their workplace, most workers reported that they had good knowledge of how co-workers performed. About two-thirds rated observability above seven on a scale from zero to ten. Asked what they would do if they saw a fellow employee not working up to speed, about one-third of workers

14. Between 1975 and 2005 the number of workers covered by just ESOP plans alone increased from 250,000 to 10,150,000. This does not include the many other types of employee ownership, profit and gain sharing, and broad-based stock options that have also grown.

15. See Bonin and Putterman (1987) and Nalbantian (1987, 26). Tracing the idea back further, Columella, the most important historian of Roman agriculture in the first century AD, described how free tenant farmers who had access to the full profits of their labor were more productive than other forms of labor when the owner of the lands was not available to monitor the work on the lands directly. Columella also stressed the importance of the owner treating the worker courteously and with goodwill while being flexible and respectful of their rights, and having a long-term relationship with the free tenant farmers. (See Columella 1941, Book I: VI, 79–83.) We acknowledge the assistance of Professor Heinrich von Staden of the Institute of Advanced Study with this insight.

reported that they would speak to the shirker or report the behavior to a supervisor. Many said that they had done that in the past. Critical to our analysis, proportionately more workers paid by some form of shared capitalism said they would act against a shirker than did other workers. Workers with larger profit-sharing or gain-sharing bonuses and those who recently received a stock option grant were the most likely to so act.

Looking at self-proclaimed motivation, workers paid under shared capitalist compensation were more likely than other workers to explain their intervention on the grounds that the shirking behavior was costing them money. In establishments where workers as a group reported more anti-shirking behavior, they also reported that co-workers worked harder and were more encouraging to each other, which produced a more effective facility, than did workers in other establishments. Finally, our data show that anti-shirking behavior and the effect of shared capitalism on that behavior depend in important ways on other workplace labor practices and policies—a point we develop as take away message six following, as it runs through virtually every analysis in the book.

As we were conducting our survey of the workers of one company, serendipity provided a natural experiment that gives us an independent "before/after" test of conclusions based on cross-section comparisons of workers with more/less shared capitalist pay. One firm announced that it was going to introduce a new profit-sharing plan shortly after its workers took our survey. We asked if we could conduct a follow-up survey after the firm put in the new scheme. The firm agreed, which gave us an exciting and unanticipated natural experiment. There were two outstanding differences between the before and after surveys: first, the proportion of employees who said they would talk to shirking co-workers went up; second, the proportion who said that they would do so because shirking affected their bonus went up also. There was no difference in the other relevant responses.

Our analysis illuminates only part of the co-monitoring story. It does not explore in depth the factors that lead one person to act against a shirker instead of seeking to free ride off of someone else's intervening. It does not measure free riding behavior before and after co-monitoring becomes important. What it does do is demonstrate that co-monitoring is real, measurable, and responds to the incentives of shared capitalist compensation. It is also possible that the increased co-monitoring of workers can allow companies with shared capitalism and supportive work practices to cut their supervisory budget, thus creating savings in labor expenses that might affect productivity. This is another issue that needs to be explored in depth.

3. The Extra Risk of Shared Capitalism is Manageable

Some analysts view risk as the Achilles Heel of shared capitalism. Workers in shared capitalist firms invest too much of their wealth in the firm, contrary to the principle of diversification, and thus take on too much risk for their own good. Evidence that a sizable number of workers in the United States place large fractions of their wealth in company stock shows that this is a real problem. In a survey of 401(k) plan participants Hewitt and Associates found that more than 27 percent of the nearly 1.5 million employees surveyed who could invest in company stock had 50 percent or more of their 401(k) plan assets invested in those shares (Sammer 2006). In the NBER firm sample, about 20 percent of workers clearly held too much of their wealth in their firm to meet any plausible diversification strategy (Blasi, Markowitz, and Kruse, chapter 3). The reason workers invest heavily in their own firm is not because they are risk lovers. Most workers in the NBER survey are risk averse, and the more risk averse are less likely to want to participate in shared capitalist modes of compensation than other workers. Nevertheless, workers seem to find the notion of being in an ownership or shared capitalist position at their workplace exceedingly attractive. Two-thirds of the most risk averse employees want shared capitalism as part of their pay package (Kruse, Blasi, and Park, chapter 1).

Blasi, Kruse, and Markowitz (chapter 3) ask whether the risk in shared capitalism makes shared capitalism unwise for most workers or whether the risk can be managed to limit much of the loss of utility from holding the extra risk. They create an index of financial security based on how much each worker's wealth represents relative to their annual salary and whether the worker has reason to believe that the firm substitutes shared capitalist compensation with the associated risk for normal fixed wages. Workers who feel financially insecure exhibit less of the positive outcomes associated with shared capitalism and are less interested in receiving more profit sharing or employee ownership in their workplaces than other workers.

Portfolio theory suggests that any risky investment—including stock in one's company—can be part of an efficient portfolio as long as the overall portfolio is properly diversified. Someone with considerable assets in their firm should invest other parts of their portfolio in assets negatively correlated with the firm's share prices. The loss of utility from the diversified portfolio should be balanced against the gains from shared capitalism to determine the "optimal" investment strategy. In the case of 401(k)'s, in 2006 16 percent of firms that offer company shares in 401(k) plans chose to limit the amount of investment in their shares or eliminate it as an option altogether (Sammer 2006). Blasi, Kruse, and Markowitz stress that an example of a better strategy for the firm would be to personalize individual portfolios on the basis of worker characteristics and preferences. Financial advisors with information on the worker's entire investment portfolio could develop investment strategies that would diversify the portfolio in ways consistent with individual risk preferences. Given estimates of risk aversion parameters, workers could prudently hold up to 10 to 15 percent of their assets in ownership or related financial linkage to their firm with only a modest loss in utility due to risk. Finally, insecurity about shared capitalist risk and its effect on behavior seems to depend on other workplace labor practices and policies. Combining less risky forms of shared capitalism such as profit sharing and stock options with reasonable amounts of employee stock ownership and complementary work practices captures many of the positive impacts of the research results while minimizing some of the jeopardy. Aside from limiting the overall amount of employee stock ownership to tolerable amounts, one important method to reducing risk is to avoid financing employee stock ownership with worker savings or wage substitution, since our findings show that workers respond poorly to wage substitution.

4. Shared Capitalism Improves the Performance of Firms

The sine qua non in most economics and business discussions of shared capitalism is that it improves the performance of firms. Four chapters in this volume examine the relation between shared capitalist modes of pay and the economic outcomes of firms. Chapters 4 and 7 use the NBER firm survey and the GSS survey. Chapter 5 uses two other data sets for the United States and Chapter 6 uses a data set for the United Kingdom to estimate the impact of shared capitalism on firm outcomes. By estimating similar models with different data sets and in the UK as well as in the US we test the generality and robustness of our findings. Results consistent across data sets and economies presumably reflect the most fundamental aspects of economic behavior. Results that vary across data sets/countries suggest more subtle relations, in which unobservable factors may be influencing the observed patterns.

Blasi, Freeman, Mackin, and Kruse (chapter 4) find that measures of shared capitalist pay are associated with a host of workplace outcomes beneficial to firms in the NBER firm and GSS surveys. More workers report that they are "not likely to search for a new job," "would turn down another job for more pay," have "loyalty to the company," and are "proud to be working for the employer" when they are paid with shared capitalist compensation than otherwise. The workers with shared capitalism are also more likely to report that "co-workers work hard," that they personally "are willing to work harder to help the company," that "co-workers have enough interest in company issues to get involved," and are more likely to make suggestions to improve the business. The only outcome that is adversely linked with shared capitalism is number of days absent, which is higher with shared capitalist compensation than otherwise, but not when shared capitalism is accompanied by complementary workplace practices.

To illuminate the motivation behind the positive worker responses to shared capitalism, we asked workers on the NBER survey how their desire to improve the business success of their employer would be affected by various forms of shared capitalist incentives. Employees said that cash incentives and stock options would motivate them the most, followed by shares in the ESOP. Respondents said that they would be motivated less if the shared capitalist policy involved buying shares with company discounts and said they would be motivated the least by buying shares in the open market. The implication is that the context or form in which the firm makes its shared capitalist compensation greatly influences how shared capitalist pay affects behavior. Consistent with this, Blasi, Freeman, Mackin, and Kruse show that the effects of shared capitalism on the diverse outcomes given before vary depending on other labor policies and practices.

Dube and Freeman (chapter 5) examine the links between modes of shared compensation in pay and employee involvement and other forms of shared decision making with various measures of productivity in the 1994–95 Workplace Representation and Participation Survey (WRPS) that asked workers about their workplace activities and modes of compensation, and in the 2003 California Establishment Survey that asked firms about compensation and decision-making practices. They find weaker links between shared capitalist modes of pay—when examined alone—and worker behavior likely to benefit firms than are found in the NBER and GSS surveys. Shared capitalist pay has positive but generally statistically insignificant effects on behavior likely to raise firm output. Since every firm has a set of workplace practices, looking at the combination of shared capitalism with such practices is the key to our analysis. The labor practice that has a big effect on behavior is an employee involvement committee, which increases employee participation in decision making. Shared capitalist forms have their impact on outcomes by augmenting the effect of involvement committees. For instance, in the WRPS an employee involvement committee by itself increases the probability that a worker will likely stay with the firm by 0.10 percentage points, whereas combined with profit sharing and employee ownership, the effect is increased to 0.18 percentage points (chapter 5, table 5.4). Similarly, in the establishment-based data set, having an employee involvement committee by itself increases productivity by 0.12 percentage points, whereas combined with profit sharing and employee ownership, the productivity effect nearly doubles to a 0.23 percentage point gain.

In the late 1990s the United Kingdom enacted tax laws that privileged employee share ownership at the expense of profit-related pay, which it had previously tax-advantaged. One reason for the change was the belief that firms were exploiting the profit-related pay system by claiming the tax break when in fact they were not truly creating pay that varied with profits. Most studies of shared capitalism linked the mode of wage payment to management perceptions of the productivity of their workplace and found modestly positive effects, which, however, differed over time and among studies. Bryson and Freeman (chapter 6) supplement management reports on labor productivity with data on sales per employee and value added per employee data for establishments in the 2004 British Workplace Employment Relations Survey (WERS) in the period following the change in tax laws. They find that stock ownership plans are positively correlated with productivity while other forms of shared capitalism have modest and generally not significant effects. But, as in analyses of US data, the biggest effects occur when shared capitalist forms of pay are combined with policies that increase worker decision making. They reference a UK Treasury study of a much larger sample of firms that yields consistent results.

As information and knowledge work have moved to the forefront of economic activity in advanced economies, it is important to determine how well, if at all, shared capitalism fits in this "new economy." The NBER survey contained a module of questions focused on innovative activity by workers. It asked workers, for instance, whether they "would be willing to be more involved in efforts to develop innovative products and services" and whether in their firm "innovative ideas are carefully considered and fairly evaluated." Using the largest company in the NBER dataset, with over 27,000 employee respondents and 280 different work sites in twenty-two countries, Harden, Kruse, and Blasi (chapter 7) examine the relation between workers' engagement in innovative behavior and shared capitalist rewards. Workers with shares in the firm perceive a more innovative culture and have a greater willingness to engage in innovative activity. The combination of shared capitalism and high performance workplace policies had the strongest impact on innovation culture and willingness to innovate. This is true for both a measure of coverage by different policies, and a measure of the effectiveness of high performance policies in one's immediate work group or team.

In sum, differences in the source and type of data notwithstanding, these chapters tell a consistent story that supports and enriches the earlier production function analyses of the relation between shared capitalism and company performance of firms, and show that its effects vary with other aspects of the firm's policies and practices.

5. Shared Capitalism Benefits Workers

The four chapters of the book that examine the relation between shared capitalism and worker well-being show that shared capitalism benefits workers along a host of dimensions. Shared capitalism is associated with better working lives and greater wealth relative to otherwise comparable workers paid by conventional means. Most workers appear to have sufficiently accurate information about shared capitalist compensation to motivate the various behavioral responses found throughout the book. At the same time, because shared capitalism does not cover many of the lowest paid workers in society it does little to reduce earnings inequality at those income levels in our society.

To begin with, workers with shared capitalist modes of pay report better outcomes on both the NBER firm survey and the GSS in such areas as participation in decisions, management treatment of employees and supervision, formal and informal training opportunities, pay and benefits, co-worker relations, job security, and labor management-relations broadly (Kruse, Freeman, and Blasi, chapter 8). Profit sharing is most consistently linked to such positive outcomes, though gain sharing, stock options, and employee ownership also affect outcomes positively. For some outcomes the positive effect is related to the worker being covered by a policy (e.g., being eligible for profit sharing, or being an employee-owner), but for other outcomes the effect is tied to the size of the financial stake involved (e.g., size of the most recent bonus, or value of employer stock or potential profit on stock options). Workers report higher job satisfaction when shared capitalism is combined with high performance work practices and low supervision, and report high participation in decisions and satisfaction with participation under similar circumstances. By contrast, the combination of close supervision with shared capitalism has negative effects on almost every outcome. And the impacts of shared capitalism are diluted for workers who believe that they are paid below the market rate for their job. This presumably reflects worker concern that shared capitalism has replaced fixed pay with less desirable variable pay. In the WRPS, employee involvement has a greater impact than shared capitalist forms on worker satisfaction related outcomes, as it did on productivity, with shared capitalism substantially augmenting the effect of involvement on such outcomes as satisfaction with influence at the workplace, job satisfaction, trust in the firm, and assessment of management (Dube and Freeman, chapter 5). Overall the results in the various studies support the idea that workers gain by sharing, but that the effect depends on other workplace policies as well.

Workers' knowledge of the benefits their firm offers them (Gustman and Steinmeier 2001; Chan and Stevens 2003) and of labor protections more broadly (Freeman and Rogers 2006) is often sparse and in some cases inaccurate. In the case of pension rights, Chan and Stevens have found that inaccurate understanding of pension systems leads some workers to choose their retirement in ways against their self-interest: they choose optimally on the basis of their inaccurate knowledge of the plans. Given this finding, Budd (chapter 9) examined whether employees in the NBER firm survey had accurate information about the shared capitalist forms of compensation at their firm by comparing their reports to company information about the plans. This comparison found that 18 to 25 percent of employees reported involvement in company plans that differed from company reports on whether they should or should not participate on the basis of the characteristics of the plans. At first, this seemed consistent with the pension results as reflecting employee ignorance about the participation, which should dampen the effects of company plans on firms and workers. But at our research conference, company representatives said they were unsure about who is covered by their own plans, particularly at the establishment level. Thus, the differences between what workers said and what we garnered from the firms appears to reflect both inaccurate worker information and management uncertainty about the implementation of plans.

Stories about ordinary workers who became millionaires through shares in a small start-up or a growing firm that prospered abound in Silicon Valley and related places. Surely most workers in shared capitalist enterprises are not so lucky, but employees with ownership stakes do develop on average greater wealth as a result of their ownership than do employees in other types of enterprises. In the NBER firm survey employee-owners have an average stake of nearly $62,000; in the GSS employer owners report nearly $48,000 in wealth from their firm. At the time the surveys were taken, stock option holders had an average $283,000 in potential stock option profits if their options could be sold. While in some cases these stakes substitute for other wealth, Buchele, Kruse, Rodgers, and Scharf (chapter 11) indicate that employee ownership does not generally come at the expense of pay and other benefits and appears to add to employees' wealth on average.[16] Comparisons of the distribution of stock between the NBER company data and national data show that broad-based employee ownership plans expand stock ownership for workers in the middle of the distribution.[17] Employee ownership constitutes about 5 percent of the median employee's wealth in the NBER companies, which means that it can have only a modest impact on the overall wealth distribution, but at the same time does not give the median worker an unduly risky portfolio.

If all workers were equally covered by shared capitalist modes of pay and if firms with shared capitalist compensation had lower inequality among their employees than other firms, then shared capitalist pay would likely be associated with lower overall inequality. In fact, shared capitalist arrangements are disproportionately distributed in the economy. While there is little difference by gender in participation in these plans, African-Americans and men with disabilities are less likely to be paid by shared capitalism than other workers. The financial values of capital income accounts are also lower for some of these groups. The primary reason for this stratification is the different distribution of persons among occupations. At the same time, shared capitalism and the employee involvement that often accompanies it appear to affect similarly the behavior and attitudes of workers with different demographic characteristics, as found by Carberry (chapter 10). Thus, firms

16. Even Frederick Taylor, whose system of scientific management emphasized high supervision and low participation by workers, strongly held the notion that "Men [and women] will not do an extraordinary day's work for an ordinary day's pay." He spent much of his life searching for the simple premium on top of normal pay that would spur workers to greater productivity even in the absence of an engaging corporate culture (Kanigel 1997, 212–13).

17. Workers may have gotten lucky with good performance of their employee-owned stock, but these results suggest that even if the stock had performed poorly, they would have been no worse off without the stock since there was little or no substitution with pay, benefits, or other wealth.

can expect reductions in turnover, increased loyalty to the firm, increased willingness to work hard, and related behaviors to improve if shared capitalist pay arrangements were extended to groups underrepresented in current plans.

6. Shared Capitalism Complements Other Labor Policies and Practices

The single overriding empirical result in this volume, which shows up in virtually all outcomes and data sets, is that combinations of policies—shared capitalism, employee involvement, and other positive labor practices—are complementary. There are some independent effects of shared capitalism but it is the combination of compensation and labor policies that seems to be the key feature of shared capitalism's success.

The evidence for the complementary effect is twofold. First, we find that firms with shared capitalist pay are more likely than other firms to have employee involvement committees and to devolve decisions to workers and other policies associated with high performance workplaces (Kruse, Blasi, and Park, chapter 1; Dube and Freeman, chapter 5; Bryson and Freeman, chapter 6). Second, as noted in preceding summary points, we find that the combination of shared capitalist pay and other policies has a greater impact on outcomes than policies taken separately. Workers are more likely to undertake anti-shirking behavior when shared capitalism is combined with higher trust in management, low levels of supervision, high performance work policies, and wages at or above market levels (chapter 2). Workers in workplaces with poor employee relations and a lack of high performance work policies view their economic position as inherently more risky and are less positively inclined toward shared capitalist modes of pay (chapter 3). Workers with shared capitalist practices and high performance work policies, low levels of supervision, and fixed wages that are at or above the market level had lower expected turnover, higher loyalty, higher willingness to work hard, and a greater frequency of suggestions (chapters 4, 7). In the UK and US establishment production function data, the combinations produce higher productivity (chapters 5, 6). Similarly, workers in firms that combine shared capitalism with other practices report greater participation in decisions, lower levels of supervision, better management treatment of employees, formal and informal training opportunities, pay and benefits, co-worker relations, job security, and job satisfaction (chapter 5, 8).

The interaction of the effects of shared capitalism with other corporate policies suggests that the various shared capitalist and other policies may operate through a latent variable, "corporate culture."

Conclusion

The findings summarized previously give a favorable picture of shared capitalism. Firms have managed to overcome the incentive to free ride that threatens to undermine any form of group pay and have increased the shared capitalist modes of pay to nearly half of the US workforce at the turn of the twenty-first century. While some workers hold too much wealth in their firm, the median worker who receives shared capitalist pay does not do so. Diversification can reduce the potentially excessive risk of linking labor market and capital market outcomes in the same firm. The chapters on workplace performance show substantial and statistically significant positive relations between shared capitalism and almost all outcomes. In most cases, the biggest effects come when shared capitalism is accompanied by other identifiable policies. The chapters on worker outcomes tell a similar story about the benefits that accrue to workers. Overall, the volume shows that shared capitalism works best when it combines monetary incentives with employee decision-making and personnel and labor policies that empower and encourage employees.

The shared capitalism vision of the US economy differs in important ways from the vision of capitalism as dependent primarily on concentrating rewards with superstar entrepreneurs and CEOs and a thin slice of executives and managers at the top of firms. Our analysis differs in important ways from the economic theories that stress the behavior of the superstar manager over that of workers more broadly or from theories of the firm that hold that profits should go to a central owner for optimal incentives to monitor work.[18] To the extent that workers monitor workers better than do managers, and that shareholders cannot write contracts that align management interests with their interests, much less with the interests of workers, shared capitalist modes of pay may offer better solutions to principal/agent problems and to the division of the rewards of joint activity than traditional capital versus labor divisions. Giving employees shared capitalism with significant discretion or residual control over how they do their jobs may be more efficient than lodging such control in management or shareholders as residual claimants, at least in some sectors.

As this summary and ensuing chapters make clear, our research has answered some questions about shared capitalist enterprises and highlights other important questions that require additional data and research. We direct attention in particular to three issues. First, there is the way shared capitalist pay and organization of work that empowers workers complement each other. This seems to reflect the elusive concept of corporate culture, which we view as potentially the latent variable behind the interactions between shared capitalism and other policies found throughout the volume. Second, there is how co-monitoring helps shared capitalist enterprises overcome free-riding tendencies. Our analysis has just scratched the surface of this phenomenon, which can potentially illuminate the deep social science problem of explaining the seemingly inordinate success of cooperative solu-

18. This theory is stated most prominently in Alchian and Demsetz (1972).

tions in economic life. Third, there is the way the risk of shared capitalism can be minimized when workers do not pay for employee stock ownership through reduced wages and lower savings; when less risky forms of shared capitalism such as cash profit sharing and stock options are combined with riskier forms such as company stock; when workers wealth portfolios hold a prudent share of ownership in their firm, and the rest of the portfolio is diversified. From the perspective of economic theory, the success of shared capitalism engages fundamental mainstream issues pertaining to risk aversion and portfolio theory, game theory and the free rider problem, behavioral finance, and theories of compensation, such as efficiency wage theories. From the perspective of policy, we hope the volume provides some evidence and guidance for business and labor leaders, as well as analysts and policymakers about ways to think about shared capitalist firms and to devise policies to help them contribute to economic well-being.

Studying Shared Capitalism

In the rest of this introduction we provide an overview of the two main surveys used in this book. We discuss the strengths and weaknesses of the surveys, the ways in which they complement each other, some of the methodological problems in researching shared capitalism, and the ways we have addressed those problems. Readers mainly interested in the results should go straight to chapter 1.

The NBER Company Survey

For an intensive look inside companies that use shared capitalism, the NBER project members recruited fourteen companies with a variety of shared capitalist programs, and employee surveys were conducted over the 2001 to 2006 period in 323 worksites. We drew up a sample of firms varying in size, industry, and type of program, and contacted them in various ways to participate. As is usual in this sort of research, we were able to convince only some firms to participate. Two firms that agreed to participate were bought out by other firms who did not want to cooperate with the study.

The basic characteristics of the fourteen firms are described in table 1 (only broadly so as not to leave open the possibility of someone identifying the firms). All of the firms have some sort of broad-based employee ownership plan, but the plan types vary: eight have standard Employee Stock Ownership Plans (ESOPs), one has a 401(k) ESOP, four have Employee Stock Purchase Plans (ESPPs), and three have 401(k)'s with company stock. Eleven of the firms have broad-based profit-sharing plans, while five have broad-based stock option plans. Most have combinations of these plans, reflecting the combinations we observe in the American labor market in general (Kruse, Blasi, and Park, chapter 1, table 1.1). While each of these fourteen firms has some type of shared capitalist plan, the plans and details differed enough among the firms and among workers and establishments

Table 1 **NBER survey companies**

	Broad-based profit sharing	Broad-based employee ownership	Broad-based stock options
Manufacturing			
<1,000 employees			
Company 1	Yes	ESOP	No
Company 2	Yes	ESOP	No
Company 3	Yes	ESOP	No
Company 4	Yes	ESOP and ESPP	Yes
1,000–9,999 employees			
Company 5	Yes	ESOP	No
Company 6	Yes	401(k) ESOP	No
Company 7	Yes	ESOP	No
10,000+ employees			
Company 8	Yes	401(k) w/co. stock	No
Service/financial			
<1,000 employees			
Company 9	No	ESOP	No
1,000–9,999 employees			
Company 10	No	ESOP	No
Company 11	No	ESPP and 401(k) w/co. stock	Yes
10,000 employees			
Company 12	Yes	ESPP and 401(k) w/co. stock	Yes
Hi-tech/Internet			
<1,000 employees			
Company 13	Yes	ESPP	Yes
10,000+ employees			
Company 14	Yes	ESPP	Yes
Total companies with plans	11	14	5

within those firms to allow us to analyze the effects of these modes of compensation and other management labor practices on outcomes.

As noted earlier, the companies vary in industry group and size. There are eight manufacturers (seven small or medium-sized and one large), two high technology firms (one medium-sized and one large), one large financial services firm, and three service firms (one small, one medium-sized, and one large).

Once firms agreed to the survey, we surveyed either all employees or a random sample of employees. Each survey had 80 to 100 questions, including core questions common across all companies and some questions of special concern to each participating company (for which we provided analysis gratis). To help ensure validated questions and useful comparisons, a number of the core questions were drawn from other surveys, including questions on job security and turnover intention from the General Social Survey, and questions on employee involvement from the Workplace Representation and Participation Survey (Freeman and Rogers 2006). The core survey questions also included new comprehensive measures of every identifiable form of profit, equity, and bonus sharing. Measures of employee ownership include participation in ESOPs and ESPPs, company stock in 401(k) plans and deferred profit-sharing plans, stock held after exercising stock options, stock grants, and open market purchases. The bonus measures cover all types of bonuses, including those linked to company performance (profit sharing), department or team performance (gainsharing), and individual performance. Appendix A reproduces the questions and gives descriptive statistics for the presence of different practices and their intensity (i.e., as a percent of salary or wealth). Appendix B describes our summary measure of shared capitalism. We create the summary measure because our surveys are virtually the only ones that include all forms of shared capitalism and remuneration. Given how widespread bundles of shared capitalist practices are in the US economy, some past studies may have only measured the variable of interest and ignored other important shared capitalist variables.

Six company surveys were conducted over the web, seven company surveys were done on paper, and one survey was done using both the web and paper surveys. The web surveys were on a university-sponsored server, not on the company server, so that workers knew this was not a company activity. When we administered surveys in person, to protect confidentiality the surveys were gathered by either members of our team or a committee of three nonmanagement employees, who administered them in one room, collected them in sealed envelopes in a box, and brought them immediately to an express mail facility and sent them directly to the NBER research team for analysis. Workers were informed about these procedures for their protection on the cover of each survey. The company response rates ranged from 11 to 80 percent, with an average of 53 percent across the fourteen companies. A total of 41,206 respondents provided usable surveys, in 323 establishments. Most of the workers (31,994) were based in the United States, though as noted the three US multinationals in the study encouraged their workers around the world to take the survey. Most of the workers could be matched to specific establishments, enabling some site-level analysis.

As noted earlier, we initially sought to find and survey paired comparison competitor companies for each company in our data set. This did not work out, both because many of the prospective comparison firms also had some form of shared capitalism, and because managers in many of the firms did not want to simply serve as controls. We nonetheless found that there was substantial variation in shared capitalism and complementary practices both within and among our fourteen firms, 323 establishments, and 41,206 workers, allowing us ample opportunity to explore the effects of shared capitalism.

General Social Survey

As noted earlier, the main limitation of the survey of firms is that it is based on a self-selected nonrandom sample of firms. This raises questions about the generalizability of the results that must be addressed head-on.

We note first that these are mainstream companies operating in the highly competitive US market, not strange entities operating under peculiar rules or regulations (per the worker-managed firms in old Yugoslavia). To the extent that our questions relate to issues that face all firms and reflect basic human nature, there are reasons to expect the findings to generalize to a broader population. But expectation/argumentation is not evidence. To see if in fact some of the main results from our firm survey hold in a representative sample of firms, we arranged to add a special module on shared capitalism on the nationally representative General Social Survey (GSS) in 2002 and 2006 by submitting a research proposal to the board of the GSS. The GSS is a national area probability sample of noninstitutionalized adults conducted by the National Opinion Research Center of the University of Chicago. The GSS started in 1972 and has been conducted every year or two since then (currently every other year). It is the major ongoing source of information on the changing attitudes and experiences of Americans over the past four decades. "Except for the US Census, the GSS is the most frequently analyzed source of information in the social sciences" (http://www.norc.org/gss+website/about+gss). The 2002 GSS had a sample of 1,145 employees, and the 2006 GSS had a sample of 1,081 employees, in for-profit companies. The response rates were 70.1 percent for the 2002 survey and 71.2 percent for the 2006 survey. The 2010 GSS with related questions is being administered as this book goes to press.

We placed questions on the GSS about the incidence of shared capitalism and replicated the questions from the NBER company survey on whether workers observed how fellow employees performed and how they reacted to someone not working as hard as they should. As noted before, we also put some standard GSS questions on the NBER survey (e.g., job security, turnover intention). Thus, the GSS provides a validation check on some results in the company survey, as well as a representative group of workers without shared capitalism that can serve as "controls" for our NBER firm surveys. An additional advantage of the GSS is that in both 2002 and 2006 there were special work modules with a wide variety of questions on work attitudes and experiences, allowing a broader look at the relationship of shared capitalism to workplace variables. The GSS questions analyzed in this book are described in appendix A. These data are available on the GSS web site (http://www.norc.org/GSS+Website/) and can be readily downloaded and analyzed by other researchers. The GSS contains information on many aspects of social life that we did not explore, which creates potential for other investigators to illuminate the relation of shared capitalism to other parts of US society.

Survey Strengths, Weaknesses, and Complementarities

Correlation between variables in nonexperimental survey research does not imply causation. There may be a variety of explanations for a positive association between two variables. A positive association between employee participation in shared capitalism and feelings of organizational commitment, for example, could reflect the effect of shared capitalism on commitment, or the placement of committed employees into positions with shared capitalism, or simply the dependence of both variables on a third factor. In these latter two cases the shared capitalism variable would be endogenous—determined by other variables in the system so that we could not reliably infer from the statistical association that independent changes in shared capitalism would create the observed correlation between the variable and organizational commitment.

Many of these problems could be solved by a true experiment, where subjects are randomly assigned to treatment and control groups, with the treatment carefully constructed and manipulated by the researchers. We would certainly like to be able to impose a variety of shared capitalism plans on 1,000 randomly-selected companies, and compare their outcomes to those of another randomly-selected 1,000 companies in a control group. As nice as this would be from a research standpoint, obviously we have neither the authority nor the resources for such a vast experiment. Instead we rely on a quasi-experimental approach (Cook and Campbell 1979), examining how naturally-occurring variation is related to outcomes of interest, while attempting to control as well as possible for potential sources of bias. It is noteworthy that the largely (though not uniformly) positive outcomes for shared capitalism in this book are consistent with laboratory experiments comparing behavior in employee-owned versus conventionally-owned "firms" (collections of randomly-assigned subjects)(Frohlich et al. 1998). Our approach has an advantage over laboratory experiments by showing the real-world existence and relevance of these findings to actual firms and workers. A recent field experiment provides corroborating evidence by randomly assigning profit-sharing plans to three stores in a twenty-one-store fast food company, with the result that profits and productivity rose and turnover fell in the profit-sharing stores relative to the control group (Peterson and Luthans 2006). By using random assignment, both of these studies provide some assurance that the findings in this book are not due to an array of potential biases.

In the rest of this chapter we discuss some of the potential biases more thoroughly, and how the studies in this book attempt to minimize them.

Employee-Reported versus Objective Data

One potential limitation of these data is that almost all of the policies, experiences, attitudes, and behaviors are reported by employees, so there may be a subjective component that muddies the analysis. Particularly when analyzing workplace performance, it is valuable to have objective data—measures of actual output or turnover behavior, for instance, rather than reported productivity or intention to leave a company. Indeed, much of the shared capitalist literature has used establishment data to examine such patterns. There have been over 100 studies of workplace performance under shared capitalism (reviewed in Weitzman and Kruse [1990], Kruse [1993]; OECD [1995]; Doucialiagos [1995]; Kruse and Blasi [1997]; Blasi, Kruse, and Bernstein [2003], Kaarsemaker [2006a, 2006b]; and Freeman [2007]). These studies show that shared capitalism is associated with better firm performance on average, but that there is enough variation in outcomes so that a positive outcome is by no means automatic. This suggests that the effects of shared capitalism may be conditioned by a variety of workplace factors such as human resource policies, the quality of employee relations, the nature of supervision, and how the job is constructed. Rather than do another large-scale survey of firms, we wanted to try a new approach, delving more deeply into the "black box" of shared capitalism in ways that might illuminate the factors that might condition the effects of shared capitalism.

Since relatively few studies have looked at shared capitalism from the workers point of view, we designed the NBER project to find out directly from workers how they experience work, and how shared capitalism fits into that experience. The workers reported on a number of attitudes and behaviors for which they are the only source (e.g., job satisfaction, turnover intention, and company loyalty). Of course it would be ideal to have objective performance data that could be matched to each individual worker, but: (a) companies do not have individual-level objective performance data for most jobs; and (b) even if they did have such individual-level data, we could not have matched to survey data without compromising anonymity. In their own right, moreover, employee reports are meaningful both as measures of subjective attitudes and as predictors of future behavior, as shown by meta-analyses of prior studies, which find that many employee-reported attitudes and behaviors are linked to important outcomes—for example, turnover intention predicts actual turnover, and employee engagement predicts behaviors that improve objective outcomes (Griffeth, Hom, and Gaertner 2000; Harter, Schmidt, and Hayes 2003). In sum, our bottom-up approach measures attitudes and behaviors that cannot be easily measured in any other way, and that are not purely subjective but are also related to behavioral outcomes.

Selectivity Bias

Many of the difficulties in reaching valid conclusions in nonexperimental research are due to potential statistical bias from self-selection of respondents. A classic experiment generally removes such selectivity bias by randomly assigning subjects to treatment and control groups (though such bias may still occur in who volunteers to be part of the experiment, and who drops out before the experiment is done). In field research like this, a number of types of selectivity bias can be at work in: (a) how those who participate in the study may be different from those who do not; and (b) how those who select, or are selected into, the treatment of interest may differ from those without the treatment. Selectivity bias can lead to biased conclusions regarding the sample being analyzed (internal validity) and problems in generalizing to the universe of interest (external validity) (Cook and Campbell 1979). In these two surveys, selectivity bias can operate at both the firm and individual levels.

Selectivity Bias in Who Participates in Study

As noted before, the firms agreeing to cooperate with the NBER survey are clearly not a random sample of all shared capitalism firms, and there may be something "special" about them that influences the results. It is possible that some special characteristic of these firms conditions the relationships observed in these firms, so that the relationships cannot be generalized to other firms with similar policies of interest. For example, perhaps the managers in the studied firms are especially knowledgeable about how to implement shared capitalism in an effective way, whereas managers in other shared capitalism firms (not part of our study) are not as effective in implementing it. Or perhaps the employees in the studied firms especially like shared capitalism and respond well to it. Similarly, there may be selectivity bias in the types of employees who respond to the survey: perhaps employees who are motivated by shared capitalism are more likely to respond to the survey.

Our principal method to check for such selectivity bias in our NBER sample is to compare results to those in the GSS national sample to see if the relationships hold among other employees with shared capitalism. As will be seen, this is largely the case, providing some reassurance that our NBER firms and employees are not atypical of other shared capitalism firms and employees. Still, at the individual level, it is possible that employees who responded to the survey may be unlike nonrespondents in some way, making it difficult to achieve valid conclusions and generalize the results. One basic method to minimize this bias is to create the highest response rate possible. As noted previously, the average response rate across the NBER surveys is 53 percent, and the response rate for the GSS is 70 percent in 2002 and 71 percent in 2006, which are all considered good response rates in individual survey research. We used two additional methods to check for selectivity bias at the individual level in the NBER surveys. In addition to the 41,206 employees who completed usable surveys, an additional 5,701 started the survey but did not complete enough of it to be usable.[19] We found that this latter "nonrespondent" group had lower average levels of shared capitalism, but the relationships between shared capitalism and outcome variables were generally similar for this group as for those included in the full analysis.[20]

19. Surveys were deemed not usable if respondents did not answer at least half of eighteen basic job and demographic questions.

20. The nonrespondent group had an average score on the shared capitalism index (described in Appendix B) that was 3.5 points lower than for the respondent group. The regressions including the nonrespondent group excluded the demographic controls, since these were based on

Selectivity Bias in Who Participates in Shared Capitalism

An even thornier type of selectivity bias concerns what types of firms and employees choose shared capitalism. Are they also different in some other way that affects the results? The firms that choose to implement shared capitalism may be better-performing companies in general, or have unmeasured policies or other qualities that affect the outcomes of interest. One solution is to do pre/post studies that hold constant any fixed unobservable qualities of the company (e.g., comparing company performance before and after the adoption of profit sharing as in Kruse [1993] or company performance and pay levels before and after the adoption of ESOPs in Kim and Ouimet [2008]). In this project we have an example of a pre/post study in which the NBER survey was administered twice at one company, the first time before a profit-sharing plan was implemented and the second time several months later after it was implemented. The results are analyzed in chapter 2.

Our primary method of avoiding much of the potential selectivity bias at the firm level is to do within-company comparisons: seeing how outcomes differ among workers with greater and lesser amounts of shared capitalism while controlling for a variety of job and personal characteristics, and effectively holding constant any firm characteristic that is common to all workers. In other words, in contrast to the many cross-sectional studies comparing firms with and without shared capitalism programs, these results here are not biased by unmeasured between-firm differences in management, policies, or anything else. By comparing to the GSS national sample, as noted before, we can be more confident that the relationships we find apply across shared capitalism firms in general. Even if the relationships hold among all shared capitalism companies, however, it remains possible that they will not generalize to firms without shared capitalism—that is, we would not get the same results if we could somehow convince or require all firms to have shared capitalism plans.

There may also be selectivity bias in the type of worker who joins a shared capitalism firm. Workers who are especially interested in performance-based pay, for example, may be especially likely to join shared capitalism firms, and these workers may have other special personal qualities that affect their attitudes and behavior at work. There is little direct evidence on this question. Weiss (1987) finds that both the initially high and low performers were more likely to quit the company after their pay became tied to group incentives—suggesting that there is some self-selection in group incentives—but this self-selection imparts no general upward or downward bias to estimates of the effects of group incentive systems.

questions at the end of the survey that very few nonrespondents answered. In addition, we used information from the "nonrespondent" group to create standard Heckman selection corrections (Heckman 1976), and found little change in the estimated relationships of shared capitalism to outcome variables.

In our NBER companies, all of the employees have chosen to join a firm with broad-based shared capitalism, but there may still be systematic within-company differences between the employees with and without shared capitalism. It may be, for example, that employees who display the best attitudes are put in positions where they are eligible for shared capitalism plans, and the positive link between shared capitalism and attitudes simply reflects this preexisting individual difference. Or certain jobs may be deemed appropriate for shared capitalism compensation and those same jobs may be structured to require certain behaviors (e.g., monitoring co-workers), but there is no causal connection between the shared capitalism and behaviors.

Selectivity bias can result from self-selection on observable or unobservable variables. The most straightforward method of minimizing selectivity bias is simply to control for a rich array of observable individual and job variables that may determine selection. One advantage of our detailed NBER surveys is that we can observe variables that many studies have had to treat as unobservable. In addition to standard demographic and job controls, we had access to variables available in few or no other studies, such as level of risk aversion, closeness of supervision, ease of seeing co-workers, and total wealth. A common supposition, for example, is that workers who choose to work in shared capitalism programs have higher tolerance for risk than do other workers, and this may be related to a variety of other personal attitudes and characteristics that affect responses to shared capitalism. The rich array of individual-level variables helps reduce the potential for selectivity bias to account for differences found in the individual-level analysis.

But there remains the possibility of self-selection on unobservable variables—for example, the employees with shared capitalism may simply have greater ability or "spunk" or other intangible qualities that affect their attitudes and behavior. One way to control for selectivity bias due to unobservable individual qualities is to do pre/post comparisons at the individual level (e.g., comparing pay and benefits of workers before and after joining profit-sharing plans, as in Kruse [1998]), but we are not able to follow individuals over time with the anonymous NBER surveys or the 2002 and 2006 cross-sectional GSS surveys. Another way to deal with selectivity bias is to use instrumental variables that substitute a predicted value for the actual value of the variable of interest, in order to remove the correlation with the error term. This requires finding some exogenous variables that predict the variable of interest (e.g., shared capitalism) but that do not directly affect the outcome of interest (e.g., response to shirkers). For example, given that shared capitalism introduces compensation risk, it is plausible that our measures of personal risk aversion might serve as exogenous variables predicting participation in shared capitalism by workers without directly predicting the workplace outcome of interest. We tested risk aversion and a variety of other variables as exogenous variables in instrumental variables models, but could not identify any that consistently met tests of exogeneity. Without a genuine controlled experiment or some natural experiment that closely mimics a controlled experiment econometrics does not enable us to rule out the effect of unobserved factors on our results. However, the case for a causal effect of shared capitalism is supported by the workers' own views about the effects of shared capitalism (chapters 2 and 4), the one pre/post study (chapter 2), and the detailed controls available in the NBER survey. In addition, as noted before, the results in this book are broadly consistent with the findings noted previously from the true experiment of Frohlich et al. (1998), where many forms of selection bias were removed by the random assignment of subjects.

Ecological Correlation Bias

There is one other difficulty that runs through many of the analyses of the NBER company data sets that we flag here. The difficulty is that correlations obtained at the level of individuals in our data set may not hold at the level of worksites where shared capitalist and other labor policies are implemented. For example, one worker could report lots of shared capitalist pay and work effort at his firm while a co-worker could report little shared capitalism and little effort. The result would be a strong positive correlation between shared capitalism and reported effort among individuals in the data set but no correlation at the possibly more appropriate establishment level of analysis. Readers familiar with the ecological correlation bias (in which correlations among aggregate units may not carry over for individuals within the units) can view this disaggregation correlation bias as a parallel problem in the opposite direction. To deal with it, we aggregated individual worker reports into worksite level averages and examined the link between the establishment level variables. To the extent that some of the individual variation within an establishment reflects real variation in conditions—for example, one part of the establishment has gain sharing or a stock option plan and another part does not—the results from the establishment level analysis may understate the true effects of shared capitalism while the results from analysis of individuals may overstate it. Where appropriate, the chapters test the link between shared capitalist pay and outcomes at both the individual and establishment levels.

Conclusion on Methodology

These two new surveys represent the most extensive "bottom-up" approach to the study of shared capitalism to date, going straight to workers to find out how they experience and respond to shared capitalism, as opposed to the largely "top-down" approach of most prior studies that rely on company-level data that is often manager-reported or administrative data from government data sets created as a result of company reporting requirements.

Neither survey is ideal. The GSS is nationally representative, but has limited numbers of persons with different forms of compensation arrangements, which makes it hard to reach statistically valid conclusions in some areas. Because it is a small national sample, workers are likely to all be employed by different firms so that we view comparisons among workers as comparisons across firms. It is not longitudinal. The NBER has a large number of respondents, but they are taken from a sample of firms that is nonrandom. Because the NBER survey covers a small number of firms, much of the variation comes from variation among workers within firms, and we generally include firm fixed effects in analyses to focus on this variation. By combining analyses of the small national sample that lives on cross-company variation and the larger nonrandom sample of workers from participating companies that lives on within-company variation, we hopefully surmount these weaknesses and reach conclusions that have general validity.

References

Adams, H. B. 1888. *History of cooperation in the United States.* Baltimore, MD: Johns Hopkins University and N. Murray.

Alchian, A. A., and H. Demsetz. 1972. Production, information costs, and economic organization. *American Economic Review* 62 (5): 777–95.

Bemis, E. W. 1886. Cooperation in the Northeast. *Publications of the American Economic Association* 1 (5): 7–136.

Beyster, J. R., and P. Economy. 2007. *The SAIC solution: How we built an $8 billion employer-owned technology company.* New York: John Wiley and Sons.

Blasi, J. 1987. *Employee ownership through ESOPs: Implications for the public corporation.* Work in America Institute Studies in Productivity. New York: Pergamon Books.

———. 1988. *Employee ownership: Revolution or ripoff?* New York and Cambridge: Harper and Row, Ballinger Books.

Blasi, J., and D. Kruse. 1991. *The new owners: Employee ownership in public companies.* New York: HarperCollins.

———. 2008. An early case study in shared capitalism: The Pillsbury story. *Journal of Employee Ownership Law and Finance* 20 (2): 123–38.

Blasi, J., D. Kruse, and A. Bernstein. 2003. *In the company of owners: The truth about stock options and why every employee should have them.* New York: Basic Books.

Bonin, J., and L. Putterman. 1987. *Economics of cooperation and labor managed economies.* New York: Cambridge University Press.

Bullock, R. J., and M. E. Tubbs. 1990. A case meta-analysis of gainsharing plans as organizational development interventions. *Journal of Applied Behavioral Science* 26 (3): 383–404.

Carey, R. 2004. *Democratic capitalism.* Bloomington, IN: Author House.

Chan, S., and A. H. Stevens. 2003. What you don't know can't help you: Pension knowledge and retirement decision making. NBER Working Paper no. 10185. Cambridge, MA: National Bureau of Economic Research, December.

Clark, J. B. 1886. *The philosophy of wealth: Economic principles newly formulated.* Boston: Ginn and Company.

Columella. 1941. *On Agriculture, Books I–IV.* Translated by H. B. Ash. Cambridge, MA: Harvard University Press.
Cook, T. D., and D. T. Campbell. 1979. *Quasi-experimentation: Design and analysis issues for field settings.* Boston: Houghton Mifflin.
Dahl, R. 1985. *A preface to economic democracy.* Berkeley: University of California Press.
Domar, E. 1966. The Soviet collective farm as a producer cooperative. *American Economic Review* 56 (September): 743–57.
Doucouliagos, C. 1995. Worker participation and productivity in labor-managed and participatory capitalist firms: A meta-analysis. *Industrial and Labor Relations Review* 49 (1): 58–77.
Dow, G. 2003. *Governing the firm: Workers' control in theory and practice.* Cambridge: Cambridge University Press.
Drucker, P. 1976. *The unseen revolution: How pension fund socialism came to America.* New York: HarperCollins.
Foerster, R., and E. Dietel. 1927. *Employee stock ownership in the United States.* Princeton, NJ: Princeton University, Industrial Relations Section, Department of Economics.
Freeman, R. 2008. When workers share in profits: Effort and responses to shirking. *Revista de Politica Economia* 97 (6): 9–36.
Freeman, R., and J. Rogers. 2006. *What workers want,* 2nd ed. Ithaca, NY: ILR Press Books.
Freeman, S. F. 2007. Effects of ESOP adoption and employee ownership: Thirty years of research and experience. Working Paper no. 07-01, Organizational Dynamics Programs, University of Pennsylvania.
Frohlich, N., J. Godard, J. A. Oppenheimer, and F. A. Starke. 1998. Employee versus conventionally-owned and controlled firms: An experimental analysis. *Managerial and Decision Economics* 19 (4/5): 311–26.
Griffeth, R. W., P. W. Hom, and S. Gaertner. 2000. A meta-analysis of antecedents and correlates of employee turnover: Update, moderator tests, and research implications for the next millennium. *Journal of Management* 26 (3): 463–88.
Gustman, A. L., and T. L. Steinmeier. 2001. What people don't know about their pensions and Social Security. In *private pensions and public policies,* ed. W. G. Gale, J. B. Shoven, and M. J. Warshawsky, 57–125. Washington, DC: Brookings Institution.
Harter, J. K., F. L. Schmidt, and T. L. Hayes. 2002. Business-unit level relationship between employee satisfaction, employee engagement, and business outcomes: A meta-analysis. *Journal of Applied Psychology* 87 (2): 268–79.
Harrison, D. A., D. A. Newman, and P. L. Roth. 2006. How important are job attitudes? Meta-analytic comparisons of integrative behavioral outcome and time consequences. *Academy of Management Journal* 49 (2): 3.
Heckman, J. 1976. The common structure of statistical models of truncation, sample selection, and limited dependent variables and a simple model for such models. *Annals of Economic and Social Measurement* 5 (4): 475–92.
Kaarsemaker, E. C.A. 2006a. Employee ownership and human resource management: A theoretical and empirical treatise with a digression on the Dutch context. Doctoral Dissertation. Radboud University Nijmegen, Nijmegen, Netherlands.
———. 2006b. Employee ownership and its consequences: Synthesis-generated evidence for the effects of employee ownership and gaps in the research literature. York, UK: University of York.
Kanigel, R. 1997. *The one best way: Frederick Winslow Tayor and the enigma of efficiency.* New York: Viking.

Kelso, L. O., and M. J. Adler. 1958. *The capitalist manifesto.* New York: Random House.
Kim, E. H., and P. Ouimet. 2008. Employee capitalism or corporate socialism? Broad-based employee stock ownership. Ross School of Business, University of Michigan. Working Paper, October.
Kruse, D. 1993. *Profit sharing: Does it make a difference?* Kalamazoo, MI: W. E. Upjohn Institute for Employment Research.
———. 1998. Profit sharing and the demand for low-skill workers. In *Generating jobs: Increasing the demand for low-skill workers,* ed. R. Freeman and P. Gottschalk, 105–53. New York: Russell Sage Foundation.
Kruse, D., and J. Blasi. 1997. Employee ownership, employee attitudes, and firm performance: A review of the evidence. In *Handbook of human resource management,* ed. D. J. B. Mitchell, D. Lewin, and M. Zaidi, 113–51. Greenwich, CN: JAI Press.
———. 1999. Public opinion polls on employee ownership and profit sharing. *Journal of Employee Ownership Law and Finance* 11 (3): 3–25.
Kurland, N. G., M. D. Greaney, and D. K. Brohawn. 2004. *Capital Homesteading.* Washington, DC: Center for Economic and Social Justice.
Logue, J., and J. Yates. 2002. *The real world of employee ownership.* Ithaca, NY: Cornell University Press.
Malmendier, U., and G. Tate. 2008. Superstar CEOs. NBER Working Paper no. 14140. Cambridge, MA: National Bureau of Economic Research, June.
Mason, R. 1982. *Participatory and workplace democracy: A theoretical development in critique of liberalism.* Carbondale and Edwardsville, IL: Southern Illinois University Press.
Mishel, L., J. Bernstein, and S. Allegretto. 2007. *The state of working America 2006/2007.* Ithaca, NY: Cornell University Press.
Nalbantian, H. 1987. Incentive compensation in perspective. In *Incentives, cooperation, and risk sharing,* ed. H. Nalbantian, 3–46. Totowa, NJ: Rowman and Littlefield.
National Center for Employee Ownership (NCEO). 2007. *ESOPs and corporate governance.* Oakland, CA: National Center for Employee Ownership.
Organization for Economic Cooperation and Development (OECD). 1995. Profit sharing in OECD countries. *OECD Employment Outlook* (July): 139–69.
Pateman, C. 1970. *Participation and democratic theory.* New York: Cambridge University Press.
Peterson, S. J., and F. Luthans. 2006. The impact of financial and nonfinancial incentives on business-unit outcomes over time. *Journal of Applied Psychology* 91 (1): 156–65.
Putterman, L., and G. Skillman, Jr. 1988. The incentive effects of monitoring under alternative compensation schemes. *International Journal of Industrial Organization* 6 (1): 109–19.
Rosen, C., J. Case, and M. Staubus. 2005. *Equity: Why employee ownership is good for business.* Boston: Harvard Business Press.
Sammer, J. 2006. Too much of a good thing. *Journal of Online Accountancy* (April). Available at: www.aicpa.org/jofa/apr2006/sammer.htm.
US Senate, Subcommittee of the Committee on Finance. 1939. *Survey of experiences in profit sharing and possibilities of incentive taxation.* Washington, DC: Government Printing Office.
Walker, F. A. 1876. *The wages question: A treatise on wages and the wages class.* New York: MacMillan and Company.
Ward, B. 1958. The firm in Illyria: Market syndicalism. *The American Economic Review* 48 (4): 566–89.

Weiss, A. 1987. Incentives and worker behavior: Some evidence. In *Incentives, cooperation, and risk,* ed. H. R. Nalbantian, 137–50. Totowa, NJ: Rowan and Littlefield.
Weitzman, M. 1984. *The share economy.* Cambridge, MA: Harvard University Press.
Weitzman, M. and D. Kruse. 1990. Profit sharing and productivity. In *Paying for productivity: A look at the evidence,* ed. A. Blinder, 95–141. Washington, DC: Brookings Institution.
Welbourne, T. M., and L. R. Gomez Mejia. 1995. Gainsharing: A critical review and a future research agenda. *Journal of Management* 21 (3): 559–609.

I

The Extent and Operation of Shared Capitalism

1

Shared Capitalism in the U.S. Economy
Prevalence, Characteristics, and Employee Views of Financial Participation in Enterprises

Douglas L. Kruse, Joseph R. Blasi, and Rhokeun Park

In the past several decades the United States and other advanced countries have seen growth in direct employee participation in the financial performance of capitalist enterprises. This participation can take many forms, including profit sharing, gain sharing, bonuses, employee stock ownership, and broad-based stock options. All of these approaches have one thing in common: offering the worker a share in profits or stock appreciation when the company makes a profit. Our broad label for this participation is "shared capitalism."

This growth is driven in part by evolution of the corporate form under capitalism, increased competitive pressures, environmental volatility, and rapid technological change, which have led firms to implement new forms of workplace organization and human resource practices. These changes include increased teamwork, employee participation in decisions, and other practices that can work in conjunction with financial participation to increase worker productivity, skills, commitment, and job security. Shared capitalist institutions with new forms of high performance work organization, not traditional labor-management relations, may be the emerging form of employee relations under capitalism.

This raises a number of important questions for firms, workers, and economic policymakers:

Douglas L. Kruse is a professor of human resource management and labor studies and employment relations at the Rutgers School of Management and Labor Relations, and a research associate of the National Bureau of Economic Research. Joseph R. Blasi is a professor of human resource management and labor studies and employment relations at the Rutgers School of Management and Labor Relations, and a research associate of the National Bureau of Economic Research. Rhokeun Park is an assistant professor of College of Business Administration at the Kwangwoon University.

- To what extent are these new modes of financial participation and decision-making related?
- Are they likely to increase or decrease economic inequality?
- Do they generally supplement or substitute for standard forms of compensation?
- How can they best improve productivity in ways that will benefit both firms and ordinary workers?
- Do employees welcome shared capitalism or are they uneasy about the increased financial risk and responsibility that this places on them?
- Are the new forms of participation likely to continue to grow?

Following a discussion of why shared capitalism exists at all, we summarize data on the current forms and extent of shared capitalism in the US economy. We then provide an overall portrait of shared capitalism using the General Social Survey (GSS) and NBER data sets that will be used to answer the previous questions in the other chapters of this book, along with an initial exploration of how shared capitalism is related to job and company characteristics, work organization, risk aversion, and worker preferences.

1.1 Why Share with Workers?

Standard economic analysis outlines two key problems with shared capitalism plans that argue against their use. Principal-agent analysis says that owners/managers can improve employees' performance by giving employees pay contingent on performance, but group incentives suffer from the free rider or "1/N" problem due to the increasingly weak link between individual performance and rewards as the size of the group expands. Economic analysis therefore predicts that firms will favor tying financial rewards to local economic performance and outcomes rather than to company-wide outcomes. This is because profit sharing or gain sharing based on workplace outcomes can motivate workers in a small group, who can influence the costs and revenues of that group. Hence, the argument suggests that firms that introduce financial sharing should eschew company-wide sharing, since there is virtually nothing the local group can do to affect the share price of the firm.

A second key problem with shared capitalism plans is income variability for risk-averse workers. Firms are predicted to select the least costly form of rewarding workers. In traditional analyses where firms are risk-neutral and workers are risk-averse, this means paying employees wages or salaries, rather than with variable pay dependent on company performance. Firms that offer more risky modes of wage payment should have to compensate workers for risk.

Given these (and other[1]) problems, why are there any shared capitalism plans? The major reasons for adopting shared capitalism can be categorized as productivity- or flexibility-related.

1.1.1 Productivity Reasons for Shared Capitalism Plans

Firms may find that group incentives are better than individual incentives for encouraging productive teamwork and information sharing, especially where centralized supervision is costly. The free rider problem may be overcome by creation of an implicit cooperative agreement among employees to work hard, enforced by monitoring co-worker performance and applying peer pressure where needed (Weitzman and Kruse 1990). What it takes to create and maintain such an agreement is unclear and may vary from workplace to workplace—it is likely that company human resource policies, employee relations, and general corporate culture play a large role. A growing body of literature finds that combinations of workplace policies may induce behaviors that improve performance (see, e.g., Ichniowski et al. [1996]; Becker, Huselid, and Ulrich [2001]). It has been demonstrated that globalization in specific industries and firms is linked to the adoption of high performance work practices (Blasi and Kruse 2006).

A productivity motivation for adopting and maintaining shared capitalism plans is directly expressed by many firms (US GAO 1986, 20; Kruse 1993, 33), and is supported by several findings in studies of adoption.[2] Studies generally find, however, that profit-sharing and employee ownership plans are more common in large firms, which runs counter to the idea that the free rider problem will favor greater productivity in small firms.[3]

1. While these are the two most common theoretical objections to shared capitalism plans, there are others as well. These include the possibility that diluting the economic surplus received by the owner will decrease performance by weakening the owner's incentive to monitor workers closely (Alchian and Demsetz 1972), and the objection that profit sharing will decrease the firm's incentives to make capital investments (Summers 1986). See Putterman and Skillman (1988) and Weitzman (1986) for responses to these, and Bonin and Putterman (1987) and Dow (2003) for additional theoretical arguments for and against shared capitalism plans.

2. Pendleton (2006) finds that employee discretion over methods and pace of work positively predicts the use of broad-based employee ownership plans, and that such discretion also predicts using employee ownership and individual incentives in combination. Oyer and Schaefer (2005) find that adoption of broad-based stock option plans can be explained by retention and sorting, but not incentive effects. Kruse (1996) finds that R&D levels are higher among old profit-sharing firms, and job enrichment plans were more likely to be adopted just before new profit-sharing plans, suggesting complementarities aimed at improving productivity. Beatty (1994) finds that risk variables suggest a productivity motivation for adoption of ESOPs. Ichniowski and Shaw (1995) find that group incentives are more likely to be adopted when they are part of a package of complementary policies to improve productivity, and also find evidence of large switching costs that discourage firms with established technologies and workplace relationships from adopting new practices. Kim (2005) finds that reducing nonlabor costs and improving employee relations are predictors of adoption of gain-sharing plans.

3. See Gregg and Machin (1988); Poole (1989); Fitzroy and Kraft (1995); Kruse (1996); and Pendleton (2006).

Shared capitalism does appear to create productive cooperation, at least in some companies. Existing evidence from over sixty studies indicates a positive association on average between shared capitalism programs and company performance, but with substantial dispersion in results (Kruse and Blasi 1997; Kruse 2002). The average estimated increase in productivity associated with employee ownership and profit sharing is about 4.5 percent, and is maintained when using pre/post comparisons and attempts to control for selection bias. Boning, Ichniowski, and Shaw (2001) find positive effects of group incentives, particularly when combined with problem-solving teams. Other studies of gain sharing also find positive results, particularly when there is high employee involvement in design and operation, shorter payout periods, controllable targets, and perceptions of procedural and distributive justice (Bullock and Tubbs 1990; Welbourne and Mejia 1995; Collins 1998). There may be a number of pathways through which shared capitalism has effects on performance, and these pathways and complementarities may differ among types of shared capitalism (Robinson and Wilson 2006). Many of the effects of shared capitalism plans on performance are likely to work through employee attitudes and behaviors.[4] Most studies find that organizational commitment and identification are higher under employee ownership, while giving mixed results between favorable and neutral on motivation and behavioral measures (Kruse and Blasi 1997). The results are consistent with opinion polls, which find that most members of the public think that workers in employee ownership firms work harder and better (reviewed in Kruse and Blasi [1999]).

1.1.2 Flexibility Reasons for Shared Capitalism Plans

Firms may also adopt shared capitalism plans for flexibility-related reasons. These plans can provide something of value to workers without a fixed obligation (such as a wage or salary increase) that the company may have difficulty meeting depending on future performance and the competitive environment. A flexibility motivation is supported by the finding that increased volatility in profits helps predict adoption of profit-sharing and employee ownership plans (Kruse 1996), although another study found that low-risk firms are more likely to provide company stock matches in 401(k) plans (Brown, Liang, and Weisbenner 2004).

Some of the firm's financial risk is being shared with workers, which as noted before, may disadvantage risk-averse workers unless they are compensated for the risk. Consistent with the idea that workers are risk averse, most prefer straight wage salary to company-wide or individual incentives; however, a majority express positive views toward employee ownership and profit sharing, and would like at least part of their next raise to be in company stock (summarized in Kruse and Blasi [1999]). The extant evidence

4. Bartel et al. (2003) find that employee attitudes affect a variety of workplace outcomes.

indicates that workers generally do not sacrifice pay and benefits for shared capitalism plans: wages and compensation tend to be higher on average for workers in employee ownership and profit-sharing plans (Blasi, Conte, and Kruse 1996; Kardas, Scharf, and Keogh 1998; Kruse 1993, 113–14; Kruse 1998; Scharf and Mackin 2000). In exchange for the financial risk, workers may benefit through lower risk of displacement: prior studies find that employee ownership firms tend to have more stable employment and higher survival rates than other firms (Craig and Pencavel 1992, 1993; Blair, Kruse, and Blasi 2000; Park, Kruse, and Sesil 2004). The prediction by Weitzman (1984) that profit sharing should stabilize firm employment has also received support in many, though not all, studies.[5]

1.1.3 Other Reasons for Shared Capitalism Plans

There are several reasons that firms may adopt shared capitalism plans apart from those that are productivity- or flexibility-related. First, firms may adopt such plans due to tax and regulatory incentives—for example, Employee Stock Ownership Plans (ESOPs) enjoyed substantial tax incentives in the 1980s, and retiring owners can still avoid capital gains taxes if they sell their stock to an ESOP. Second, some employee ownership plans were adopted in the 1980s in response to hostile takeover threats (Blasi and Kruse 1991). Both takeover threats and tax incentives were clearly a factor in some 1980s ESOP adoptions (Blasi and Kruse 1991; Beatty 1994). Third, firms may adopt employee ownership or profit sharing out of a desire to discourage unionization by increasing employee identification with the company. Profit-sharing plans are less common among unionized workers, which at least partly reflects firms dropping such plans after a union drive (Freeman and Kleiner 1990; Mitchell, Lewin, and Lawler 1990; Kruse 1996). Findings are mixed on the relation between unionization and employee ownership.[6]

Finally, shared capitalism plans may be adopted and promoted for moral or social reasons. Albert Gallatin, a signer of the Declaration of Independence and Secretary of the Treasury under Thomas Jefferson, set up a profit-sharing plan at the Pennsylvania Glass Works in 1795, stating that the "democratic principle upon which this Nation was founded should not be restricted to the political processes but should be applied to the industrial operation" (quoted in US Senate [1939, 72]). Workers who started the first unions in colonial American coastal cities set up some worker cooperatives

5. Studies of Weitzman's prediction that profit sharing should stabilize firm employment have produced mixed findings: a majority support the proposition that firms view profit sharing differently from fixed wages in making employment decisions, while half of the studies find greater employment stability associated with profit sharing and the other half find either no greater stability or greater stability only in some samples (summarized in Kruse [1998, 109–13]).

6. Gregg and Machin (1988) and Poole (1989) find employee ownership is more common in unionized companies in the United Kingdom, while Kruse (1996) finds that ESOP adoption was equally likely in union and nonunion establishments in the 1970s and 1980s.

as alternatives to the craft firms where some master craftsmen were attempting to introduce more division of labor in order to deskill traditional craft workers and reduce their pay. A century later, some labor organizations set up worker cooperatives as part of a political challenge to how capitalism was developing, while others saw employee ownership and profit sharing as a means to build support for capitalism in opposition to the competing communist and socialist systems—arguing that it would help cure "unrest" and "irrational agitation" in capitalism, and that the "great uplift and inspiration that sharing of profits cultivates in the employee" would lead to "harmony and contentment" (Askwith 1926, 20). John D. Rockefeller and other corporate leaders in 1919 encouraged employee ownership, employee involvement in corporate decision-making, and profit sharing as part of a grand plan for "welfare capitalism" that spread in the 1920s. Profit sharing was promoted in the 1930s in Congressional hearings in the 1930s by Republican Senator Arthur Vandenberg, and ESOPs were promoted by investment banker Louis Kelso in conjunction with Democratic Senator Russell Long of Louisiana in the 1970s, as ways to broaden participation in the economic system.[7]

In sum, the two key objections to group incentives—the free rider problem and worker risk aversion—have not been sufficient to quash shared capitalism plans. They continue to be adopted and maintained, providing a fertile ground for examining outcomes for both firms and workers. As will be seen, such programs now involve almost half of adult workers in the economy, albeit at different levels of intensity and with different combinations of work practices. The next section reviews current data on the prevalence of shared capitalism plans, followed by a more intensive look at the kind of company policies associated with shared capitalism that can shed light on how they are used by companies.

1.2 Prevalence of Shared Capitalism Programs

There are a variety of forms that shared capitalism programs can take, which we break into four broad categories: profit sharing, gainsharing, employee ownership, and stock options. The NBER Shared Capitalism program sponsored several questions on shared capitalism in the 2002 and 2006 General Social Surveys and the 2003 National Organizations Survey, providing the most recent representative data available. The results from these surveys are summarized in table 1.1, while Appendix table 1A.1 summarizes other nationally representative surveys and administrative data over the past fifteen years. All of the surveys have high response rates. Four of the surveys were conducted by the US Census Bureau (the two National Employer Surveys, the National Compensation Survey, and the National Longitudinal Survey of Youth), two surveys were conducted by the National Opinion Research Center of the University of Chicago (General

7. For a more extensive history of shared capitalism see Blasi, Kruse, and Bernstein (2003).

Table 1.1 Current prevalence of shared capitalism plans

	(1)	(2)	(3)
Source	GSS	GSS	NOS
Year	2002	2006	2002
Type of data	Employee survey	Employee survey	Firm survey
Profit sharing			
Percent of employees covered			
Eligible for bonuses based on company performance	34	38	46
Received bonus last year based on company performance	24	30	
Percent of firms with plans			
Any employees eligible for bonuses based on company performance			62
Gain sharing			
Percent of employees covered			
Eligible for bonuses based on department or team performance	23	27	23
Received bonus last year based on department or team performance	17	21	
Percent of firms with plans			
Any employees eligible for bonuses based on department or team performance			35
Employee ownership			
Percent of employees covered			
Own company stock	21	18	16
Percent of firms			
Any employees own company stock			33
Stock options			
Percent of employees covered			
Hold stock options	13	9	
Granted stock options last year		5	
Percent of firms			
Any employees granted stock options last year			14
Combinations			
Any of above	43	47	
Just one form:			
Rec'd profit- or gain-sharing bonus last year	14.6	21.2	
Hold company stock	5.0	3.8	
Hold stock options	0.7	0.7	
Two forms:			
Hold co. stock and rec'd profit- or gain-sharing bonus last year	3.7	5.3	
Hold co. stock and stock options	6.1	3.2	
Hold stock options and rec'd profit- or gain-sharing bonus last year	0.4	0.6	
All three forms	6.1	4.6	
Sample size	1,257	1,173	312

Notes: GSS = General Social Survey; NOS = National Organizations Survey.

Social Survey and National Organizations Survey), and two were conducted by professional survey organizations (the Worker Representation and Participation Survey by Princeton Survey Research Associates, and the Employee Benefits Research Institute survey by Gallup). All surveys are based on the full private sector, except the National Employer Surveys, which are limited to private for-profit firms.[8]

1.2.1 Profit Sharing Prevalence

There is no hard and fast definition of profit sharing. Many firms have formal plans that are called profit sharing, but there is variation in (a) how profits are defined, (b) whether profits must meet a threshold level, (c) whether some or all of the profit share is discretionary, and (d) whether the profit share is paid in cash or is deferred (put into a defined contribution pension plan). In addition, firms may have bonus plans that are not called profit sharing, but that effectively share profits since the bonus is affected by how well the company is doing. As shown in table 1.1, just over one-third of employees say that they are covered by profit sharing in 2002 (34 percent) and 2006 (38 percent), which is in line with earlier employee surveys in table 1A.1. Employers reported a higher percentage of employees eligible for bonuses based on company performance (46 percent), though another survey using a more restricted definition showed lower figures (30 percent of workers are in a deferred profit-sharing plan while 5 percent are in a cash profit-sharing plan, in table 1A.1).

1.2.2 Gain Sharing Prevalence

Gain-sharing plans typically tie employee compensation to a group-based operational measure—such as physical output, productivity, quality, safety, customer satisfaction, or costs—rather than to a company-wide financial measure such as profitability or returns. These plans often involve employees in some formal way to develop ideas and skills for improving performance. The three most popular types are Scanlon, Rucker, and ImproShare plans, although there is a growing number of custom-designed plans. As shown in table 1.1, employee and company surveys agree that about one-fourth (23 to 27 percent) of employees are eligible for bonuses based on group or workplace performance.[9]

8. The full private sector figures include nonprofit organizations. While these organizations cannot have employee ownership and stock options, they can have organization- and group-based bonuses that are equivalent to profit sharing and gain sharing, so their inclusion provides the best estimates of the extent to which shared capitalism has permeated the entire private sector. Other chapters in this volume restrict attention to for-profit firms.

9. About two-fifths (43 percent) of Fortune 1000 surveyed companies have gain-sharing plans somewhere in the company, although most include less than 20 percent of employees (Lawler, Mohrman, and Ledford 1995, 19). Broader surveys of compensation and human resource managers have found that only about one-eighth (13 percent) have formal gain sharing plans (Collins 1998).

1.2.3 Employee Ownership Prevalence

Employee ownership of company stock can occur in a variety of ways. Combining all the ways, the GSS surveys in table 1.1 show that roughly one-fifth of employees report owning some company stock (21 percent in 2002 and 18 percent in 2006, which is in line with earlier surveys in table 1A.1). The most popular type of plan is the ESOP (Employee Stock Ownership Plan). The ESOP is distinguished by the fact that workers do not have to use their own money to buy the stock (unless stock was traded for wage and work rule changes, which happens only in a very small minority of ESOPs). Federal legislation allows companies to borrow money from a bank to fund the worker stock and pay for it in installments from company revenues. About 5 percent of employees are part of ESOPs (table 1A.1). Employees may also own company stock through other types of defined contribution plans. Many employees have bought stock through their company 401(k) plan, a retirement plan where they make pretax contributions from their paycheck. Sometimes corporations will match employee contributions to 401(k) plans with company stock, so this one limited aspect of 401(k)-based employee ownership is closer to the ESOP because workers do not buy it. About 20 percent of workers are eligible for a defined contribution plan that holds employer stock (table 1A.1). These non-ESOP pension plans also include various Employee Retirement Income Security Act (ERISA)-covered stock bonus plans and deferred profit-sharing trusts (often combined with 401(k) plans), which actually hold some of their assets in company stock.

Employees can also own company stock outside of pension plans. Employee Stock Purchase Plans (ESPPs) allow workers to buy stock with deductions from their paycheck with a discount from the market price, and some corporations provide employees direct grants of stock as part of a stock bonus plan. Employees may also hold onto stock after exercising stock options, or own stock through open market purchases. These plans combine with the pension plans to make about one-fifth of private sector employees into employee-owners.

1.2.4 Stock Options Prevalence

Stock options represent a kind of hybrid between profit sharing and employee ownership. A stock option is the right to buy the stock at a set price for ten years into the future. The worker does not have to purchase the stock. Receiving one hundred stock options to purchase Biotech Inc. stock at $10 per share gives the worker the right to exercise these options anytime over ten years if the stock price goes above $10 per share. During the ten years, the worker can, for example, buy a stock trading at $15 a share for $10 per share, then sell the stock, and pocket the $5 profit after taxes. While stock option excesses have been abused among higher executives, for other managers and workers, a stock option has less risk than using one's savings to buy the stock and really involves the right to the upside gain without the risk of losing one's capital. The GSS surveys show a decline in stock option holding from 13 percent in 2002 to 9 percent in 2006, which we believe is due to the Security and Exchange Commission's implementation of stock option expensing that led some companies to cut back on broad-based plans.[10] Only 14 percent of companies reported making stock option grants in 2002 and 5 percent of employees in the 2006 GSS reported actually receiving a stock option grant in the prior year (table 1.1), while other surveys showed that 8 percent of employees are eligible to receive stock options (table 1A.1).[11]

1.2.5 Overall Prevalence and Overlap Among Types of Shared Capitalism

The prevalence of any type of shared capitalism is high: the GSS surveys showed that 43 percent of employees reported participating in one or more of the above plans in 2002, rising to 47 percent in 2006 (table 1.1). The rise in profit-sharing and gain-sharing eligibility more than offset the declines in employee ownership and stock option holding between these two years. Earlier surveys show that between 41 percent and 75 percent of firms have shared capitalism plans (table 1A.1).

What is the overlap among the different types of shared capitalism? This issue has never been comprehensively explored until the 2002 and 2006 General Social Surveys. As shown in table 1.1, close to 15 percent of employees in the 2002 survey received a profit- or gain-sharing bonus in the prior year but do not own company stock or hold stock options, rising to 21 percent in 2006. There were 4 to 5 percent who just own company stock and less than 1 percent who just hold stock options. About 10 percent had two of the three forms of shared capitalism in both years, while 5 to 6 percent had all three. The important point here is that employee ownership and stock option holding are uncommon on their own, and typically paired with another type of shared capitalism. Over three-fourths of the employee-owners also have profit-gain-sharing bonuses and/or stock options, while almost all of the 13 percent who hold stock options also have profit-gain-sharing bonuses and/or employee ownership. This high overlap suggests that firms may believe that it is worthwhile to develop employee ownership and stock options in combination with each other and profit/gain sharing by placing together forms of shared capitalism that are less risky for workers (cash profit sharing or stock options) with those that are more risky for workers (owning company

10. This drop in stock option holding likely accounts for the drop in the percent of workers in the computer services industry who own company stock (from 58.3 percent to 31.9 percent). Because employee ownership often comes about as a result of being granted stock options, this drop is likely an unintended consequence of the employee stock option expensing.

11. The figure stayed at 8 percent in the 2006 survey (BLS 2006). The 2006 numbers are not presented in the table since there are no figures on deferred profit sharing or employee ownership.

stock). Such combinations also reflect a pairing of short-term and long-term incentives.

Employee ownership and profit sharing have also received substantial attention in other advanced countries and transition economies. With coverage similar to that in the United States, between 20 and 30 percent of workers in France, Great Britain, Italy, and Japan are covered by some form of profit sharing, while smaller numbers are covered by employee stock ownership (Del Boca, Kruse, and Pendleton 1999; Jones and Kato 1995). Across the European Union, between 5 and 43 percent of firms within each country have profit-sharing plans, between 1 and 22 percent have employee share ownership, and between 5 and 38 percent have team-based bonuses (European Foundation for the Improvement of Living and Working Conditions 1997; Poutsma 1999; Pendleton et al. 2003; Poutsma, Kalmi, and Pendleton 2006). Some employee ownership is also found in Korea and Taiwan (Cin, Han, and Smith 2003, Kato et al. 2005) and in some socialist countries transiting to private ownership, including China (Tseo 1996; Chiu et al. 2005), Russia (Blasi, Kroumova, and Kruse 1997), and the countries in central and eastern Europe (Uvalic and Vaughan-Whitehead 1997; Smith, Cin, and Vodopivec 1997). Broad-based stock options have appeared in stock market companies and high tech firms in Asia and are newly emergent in China and India.

1.2.6 Employee Participation in Decision Making

Employee participation in decision making is often seen as complementary to financial participation, most basically because financial participation provides the incentive to improve performance while participation in decision making can provide a means to improve performance. Before looking at their overlap in the next section, table 1.2 summarizes the most recent survey data on the overall prevalence of employee participation in decisions. There is a lot of variation in the types and measures of employee participation. About two-fifths of employees report having a lot of influence in decisions or say they often participate with others in job decisions in both 2002 and 2006, while one-third of employees report being in an employee involvement team (30 percent) or self-managed work team (33 percent). Firms report a lower number of employees in these plans (17 percent each), while about two-fifths of firms report having these plans at all. Data from earlier surveys in table 1A.2 show great dispersion using different measures, from a low of 13 to 16 percent of employees in self-managed teams to a high of 52 to 55 percent of employees in work-related meetings for nonmanagers.

1.3 Looking Inside the Shared Capitalism Firms

The NBER project was established to take a closer look at shared capitalism plans, providing a more complete portrait along with an analysis of their causes and effects. We complement the broad representative data from

Table 1.2 **Current prevalence of employee participation in decisions**

	(1)	(2)	(3)
Source	GSS	GSS	NOS
Year	2002	2006	2002
Type of data	Employee survey	Employee survey	Firm survey
Percentage of employees covered			
Employee involvement team			
Self-managed team		30	17
Quality circles or employee involvement committees		33	17
Often participate with others in making decisions that affect job	42	38	
Often participate with others in helping set how things are done on job	45	42	
Percentage of firms with plans			
Self-managed teams for nonmanagers			39
Quality circles or employee involvement committees			42
Worker safety committees			49
Sample size	1,257	1,173	312

Notes: GSS = General Social Survey (from National Opinion Research Center, analyzed by authors) (all private sector); NOS = National Organizations Survey (from National Opinion Research Center, analyzed by authors) (all private sector).

the 2002 and 2006 GSS with an intensive analysis of employee survey data from fourteen companies that have a variety of shared capitalism programs, which we refer to as the NBER data set. Both data sets are described in the "Studying Shared Capitalism" section of the introduction to this volume.

We first focus on the size of the financial stakes in shared capitalism, then examine the types of jobs covered and the types of companies that participate, then assess the relationship to work organization and company policies, and finally describe the risk profile of participants and nonparticipants using new measures of risk aversion in the NBER data set.

1.3.1 Size of Financial Stakes in Shared Capitalism

The extent and characteristics of shared capitalism programs in the GSS and NBER data sets are presented in table 1.3. This table combines the 2002 and 2006 GSS prevalence figures from table 1.1 (showing about one-third of workers covered by profit sharing, one-fourth covered by gain sharing, one-fifth holding company stock, and one-ninth holding stock options), and adds detail on the financial stakes involved. The monetary value appears to be significant for covered employees. The median profit-sharing and gain-sharing bonus in the GSS is $1,500, or 4.6 percent of annual pay, and their entire employer stock estate value totals $10,000 or 23 percent of annual pay for the median employee-owner.

Table 1.3 Shared capitalism types and intensities in GSS and NBER data sets

	General Social Survey 2002–2006	NBER company data set	Sample sizes GSS	Sample sizes NBER
Bonus eligibility				
Profit sharing	35.9%	71.3%	2,386	41,018
Gain sharing	24.9%	20.7%	2,386	41,023
Size of most recent bonus, if eligible for any				
Mean dollar value	$6,265	$11,329	693	26,113
Median dollar value	$1,500	$2,000	693	26,113
Mean % of pay	8.9%	12.1%	645	22,019
Median % of pay	4.6%	5.7%	645	22,019
Employee ownership				
Own employer stock in any form	19.4%	64.0%	2,406	41,206
Own employer stock through:				
Employee Stock Ownership Plan		8.1%		41,109
Employee Stock Purchase Plan		17.6%		40,990
401(k) plan		33.5%		40,885
Exercising options and keeping stock		5.0%		41,032
Open market purchase		7.3%		41,145
Value of employer stock, if own stock				
Dollar value: Mean	$63,130	$60,078	318	25,447
Dollar value: Median	$10,000	$14,375	318	25,447
% of pay: Mean	81.7%	65.0%	302	22,715
% of pay: Median	23.0%	30.6%	302	22,715
% of wealth: Mean		19.6%		23,141
% of wealth: Median		10.0%		23,141
Stock options				
Currently hold stock options	11.3%	21.9%	2,392	41,166
Ever granted stock options		22.3%		41,166
Granted stock options last year		20.4%		41,158
Value of stock options, if hold options:				
Mean dollar value of unvested options		$112,882		8,390
Mean dollar value of vested options		$143,117		8,497
Total dollar value: Mean		$249,901		8,656
Total dollar value: Median		$75,000		8,656
% of pay: Mean		183.7%		8,403
% of pay: Median		100.0%		8,403
% of wealth: Mean		60.3%		8,104
% of wealth: Median		28.6%		8,104
Any of above programs	44.9%	85.7%	2,430	41,206

The column labeled "NBER company data set" naturally gives higher figures for the shared capitalist modes of compensation since we selected these firms on the basis of having these programs. Of the workers in the firms, 71 percent report being paid by profit sharing, 21 percent report gain sharing, 64 percent report owning employer stock, and 22 percent report holding stock options. Overall, 86 percent of surveyed workers report having at least one of these programs. The size of the median profit-sharing and gain-sharing stake are only somewhat higher among the NBER companies than in the GSS (5.7 percent compared to 4.6 percent), as is employee ownership as a percent of pay (30.6 percent compared to 23.0 percent). The median stock option holding is $75,000 (counting the estimated profit on both vested and unvested stock options if they were exercised on the day of the survey), representing 100 percent of annual pay and 29 percent of total wealth. These stakes should be large enough to detect effects on worker and firm outcomes, if such effects exist.

1.3.2 Participation by Type of Job and Company

Where are shared capitalism plans most likely? Theory broadly suggests that they are most likely to be adopted in jobs and companies where performance is most sensitive to employee effort, or where the need for flexibility is greatest. Table 1.4 provides participation rates by basic job and company characteristics, using both the representative GSS data set and our larger NBER data set, with more extensive measures.

The idea that shared capitalism is most likely in performance-sensitive jobs is supported by the finding that profit/gain sharing is most common among sales and management employees (48 percent and 56 percent, in column [1]), but the incidence remains substantial among all but service employees (19 percent). Managers are also the most likely to own company stock (27 percent, column [2]), but are not particularly more likely to hold stock options (14 percent, column [3]). The NBER data show high levels of participation in profit/gain sharing and employee ownership for all occupational groups, and low levels of stock options only among production workers and service employees (since the NBER stock option companies had few production or service employees, although this is not true for all stock option firms in the United States).

Those who have been at their jobs for less than one year are the least likely to participate in shared capitalism, partly reflecting probationary periods (e.g., employees only become eligible for an ESOP after six months or one year). The exception is that new employees are more likely than older employees to hold stock options in the NBER data set, probably reflecting the use of stock options to lure workers into the jobs.

Not surprisingly, shared capitalism is more common among full-time employees in both the GSS and NBER data—such employees are more likely to be core employees whose commitment and effort are important to workplace performance. Also not surprisingly, union members are less likely than nonunion employees to be part of profit-gain-sharing plans (38 percent versus 14 percent, in column [1]). Unions tend to resist profit sharing due to concerns that management can manipulate profit figures, and that such pay can create inequality among workers (Zalusky 1990). Given the resistance of some union representatives to variable rewards, it is striking that union

Table 1.4 **Participation in shared capitalism by job and company characteristics**

	GSS, 2002–2006 Percent of those at left who:			NBER Percent of those at left who:			Sample sizes	
	Are eligible for profit or gain sharing (1)	Own co. stock (2)	Hold stock options (3)	Are eligible for profit or gain sharing (4)	Own co. stock (5)	Hold stock options (6)	GSS (7)	NBER (8)
Overall	37.2	19.4	11.3	76.4	64.0	21.9	2,430	41,206
Occupation								
Production	32.8	17.2	9.2	72.1	51.6	1.8	638	18,227
Admin. support	35.8	23.5	15.5	68.5	63.8	18.1	340	2,246
Professional/technical	36.7	21.9	13.7	82.9	78.8	44.1	443	11,582
Sales	47.6	21.5	12.9	64.8	75.7	49.6	299	2,220
Service	19.2	6.5	4.1	71.4	50.8	0.0	322	1,105
Management	55.8	26.5	13.6	90.6	78.6	42.3	368	4,836
Lower mgt.				88.4	83.7	60.3		4,214
Middle mgt.				88.9	79.4	48.3		2,946
Upper mgt.				90.4	74.4	46.8		856
Tenure								
1 year or less	30.5	7.5	4.4	62.3	51.2	33.1	775	6,029
> 1, < = 5 years	39.7	20.3	11.6	75.2	61.1	24.5	828	10,602
More than 5 years	41.8	30.3	17.8	80.8	69.1	18.2	805	23,639
Hours of work								
Part-time (< 35)	20.7	8.2	4.9	54.8	45.9	13.1	447	588
Full-time (35+)	40.9	22.0	12.7	76.7	64.2	21.6	1,983	39,625

(continued)

Table 1.4 (continued)

	GSS, 2002–2006 Percent of those at left who:			NBER Percent of those at left who:			Sample sizes	
	Are eligible for profit or gain sharing (1)	Own co. stock (2)	Hold stock options (3)	Are eligible for profit or gain sharing (4)	Own co. stock (5)	Hold stock options (6)	GSS (7)	NBER (8)
Union member								
No	38.0	19.0	10.9	80.9	70.3	25.2	1,455	35,547
Yes	14.0	24.2	12.4	46.7	22.4	0.7	161	5,001
Establishment size								
1 to 9	26.0	8.9	4.2				505	
10 to 49	35.6	12.3	7.1				604	
50 to 99	40.5	20.3	13.8				329	
100 to 999	44.1	26.9	16.0				656	
1,000+	44.8	36.8	20.1				300	
Industry								
Ag./mining/constr.	22.3	11.1	5.2				183	
Manufacturing	52.0	29.1	18.3				399	
Trans./comms./utilities	43.8	37.9	23.7				214	
Wholesale/retail	32.7	14.0	8.3				553	
Finance/insurance	55.0	35.5	18.8				198	
Computer services	65.2	43.4	40.3				52	
Other services	28.6	9.9	4.0				771	

members in the GSS are actually slightly more likely than nonunion employees to report owning company stock and holding stock options. While there have been some noteworthy examples of unions leading employee buyouts (which make up a very small percentage of firms with employee ownership), this employee ownership result more likely reflects the greater likelihood of retirement plans among union employees, many of which invest in company stock.

The free rider problem predicts that these plans will be most advantageous in small workplaces, and some evidence in chapter 2 indicates that this is true. But while this would lead one to expect a greater prevalence of shared capitalism plans in small establishments, their prevalence is actually higher among larger establishments (columns [1] through [3]). All three types of shared capitalism are most common in establishments with 1,000 or more employees. This may be explained by the existence of fixed costs in setting up plans, which can be spread across a larger number of employees in larger establishments. These large establishment sizes strongly suggest that if these companies want to use shared capitalism to enhance performance, they need to take steps to counter the free rider problem.

Finally, shared capitalism is well-represented in every broad industry. Profit/gain sharing is most common in manufacturing, finance, and computer services (> 50 percent in each), while employee ownership and stock options are most common in transportation/communications/utilities, finance, and computer services. The figures are consistently highest in computer services, reflecting the strong use of these incentives in new economy companies that rely heavily on human skill and ingenuity (Blasi, Kruse, and Bernstein 2003). The growth of high performance work practices and self-managed work teams in manufacturing also suggests that reliance on human skill and ingenuity is now more widely relevant in traditionally blue-collar industries. This is not consistent with the notion that shared rewards (especially employee ownership) will only work with professional groups such as lawyers or more specialized service firms (Hansmann 1996). Shared capitalism appears to be least prevalent in the agriculture/mining/construction industry group, yet this requires closer examination. Profit sharing is quite common in these industries, and it has been reported that many large construction firms use shared capitalism practices. An analysis of incidence in the three separate industries making up this grouping is probably required.[12]

1.3.3 Work Organization and Shared Capitalism

How are these jobs structured, and what policies accompany shared capitalism plans? Table 1.5 uses the GSS and NBER data to explore how shared capitalism relates to several aspects of work organization and policies,

12. The newsletters of the National Center for Employee Ownership have reported on the construction industry. For example, see www.nceo.org/library/esop-construction-industry.html.

Table 1.5 **Work organization by type of shared capitalism**

	GSS (2002–2006)				NBER			
	All employees (%) (1)	Eligible for profit or gain sharing (%) (2)	Own co. stock (%) (3)	Hold stock options (%) (4)	All employees (%) (5)	Eligible for profit or gain sharing (%) (6)	Own co. stock (%) (7)	Hold stock options (%) (8)
Total	100.0	100.0	100.0	100.0	100.0	100.0	100.0	100.0
Work as part of team	57.8	60.8**	60.4	64.8**	59.3	60.8**	57.9**	64.7**
Ease of observing co-worker performance								
Hard	15.5	12.5**	16.1	11.9	18.3	17.8**	19.2**	26.3**
Medium	14.4	14.1	13.5	16.2	32.7	33.3**	33.8**	37.7**
Easy	70.1	73.3**	70.4	72.0	49.0	48.9	47.1**	36.0**
Closeness of supervision								
Low supervision					47.5	50.5**	53.9**	66.6**
Medium supervision					33.7	33.1**	32.0**	24.8**
High supervision					18.7	16.4**	14.1**	8.7**
Participation in decisions								
Employee involvement team					34.7	37.9**	37.7**	37.7**
Lot of involvement in job decisions					50.5	53.5**	56.5**	71.2**
Lot of involvement in setting dept. goals					21.3	22.6**	23.8**	33.2**
Lot of involvement in co. decisions								
A lot of say about what happens on job	24.6	30.8**	28.4*	28.7				
Often help set way things are done on job	39.7	46.8**	47.5**	49.0**				
Often make decisions with others	43.5	50.1**	49.4**	52.1**				
Training/multiskilling								
Have training opportunities I need	60.3	62.7*	61.6	60.6				
Formal training in past year					56.4	59.2**	61.8**	76.3**
Frequently participate in job rotation					11.2	11.4*	11.5*	6.2*
High job security	88.3	92.7**	91.7*	91.3	84.3	86.9**	87.8**	92.0**
See myself working here a long time					81.7	83.6**	84.8**	88.3**
Current job is part of long-time career					76.2	78.0**	79.1**	83.5**
Sample size	2,430	908	470	275	41,206	31,351	26,390	9,019

**Difference between those who are and are not covered by this policy is significant at the 5 percent level.

*Significant difference at the 10 percent level.

shedding some light on the role these plans may play in companies. The figures in table 1.5 are simple cross-tabulations—these relationships are analyzed using probit regressions in table 1.6.

Consistent with the idea that shared capitalism can encourage cooperative teamwork, profit/gain sharing employees are more likely to work in teams, to be able to observe co-worker performance, and to have low levels of supervision (columns [2] and [6]). The patterns are mixed, however, for employee-owners and stock option holders. The stock option holders are more likely to work in teams and to have low levels of supervision, but are no more likely (and may be less likely) to easily observe co-worker performance (columns [4] and [8]). This may have to do with their concentration in high tech and computer industry firms. Employee-owners are not more likely to work in teams or to find it easy to observe co-workers, although they are more likely to have low levels of supervision (columns [3] and [7]). This suggests that profit/gain sharing may be the primary method for encouraging cooperative teamwork in day-to-day work, while employee ownership and stock options may affect other outcomes (e.g., identification, loyalty, turnover). This is a good example of how we can learn from the analysis of prevalence. It could possibly be the basis of an argument for combining short-term forms of shared capitalism like profit/gain sharing with longer horizon forms such as employee ownership and stock options. Whether these forms do have the effects suggested by the prevalence figures is the job of other chapters to sort out.

Participation in decisions may, as discussed earlier, be an important complement to shared capitalism programs in affecting workplace performance. Such participation can give employees the means to improve performance, while shared capitalism provides the incentives. The data in table 1.5 generally support the idea of complementarity, with shared capitalism employees having higher levels on both the objective measure of participation (being in an employee involvement team) and the subjective measures (having say/influence in one's job, or participating with others in decisions affecting one's job). Profit/gain sharing is consistently linked to higher participation in both data sets, while employee ownership and stock option holding show mixed results in the GSS but strong associations with participation in the NBER data.[13]

Training may be another important complementary policy, helping to develop worker skills and commitment that can be reinforced by shared capitalism. The GSS tabulations in table 1.5 show that those with profit/gain sharing are more likely to report that they have the training opportunities they need. The shared capitalism employees in the NBER firms are more likely to have had employer-sponsored training in the past year, while

13. Kalmi, Pendleton, and Poutsma (2004) find that the different plan types have different relationships to participatory practices.

profit/gain sharing employees and employee-owners—but not stock option holders—are slightly more likely to frequently participate in job rotation.

Finally, job security may be an important complementary policy—it is hard to maintain worker commitment and cooperative teamwork if employees are afraid they will be laid off. Just over 90 percent of the GSS shared capitalism employees report they are unlikely to be laid off, which is higher than the 88 percent figure for the entire sample, with significantly greater job security for profit/gain sharers and employee-owners. All three groups of shared capitalism employees report significantly greater job security in the NBER data. In addition, each of these three groups reports a higher expected likelihood of working at the company for a long time, and of seeing their current jobs as part of a long-term career.

Table 1.6 analyzes these relationships using probit regressions to predict the likelihood of participating in each of the types of shared capitalism. The NBER regressions control for company fixed effects, thereby doing within-company comparisons of who participates. Most of the simple relationships described previously are maintained when controlling for other variables. In particular, each of the plans is associated with greater participation in decisions and with employer-sponsored training in the past year. The ease of observing co-workers is a significant predictor of profit/gain sharing in both the GSS and NBER data, suggesting an important role for peer pressure. Closeness of supervision is a strong negative predictor in the NBER sample, and high job security is a strong positive predictor, indicating that freedom from supervision and job security may be complementary policies. Finally, the GSS regressions confirm that each type of shared capitalism is more likely in larger establishments (though the highest prevalence of profit/gain sharing is among establishments with 100 to 999 employees rather than the 1,000+ group).

1.3.4 Risk Aversion and Shared Capitalism

Risk aversion is clearly an important consideration in shared capitalism. We measured risk aversion with several questions on the NBER company surveys, including a self-rating on a 0 to 10 scale, how much one would pay for a bet, whether one would take a job with stable pay versus one with risky but higher pay, and whether one regularly buys and sells stock on the stock market. These are strongly related and appear to measure a common risk propensity. Here we focus on the employee's self-rating, where 0 is "hate to take any kind of risk" and 10 is "love to take risks" (see question wording in Appendix A). The average score is 5.6, but there is wide dispersion: 20 percent of employees give scores of 3 or less, and 41 percent give themselves scores of 7 or more. Of course these employees are not representative of the overall workforce, since they have chosen to work in companies with shared capitalism and 85 percent are covered by some type of shared capitalism plan. We can nonetheless learn something about the role of risk aversion

Table 1.6 **Predicting participation in shared capitalism**

	GSS			NBER		
	Eligible for profit or gain sharing (1)	Own co. stock (2)	Hold stock options (3)	Eligible for profit or gain sharing (4)	Own co. stock (5)	Hold stock options (6)
Occupation						
Production (excl.)						
Admin. support	0.058 (0.041)	0.080 (0.036)**	0.083 (0.031)***	–0.010 (0.010)	0.023 (0.011)**	0.044 (0.017)***
Prof./technical	0.041 (0.043)	0.075 (0.036)**	0.059 (0.027)**	0.019 (0.006)***	0.064 (0.006)***	0.141 (0.011)***
Sales	0.214 (0.044)***	0.096 (0.039)***	0.074 (0.032)***	–0.240 (0.014)***	0.035 (0.012)***	0.147 (0.022)***
Service	–0.056 (0.045)	–0.031 (0.036)	0.012 (0.031)	–0.022 (0.013)*	–0.016 (0.015)	
Management	0.224 (0.041)***	0.099 (0.036)***	0.049 (0.026)**			
Lower mgt.				0.033 (0.008)***	0.039 (0.010)***	0.146 (0.018)***
Middle mgt.				0.062 (0.008)***	0.072 (0.010)***	0.473 (0.020)***
Upper mgt.				0.085 (0.012)***	0.045 (0.017)**	0.741 (0.018)***
Tenure (years)	0.000 (0.002)	0.006 (0.001)***	0.002 (0.001)***	0.004 (0.000)***	0.009 (0.000)***	0.005 (0.000)***
Full-time	0.144 (0.029)***	0.089 (0.019)***	0.036 (0.015)**	0.000 (0.000)***	0.000 (0.000)***	0.000 (0.000)
Union member	a	a	a	–0.343 (0.010)***	–0.390 (0.010)***	–0.100 (0.007)***
Work as part of team	0.006 (0.024)	0.003 (0.018)	0.020 (0.012)	a	a	a
Ease of observing co-worker	0.007 (0.004)**	–0.001 (0.003)	0.001 (0.002)	0.004 (0.001)***	0.002 (0.001)*	–0.002 (0.001)
Closeness of supervision				–0.004 (0.001)***	–0.011 (0.001)***	–0.009 (0.001)***
Participation index	0.114 (0.018)***	0.051 (0.013)***	0.030 (0.009)***			
Employee involvement team				0.054 (0.004)***	0.041 (0.005)***	0.012 (0.007)*
Formal training in past year				0.039 (0.005)***	0.039 (0.005)***	0.027 (0.006)***
Have needed training opps.	0.015 (0.024)	–0.004 (0.018)	–0.004 (0.013)			
High job security	a	a	a	0.083 (0.007)***	0.061 (0.007)***	0.053 (0.008)***

(continued)

Table 1.6 (continued)

	GSS			NBER		
	Eligible for profit or gain sharing (1)	Own co. stock (2)	Hold stock options (3)	Eligible for profit or gain sharing (4)	Own co. stock (5)	Hold stock options (6)
Establishment size						
1 to 9 (excl.)						
10 to 49	0.109 (0.036)***	0.034 (0.031)	0.031 (0.024)			
50 to 99	0.164 (0.042)***	0.117 (0.039)***	0.109 (0.034)***			
100 to 999	0.174 (0.036)***	0.171 (0.034)***	0.117 (0.028)***			
1,000+	0.155 (0.045)***	0.253 (0.045)***	0.142 (0.039)***			
Industry						
Ag./mining/constr.	–0.235 (0.035)***	–0.072 (0.027)**	–0.053 (0.015)***			
Manufacturing (excl.)						
Trans./comms./utilities	–0.075 (0.041)*	0.081 (0.037)**	0.038 (0.026)			
Wholesale/retail	–0.190 (0.034)***	–0.058 (0.025)**	–0.042 (0.016)**			
Finance/insurance	–0.029 (0.048)	0.070 (0.042)*	0.007 (0.024)			
Computer services	0.090 (0.090)	0.101 (0.076)	0.135 (0.071)***			
Other services	–0.208 (0.034)***	–0.128 (0.022)***	–0.098 (0.014)***			
Company fixed effects				Yes	Yes	Yes
n	2,283	2,275	2,264	34,316	34,790	30,301
Pseudo-R^2	0.12	0.165	0.156	0.194	0.211	0.815

Notes: Figures are derivatives based on probit regressions, representing effect of one-unit change in independent variable on probability of dependent variable.

[a]These variables were available only for a limited number of observations. When they are included, the significant relationships are:

Union membership in GSS: negative and significant only in column (1); High job security in GSS: positive and significant only in column (1); Work as part of team in NBER: positive and significant in columns (4–6).

***Significant at the 1 percent level.

**Significant at the 5 percent level.

*Significant at the 10 percent level.

by examining its relation to plan participation and worker views of variable pay.

Risk aversion is related to plan participation, as shown in table 1.7, but not always in expected ways. A surprising finding is that those who are eligible for profit sharing rate themselves as more risk averse (less risk loving) than those who are not eligible, both before and after controlling for demographic, pay, and wealth variables (columns [3] and [5]). One explanation of this is that profit sharing may be less risky than sinking your savings in your company stock under certain circumstances, such as where you feel you are paid at the market rate for wages and there is no wage substitution. Eligibility for gain sharing and individual bonuses, in contrast, is associated with greater risk loving. Like profit sharers, stock option holders appear slightly more risk averse after controlling for demographic, pay, and wealth variables.

Employee owners appear to like risk more on average, but this varies by type of employee ownership. Those owning stock through 401(k) plans or open market purchases are clearly more risk loving than others (table 1.7, column [6]), undoubtedly reflecting the self-selection of risk lovers buying stock or allocating 401(k) accounts toward company stock. The ESOP mem-

Table 1.7 **Risk aversion and participation in variable pay**

	Risk-loving mean values (0–10 scale)					
	Participate in plan at left				Risk loving as predictor of plan at left[a]	
	Yes (1)	No (2)	Simple difference (3)	(s.e.) (4)	Coefficient (5)	(s.e.) (6)
Profit-sharing eligibility	5.57	5.73	–0.16	(0.03)***	–0.009	(0.001)***
Gain-sharing eligibility	6.02	5.51	0.51	(0.03)***	0.004	(0.001)***
Individual bonus eligibility	6.01	5.46	0.55	(0.03)***	0.003	(0.001)***
Hold stock options	6.12	5.47	0.65	(0.03)***	–0.001	(0.001)*
Own co. stock	5.71	5.45	0.26	(0.03)***	0.003	(0.001)**
Own employer stock through:						
Employee Stock Ownership Plan	5.32	5.65	–0.33	(0.04)***	0.000	(0.001)
Employee Stock Purchase Plan	6.16	5.51	0.65	(0.03)***	0.000	(0.000)
401(k) plan	5.57	5.65	–0.08	(0.03)***	0.005	(0.001)***
Exercising options and keeping stock	6.11	5.59	0.52	(0.06)***	0.000	(0.000)
Open market purchase	6.49	5.55	0.94	(0.05)***	0.003	(0.000)***

Notes: Based on NBER data. s.e. = standard error.

[a]Controlling for age, gender, marital status (2 dummies), family size, college graduate, graduate degree, number of kids, race (4 dummies), disability status, ln(fixed pay), ln(wealth), and twenty-one country dummies.

***Significant at the 1 percent level.

**Significant at the 5 percent level.

*Significant at the 10 percent level.

bers, however, are more risk averse than non-ESOP members in a simple comparison, and risk loving is not a significant predictor of ESOP membership, or of owning stock through an ESPP or exercised stock options, after controlling for demographic, pay, and wealth variables.

Does risk aversion affect employees' views of variable pay? Most of the NBER workers would prefer to be paid in part with profit sharing, company stock, or stock options, as shown in table 1.8. Remarkably, even two-thirds (66 percent) of the most risk-averse employees would prefer this, while 86 percent of the least risk-averse prefer this. Very similar results are obtained by a question asking about the employee's next pay increase, where again two-thirds of the most risk-averse would prefer at least some of the increase to be in the form of shared capitalism pay. This would not make sense if the employees were seeing the shared capitalism pay as simply adding risk; rather, they are likely perceiving a chance for increased reward and perhaps some of the other benefits for workers analyzed in chapter 8.

About three-fourths of employees would prefer a new bonus program to be based at least in part on their individual performance, where the line of sight is clearly greatest. Almost three-fifths (58 percent), however, prefer that it also be based on company profits or performance, while only about one-third (37 percent) prefer that it be based in part on work group performance. It may be that the greater line of sight for work group bonuses is trumped by their greater perceived risk, as work group performance is probably seen as more variable than overall company performance (which averages across all work groups in the company). Those with low risk aversion are more likely to choose individual- or work group-based bonuses, while risk aversion is not related to the desire for company-based bonuses.

Most employees would not vote to sell the company to an outside investor for a 50 percent premium, but would do so for a 100 percent premium. This likelihood is lowest among those with high risk aversion, reflecting greater concern about job loss if the company were sold. While the concern about job loss is the most common reason for refusing to sell the company, about one-third of employees say they would refuse to sell because they like owning company stock (33 percent), and a similar number say they would refuse because they like the sense of community from employee ownership (37 percent). A lot more research is needed on this broader issue of employee ownership and workers' corporate governance rights since governance has always been seen by corporate finance experts as being partly about managing risk. (It is standard in investment banking to provide more governance rights when risk is higher.)

Finally, most workers say that they would be willing to accept some degree of lower regular pay in exchange for the opportunity to participate in a company-based bonus system averaging 10 percent of their pay. This willingness varies substantially, however: two-fifths (41 percent) would not accept lower pay, while one-sixth (15 percent) would accept less than 5 percent

Table 1.8 **Worker views of performance-based pay**

		Risk aversion		
	Overall	High	Medium	Low
Type of pay preferred				
All fixed wage or salary	22%	34%	25%	14%***
Paid in part with profit sharing, stock, or stock options	78%	66%	75%	86%***
n	13,199	2,090	5,069	5,953
Preference for next pay increase				
All fixed pay	27%	33%	28%	23%***
Split between fixed wages and profit sharing, stock, or options	60%	55%	61%	62%***
All profit sharing, stock, and options	13%	12%	11%	15%***
n	25,869	5,318	9,805	10,330
Would prefer new bonus plan to be based on (can pick more than one)				
Your individual performance	77%	71%	77%	79%***
Your work group performance	37%	31%	36%	40%***
Company profits or performance	58%	57%	59%	59%
n	13,379	2,144	5,133	6,002
Would vote to sell company if outside investor offered:				
50% premium	41%	36%	39%	45%***
100% premium	64%	57%	61%	68%***
Reasons for not selling for 50% premium:				
Like owning company stock	33%	35%	33%	32%
Like sense of community from employee ownership	37%	37%	36%	39%
Concerned about investor laying off employees	70%	75%	73%	65%***
Offer might mean company is worth more	39%	33%	38%	44%***
n	12,938	2,059	4,931	5,854
Lower pay accepted for company-based bonus averaging 10%				
Mean percent lower regular pay accepted (standard deviation)	3.31 (3.56)	2.28 (3.21)	3.15 (3.51)	3.91*** (3.63)
0% lower pay accepted	41%	55%	43%	33%***
Between 0% and 5% lower pay accepted	15%	15%	15%	15%
5% lower pay accepted	27%	19%	26%	31%***
More than 5% lower pay accepted	17%	11%	16%	21%***
n	29,426	5,535	11,141	12,480

***Significant difference among risk groups at the 1 percent level.
**Significant difference at the 5 percent level.
*Significant difference at the 10 percent level.

lower pay, one-fourth (27 percent) would accept 5 percent lower pay, and one-sixth (17 percent) would accept more than 5 percent lower pay. This is predictably related to risk aversion: a majority of the most risk averse would not accept any lower regular pay (55 percent), compared to only a third of the least risk averse (33 percent).

The NBER employees, of course, may not be representative of the overall workforce—in particular, they may have joined these companies because they are less risk averse and more favourably inclined toward shared capitalism than most workers. The data are broadly consistent, however, with existing representative surveys. Over half (57 percent) of workers in a 1986 BNA/Bruskin poll said they would trade their next pay increase for a share in the company, while 44 percent said this in a 1989 EBRI/Gallup poll (summarized in Kruse and Blasi [1999]). Workers in general report that, if they had company stock, they would be less likely than the NBER workers to vote to sell the company even for a substantial premium.[14] This indicates either a more rosy view of the advantages of employee ownership among the workforce in general, or more concern about an outside investor laying off workers. The public surveys do show positive views of employee ownership: strong majorities think employee-owners will work harder, have higher commitment, and be more concerned with the long-term success of the company. Participation in decisions, however, appears to be very important: most employees would prefer participation in decisions to having a share of ownership, and say that if they owned stock, they would not let management vote their shares on major corporate issues (summarized in Kruse and Blasi [1999]).

Overall, as expected, risk aversion is a key factor for shared capitalism: it appears most likely to steer workers away from positions providing gain sharing or individual bonuses, and to discourage workers from allocating 401(k) assets toward company stock or purchasing company stock on the open market. Greater risk aversion is associated with less positive views of shared capitalism pay, but even among the most risk-averse employees, two-thirds says they prefer some shared capitalism as part of their pay package.

1.4 Conclusion

Contrary to concerns about the free rider problem and worker risk aversion, a substantial number of workers participate in shared capitalism plans and are open to more shared capitalism in their firms. Nationally-representative surveys of private-sector employees and firms show that:

- One-fourth to one-third of employees are eligible for profit sharing.
- About one-fourth of employees are eligible for gain sharing.
- About one-fifth of employees own stock in their companies.
- Between one-twelfth and one-eighth of employees are eligible for stock options or hold stock options.

14. The 41 percent who would sell for a 50 percent premium is somewhat higher than the 23 percent figure for all employees from a 1989 EBRI/Gallup poll, and the 64 percent who would vote to sell for a 100 percent premium is much higher than the 36 percent figure for all employees from a 1994 EBRI/Gallup poll (summarized in Kruse and Blasi [1999]).

- Overall, between one-third and one-half of employees participate in some form of shared capitalism.

Why do firms use these plans, and why do workers accept them? This chapter broadly reviews the major reasons for adopting these plans and some of the research results. The two major categories of reasons for adopting these plans are productivity-related and flexibility-related reasons. Prior studies find that these plans tend to be associated with better company performance on average, but there is wide dispersion in outcomes. The goal of the other chapters using these data is to explain this dispersion and understand why, where, and how shared capitalism does or does not work. Limited evidence also shows that these plans tend to be associated with greater job stability, firm survival, and employee compensation—the latter finding helping to explain why employees express positive attitudes toward shared capitalism plans. The dispersion of results indicates that there is still much to learn about how these plans can play a positive role in workplaces. Research has not nailed down the complementary role that other human resource policies play in affecting worker attitudes and firm performance.

Both the NBER data set and the nationally-representative GSS data set indicate that while shared capitalism exists broadly throughout the economy, it is not distributed randomly across firms and employees. One important finding is that shared capitalism plans are more likely in larger establishments, where free riding is likely to be the highest. To counter free riding, firms may combine shared capitalism with other policies to create a cooperative culture. An initial exploration of work organization and policies supports this idea: shared capitalism employees are more likely to participate in workplace decision-making and training programs, and to have high job security and low levels of supervision. Within-company comparisons show that they are also more likely to work in teams, and profit/gain sharing employees can more easily observe co-worker performance, creating the conditions for cooperative teamwork. An examination of risk aversion in the NBER data set shows that, as expected, risk aversion is linked to lower participation in several types of plans and less positive views of shared capitalism, but even among the most risk averse employees, two-thirds prefer to have some form of shared capitalism in their pay package.

So risk aversion does not appear to be an insurmountable barrier and there appear to be conditions for productive cooperation—does this in fact occur? What other effects does shared capitalism have on both firms and employees? These relationships are probed and tested in the following chapters, using the GSS and NBER data to explore a wide variety of outcomes for both workers and firms.

Over the last few decades many economists have said about various shared capitalism practices: "If it makes so much sense then why do we not observe more firms and employees doing it?" The response put forward by these prevalence figures is: "It appears to have spread throughout the economy, so what does that mean?" This chapter has examined some of the linkages between shared capitalism practices and other employment practices. These linkages raise another series of questions: are managers in companies making the right choices about how to achieve optimal performance from shared capitalist practices, or are there patterns and combinations that work better and worse? In other words, is what we observe optimal because that is the shared capitalist arrangement that has emerged in the laboratory of real life? Or, should managers consider making substantive changes to how they organize shared capitalism because it can be done well or poorly? One needs to beware of looking at these incidence patterns with a "deterministic" frame of mind. It should not be immediately concluded that just because there are certain types of shared capitalist practices (such as company stock in 401(k) plans as a lone form of shared capitalism) or combinations of these practices with human resource policies (such as a low incidence of self-management work teams with employee ownership) that somehow managers have told us these are the best workable combinations. Firms and managers may have it wrong in some cases and right in others. (For an example of a manager's analysis, see Carey [2004].) These data will be used to explore the answers to these questions.

This NBER research program continues a long tradition of examination of shared capitalism by economists. The phenomenon was seen as being so important that John Bates Clark, a founder of the American Economic Association, wrote a book in the 1880s calling for the combination of profit-sharing and employee ownership in companies to improve business performance by motivating worker involvement (Clark 1886). With his encouragement and with the hard work of a research group organized at Johns Hopkins University to survey the nation on this question, the first volume of the journal of the American Economics Association included an article surveying shared capitalism in companies in the Northeast (Bemis 1886) and in the Midwestern city of Minneapolis (Shaw 1886; Adams 1888). Subsequent early issues covered other regions of the United States. Given that almost half of US employees currently report participating in some form of shared capitalism, it is time to take a close look again.

Appendix

Table 1A.1 Prior evidence on prevalence of shared capitalism plans

	(1)	(2)	(3)	(4)	(5)	(6)	(7)	(8)	(9)
Source	WRPS	NLSY	EBRI	NES	NES	Form 5500	NCS	NCS	NCS
Year	1994/95	1993	1994	1994	1997	1998	2003	2005	2007
Type of data	Employee survey	Employee survey	Employee survey	Firm survey	Firm survey	Admin. data	Firm survey	Firm survey	Firm survey
Profit sharing									
Percent of employees covered									
Receive any bonuses based on profit sharing	30								
Employer makes profit sharing available		35							
Deferred profit-sharing plan							21	30	
Cash profit-sharing plan							5		5
Gain sharing									
Percent of employees covered									
Receive any bonuses based on meeting workplace goals	27								
Employee ownership									
Percent of employees covered									
Participate in an employee stock ownership or ESOP plan	24								
Own company stock			21						
ESOP participant						6	5	4	
Participant in non-ESOP 401(k) w/employer stock[a]						11			
Participant in other defined con. plan w/employer stock[a]						1			

(*continued*)

Table 1A.1 (continued)

	(1)	(2)	(3)	(4)	(5)	(6)	(7)	(8)	(9)
Eligible for other defined con. plan w/employer stock[a]							20		
Participant in savings/thrift plan w/employer stock[a]								16	
Stock options									
Percent of employees covered									
Eligible to receive stock options							8		8
Combinations									
Percent of employees covered									
Any of above	57								
Percent of firms									
Profit-sharing, bonus, or gain-sharing plan				75					
Stock options or profit sharing					41				
Sample size	2,408		1,000	2,867	2,963	50,769	3,030	3,227	8,256

Notes: WRPS = Worker Representation and Participation Survey (Freeman and Rogers 1999); NLSY = National Longitudinal Survey of Youth (Kruse 1998); EBRI = Employee Benefits Research Institute (EBRI/Gallup 1994); NES = National Employer Survey (Kruse and Blasi 2000); Form 5500 = Form 5500 pension data set (Kruse 2002); NCS = National Compensation Survey (BLS 2005, 2007, 2008).

[a]At least some employees in these plans own company stock, but the employee him/herself might not own stock (e.g., if she or he declined to allocate some contributions to employer stock in a 401(k)).

Table 1A.2 Prior evidence on prevalence of employee participation in decisions

	(1)	(2)	(3)
Source	WRPS	NES	NES
Year	1994/95	1994	1997
Type of data	Employee survey	Firm survey	Firm survey
Percentage of employees covered			
Employee involvement team	31		
Self-managed team		13	16
Work-related meetings for nonmanagers		52	55
Quality circles or employee involvement committees			
A lot of influence in decisions about how job is done	57		
A lot of influence in setting group or dept. goals	32		
Percentage of firms with plans			
Self-managed teams for nonmanagers		32	34
Work-related meetings for nonmanagers		80	74
Sample size	2,408	2,867	2,963

Notes: WRPS = Worker Representation and Participation Survey (Freeman and Rogers 1999)(all private sector); NES = National Employer Survey (Kruse and Blasi 2000)(private for-profit firms).

References

Adams, H. B. 1888. *History of cooperation in the United States.* Baltimore, MD: Johns Hopkins University and N. Murray.

Alchian, A. A., and H. Demsetz. 1972. Production, information costs, and economic organization. *American Economic Review* 62 (5): 777–95.

Askwith, M. E. 1926. *Profit-sharing: An aid to trade revival.* London: Duncan Scott.

Bartel, A., R. Freeman, C. Ichniowski, and M. Kleiner. 2003. Can a work organization have an attitude problem? The impact of workplaces on employee attitudes and economic outcomes. NBER Working Paper no. 9987. Cambridge, MA: National Bureau of Economic Research, September.

Beatty, A. 1994. An empirical analysis if the corporate control, tax and incentive motivations for adopting leveraged employee stock ownership plans. *Managerial and Decision Economics* 15 (4): 299–315.

Becker, B. E., M. A. Huselid, and D. Ulrich. 2001. *The HR scorecard: Linking people, strategy, and performance.* Cambridge, MA: Harvard Business School Press.

Bemis, E. W. 1886. Cooperation in the Northeast. *Publications of the American Economic Association* 1 (5): 7–136.

Blair, M., D. Kruse, and J. Blasi. 2000. Is employee ownership an unstable form? Or a stabilizing force? In *The new relationship: Human capital in the American corporation,* ed. T. Kochan and M. Blair, 241–98. Washington, DC: The Brookings Institution.

Blasi, J., and D. Kruse. 1991. *The new owners: The mass emergence of employee ownership in public companies and what it means to American business.* New York: HarperBusiness.

———. 2006. High performance work practices at century's end. *Industrial Relations* 45 (4): 547–78.

Blasi, J., M. Conte, and D. Kruse. 1996. Employee ownership and corporate performance among public corporations. *Industrial and Labor Relations Review* 50 (1): 60–79.

Blasi, J., M. Kroumova, and D. Kruse. 1997. *Kremlin capitalism: Privatizing the Russian economy.* Ithaca, NY: Cornell University Press.

Blasi, J., D. Kruse, and A. Bernstein. 2003. *In the company of owners: The truth about stock options (and why every employee should have them).* New York: Basic Books.

Bonin, J., and L. Putterman. 1987. *Economics of cooperation and labor managed economies.* New York: Cambridge University Press.

Boning, B., C. Ichniowski, and K. Shaw. 2001. Opportunity counts: Teams and the effectiveness of production incentives. NBER Working Paper no. 8306. Cambridge, MA: National Bureau of Economic Research, May.

Bureau of Labor Statistics (BLS). 2005. *National Compensation Survey: Employee benefits in private industry in the United States, 2003.* Bulletin 2577, US Bureau of Labor Statistics, October.

———. 2006. *National Compensation Survey: Employee benefits in private industry in the United States, March 2006.* Summary 06-05, US Bureau of Labor Statistics, August.

———. 2007. *National Compensation Survey: Employee benefits in private industry in the United States, 2005.* Bulletin 2589, US Bureau of Labor Statistics, May.

———. 2008. *National Compensation Survey: Employee benefits in private industry in the United States, March 2007.* Summary 07-05, US Bureau of Labor Statistics, August.

Brown, J., N. Liang, and S. Weisbenner. 2004. 401(k) matching contributions in company stock: Costs and benefits for firms and workers. NBER Working Paper no. 10419. Cambridge, MA: National Bureau of Economic Research, August.

Bullock, R. J., and M. E. Tubbs. 1990. A case meta-analysis of gainsharing plans as organization development interventions. *Journal of Applied Behavioral Science* 26 (3): 383–404.

Carey, Raymond. 2004. *Democratic capitalism.* Bloomington, IN: Author House.

Chiu, W. C. K., X. Huang, and H. L. Lu. 2005. When Marx borrows from Smith: The ESOP in China. *Journal of Contemporary China* 14 (45): 761–72.

Cin, B.-C., T.-S. Han, and S. C. Smith. 2003. A tale of two tigers: Employee financial participation in Korea and Taiwan. *International Journal of Human Resource Management* 14 (6): 920–41.

Clark, J. B. 1886. *The philosophy of wealth.* Boston: Ginn and Company.

Collins, D. 1998. *Gainsharing and power: Lessons from six Scanlon plans.* Ithaca and London: Cornell University Press, ILR Press.

Craig, B., and J. Pencavel. 1992. The behavior of worker cooperatives: The plywood companies of the Pacific Northwest. *American Economic Review* 82 (5): 1083–1105.

———. 1993. The objectives of worker cooperatives. *Journal of Comparative Economics* 17 (2): 288–308.

Del Boca, A., D. Kruse, and A. Pendleton. 1999. Decentralisation of bargaining systems and financial participation: A comparative analysis of Italy, UK, and the US. *Lavoro e Relazioni Industriali* (Summer): 9–49.

Dow, G. 2003. *Governing the firm: Worker's control in theory and practice.* Cambridge: Cambridge University Press.

Employee Benefit Research Institute (EBRI)/Gallup. 1994. Public attitudes on employee stock ownership and benefit promises, 1994. EBRI/Gallup Poll no. G-54, Employee Benefit Research Institute, Washington, DC.

European Foundation for the Improvement of Living and Working Conditions. 1997. *New forms of work organization: Can Europe realize its potential?* Luxembourg: Office for Official Publications of the European Communities.

Fitzroy, F., and K. Kraft. 1995. On the choice of incentive in firms. *Journal of Economic Behavior and Organization* 26: 145–60.

Freeman, R., and M. Kleiner. 1990. The impact of new unionization on wages and working conditions. *Journal of Labor Economics* 8 (1): S8–S25.

Freeman, R., and J. Rogers. 1999. *What workers want.* New York: Russell Sage and Cornell University Press.

Gregg, P. A., and S. J. Machin. 1988. Unions and the incidence of performance linked pay schemes in Britain. *International Journal of Industrial Organization* 6 (1): 91–107.

Hansmann, H. 1996. *The ownership of enterprise.* Cambridge, MA: Harvard University Press.

Ichniowski, C., T. Kochan, D. Levine, C. Olson, and G. Strauss. 1996. What works at work: Overview and assessment. *Industrial Relations* 35 (3): 299–333.

Ichniowski, C., and K. Shaw. 1995. Old dogs and new tricks: Determinants of the adoption of productivity-enhancing work practices. *Brookings Papers on Economic Activity, Microeconomics:* 1–55.

Jones, D.C., and T. Kato. 1995. The productivity effects of employee stock-ownership plans and bonuses: Evidence from Japanese panel data. *American Economic Review* 85 (3): 391–414.

Kalmi, P., A. Pendleton, and E. Poutsma. 2004. The relationship between financial participation and other forms of employee participation: New survey evidence from Europe. Discussion Paper no. 3/April. Helsinki Center of Economic Research.

Kardas, P., A. L. Scharf, and J. Keogh. 1998. Wealth and income consequences of ESOPs and employee ownership: A comparative study from Washington state. *Journal of Employee Ownership Law and Finance* 10 (4): 3–52.

Kato, T., J. H. Lee, K.-S. Lee, and J.-S. Ryu. 2005. Employee participation and involvement in Korea: Evidence from a new survey and field research. *International Economic Journal* 19 (2): 251–81.

Kim, D.-O. 2005. The choice of gainsharing plans in North America: A congruence perspective. *Journal of Labor Research* 26 (3): 465–83.

Kruse, D. 1993. *Profit sharing: Does it make a difference?* Kalamazoo, MI: W. E. Upjohn Institute for Employment Research.

———. 1996. Why do firms adopt profit-sharing and employee ownership plans? *British Journal of Industrial Relations* 34 (4): 515–38.

———. 1998. Profit sharing and the demand for low-skill workers. In *Generating jobs: Increasing the demand for low-skill workers,* ed. R. Freeman and P. Gottschalk, 105–53. New York: Russell Sage Foundation.

———. 2002. Research evidence on prevalence and effects of employee ownership. Testimony before the Subcommittee on Employer-Employee Relations, Committee on Education and the Workforce, US House of Representatives, February 13.

Kruse, D., and J. R. Blasi. 1997. Employee ownership, employee attitudes, and firm performance: A review of the evidence. In *The human resource management handbook, part I,* ed. D. Lewin, D. J. B. Mitchell, and M. A. Zaidi, 131–51. Greenwich, CT and London: JAI Press Inc.

———. 1999. Public opinion polls on employee ownership and profit sharing. *Journal of Employee Ownership Law and Finance* 11 (3): 3–25.
———. 2000. The new employee/employer relationship. In *Working nation: Workers, work, and government in the new economy,* ed. D. Ellwood, 42–90. New York: Russell Sage Foundation.
Lawler, E., S. Mohrman, and G. E. Ledford. 1995. *Creating high performance organizations: Practices and results of employee involvement and quality management in Fortune 1000 companies.* San Francisco: Jossey-Bass.
Mitchell, D. J. B., D. Lewin, and E. Lawler. 1990. Alternative pay systems, firm performance, and productivity. In *Paying for productivity: A look at the evidence,* ed. Alan Blinder, 15–88. Washington, DC: Brookings Institution.
Oyer, P., and S. Schaefer. 2005. Why do some firms give stock options to all employees? An empirical examination of alternative theories. *Journal of Financial Economics* 76 (1): 99–133.
Park, R., D. Kruse, and J. Sesil. 2004. Does employee ownership enhance firm survival? In *Advances in the economic analysis of participatory and labor-managed firms,* vol. 8, ed. V. Perotin and A. Robinson, 3–33. New York: Elsevier Science, JAI.
Pendleton, A. 2006. Incentives, monitoring, and employee stock ownership plans: New evidence and interpretations. *Industrial Relations* 45 (4): 753–77.
Pendleton, A., E. Poutsma, J. Van Ommeren, and C. Brewster. 2003. The incidence and determinants of employee share ownership and profit sharing in Europe. In *Advances in the economic analysis of participatory and labor-managed firms,* vol. 7, ed. T. Kato and J. Pliskin, 141–72. New York: Elsevier Science, JAI.
Poole, M. 1989. *The origins of economic democracy: Profit-sharing and employee-shareholding schemes.* London: Routledge.
Poutsma, E. 1999. *Financial employee participation in Europe.* Nijmegen, Netherlands: Nijmegen University Business School, Report to the European Foundation for the Improvement of Living and Working Conditions.
Poutsma, E., P. Kalmi, and A. Pendleton. 2006. The relationship between financial participation and other forms of employee participation: New survey evidence from Europe. *Economic and Industrial Democracy* 27 (4): 637–67.
Putterman, L., and G. Skillman, Jr. 1988. The incentive effects of monitoring under alternative compensation schemes. *International Journal of Industrial Organization* 6 (1): 109–19.
Robinson, A. M., and N. Wilson. 2006. Employee financial participation and productivity: An empirical reappraisal. *British Journal of Industrial Relations* 44 (1): 31–50.
Scharf, A., and C. Mackin. 2000. Census of Massachusetts companies with Employee Stock Ownership Plans (ESOPs). Boston: Commonwealth Corporation.
Shaw, A. 1886. Cooperation in a Western city. *Publications of the American Economic Association* 1 (4): 7–106.
Smith, S., B.-C. Cin, and M. Vodopivec. 1997. Privatization incidence, ownership forms, and firm performance: Evidence from Slovenia. *Journal of Comparative Economics* 25 (2): 158–79.
Summers, L. 1986. On the share economy. *Challenge* (November/December): 47–50.
Tseo, G. 1996. Chinese economic restructuring: Enterprise development through employee ownership. *Economic and Industrial Democracy* 17 (2): 243–79.
US General Accounting Office. 1986. *Employee stock ownership plans: Benefits and costs of ESOP tax incentives for broadening stock ownership.* GAO/PEMD-87-8. Washington, DC: General Accounting Office.
US Senate, Subcommittee of the Committee on Finance. 1939. *Survey of experiences*

in profit sharing and possibilities of incentive taxation. Washington, DC: Government Printing Office.
Uvalic, M., and D. Vaughan-Whitehead, eds. 1997. *Privatization surprises in transition economies: Employee-ownership in Central and Eastern Europe.* Cheltenham, UK and Lyme, NH: Elgar, distributed by American International Distribution Corp., Williston, VT.
Weitzman, M. L. 1984. *The share economy.* Cambridge, MA: Harvard University Press.
———. 1986. Macroeconomic implications of profit sharing. In *NBER macroeconomics annual 1986,* ed. S. Fischer, 291–335. Cambridge, MA: MIT Press.
Weitzman, M. L., and D. Kruse. 1990. Profit sharing and productivity. In *Paying for productivity: A look at the evidence,* ed. Alan Blinder, 95–139. Washington, DC: Brookings Institution.
Welbourne, T. M., and L. R. Gomez Mejia. 1995. Gainsharing: A critical review and a future research agenda. *Journal of Management* 21 (3): 559–610.
Zalusky, J. 1990. Labor-management relations: Unions view profit sharing. In *Profit sharing and gain sharing,* ed. M. J. Roomkin, 65–78. Metuchen, NJ: Scarecrow Press.

2

Worker Responses to Shirking under Shared Capitalism

Richard B. Freeman, Douglas L. Kruse, and Joseph R. Blasi

What do workers do when they see someone slacking off in ways that reduce the productivity of their work group and enterprise?

The rational response depends on the circumstances. In a tournament race for promotion, having a competitor slack off is good news. You do not have to go all out to win the promotion. In a piece-rate pay system where the firm lowers the rate per piece when workers produce more than expected, you will also welcome the shirker. The more other workers shirk, the less

Richard B. Freeman holds the Herbert Ascherman Chair in Economics at Harvard University and is a research associate of the National Bureau of Economic Research. Douglas L. Kruse is a professor of human resource management and labor studies and employment relations at the Rutgers School of Management and Labor Relations, and a research associate of the National Bureau of Economic Research. Joseph R. Blasi is a professor of human resource management and labor studies and employment relations at the Rutgers School of Management and Labor Relations, and a research associate of the National Bureau of Economic Research.

Presented at the Russell Sage/NBER conference in New York City, October 2006. The authors wish to thank Eric Maskin and Canice Prendergast for comments on the paper at the Russell Sage/NBER conference. The discussion and footnotes in response to possible objections represent our responses to their very helpful points. An earlier version was presented at the 2004 Association for Comparative Economic Studies conference, San Diego, CA, with valuable comments from Avner Ben-Ner. This chapter is part of the National Bureau of Economic Research's Shared Capitalism Research Project, funded by the Russell Sage and Rockefeller Foundations. Additional funding for the General Social Survey questions was provided by the Foundation for Enterprise Development, the ESOP Association, the Employee Ownership Foundation, Hewitt Associates, the National Center for Employee Ownership, and the Profit Sharing Council of America. The authors wish to thank Tom Smith with the General Social Survey at the National Opinion Research Center of the University of Chicago and Peter Marsden of Harvard University with the National Organizations Study for their assistance in arranging the shared capitalism segment of both surveys. Refen Koh, Michelle Pinheiro, Rhokeun Park, and Patricia Berhau provided excellent assistance in survey scanning, entry, and verification.

likely it is that management will lower the rate per piece and make it harder to earn your weekly pay.

But when part of workers' pay comes in the form of some group incentive such as profit sharing or share ownership or stock options, a worker who does not do his or her job takes "money out of the pocket" of other workers. The group would be better off if someone acted against the shirker. But standard analysis suggests that it will rarely be rational for anyone to intervene. The costs of intervening with the shirker fall on the intervener but that person gets only part of the benefit (in an N worker group the worker who intervenes gains 1/Nth of the benefit going to workers and none of the benefit that goes to capital). The implication is that rational workers will not act against a shirker just as rational players should not cooperate in a prisoner's dilemma game. Group incentive systems are thus doomed to failure.

The facts for labor practices as for prisoner's dilemma and other games of cooperation are different. Team production and group incentive plans, which succeed only if they overcome free riding and shirking, are widespread in modern economies. Since workers often have better information than management on what fellow workers are doing, worker responses to shirking are critical to the success or failure of these schemes. Many workplaces develop cultures where workers discourage others from shirking. Lab experiments find cooperative behavior in collective goods games when game theory rationality predicts that the rational player defects. Directly relevant to our analysis, Fehr and Gachter (2000) have found that individuals punish defectors in laboratory experiments even when it is not in their individual self-interest to do so, due to norms of reciprocity that are strong among many individuals. Peer monitoring has also been found in group loans in Third World credit markets (Stiglitz 1990). Punishing free riders at a workplace may also benefit the intervener in the long run if other members of the group appreciate that person's action against free riders. They may reap long-term rewards in the form of higher esteem and greater influence within a group. Self-interest aside, the evidence from anthropologists that voluntarily "policing" cooperation occurs in many societies suggests that it may be hardwired from evolution. Some economists have suggested how ostracism can be effective in promoting cooperation (Hirshleifer and Rasmussen 1989). It is also worth noting that to the extent shirking occurs, it is not confined to group incentive systems. Shirking may happen in virtually every workplace.

This study examines worker reactions to shirking by analyzing questions on the 2002 and 2006 General Social Surveys (GSS) and the NBER surveys of fourteen companies that have some forms of group incentive plans. We asked workers about the ease of observing co-workers' performance, and the likelihood of responding to poor work performance. Our analysis of these questions, together with questions about incentive systems, firm human resource policies, and other aspects of the workplace, show:

1. Most workers believe that they can readily detect shirking by fellow employees.

2. Workers are most likely to take action against shirkers in workplaces where employees are paid by some form of "shared capitalism"—by which we mean profit sharing, gain sharing, stock options, or other forms of ownership—and they participate in decisions or work in team settings.

3. Responses to these forms of group incentive pay are largest when they trust management and have good employee management relations, and when the firm adopts high-performance human resource policies, low levels of supervision, and pays fixed wages at or above market levels along with the incentive pay.

4. Consistent with the theory of free riding, anti-shirking behavior is greater in smaller firms and is particularly strong in small firms with shared capitalist pay.

5. Workers in workplaces where there is more anti-shirking behavior report that co-workers work harder and encourage other workers more, and that their workplace facility is more effective in several dimensions related to productivity and profits.

The bottom line is that "shared capitalist" arrangements—defined broadly as those in which firms share rewards and decision-making with workers—and positive labor relations encourage workers to act against shirking behavior and thus strengthen the potential for group incentive systems and team production to overcome the free rider problem and succeed.

2.1 Group Incentives and Monitoring Colleagues

When will a worker act against a shirking fellow employee?

The natural economics answer is that a worker will so act when it pays off for that person, which almost invariably requires group incentive pay. Building on Drago and Garvey (1998), it is easy to show that workers are more likely to intervene the higher the amount of the group incentive, the higher the probability that intervening increases the performance of the co-worker, the lower the cost of intervening (which may depend on individual incentives), and the smaller the number of co-workers. In addition, workers may gain respect from fellow workers and supervisors, which can translate into greater chances of promotion in the future. Workers may discourage "shirkers" through peer pressure and nonpecuniary sanctions such as social ostracism, personal guilt, or shame (Kandel and Lazear 1992). Since the 1/N problem is smaller at small workplaces, cooperative agreements should be easier to establish and maintain in small companies than in large ones.

Workers can also engage in punishing behavior to enforce group norms of high effort, and change the behavior of free riders. Punishment may be effective in counteracting the free rider effect per the experimental results of Carpenter (2004). He explains his results by noting that an increase in the size of a group has two opposing effects: it "forces monitors to spread their resources thinner which might lead to more free riding," but "there are also more people monitoring each free rider so it is not obvious whether the total amount of punishment each free rider receives will increase or decrease" (2004, 4). Prendergast suggests that monitoring with a sufficiently low cost can negate the free rider problem but notes that "empirical evidence on peer pressure reveals behavioral responses different from those posited in the theory".[1]

Finally in the workplace setting, management may seek to develop a corporate culture that emphasizes company spirit, promotes group cooperation, encourages social enforcement mechanisms, and so forth in order to encourage cooperative actions (Weitzman and Kruse 1990; Blasi, Conte, and Kruse 1996; Blasi, Kruse, and Bernstein 2003, 226–28). Fudenberg and Maskin (1986) show how the free rider problem can be overcome in an ongoing relationship by a cooperative agreement among participants. Using artificial agent modeling with small groups, Axelrod (1984) has shown how mutual cooperation can develop among agents through reciprocity. Klos and Nooteboom (2001) explore the creation of interaction networks that have trust as a major component. Nalbantian and Schotter (1997) show how the performance of an experimental group depends on the effort norms established by the group under previous incentive schemes. Knez and Simester (2001) show how the use of autonomous work groups at Continental Airlines helped overcome free riding and encourage mutual monitoring in the presence of a company-wide bonus.[2]

Whatever model one uses to explain punishment of free riders, workers should be more likely to act against shirkers when they: (a) have some financial interest in the performance of the firm; (b) regularly participate in workplace decisions, which should also reduce the cost of speaking out; and (c) have trust in management and good labor-management relations, since in those situations, they can reasonably expect the firm to reward them for helping to reduce shirking. If you do not trust management, you can hardly be expected to report shirking to management. If you regard labor-management relations as poor, you may view shirking as a justifiable response to management's poor treatment of workers. Financial interest, participation in decisions, trust in management, and good labor-labor man-

1. Prendergast (1999) cites Weiss' study of workers in a pharmaceutical company (1987) and Hansen's examination (1997) of the incentives of telephone operators for a large financial corporation. Both found that group incentives improved the performance of workers who were less productive under individual schemes but decreased the performance of more productive workers. See also Bailey (1970) and Gaynor and Pauly (1990).

2. Also, Welbourne and Ferranti (2008) find that managers are more supportive of workers reacting to coworkers' behavior under gain sharing than under traditional merit pay, as indicated by their worker performance ratings.

agement relations should help to create and reinforce norms of reciprocity that encourage workers to take action against shirkers.

2.2 New Data on Shirking Detection and Responses

The innovation of our study is the new questions on the nationally representative GSS and the NBER company surveys about workers' ability to detect the performance of other workers at their workplace and their actions if they observed shirking. (See the "Studying Shared Capitalism" section of the Introduction for descriptions of the data sets and limitations.) We asked about the ability of workers to observe their peers' effort because that is a necessary precondition for acting against shirking:

> In your job how easy is it for you to see whether your co-workers are working well or poorly? On a scale of 0 to 10 please describe with 0 meaning not at all easy to see and 10 meaning very easy to see.

Figure 2.1, panel A, displays the frequency distribution of answers from the GSS. The distribution is concentrated at the upper end, with 49 percent of workers giving the highest possible answer about the ease of detecting how co-workers are doing, and another 28 percent giving answers in the 7 through 9 categories. Responses are also bunched at the 0 category as well, with 8 percent of workers giving this answer, but otherwise there is a paucity of responses at the low end. Thus, the vast majority of workers think they have a good idea of how hard their fellow employees are working. Looking at which employees report being able to observe co-workers shows a priori sensible variation among employees. Workers who answered with a 7 or more to the question reported disproportionately that they work in a team as opposed to by themselves, and that they rely on co-workers and supervisors for help, compared to workers who answered 3 or less on seeing how co-workers perform (data not shown but available). In addition, 13 percent who answered 7 or higher reported that they are managers, compared to 7 percent of those answered 3 or less.

Panel B of figure 2.1 displays the frequency distribution of answers from the NBER survey. The largest single group of respondents gave the maximum answer to their ability to observe their fellow employees, but the distribution is less concentrated than the distribution in the GSS, with proportionately half as many workers giving the 10 response. Still, 62 percent of respondents gave a response of 7 or more to the observability question.

Given that most workers say that they can observe the effort of co-workers, what do they do if they catch someone shirking? Our question was:

> If you were to see a fellow employee not working as hard or well as he or she should, how likely would you be to:
> A. Talk directly to the employee;
> B. Speak to your supervisor or manager;

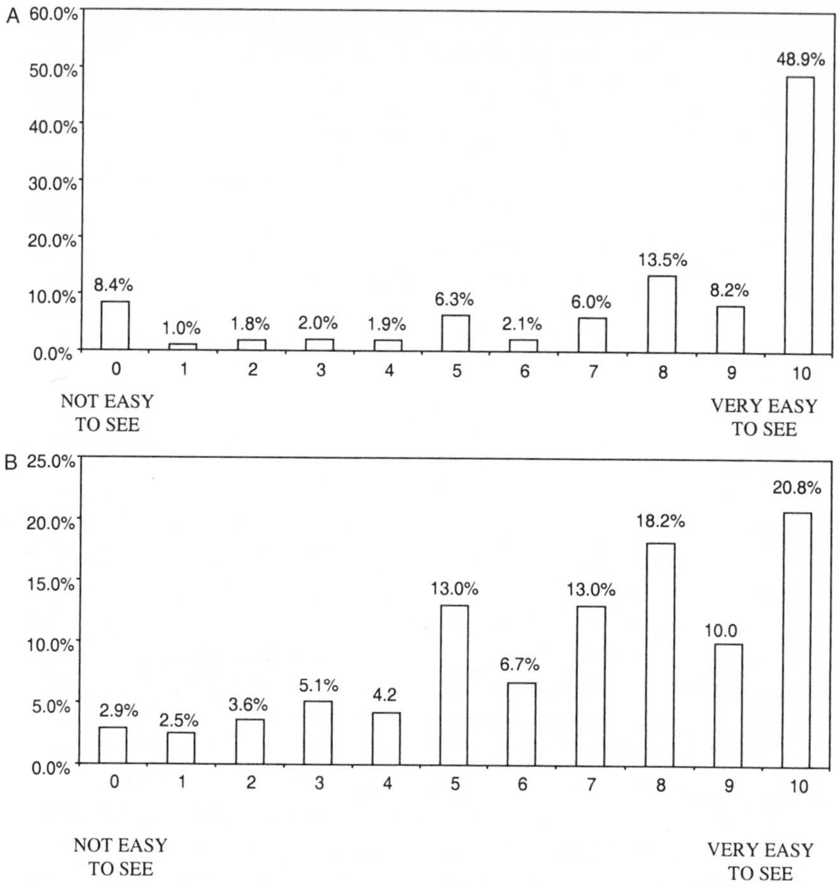

Fig. 2.1 Distribution of workers by how well they can see whether co-workers are working well or poorly: *A*, GSS; *B*, NBER

C. Do nothing;

D. (contained on only some company surveys) Talk about it in a work group or team.[3]

The responses use a four-point scale: not at all likely, not very likely, somewhat likely, and very likely. As a simple way to display the responses to these questions, we formed a summated rating anti-shirking index reflecting the likelihood of intervention against shirkers using a 1 to 4 scale, where 1 measures the lowest intervention and 4 the greatest intervention, by simply adding the values of responses across questions (Bartholomew et al. 2002). The

3. This option was not included in the 2002 GSS and the early NBER surveys.

anti-shirking index ranges from 3 to 12 for the observations based on the A to C responses and from 4 to 16 for the smaller sample for which we asked part D as well. In this ordering a 12 means that the worker reported that it was very likely they would talk to the shirking employee and very likely that they would talk to the supervisor and not at all likely that they would do nothing. A 3 means that they said it was very unlikely they would talk to the shirking employee, very unlikely they would talk to the supervisor, and very likely they would do nothing.

Figure 2.2, panel A, summarizes the responses from the GSS. It shows that the summary statistic differentiates people in a relatively continuous way. If we organize the data into five bins, grouping the 3 and 4 responses, and the 5 and 6 responses, and so on, the distribution looks roughly uniform. The anti-shirking index has a mean of 7.81 and a standard deviation of 2.94. Panel B of figure 2.2 gives the anti-shirking index for the NBER survey data. With the larger sample, the distribution has proportionately more persons in the

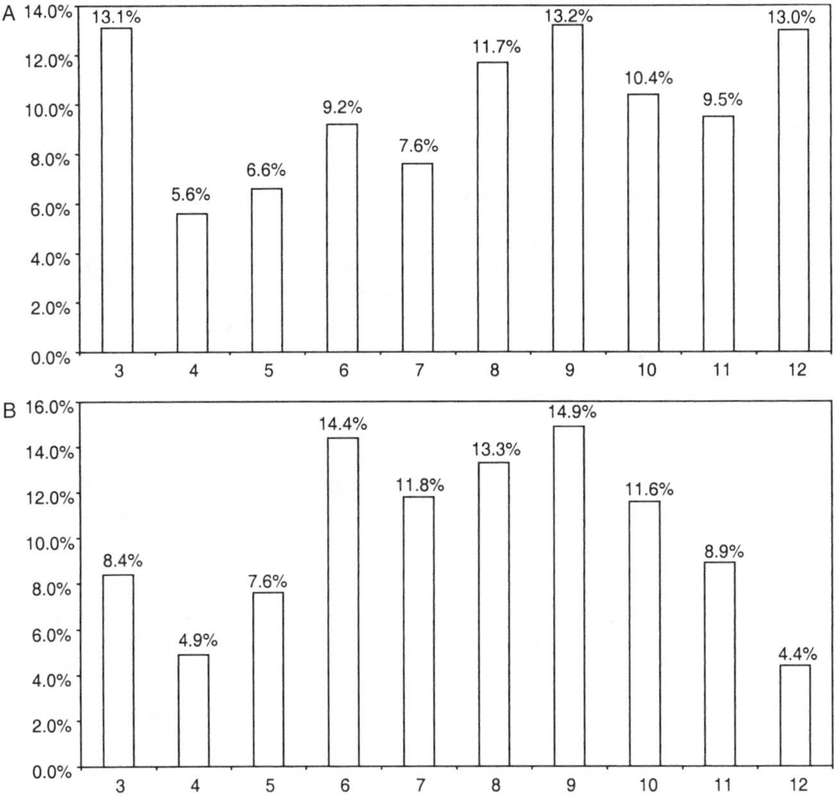

Fig. 2.2 Distribution of anti-shirking index: *A*, GSS; *B*, NBER frequency

Table 2.1 Potential employee actions against shirkers

	Response to fellow worker not working as hard or well as he or she should:			
	Talk to employee (1)	Talk to supervisor or manager (2)	Talk about it in work group or team (3)	Do nothing (4)
GSS				
Not at all likely	26.0%	28.0%	36.1%	38.8%
Not very likely	17.2%	22.4%	20.3%	20.5%
Somewhat likely	24.4%	25.1%	24.0%	17.6%
Very likely	32.4%	24.4%	19.7%	23.0%
n	2,183	2,137	1,058	2,173
NBER				
Not at all likely	28.1%	21.5%	28.6%	36.7%
Not very likely	25.4%	26.8%	26.5%	24.1%
Somewhat likely	29.9%	34.8%	31.3%	22.4%
Very likely	16.7%	17.0%	13.5%	16.8%
n	38,228	37,767	29,336	36,979

middle of the distribution, which gives it a rough normal look. But again, there is wide variation. Some people are likely to take action against a shirker and some are likely to do little. Our goal is to find out what differentiates workers in this form of behavior.

Table 2.1 shows for both data sets the proportion of workers who said it was likely or not likely that they would take one of the actions in response to shirking behavior by a fellow employee. One finding is that more workers in the GSS sample than in the NBER companies say they would be "very likely" to take action against shirkers, which would seem to go against the idea that shared capitalism encourages anti-shirking activities; this difference, however, is primarily due to the larger establishment sizes in the NBER sample, and the difference is reversed when controlling for this and other factors distinguishing the samples.[4] In addition, the table shows that the greater concentration of responses at the upper end of the distribution in the GSS than in the NBER data set is due to the great proportion in the former who say they would talk to the shirking employee: 32.4 percent in the GSS versus 16.7 percent in the NBER data set. In the GSS proportionately more workers say that it is very likely that they would talk to an employee than would talk to a supervisor or manager, whereas in the NBER data set

4. The GSS employees are also younger on average, and more likely to say they can see how well their co-workers are working. When these two variables and establishment size are used in the GSS sample to predict anti-shirking, the predicted mean for the NBER sample is less than the actual mean, indicating that the NBER employees are generally more likely than would be expected to take action against shirkers.

Table 2.2 **Past employee actions against shirkers (NBER survey)**

	Talk to employee (1)	Talk to supervisor or manager (2)	Talk about it in work group or team (3)	Do nothing (4)
Actions actually taken when saw fellow worker not working as hard or well as he or she should[a]	33.5%	46.0%	20.3%	29.3%
If said likelihood of this action was:				
Not at all likely	6.1%	12.4%	3.9%	14.8%
Not very likely	13.9%	26.6%	9.1%	17.0%
Somewhat likely	54.6%	65.3%	34.0%	41.9%
Very likely	81.7%	84.9%	52.8%	72.4%
n	18,744	18,744	18,744	18,744

[a]Workers were asked "Have you ever seen one of your fellow employees not working as hard or well as he or she should over an extended time period?" The above answers are based on the 58.6 percent who responded "yes." They were then asked "What action, if any, did you take?" In addition to the actions listed above, 5.2 percent said they would do "something else."

about the same proportion say it is very likely they would talk to the shirker as to a manager.[5]

To move from hypothetical responses to actual behavior, in some company surveys we added a question, "Have you ever seen one of your fellow employees not working as hard or well as he or she should over an extended time period?" Over half, 59 percent, of the respondents said yes.[6] We then asked what they did in response. As seen in table 2.2, 34 percent of the employees talked to the shirker, 46 percent talked to a supervisor or manager, 20 percent talked about it in a work group or team, 5 percent did something else, and 29 percent did nothing (row 1). Most important, these answers correlate highly with the respondents' reported likelihood of taking this action, as shown in rows 2 to 5: for example, 82 percent of those who said they were very likely to talk to the shirker actually did so, while only 6 percent of those who said it was not likely they would talk to the shirker actually did so.

From the tabulations in figures 2.1 and 2.2 and tables 2.1 and 2.2, we conclude the following: most workers can tell when a fellow employee is

5. Since some respondents said that they did not have a supervisor or manager, the sample size of answers to that question is smaller than the sample size for the other questions. One possible objection to the anti-shirking index is that it combines disparate behaviors that may substitute for each other—for example, a worker may choose between talking to the shirker or supervisor but not want to do both. We find, however, that the responses are highly correlated (the alpha for the index is .80 in the GSS data and .69 in the NBER data). We also present results for each response separately in table 2.4 and find results consistent with those using the anti-shirking index.

6. The mean of the anti-shirking index for the 41 percent of workers who said they have not seen a co-worker shirking is not significantly different from the mean for the 59 percent, suggesting that there is no systematic difference in willingness to take action against shirkers between these two groups.

shirking or not; there is wide variation in what they will do when faced with a situation in which someone shirks; and that this variation reflects variation in actual past behavior.

2.3 Shared Capitalist Arrangements: Group Incentives and Labor Policies

We have a wide set of measures of the group incentives and labor policies that we expect to affect worker responses to shirking behavior. As far as we know, ours is the most comprehensive survey of group incentive policies in the United States. The overall prevalence of shared capitalist compensation is presented in tables 1.1 and 1.3 of chapter 1. The most important result is that 45 percent of the for-profit private sector employees in the GSS sample report participating in some kind of shared capitalism program (36 percent in profit sharing, 25 percent in gain sharing, 19 percent in employee ownership, and 11 percent in stock options). This gives us good variation for examining the relation of these programs to worker outcomes. Regarding other work policies, the 2002 and 2006 GSS asked whether employees normally work as part of a team and how often they participate with others in determining how things are done at their job. Over half (58 percent) of private sector workers report working in a team setting, and 44 percent report that they often participate with others in helping set the way things are done on a job.

The prevalence of group incentives is necessarily higher in the NBER sample, since these firms were selected on the basis of having one or more shared capitalism programs. About two-thirds report profit sharing (71 percent) and owning company stock (64 percent), while about one-fifth report gain sharing (21 percent) and holding stock options (22 percent). The figure for working as part of a team (59 percent) is similar to that for the GSS, and about one-third (35 percent) report being part of an employee involvement team.

As a first step in assessing the relation of shared capitalism to employee outcomes, we constructed a thermometer-style index of shared capitalism, which assigns points based on coverage by shared capitalism programs and the size of the financial stakes. This index is described in Appendix B. We also present results breaking out the different forms of shared capitalism types and intensities.

2.4 Shared Capitalist Incentives and Shirking

To examine the determinants of anti-shirking behavior, we first regressed the anti-shirking index on organizational/company policy variables and job and demographic factors. As seen in table 2.3, the shared capitalism index is linked to greater anti-shirking activity in both the GSS and NBER data sets. Among the covariates, the ease of observing co-workers has a strong positive

Table 2.3 **Effects of shared capitalism on anti-shirking index**

	GSS data	GSS data	NBER data
Shared capitalism index	0.115 (.035)***	0.072 (0.034)**	0.027 (0.009)***
Ease of seeing how well co-worker is working	0.086 (.024)***	0.061 (0.024)**	0.130 (0.005)***
Work as part of team	1.060 (.059)***	0.766 (0.157)***	
High participation in decisions		1.207 (0.153)***	
Task variety		0.308 (0.103)***	
Any individual bonuses			0.199 (0.036)***
Employee involvement team			0.571 (0.028)***
Formal training			0.235 (0.028)***
Job security			0.445 (0.037)***
How closely supervised			–0.013 (0.006)**
Size 1–9 ees.	1.255 (.278)***	1.015 (0.271)***	
10–49 ees.	1.211 (.259)***	1.073 (0.250)***	
59–99 ees.	0.933 (.280)***	0.858 (0.269)**	
100–999 ees.	0.427 (.244)*	0.412 (0.235)	
1,000+ ees. (excl.)			
n	1,634	1,633	32,099
R^2	0.131	0.176	0.192

Notes: The GSS regressions include controls for occupation (7 dummies), age, years of tenure, female, black, Hispanic, education (4 dummies), full-time status, ln(yearly earnings), and dummy for survey year 2006. The NBER regressions include controls for occupation (5 dummies), mgt. level (3 dummies), hourly pay status, supervisory status, years of tenure, hours worked per week, union status, country (27 dummies), age, gender, marital status (2 dummies), family size, college graduate, graduate degree, number of kids, race (4 dummies), disability status, ln(fixed pay), and company fixed effects. ees. = employees.

***Significant at the 1 percent level.

**Significant at the 5 percent level.

*Significant at the 10 percent level.

effect on the anti-shirking index, consistent with the idea that workers will be more likely to take action the greater the observability of shirking behavior. The participation variables have a substantial positive impact on the anti-shirking index in both data sets, as does job security in the NBER data set. Job task variety also has a strong positive effect (consistent with Drago and Garvey [1998]), indicating that knowledge of how to help is greater, and the costs of helping are lower, when the worker has a broader base of skills and overlap of tasks with the shirking co-worker. Those who are supervised more closely are less likely to engage in anti-shirking behavior in the NBER data set, perhaps reflecting a belief among closely-supervised workers that dealing with shirking is the supervisor's responsibility (to be addressed in table 2.9). Finally, the data shows that the size of the workplace has a strong impact on anti-shirking behavior, with workers more likely to intervene to stop shirking in a smaller workplace, where the shirking of one co-worker is more likely to affect them than it would in a larger workplace.

The specific behaviors making up the anti-shirking index are analyzed separately in table 2.4, panels A and B. The shared capitalism index is a

Table 2.4 Specific responses to shirking (based on ordered probits)

	Likelihood of talking to shirker (1)	Likelihood of talking to sup./manager (2)	Likelihood of talking in work group (3)
	A. GSS		
Shared capitalism index	0.038 (0.015)***	0.038 (0.014)***	–0.011 (0.022)
Ease of seeing how well co-worker is working	0.033 (0.010)***	0.022 (0.010)**	0.029 (0.016)*
Work as part of team	0.426 (0.063)***	0.298 (0.062)***	0.138 (0.099)
Size 1–9 ees.	0.469 (0.112)***	0.448 (0.111)***	–0.393 (0.165)**
10–49 ees.	0.432 (0.104)***	0.417 (0.104)***	–0.166 (0.150)
59–99 ees.	0.293 (0.111)***	0.390 (0.110)***	–0.304 (0.163)
100–999 ees.	0.086 (0.101)	0.208 (0.100)**	0.007 (0.143)
1,000+ ees. (excl.)			
n	1,676	1,641	800
(Pseudo) R^2	0.058	0.034	0.019
Cut point 1	0.886 (0.379)	–0.020 (0.370)	–1.365 (0.562)
Cut point 2	1.407 (0.380)	0.598 (0.371)	–0.818 (0.561)
Cut point 3	2.077 (0.382)	1.325 (0.371)	–0.094 (0.560)
	B. NBER		
Shared capitalism index	0.010 (0.004)**	0.007 (0.004)*	0.009 (0.005)*
Any individual bonuses	0.061 (0.017)***	0.084 (0.017)***	0.050 (0.020)**
Ease of seeing how well co-worker is working	0.045 (0.002)***	0.057 (0.002)***	0.037 (0.003)***
Employee involvement team	0.224 (0.013)***	0.192 (0.013)***	0.195 (0.015)***
Formal training	0.146 (0.013)***	0.055 (0.013)***	0.065 (0.014)***
Job security	0.132 (0.018)***	0.206 (0.018)***	0.084 (0.019)***
How closely supervised	0.002 (0.003)	–0.002 (0.003)	0.007 (0.003)**
n	33,807	33,544	25,570
(Pseudo) R^2	0.071	0.049	0.022
Cut point 1	0.152 (0.254)	0.198 (0.252)	0.020 (0.664)
Cut point 2	0.907 (0.254)	1.012 (0.252)	0.700 (0.664)
Cut point 3	1.920 (0.255)	2.104 (0.252)	1.715 (0.664)

Notes: (Panel A): the regressions include controls for occupation (7 dummies), age, years of tenure, female, black, Hispanic, education (4 dummies), full-time status, ln(yearly earnings), and dummy for survey year 2006. ees. = employees.

(Panel B): the regressions include controls for occupation (5 dummies), mgt. level (3 dummies), hourly pay status, supervisory status, years of tenure, hours worked per week, union status, country (27 dummies), age, gender, marital status (2 dummies), family size, college graduate, graduate degree, number of kids, race (4 dummies), disability status, ln(fixed pay), and company fixed effects.

***Significant at the 1 percent level.

**Significant at the 5 percent level.

*Significant at the 10 percent level.

positive predictor of each type of anti-shirking behavior in both the GSS and NBER data, except for the likelihood of talking in a work group in the GSS data. It seems that many workers with shared capitalism do not wish to talk about the shirker to the group in the shirker's presence as they might find this embarrassing (consistent with concerns by workers that the shirker might resent them or other employees would react poorly, as presented in table 2.9).

2.4.1 Types of Shared Capitalism

Which shared capitalism policies are responsible for the results given in our indices? Table 2.5 uses different types and intensities of shared capital-

Table 2.5 Effects of particular forms of shared capitalist compensation on anti-shirking index

	GSS (1)	NBER (2)	NBER (3)
Profit and gain sharing			
Profit-sharing or gain-sharing eligibility	0.344 (0.183)*	0.010 (0.040)	
Profit-sharing gain-sharing bonus as % of base pay	0.742 (0.887)	1.424 (0.143)***	
Profit-sharing eligibility			–0.181 (0.045)***
Profit-sharing bonus as % of base pay			0.596 (0.202)***
Gain-sharing eligibility			0.099 (0.056)*
Gain-sharing bonus as % of base pay			0.675 (0.223)***
Individual bonus eligibility			0.250 (0.053)***
Individual bonus as % of base pay			–0.480 (0.230)**
Stock options			
Stock option holding	0.237 (0.293)	0.440 (0.075)***	–0.043 (0.110)
Stock option value as % of base pay			0.001 (0.011)
Stock option grant last year			0.212 (0.108)**
Stock option grant as % of avg. grant			0.014 (0.023)
Employee ownership			
Co. stock ownership	0.020 (0.298)	0.182 (0.038)***	0.051 (0.042)
Co. stock as % of base pay	0.141 (0.101)	0.027 (0.018)	–0.023 (0.019)
R^2	.132	.113	.195
n	1,645	34,379	30,933

Notes: Based on ordinary least squares (OLS) regressions. The GSS regression includes controls for occupation (7 dummies), age, years of tenure, female, black, Hispanic, education (4 dummies), full-time status, ln(yearly earnings), co. size (4 dummies), ease of observing co-workers, and dummy for survey year 2006. The NBER regression in column (2) contains the GSS controls from column (1) except co. size, plus company and country fixed effects. The NBER regression in column (3) includes the controls from column (2) plus hourly pay status, supervisory status, hours worked per week, union status, marital status (2 dummies), family size, number of kids, race (4 dummies), disability status, ln(fixed pay), closeness of supervision, employee involvement team, training in past year, high job security, and company fixed effects.

***Significant at the 1 percent level.

**Significant at the 5 percent level.

*Significant at the 10 percent level.

ism to predict taking action against shirking. In the GSS data, the most important factor behind anti-shirking activity is the presence of profit sharing and gain sharing (column [1]). In the NBER data where we actually have detailed information on the extent of profit sharing, it is the intensity rather than the presence of profit sharing and gain sharing that seems to matter. The NBER results in column (2) show a very strong effect of the profit-gain-sharing bonus size (not eligibility), along with strong positive effects of stock option holding and owning any company stock.

When the richer NBER data are used for a more detailed breakdown of shared capitalism in column (3) (along with more extensive controls, mirroring the specification in table 2.3), anti-shirking activity is strongly related to both profit-sharing bonus size and gain-sharing bonus size. There is one seemingly odd result, however. The negative coefficient on eligibility combined with the positive coefficient on bonus size indicate that when the profit share is small, those eligible for profit sharing are less likely than noneligible employees to take action. As will be seen in table 2.9, shared capitalism appears to increase the fear that co-workers will resent any anti-shirking action, so that low levels of profit sharing may have a negative effect on anti-shirking activity, but this reluctance is apparently overcome as the bonus grows larger. For gain sharing, by contrast, simple eligibility increases anti-shirking behavior. On this issue, note that gain-sharing can appear as a compact within a specific small group or department within the firm.

Consistent with the results of Drago and Garvey (1998), the effect of greater individual bonuses is negative and significant on anti-shirking behavior (column [3]). Apparently, individual bonuses focus workers on their own work and may lead them to see co-workers as competitors (or at least not cooperators). By contrast, workers who received a stock option grant last year were more likely to take action against shirkers, although the size of the grant, and of one's holdings, do not seem to make a difference (column [3]). Owning company stock is no longer a significant predictor in column (3), although in supplementary regressions (not reported here) we have positive associations with some forms of ownership—Employee Stock Purchase Plan (ESPP) participation, holding stock after exercising options, holding stock purchased on the open market, and Employee Stock Ownership Plan (ESOP) membership (this latter result only when company fixed effects are not used[7]).

That ownership appears to operate through simply owning stock and not the size of one's stake is consistent with findings from several other studies of higher organizational commitment (reviewed in Kruse and Blasi [1997]).

7. Company fixed effects are probably inappropriate to use in analyzing the effects of ESOP membership, since Employee Retirement Income Security Act (ERISA) rules provide strict guidelines to ensure broad coverage. The small number of non-ESOP members are likely to be very different from the ESOP members within a firm, and the effects of ESOP membership may be better judged by comparing ESOP members to otherwise-similar workers in other firms.

This suggests that employee ownership may operate largely by changing the psychological contract between the employer and employees (Rousseau and Shperling 2003), getting employees to think like owners through a change in status rather than a change in direct financial incentives. Such incentives may nonetheless be part of the psychological context, since eight out of ten of the workers reporting employee ownership in the 2002 GSS report they also have some form of profit/gain sharing or stock options, which indicates that some managers recognize the value of combining short-term rewards and long-term equity (Blasi, Kruse, and Freeman 2006, 7).

2.4.2 Before/After on Profit Sharing

The cross section data presented so far are consistent with the theory that shared capitalism affects the response of workers to shirking co-workers but cannot rule out the possibility that there are missing variables or other processes that affect results. As we were conducting our survey, one firm told us that they intended to introduce a new profit-sharing plan which offered the chance to conduct a before/after analysis as well as a cross-section analysis of worker responses to group incentives. Accordingly, we administered our survey twice at this firm, six months apart, with the first survey coming before the firm introduced a new profit-sharing plan, and the second survey coming after the firm had introduced the new plan.[8]

As shown in table 2.6, the introduction of the profit-sharing plan led to a jump in the percent of employees saying they are eligible for profit sharing from 59 percent at the first survey to 88 percent at the second survey. Apart from this, only two variables in the entire survey showed significant changes between the surveys: the percent who say they were very likely to talk to a shirking co-worker (increase from 42 percent to 55 percent), and the percent who say that they would do something about a shirker because poor performance would hurt the bonus or stock value (from 39 percent to 56 percent). The fact that these are the only three variables that changed between the surveys indicates that there were not compositional changes or other policy changes that affected the results. These results lend support to the prior findings, pointing toward a positive effect of profit sharing in attempts to combat co-worker shirking.

2.4.3 Complementarities

Analysis of the decision equation for workers to intervene against shirking suggests that some of the factors that influence behavior should enter equa-

8. The analyses presented so far use only the responses to the second survey at this company, to avoid having more than one survey from some employees. The surveys did not have individual identifiers so respondents could not be tracked across the two surveys. The higher response rate in the second survey is due in part to the provision of a five-dollar bill accompanying this survey, but the surveys appear equally representative since the means on all variables (apart from those highlighted in table 2.6) were not significantly different between the two surveys.

Table 2.6 **Longitudinal evidence: Two waves of same company**

	2004 (profit sharing announced) (1)	2005 (profit sharing in place) (2)	Change
Profit sharing	58.6%	87.9%	29.2%***
Very/somewhat likely to take action against shirker			
Talk to shirking employee	42.1%	54.5%	12.4%***
Talk to supervisor or manager	64.3%	68.1%	3.9%
Talk about it in work group	47.3%	48.8%	1.5%
Do nothing	34.1%	33.7%	–0.4%
Why you are likely to take action			
I like helping others	47.4%	49.6%	2.3%
Employee might help me in the future	30.6%	33.5%	2.9%
Poor performance will cost me and other employees in bonus or stock value	38.8%	56.1%	17.3%***
Other employees appreciate it when someone steps forward	34.3%	34.4%	0.1%
Want to keep work standards high	59.3%	59.6%	0.3%
Employee's poor performance could affect my own job	57.1%	56.3%	–0.8%
Other (What?)	14.2%	10.0%	–4.2%
n	273	428	

***Significant at the 1 percent level.
**Significant at the 5 percent level.
*Significant at the 10 percent level.

tions in an interactive rather than linear way. The worker decides to intervene against a shirker when the expected benefits of intervening exceed the costs: $p\ (G) - \text{Cost}$, where p is the probability that the intervention will succeed, G is the gain to the worker, and C is the cost. The financial incentive would affect G; participation should affect p and the cost. Labor-management relations L-M might affect both G and p. More complicated analyses, in which the worker is assumed to take account of the possible behavior of other employees, lead to even more complexity, which we will ignore. Instead, we have looked for potential interactions among key variables in determining anti-shirking behavior.

Using the nationally representative GSS data, table 2.7 examines how shared capitalism interacts with company size, and table 2.8 examines how it interacts with other company policies. Shared capitalism is most strongly associated with taking action against shirkers in the smallest workplaces, as shown in column (1) of table 2.7. The supports the idea that the 1/N problem will be lower in smaller workplaces (note that the base estimates continue to show more anti-shirking activity among workers in small companies with-

Table 2.7 **Company size and employee-management relations as moderators of shared capitalism**

	GSS data		NBER data
	(1)	(2)	(3)
Shared cap. index * co. size of:			
1–9 ees.	0.281 (0.085)***		
10–49 ees.	0.117 (0.068)*		
59–99 ees.	0.195 (0.085)**		
100–999 ees.	0.029 (0.057)		
2,000+ ees.	0.045 (0.076)		
Shared cap. index * mgt. is trustworthy			
Strongly disagree (D or F in col. [3])		0.043 (0.165)	0.048 (0.014)***
Disagree (C in col. [3])		0.117 (0.072)	–0.001 (0.013)
Agree (B in col. [3])		0.083 (0.048)*	0.014 (0.010)
Strongly agree (A in col. [3])		0.179 (0.064)***	0.054 (0.013)***
Mgt. is trustworthy:			
Strongly disagree (excl.)			
Disagree	0.057 (0.181)	–0.053 (0.414)	0.499 (0.064)***
Agree	–0.249 (0.210)	0.122 (0.374)	0.710 (0.065)***
Strongly agree	–0.199 (0.313)	0.208 (0.398)	0.838 (0.081)***
Size 1–9 ees.	0.855 (0.345)**	1.179 (0.283)***	
10–49 ees.	1.005 (0.336)***	1.143 (0.259)***	
59–99 ees.	0.585 (0.366)	0.885 (0.281)***	
100–999 ees.	0.403 (0.317)	0.407 (0.244)*	
1,000+ ees. (excl.)			
n	1,631	1,627	31,770
(Pseudo) R^2	0.137	0.132	0.205

Notes: Dependent variable = anti-shirking index. The GSS regression includes controls for occupation (7 dummies), age, years of tenure, female, black, Hispanic, education (4 dummies), full-time status, ln(yearly earnings), ease of observing co-workers, work as part of team, and dummy for survey year 2006. The NBER regressions include controls for occupation (5 dummies), mgt. level (3 dummies), hourly pay status, supervisory status, years of tenure, hours worked per week, union status, country (27 dummies), age, gender, marital status (2 dummies), family size, college graduate, graduate degree, number of kids, race (4 dummies), disability status, ln(fixed pay), employee involvement team, training in past year, job security, ease of observing co-workers, closeness of supervision, individual bonuses, and company fixed effects. ees. = employees.

***Significant at the 1 percent level.

**Significant at the 5 percent level.

*Significant at the 10 percent level.

out shared capitalism, indicating that shirking may be perceived as more of an economic threat in small enterprises generally). The shared capitalist index effect is also significant in the next two larger size classes, and positive (although not significant) in the two largest classes. (As noted in chapter 1, the greater prevalence of shared capitalism in larger establishments may be explained in part by fixed costs in setting up these plans.) An equally or even more important factor in taking action against shirkers, however,

Table 2.8 **Company policies as moderators of shared capitalism**

	(1)	(2)
Shared capitalism index	0.028 (0.010)***	–0.018 (0.018)
Employee involvement team	0.544 (0.030)***	
Formal training	0.232 (0.029)***	
Job security	0.431 (0.040)***	
High perf. policy index		0.259 (0.030)***
*shared capitalism index		0.035 (0.006)***
How closely supervised	–0.014 (0.006)**	0.030 (0.010)***
*shared capitalism index		–0.013 (0.002)***
Fixed pay at or above market	0.181 (0.028)***	0.043 (0.050)
*shared capitalism index		0.034 (0.010)***
n	28,424	28,424
(Pseudo) R^2	0.193	0.194

Notes: Dependent variable = anti-shirking index. Based on NBER data. The regressions include controls for occupation (5 dummies), mgt. level (3 dummies), hourly pay status, supervisory status, years of tenure, hours worked per week, union status, country (27 dummies), age, gender, marital status (2 dummies), family size, college graduate, graduate degree, number of kids, race (4 dummies), disability status, ln(fixed pay), ease of observing co-workers, individual bonuses, and company fixed effects.

***Significant at the 1 percent level.

**Significant at the 5 percent level.

*Significant at the 10 percent level.

appears to be the quality of the relationship with management. As shown in column (2), shared capitalism is associated with anti-shirking activity most strongly when combined with a high level of trust in management. While this could simply reflect column (1)'s finding of a more positive effect in small companies, the results in column (2) are maintained when the smallest companies are deleted (not shown here). Similar results are obtained when shared capitalism is interacted with the view of employee-management relations.[9] These results indicate that employees are likely to take action to increase productivity only when they are confident that any gains will in fact be shared with workers. This suggests that large companies can use improved employee-management relations to counteract the 1/N problem.[10]

9. The correlation between trust in management and view of employee management relations is .60, indicating they appear to represent a common attitude.

10. We examined other ways in which shared capitalism arrangements may interact with workplace policies. The positive shared capitalism effect on the likelihood of taking action against shirkers is lower among those who plan to look for a new job in the next year (presumably because they will not be around to receive the profit share), and in companies with high injury rates (which could worsen management employee relations and decrease expected tenure). While some models predict that financial participation will have a positive interaction with participation in decision-making in affecting worker motivation and performance (e.g., Ben-Ner and Jones 1995), we do not find significant interactions using the GSS participation

This result does not, however, carry over to within-company comparisons in the NBER data. The most positive effect of shared capitalism on anti-shirking activity still occurs among employees with the most trust in management, but the shared capitalism index has a positive effect even when the NBER employees disagree that management is trustworthy. We do not have a ready explanation for the difference between the two data sets. Because almost all employees in the GSS sample work in different companies, we do not know if the positive interaction between shared capitalism and employee-management relations in that data set reflects the effect of companies with good employee-management relations in general, or of individuals who perceive good relations within a company (even if their co-workers do not). We did some exploration of company and individual differences in the NBER data and found that anti-shirking behavior is generally strong in companies with higher average grades of employee-management relations and trust in management, no matter the individual employee's grades of these items. This suggests the importance of company culture in fostering an environment encouraging peer pressure.

The role of complementary company policies is explored with the NBER data in table 2.8. Column (1) essentially replicates the specification from table 2.3, adding a control for the worker's perception that his or her fixed pay is at or above market level. The strong positive effect of the wage variable is consistent with efficiency wage theories, which posit that worker performance can be improved through better pay. The negative effect of close supervision suggests that the gift exchange version of efficiency wage theory is more relevant than the shirking version, since in the shirking version close monitoring should have positive effects on worker behavior. The shared capitalism index remains a positive predictor as the wage variable is introduced. The effect appears to be contingent, however, on other workplace policies. The shared capitalist index has a strong positive interaction with a high performance policy index (column [2]), supporting the idea of complementarities among these policies in affecting worker behavior.[11] The shared capitalist index also has a strong negative interaction with closeness of supervision, and a positive interaction with having fixed pay at or above market level. The negative supervision interaction may reflect a negative reaction to the mixed message received by workers: we want you to work

measures (which are subjective and may mediate the effects of shared capitalism). Further, we did not find that employee stock ownership or holding stock options alone were related to anti-shirking behavior. This is consistent with the research literature and our findings in this and related papers in the NBER project that employee ownership and stock options generally interact with company culture in impacting performance, although there is evidence that employee ownership directly improves commitment. Also, as noted, it is possible that some managers combine profit sharing and equity participation in order to get synergy between them.

11. These results showing the value of embedding such participation in a system of high performance work policies are consistent with the analysis of Appelbaum et al. (2000) and Huselid (1995).

harder due to company-based pay, but we are nonetheless going to watch you very closely. In this case the shared capitalism might be perceived by workers as primarily risk-sharing. The positive interaction with having fixed pay at or above the market level may reflect a more positive response by workers when the company seems to be truly sharing, and not asking the worker to sacrifice pay levels in exchange for shared capitalist incentives. Forms of employee ownership that are combined with below-market pay might not be optimal for anti-shirking behavior because the incentive is diluted through what workers perceive as wage substitution.

These interaction results for supervision and high-performance policies are illustrated in figure 2.3. This figure shows how there is a positive relation between shared capitalism and the anti-shirking index only when there are high-performance policies and average or low levels of supervision. Otherwise the relationship is negative.

Thus, incentive intensity is strongly related to anti-shirking activity, but appears to work best as part of a high-performance work system where workers are paid well and not supervised too closely. These results are consistent with the findings of Ichniowski, Shaw, and Prennushi (1997) that workplace productivity is improved by combining several high-performance human resource policies, and show that worker response to shirkers is likely an important mechanism in the higher productivity.

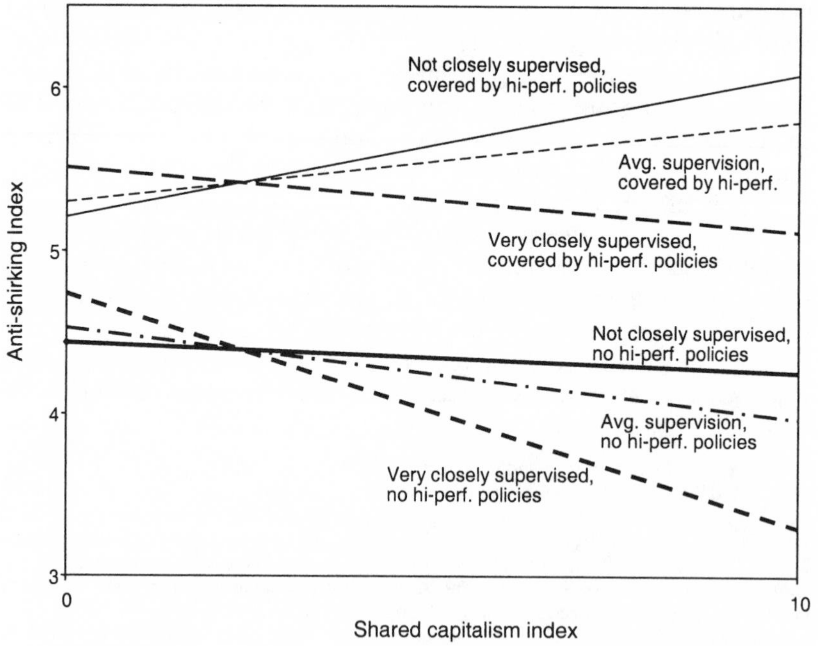

Fig. 2.3 The contingent effects of shared capitalism on anti-shirking activity

2.4.4 Reasons For/Against Acting Against Shirkers

The dynamics underlying taking action against shirkers are explored more fully in table 2.9, which records employee responses to questions about why they might or might not do something about a shirking co-worker. These questions were asked on only some of our company surveys. Over half of workers said they would be likely to do something because the employee's performance could affect their own jobs (56 percent), reflecting interdepen-

Table 2.9 Why people do/do not act against shirkers

		Position in shared capitalism[a]			
	All (1)	Lower (2)	Middle (3)	Upper (4)	Coefficient on SC index[b] (5)
Why you might do something					
I like helping others	44.9%	47.2%	43.2%	42.8%	0.001
Employee might help me in the future	31.0%	32.0%	30.5%	29.7%	0.003
Poor performance will cost me and other employees in bonus or stock value	42.9%	32.0%	48.5%	58.2%	0.038***
Other employees appreciate it when someone steps forward	23.9%	19.9%	24.9%	32.0%	0.008***
Want to keep work standards high	46.6%	41.6%	46.6%	58.9%	0.015***
Employee's poor performance could affect my own job	55.9%	53.2%	56.9%	61.3%	0.010***
Other (What?)	6.8%	5.7%	7.0%	8.9%	0.003***
n	32,386	13,991	12,514	5,463	
Why you might do nothing					
Employee not working well would resent it	41.3%	37.9%	43.2%	44.7%	0.015***
Other employees would react poorly	23.4%	24.3%	23.3%	21.8%	0.000
It's the supervisor's job, not mine	44.7%	45.0%	46.8%	39.7%	0.001
Some other employee will probably take action	8.4%	10.5%	7.2%	6.1%	0.000
There's no financial benefit for me	7.7%	10.2%	6.6%	4.9%	–0.003***
Nothing in it for me personally	11.0%	13.3%	10.1%	8.0%	–0.003**
Other (What?)	12.4%	8.8%	13.3%	19.0%	0.007***
n	30,363	12,236	12,284	5,444	

Note: Based on NBER data.

[a]Shared capitalism index of 5 or greater = "upper," 3 to 4 = "middle," and 0 to 2 = "lower."

[b]Based on linear probability models predicting whether employee checked this reason, controlling for ease of observing co-worker, closeness of supervision, occupation (5 dummies), mgt. level (3 dummies), hourly pay status, supervisory status, tenure in years, hours worked per week, union status, age, gender, marital status (2 dummies), family size, college graduate, graduate degree, number of kids, race (4 dummies), disability status, ln(fixed pay), and company fixed effects.

***Significant at the 1 percent level.

**Significant at the 5 percent level.

*Significant at the 10 percent level.

dent work where cooperation can be especially productive. Almost half of workers said they would do something because they would want to keep work standards high (47 percent), which can be seen as reflecting a cooperative solution to reinforce high work norms. Almost as many workers expressed a financial incentive, saying the poor performance would lead to lower bonus or stock value (43 percent), while 45 percent said they simply like helping others, and 31 percent said the employee might help them in the future.

The responses are related to the level of participation in shared capitalism. For example, the percent saying that poor performance would lead to lower bonus or stock value is almost twice as high among those with a high value on the shared capitalism index (58 percent in column [4]) relative to those with a low value on the index (32 percent in column [2]). Similarly, the former group is more likely to say they would do it to keep work standards high (59 percent compared to 42 percent). Column (5) shows that the shared capitalism index is a strong predictor of five of the reasons for taking action.[12]

The predominant reason for not taking action against shirkers is that it is seen as the supervisor's job (45 percent), followed closely by the fear that the shirking employee would resent it (41 percent). About one-fourth (23 percent) feared that other employees would react poorly, while less than one-tenth (8 percent) directly expressed free ridership by saying that some other employee would probably take action. The shared capitalism index is a strong predictor of the fear that the shirking employee would resent the action, perhaps because the intervener would be seen as acting out of a financial concern rather than out of concern for the worker. As noted earlier, this may help explain why very low levels of profit sharing appear to be associated with reduced likelihood of taking action against shirkers—an effect that is more than counterbalanced by other reasons as the bonus size grows. The shared capitalist index also, not surprisingly, predicts a lower likelihood that the employee will say there is no financial benefit or "nothing in it for me personally" (column [5]). Therefore these data are consistent with the idea that shared capitalism can affect worker behavior.

2.4.5 Outcomes of Anti-Shirking Activity

What happened as a result of the action? The data in table 2.10 point up one of the dangers of taking action, as one-third (35 percent) of the workers said that the employee who was not working well resented it. The

12. One possible objection to our focus on shared capitalism is that there are many reasons workers take action against shirkers, as shown in this table. Of course, workers report and probably have a variety of reasons—which may also include simply noticing incompetence, as noted by Eric Maskin in discussing our chapter—and we do not pretend that workers have the simple motive of "anti-shirking" in their minds, or that shared capitalism is the only motivator. These results show that shared capitalism is not related to two of the key reasons for taking action ("I like helping others" and "Employee may help me in the future"), but is clearly related to several reasons that reflect a concern with site performance efficiency.

Table 2.10 Responses to anti-shirking actions

	Yes (%)	No (%)	Don't know (%)	*n*
What was the outcome of your actions?				
Employee not working well resented it	34.7	19.1	46.2	14,125
Other employees appreciated it	45.0	11.4	43.6	13,676
Supervisor appreciated it	40.1	15.5	44.4	13,845
Employee not working well improved	35.7	38.9	25.4	14,254
Other	28.3	9.9	61.8	2,923

Notes: Based on NBER data. Workers were asked "Have you ever seen one of your fellow employees not working as hard or well as he or she should over an extended time period?" If yes, they were then asked "What action, if any, did you take?" Those who reported taking some action (see table 2.2) were then asked the above question about the outcome.

most likely outcome, however, was that other employees appreciated the action (45 percent), while almost as many said the supervisor appreciated it (40 percent), and just over one-third said that the employee's performance improved (36 percent).

Does it help economic performance? Only a minority of workers report that the employee's performance improved, but this may still be enough to make a difference in workplace performance. Also, apart from actual anti-shirking actions, people may work harder simply knowing that their co-workers are likely to do something if they see signs of shirking. We do not have hard performance data, but we do have several survey measures of co-worker and facility performance that show a strong relationship with our anti-shirking measures. Table 2.11 shows that those who report a higher likelihood of talking to a shirker, and a lower likelihood of doing nothing, rate their co-workers' effort higher on a 0 to 10 scale. The anti-shirking index is very strongly related not just to this measure, but also to a perception that workers tend to encourage each other, and to ratings of the facility on five specific measures of performance. Since several of these measures involve workers reporting on the behavior of others, it lessens the probability that that the interveners are putting a good spin on their behavior by reporting higher performance, as one reviewer has cautioned. To check the possibility that this simply reflects individual characteristics (e.g., greater optimism about company performance among those who say they would take action against shirkers), we also calculated these relationships at the site level and found that worksites with higher average scores on the anti-shirking index also had significantly higher average evaluations of workplace performance. This is illustrated in figure 2.4 for one of our performance measures (evaluations of co-workers' performance).[13] Therefore, this does not simply reflect

13. We also find that site-level averages of the anti-shirking index are strongly related to site-level averages of a worker-reported performance index (containing the five items from the

Table 2.11 **Relation of anti-shirking behavior to co-worker performance**

A Average ratings of co-worker effort (0–10 scale)

	Anti-shirking action		
	Talk to shirker	Talk to sup./man.	Do nothing
Not at all likely	6.7	6.8	7.2
Not very likely	7.0	7.1	7.1
Somewhat likely	7.3	7.2	7.0
Very likely	7.5	7.1	6.6

B Anti-shirking index as predictor of workplace performance

Dependent variable	Summated rating coefficient	(s.e.)	T or Z	*n*
Rating of co-worker effort (0–10 scale, OLS)	0.109	(0.004)	25.24	35,637
Workers encourage each other (–1, 0, 1, ordered probit)	0.135	(0.005)	27.14	12,659
Grade of facility performance (0–4 scale, OLS):				
A. Getting the job done that has to get done efficiently	0.050	(0.002)	21.12	22,810
B. Practicing accountability	0.066	(0.003)	23.32	22,705
C. Delivering customers' products on time	0.021	(0.003)	7.68	22,700
D. Delivering highest quality customer products	0.044	(0.003)	17.69	22,704
E. Being the market leader in its products	0.032	(0.003)	13.18	22,569

Note: Based on NBER data. s.e. = standard error.

an individual reporting phenomenon: shared views of higher performance in a workplace are related to shared commitments to take action against shirkers. It appears that the propensity for anti-shirking activity does make a difference in performance.

One possible objection to these findings is that some production processes are difficult to supervise by managers so that work is arranged to rely on peer intervention. Shared capitalism may be used not to encourage anti-shirking behavior, but directly to deter shirking, so that peer intervention and shared capitalism are both consequences of technologies rather than causally related to each other. Our pre/post results in table 2.6 go against this explanation. We also tested this by examining the relationship in different industries, and by controlling for detailed manufacturing technologies (in our diversified multinational firm with diverse technologies such as plastics and aerospace). The shared capitalism effect does not disappear, but in fact gets slightly stronger with more detailed controls for production technol-

bottom of table 2.11) and employee loyalty to the organization, although there is no strong relationship to site-level averages of willingness to work hard and turnover intention. For one large multinational, the data set has a number of hard operational measures of efficiency, but only at an aggregate division level, which makes analysis problematic.

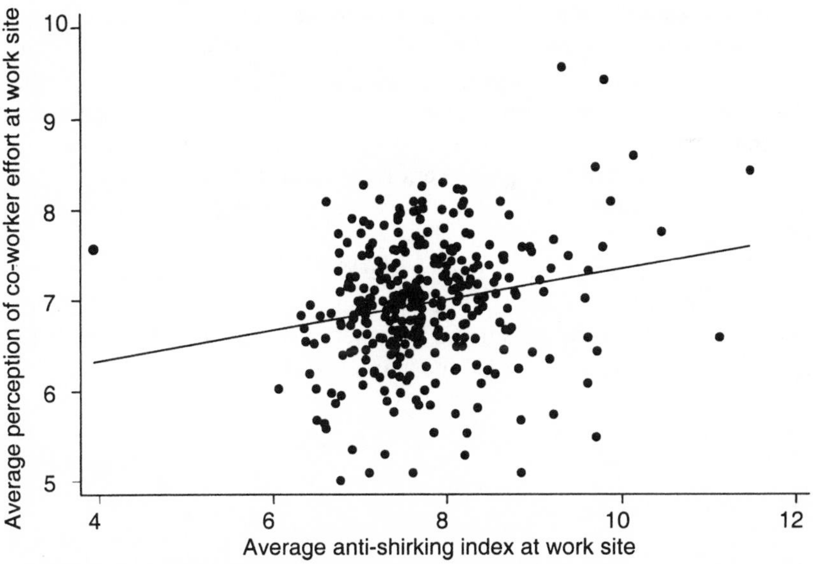

Fig. 2.4 Anti-shirking and worker effort at site level

ogies, making us more confident that anti-shirking intentions and behavior are a result of shared capitalism and company culture.[14]

2.5 Conclusion

This study has examined employee responses to new questions on the 2002 and 2006 General Social Surveys and a large database of more detailed NBER employee surveys on whether workers can easily observe whether co-workers are shirking and how workers respond to shirking. The answers to the new questions provide valuable insight into the likely magnitude of mutual monitoring and peer pressure against shirking behavior. They show that most workers believe that they are able to observe the effort/activity of fellow workers, which is the first prerequisite for mutual monitoring and peer

14. One limitation of our study is the lack of a measure of shirking per se. However, we did ask each employee in two companies to respond on a 1 to 5 scale whether "There are days when I don't put much effort into my job." Analysis of this variable indicates that workers reporting high effort are the ones who are more likely to intervene against shirkers. Moreover, there is no direct relationship between the shared capitalism index and increased individual effort. This reflects the finding that the principal impact of shared capitalism appears to work in combination with various aspects of company culture such as trust, high performance work systems, and fixed wages at or above market. This suggests that neither shared capitalism alone nor unique production systems dependent on technologies are creating anti-shirking work systems, but rather that shared capitalism enhances anti-shirking together with company culture, and shared capitalism and positive company culture also impact the potential shirker's level of effort. These additional analyses are available from the authors.

pressure against shirking to work. In addition, about half of the workforce says that they would be very likely to respond to poor job performance by co-workers, with more saying that they would talk to the shirker rather than reporting the behavior to management. While there are some demographic correlates to responding against shirking, workplace factors are more strongly related to employee efforts to reduce shirking. This conflicts with the claim that broad-based incentives will be weak for everyone because of free riding.[15]

Employees respond more against shirking in workplaces with shared capitalism institutions, and the findings suggest important complementarities between shared capitalism and high-performance policies, supervision intensity, and being paid at least the market wage.

References

Appelbaum, E., T. Bailey, P. Berg, and A. Kalleberg. 2000. *Manufacturing advantage: Why high-performance work systems pay off.* Ithaca, NY: Cornell University Press.

Axelrod, R. M. 1984. *The evolution of cooperation.* New York: Basic Books.

Bailey, R. M. 1970. Economies of scale in medical practice. In *Empirical studies in health economics,* ed. H. Klarman, 255–73. Baltimore, MD: Johns Hopkins University Press.

Bartholomew, D., J. Galbraith, I. Moustkaki, and F. Steele. 2002. *The analysis and interpretation of multivariate data for social scientists.* Chapman and Hall/CRC.

Ben-Ner, A., and D.C. Jones. 1995. Employee participation, ownership, and productivity: A theoretical framework. *Industrial Relations* 34 (4): 532–54.

Blasi, J. R., M. Conte, and D. Kruse. 1996. Employee stock ownership and corporate performance among public companies. *Industrial and Labor Relations Review* 50 (1): 60–79.

Blasi, J. R., D. Kruse, and A. Bernstein. 2003. *In the company of owners: The truth about stock options (and why every employee should have them).* New York: Basic Books.

Blasi, J., D. Kruse, and R. Freeman. 2006. Shared capitalism at work: Impacts and policy options. In *America at work,* ed. E. Lawler and J. O'Toole, 275–96. New York: Palgrave/Macmillan.

Carpenter, J. 2004. Punishing free riders: How group size affects mutual monitoring and the provision of public goods. IZA Discussion Paper no. 1337, Institute for the Study of Labor.

Drago, R., and G. T. Garvey. 1998. Incentives for helping on the job: Theory and evidence. *Journal of Labor Economics* 16 (1): 1–25.

Fehr, E., and S. Gächter. 2000. Cooperation and punishment in public goods experiments. *American Economic Review* 90 (4): 980–94.

15. The standard theory does not predict no anti-shirking intervention but only that it is likely to be suboptimal. As our discussant Eric Maskin noted, there is "no way of telling what optimal intervention would be." Our study does suggest, however, how the corporation can be structured to increase anti-shirking behavior and performance.

Fudenberg, D., and E. Maskin. 1986. The folk theorem in repeated games with discounting or with incomplete information. *Econometrica* 54 (3): 533–54.
Gaynor, M., and M. Pauly. 1990. Compensation and productive efficiency in partnerships: Evidence from medical group practice. *Journal of Political Economy* 98 (3): 544–74.
Hansen, D. G. 1997. Worker performance and group incentives: A case study. *Industrial and Labor Relations Review* 51 (1): 37–49.
Hirshleifer, D., and E. Rasmussen. 1989. Cooperation in a repeated prisoners' dilemma with ostracism. *Journal of Economic Behavior and Organization* 12 (August): 87–106.
Huselid, M. 1995. The impact of human resource management practices on the turnover, productivity, and corporate financial performance. *Academy of Management Journal* 38:635–72.
Ichniowski, C., K. Shaw, and G. Prennushi. 1997. The effects of human resource management practices on productivity: A study of steel finishing lines. *American Economic Review* 87 (3): 291–313.
Kandel, E., and E. P. Lazear. 1992. Peer pressure and partnerships. *Journal of Political Economy* 100 (4): 801–17.
Klos, T. B., and B. Nooteboom. 2001. Agent-based computational transaction cost economics. *Journal of Economic Dynamics and Control* 25 (3–4): 503–26.
Knez, M., and D. Simester. 2001. Firm-wide incentives and mutual monitoring at Continental Airlines. *Journal of Labor Economics* 19 (4): 743–72.
Kruse, D., and J. Blasi. 1997. Employee ownership, employee attitudes, and firm performance: A review of the evidence. In *The human resources management handbook, part 1,* ed. D. Lewin, D. J. B. Mitchell, and M. A. Zaidi. Greenwich, CT: JAI Press.
Nalbantian, H., and A. Schotter. 1997. Productivity under group incentives: An experimental study. *American Economic Review* 87 (3): 314–41.
Prendergast, C. 1999. The provision of incentives in firms. *Journal of Economic Literature* 37 (1): 7–63.
Rousseau, D. M., and Z. Shperling. 2003. Pieces of the action: Ownership and the changing employment relationship. *Academy of Management Review* 28 (4): 553–70.
Stiglitz, J. E. 1990. Peer monitoring and credit markets. *World Bank Economic Review* 4 (3): 351–66.
Weiss, A. 1987. Incentives and worker behavior. In *Incentives, cooperation, and risk sharing,* ed. H. Nalbantian, 137–50. Totowa, NJ: Rowman and Littlefield.
Weitzman, M., and D. Kruse. 1990. Profit sharing and productivity. In *Paying for productivity: A look at the evidence,* ed. A. S. Blinder, 95–141. Washington, DC: Brookings Institution.
Welbourne, T. M., and C. J. Ferrante. 2008. To monitor or not to monitor. *Group and Organization Management* 33 (2): 139–62.

3

Risk and Lack of Diversification under Employee Ownership and Shared Capitalism

Joseph R. Blasi, Douglas L. Kruse, and
Harry M. Markowitz

I am in favor of having as large a unit as market conditions will allow. . . . To suppose that safety-first consists in having a small gamble in a large number of different [companies] where I have no information to reach a good judgment, as compared with a substantial stake in a company where one's information is adequate, strikes me as a travesty of investment policy.
—John Maynard Keynes Letter to F. C. Scott on February 6, 1942 (Keynes 1983). (Keynes managed the investments of a large British insurance company and the endowment funds of Kings College Cambridge [quoted in Bernstein (1992, 48)]).

The correlation among returns is not the same for all securities. We generally expect the returns on a security to be more correlated with those in the same industry than those of unrelated industries. Business connections among corporations, the fact that they service the same area, a common dependence on military expenditures, building activity, or the weather can increase the tendency of particular returns to move up and down together. To reduce risk it is necessary to avoid a portfolio whose securities are highly correlated with each other.
—Harry M. Markowitz, *Portfolio Selection* (1991, 5)

As we saw in chapter 1, a substantial proportion of private sector workers participate in some form of shared rewards and there is evidence that shared

Joseph R. Blasi is a professor of human resource management and labor studies and employment relations at the Rutgers School of Management and Labor Relations, and a research associate of the National Bureau of Economic Research. Douglas L. Kruse is a professor capitalism plays a positive role in economic performance (Kruse, Blasi, and Park 2008; Freeman Kruse, and Blasi 2008; Blasi et al. 2008; Harden, Kruse, and Blasi 2008). With this level of incidence and these potential outcomes, it is incumbent on scholars to figure out whether and under what conditions such practices make sense or are really ill-advised. Since shared capitalism, especially in the form of employee stock ownership and stock options, is an investment, we need to examine it from the critical perspective of risk. This chapter considers two questions: what is the impact of subjective risk on workers' attitudes, preferences, and behaviors under shared capitalism? Can employee ownership and other forms of worker equity participation be consistent with proper diversification? While the possible jeopardy from employee stock ownership constitutes a major objection by economists, the impact of subjective risk under shared capitalism and the resolution of the empirical question "How much is too much?" in a portfolio has never been comprehensively addressed.

Many economists have seriously worried about the phenomenon of employee stock ownership because it possibly "puts all one's eggs in one basket." Workers risk losing both their job and their investments in the same firm. Looking at subjective worker behavior, Benartzi and Thaler's incisive study (2001) found that workers put about 42 percent of their assets in the company stock account and then split the remaining assets fairly evenly between nonemployee ownership equities and fixed income securities with the result that the workers in the companies with employee ownership are over 70 percent invested in equities, in effect, further adding to lack of diversification in their portfolios. Benartzi (2001) has shown that workers in large corporate defined contribution retirement plans (such as 401(k) plans) increase the proportion of their holdings in employee ownership of company stock after the company's equity performs well on the market, allocating four times more new investments to company stock in the future when the company stock had done well in the past. He concludes that this violates a cardinal law of economics, portfolio diversification. Meulbroek

of human resource management and labor studies and employment relations at the Rutgers School of Management and Labor Relations, and a research associate of the National Bureau of Economic Research. Harry M. Markowitz is a professor of finance at the Rady School of Management, University of California, San Diego.

The original version of this chapter was prepared for the Russell Sage/NBER conference in New York City, October 2006. This chapter is part of the National Bureau of Economic Research's Shared Capitalism Research Project, funded by the Russell Sage and Rockefeller Foundations from 2001 to 2007. Additional funding for the General Social Survey questions was provided by the Foundation for Enterprise Development, the ESOP Association, the Employee Ownership Foundation, Hewitt Associates, the National Center for Employee Ownership, the Profit Sharing Council of America, and American Capital Strategies. The authors wish to thank Tom Smith with the General Social Survey at the National Opinion Research Center of the University of Chicago and Peter Marsden of Harvard University with the National Organizations Study for their assistance in arranging the shared capitalism segment of both surveys. The authors wish to thank Daniel Kahneman of Princeton University for several generous discussions and communications with us about our ideas.

(2002) compares the risk of holding one company's stock to a diversified portfolio for all stocks listed in the Center For Research on Securities Prices (CRSP) and concludes that "on average 42% of the stock's market value will be sacrificed by failing to diversify" (29). She looked at expectations of what could happen rather than the specific tracking of actual data on employee investments in company stock and considered the extreme case of 100 percent employee investment in company stock. Meulbroek sees no rational basis for company stock ownership by employees whatsoever (2002, 14) and makes a strong recommendation against any employee ownership at all in the economy.

3.1 Data and Methods

Our analysis uses the NBER data set (described in the "Studying Shared Capitalism" section of the Introduction). Within this data set 81.5 percent of the workers had one or more forms of shared capitalist rewards, and analyses are conducted on only these workers (35,429 employees). This data set is particularly useful to examine risk because it provides a comprehensive description of the possible ways a worker can share in the profits or equity of the company plus detailed information on their income and wealth, organization of work, specific measures of their attitudes toward shared capitalism, their preferences for more or less shared capitalism, and their behavioral responses to shared capitalism (loyalty, turnover, and willingness to work harder for the company). These measures of worker attitudes, preferences, and behavioral responses are the main dependent variables of the study. Moreover, variables on empowerment and employee relations and work structure allow us to examine their role in the story. To deal with the nonrepresentative firm problem, we include company fixed effects in our calculations.

The economic insecurity score is the main independent variable of the study. The three components of a worker's economic insecurity score are the size of each worker's fixed annual pay, how many multiples each worker's total wealth (minus debt) is relative to that worker's fixed annual pay, and the extent to which each worker perceives they are competitively paid in the firm where they work. Briefly put, the score expresses how much cushion each worker's current capital offers them relative to their annual income, taking into account whether the worker feels fairly compensated or not based on expectations from the local labor market. If a worker perceives he or she is underpaid, then profit sharing or employee stock ownership may be perceived as wage substitution. The higher the score the more the worker's economic insecurity and the more the worker's capital is in danger. The construction of the economic insecurity score is explained in detail in the appendix.

Here is a concrete example of economic insecurity and economic security.

Table 3.1 **The economic insecurity score**

Score	Percent	Number
0	0.26	59
1	2.62	603
2	7.56	1,737
3	12.15	2,792
4	14.54	3,341
5	16.22	3,728
6	16.50	3,792
7	14.13	3,248
8	9.73	2,237
9	4.40	1,010
10	1.88	433

Note: Mean = 5.28; Median = 5; s.d. = 2.12; n = 22,980.

At one extreme, that of the high economic insecurity score, is a worker with fixed annual pay of $25,000, whose total wealth (minus debt) is less than $25,000, and who perceives that she or he is being paid significantly below market for their job position relative to comparable workers. We hold that the more insecure worker—just as Adam Smith predicts from his observations of the French sharecroppers in the Theoretical Perspectives section following—will be resistant to risking his or her own capital in the firm. At the other extreme, that of the low economic insecurity score (i.e., high economic security), is a worker with fixed annual pay of $75,000, whose total wealth is four multiples of annual pay at $300,000, and who perceives that he or she is being paid significantly above the market rate. We hold that this worker will be more comfortable with shared capitalism because their higher salary creates less immediate economic insecurity, their wealth cushions a significant amount of potential insecurity, and their perception that they receive a fixed wage above the market, for them, does not frame their shared capitalism as wage substitution. Obviously, however, both workers are vulnerable to the same peril of job loss. Table 3.1 shows the economic insecurity scores for the sample. There is a lot of variation in the sample. Because some components of the score were not contained in all company surveys, the score is only available for 22,980 workers.

3.2 Theoretical Perspectives

What we expect to find about the impact of risk on the attitudes, preferences, and behavioral outcomes of workers in firms under shared capitalism has been inspired by the work of Adam Smith, which provides important background to this discussion. A key theme of Smith's economics is that capitalism would result in better economic performance as a result of more effort, productivity, and wealth. While he did not deal with portfolio diversification per se, Smith wrote about the evolution from feudalism to the new market system as part of a long line of economists who stressed that capitalism also involved greater risk and speculation. The principal advantage of feudalism for the worker was the protection it provided from such danger (see Smith [1776, Book III, 2.2–2.21]). Adam Smith, however, definitely recognized that a worker could be interested in shared rewards, but that it was not a common arrangement at that time. He wrote:

> It sometimes happens, indeed, that a single independent workman has stock sufficient both to purchase the materials of his work, and to maintain himself till it be completed. He is both master and workman, and enjoys the whole produce of his own labour, or the whole value which it adds to the materials upon which it is bestowed. It includes what are usually two distinct revenues, belonging to two distinct persons, the profits of stock, and the wages of labour. (Smith 1776, Book I. 8.9–10)

Smith recognized the incentive value of such shared capitalist rewards and cited its role in improved economic performance. In writing about the French Metayers or sharecroppers as one example of a shared capitalist institution, he said:

> The proprietor furnished them with the seed, cattle, and instruments of husbandry, the whole stock, in short, necessary for cultivating the farm. The produce was divided equally between the proprietor and the farmer, after setting aside what was judged necessary for keeping up the stock, which was restored to the proprietor when the farmer either quitted, or was turned out of the farm. Land occupied by such tenants is properly cultivated at the expense of the proprietor as much as that occupied by slaves. There is, however, one very essential difference between them. Such tenants, being freemen, are capable of acquiring property, and having a certain proportion of the produce of the land, they have a plain interest that the whole produce should be as great as possible, in order that their own proportion may be so. A slave, on the contrary, who can acquire nothing but his maintenance, consults his own ease by making the land produce as little as possible over and above that maintenance. (Smith 1776, Book III, chapter 2, 11–12) (as quoted in Laffont and Martimort [2002, 10])

However, Smith identified a critical problem with the idea in addressing risk under such shared capitalist arrangements when he identified the moral hazard problem of sharecropping: sharecroppers do not desire to risk their own capital. Thus he wrote:

> It could never, however, be the interest even of this last species of cultivators to lay out, in the further improvement of the land, any part of the little stock which they might save from their own share of the produce, because the lord, who laid out nothing, was to get one-half of whatever it produced. . . . It might be the interest of a metayer to make the land

> produce as much as could be brought out of it by means of the stock furnished by the proprietor; but it could never be his interest to mix any part of his own with it. In France, where five parts out of six of the whole kingdom are said to be still occupied by this species of cultivators, the proprietors complain that their metayers take every opportunity of employing the master's cattle rather in carriage than in cultivation; because in the one case they get the whole profits to themselves, in the other they share them with their landlord. (Smith 1776, Book III, chapter 2, 13)(as quoted in Laffont and Martimort [2002, 10])

While he did not envision how such shared capitalist incentives would be structured in a complex economy, Smith clearly saw the advantages of shared capitalism. This analysis suggests that the incentive effect would be diminished if the worker's own capital was subject to excessive risk. We expect that workers will be risk averse in mixing their own capital with that of the firm. Smith's discussion is one of the inspirations for our economic insecurity variable.

While Smith's notion is based on salient historical observations, Daniel Kahneman and Amos Tversky's prospect theory (1979, 2000) inspired us to develop a unique way to explore the issues at hand. Prospect theory holds that people decide about outcomes based on a reference point (reflecting their status quo) rather than based upon some "objective" final situation or status. In their view, this status quo "frames" their decision. They note that different attitudes toward risk will emerge when a person perceives gains relative to their reference point or losses relative to their reference point and that people will care more about potential losses than potential gains. The economic insecurity score provides one measure of a worker's status quo and is directly influenced by Adam Smith's observation that a worker will not want to risk his or her own capital in a shared capitalist arrangement.

3.3 Hypotheses

Reflecting Adam Smith's perspective that workers will not jeopardize their own capital, this part of the chapter explores subjective risk, namely, how workers in shared capitalist arrangements respond to variations in their economic insecurity. People are risk averse. Our first hypothesis is:

HYPOTHESIS ONE: *As the economic insecurity score increases, attitudes toward shared capitalism, preferences for variable pay, and workplace outcomes (behaviors) under shared capitalism will worsen.*

Next we examine the impact of company culture. A worker's economic insecurity and response to shared capitalism are likely to be related to worker empowerment (influence over one's job and the workplace) and perceived fairness. In the absence of empowerment, shared capitalism may easily be seen as nothing more than increased income exposure, whereas empowerment creates a greater sense that one can affect workplace performance and rewards under shared capitalism. Regarding fairness, a number of scholars have argued that economists should add to their analyses the "preferences that people have for being treated fairly" (Kahneman, Knetsch, and Thaler [1986a, 1986b, S285–6]; see also Akerlof [1979] and Arrow [1973]). Good employee-management relations, where employees feel they are treated fairly, may be an important condition to create cooperation and higher performance under shared capitalism. Workers may therefore respond better to shared capitalism when they have greater empowerment and perceive better employee relations, diminishing the negative effects of economic insecurity. This is consistent with the idea that under the right conditions, shared capitalism can strengthen the "psychological contract" between employees and the firm (Rousseau and Shperling 2003). The second hypothesis is:

HYPOTHESIS TWO: *Lack of empowerment and poor employee relations help explain the negative relationship between the economic insecurity score and attitudes toward shared capitalism, preferences for variable pay, and behavioral outcomes under shared rewards.*

Several researchers have linked a bundle of high performance work practices to either improved operating performance of individual facilities or better productivity, lower turnover, and better total shareholder return of firms (Appelbaum et al. 2000; Becker, Huselid, and Ulrich 2001; Cappelli and Neumark 2001; Ichniowski, Shaw, and Prennushi 1995). These bundles are characterized by a coordinated integration of the various "high performance people management" systems inside the firm and involve: selective recruitment, intensive training and performance management, self-directed work teams, employee involvement, and performance sharing.[1] These bundles may interact with shared capitalism in the same way as previously hypothesized for employee empowerment and employee relations: such practices can help create the means for employees to positively affect performance, and strengthen the psychological contract between employees and the firm. This is likely to make employees more receptive to shared capitalism, and diminish the negative effects of economic insecurity. Put simply, we hypothesize that a more engaging work system will buffer worker response to economic uncertainty and insecurity. The third hypothesis is:

HYPOTHESIS THREE: *The presence of a high performance work system will reduce the negative effect of high economic insecurity on attitudes toward shared capitalism, preferences for variable pay, and outcomes under shared rewards.*

1. The authors are indebted to Mark Huselid for suggesting what themes and wording should be considered as critical for our questions regarding the measurement of alignment with the company's strategy. While we did some editing to make the questions accessible to the wide variety of workers and firms in the study, they basically follow his ideas.

3.4 Results

Risk aversion is the general norm for workers. Using the employee surveys of the NBER Shared Capitalism data set we can briefly review findings on the general preference for risk aversion or risk seeking among the workers in the sample based on demographic group and job characteristics. This is based on responses to the question:

> Some people like to take risks and others dislike taking risks. Where would you place yourself on a scale of how much you like or dislike taking risks, where 0 is hating to take any kind of risk and 0 is loving to take risks?
>
> Hate to take risks Love to take risks
>
> 0 1 2 3 4 5 6 7 8 9 10

The sample tends toward risk seeking: the mean is 5.6, with only one-quarter (26 percent) giving an answer of 4 or below, while 55 percent gave an answer above 5. Those with low earnings are predictably more likely to say they are risk averse, with 53 percent giving scores of 5 or below, compared to 27 percent of the high earners. The results are similar when breaking the figures down by wealth categories.

Another measure of risk aversion comes from the survey question:

> You are offered a bet. You have a 10 percent chance of winning $1,000. Would you take the bet if it cost you: (mark highest price you would pay)
>
> ☐$150 ☐$100 ☐$50 ☐$20 ☐$10 ☐$1
> ☐Would not pay anything

One-third (33 percent) of the individuals indicated extreme risk aversion, saying they would pay nothing or only $1 for the bet, while at the other extreme, 7 percent would pay $100 and 2 percent would pay $150 (above the expected value of the bet, indicating extreme risk loving). This is also related to earnings: 41 percent of the low earners would pay no more than $1, compared to 19 percent of high earners. It is noteworthy, however, that there is a good deal of dispersion even within the low-earning and high-earning groups. With this perspective on the general risk aversion of workers, let us now examine the results.

HYPOTHESIS ONE: *As the economic insecurity score increases, attitudes toward shared capitalism, preferences for variable pay, and workplace outcomes (behaviors) under shared incentives will worsen.*

The sample is workers who say that they participate in any kind of shared capitalist practice, including company stock ownership of any kind, stock options, profit or gain sharing, or any combination of these. Table 3.2 shows the results and reports on a number of individual variables that measure attitudes toward shared rewards, preferences for more shared rewards, and

Table 3.2 **Economic insecurity score and attitudes, preferences, and outcomes for workers with any shared capitalist practice**

	Line	Coefficient	*T*-stat.	*n*	R^2
Attitudes					
Summative attitudes measure (0–20, ordered probit)	1	–0.109***	–20.56	17,922	0.044
Important to work in a company that provides stock ownership or stock options to its employees (0–10, ordered probit)	2	–0.062***	–11.27	17,967	0.032
Feel like an owner (1–10, ordered probit)	3	–0.125***	–22.90	17,954	0.060
Ownership important to me (1–10, ordered probit)	4	–0.050***	–6.83	10,426	0.032
How important stock options were in attracting you to work for the company (1–4, ordered probit)	5	–0.034***	–3.66	6,964	0.021
Importance of Employee Stock Purchase Plan in attracting you to work at the company (0–4, ordered probit)	6	–0.063***	–5.77	5,210	0.025
How important the ESOP was in attracting you to work for the company (1–4, ordered probit)	7	–0.024	–1.37	1,898	0.034
Extent to which a cash incentive would increase your motivation to improve the business success of the company (0–4, ordered probit)	8	0.059***	6.65	7,727	0.008
Extent to which open market purchases of company stock would increase your motivation to improve the business success of the company (0–4, ordered probit)	9	–0.050***	–5.46	6,430	0.013
Extent to which stock options would increase your motivation to improve the business success of the company (0–4, ordered probit)	10	–0.050***	–5.15	6,462	0.040
Extent to which buying company stock in an Employee Stock Purchase Plan would increase your motivation to improve the business success of the company (0–4, ordered probit)	11	–0.050***	–5.28	6,436	0.025
Extent to which an ESOP would increase your motivation to improve the business success of the company (0–4, ordered probit)	12	–0.054***	–3.03	1,902	0.029
Ranking of the following relative to the other incentives in affecting one's motivation to improve the business success of the company (0–3 lowest-highest rank, ordered probit)					
cash bonus	13	0.036**	2.44	3,067	0.055
fixed wage increase	14	0.063***	4.23	3,112	0.033
401(k) company stock match	15	–0.060***	–4.12	2,908	0.031
company-wide profit-sharing plan	16	–0.038***	–2.75	3,120	0.044
Preferences					
Summative preferences measure (0–4, ordered probit)	17	–0.012	–1.58	10,707	0.037
Preference of variable pay, a 50/50 chance to make 10% more or 5% less over fixed pay (0–1, probit)	18	–0.010	–1.27	14,194	0.121
Preference of variable pay, a 50/50 chance to make 50% more or 25% less over fixed pay (0–1, probit)	19	–0.076***	–4.75	3,385	0.122
Preference for next pay increase as all fixed wages, a mixture of fixed and performance-based, or all performance-based pay (1–3, ordered probit)	20	–0.021**	–2.77	11,549	0.016

(*continued*)

Table 3.2 (continued)

	Line	Coefficient	*T*-stat.	*n*	R^2
Preference of company stock or stock options over cash incentive plan for some of your compensation (1–5, ordered probit)	21	–0.100***	–10.84	6,434	0.033
Preference of variable pay using company stock, profit sharing or stock options over only fixed pay (0–1, probit)	22	–0.105***	–8.17	7,997	0.167
% less regular pay worker is willing to accept to get a possible performance bonus of 10% on average of regular pay annually with the risk it could be higher or lower in any given year (0–100%, OLS)	23	–0.222***	–11.62	15,261	0.071
Ranking of the following as part of a pay raise (0–3 lowest-highest rank, ordered probit)					
Stock options	24	–0.020	–1.32	1,178	0.013
Fixed wage increase	25	0.067***	2.85	1,738	0.019
Company stock	26	–0.072***	–4.00	1,691	0.015
Company-wide profit-sharing plan	27	0.024	1.33	1,697	0.032
Would not opt to receive 50% of ESOP in cash right away or transfer it to another retirement fund versus keeping it entirely in company stock (0–1, probit)	28	–0.014	–0.58	1,297	0.042
Outcomes					
Summative outcomes rating (0–20, ordered probit)	29	–0.109***	–19.93	17,469	0.033
Not likely to look hard for a job (0–3, ordered probit)	30	–0.115***	–18.33	17,940	0.036
Feel loyalty to the company (0–3, ordered probit)	31	–0.108***	–17.45	17,735	0.060
See myself working here a long time (0–1, probit)	32	–0.091***	–11.18	17,953	0.043
See current job as part of career (0–1, probit)	33	–0.048***	–6.39	17,979	0.078
Will work harder for company (0–4, ordered probit)	34	–0.063***	–11.05	17,968	0.040
Number of days absent (#, tobit)	35	0.171**	2.36	17,676	0.018
It's part of my job to find out how to improve my work group or team's performance (0–4, ordered probit)	36	0.004	–0.11	592	0.078
Days in which I don't put much effort into my job (0–4, ordered probit)	37	–0.011	–1.17	6,840	0.017
Suggestion meeting frequency (0–4, ordered probit)	38	–0.054***	–3.48	2,224	0.033
Offering suggestions frequency (0–4, ordered probit)	39	0.011	1.42	12,643	0.072

Notes: Each line represents a separate regression, containing coefficient and *T*-statistic for Economic Insecurity Score in predicting the dependent variable at the left. Controls are noted at bottom. OLS = ordinary least squares.

See the appendix for variable definitions and descriptive statistics. Regressions include only workers who said they participated in at least one shared capitalist practice (owning company stock, participating in a profit-sharing or gain-sharing plan, or currently holding or receiving company stock options in the past year). Control variables include age, sex, marital status, children, family size, disability status, education, occupation, full-time status, payment on an hourly rate, hours worked per week, tenure, supervisory status, and log of fixed annual pay.

***Significant at the 1 percent level.

**Significant at the 5 percent level.

*Significant at the 10 percent level.

workplace outcomes (behaviors) under shared reward situations. Some of the dependent variables are also grouped into summative attitude, preference, and outcome variables where a large sample size is amenable to such a grouping:

Summative attitudes variable—measures (a) how important it is to work in a company with employee ownership, and (b) how much the worker feels like an owner.

Summative preferences variable—measures (a) preference for variable pay (a 50/50 chance to make 10 percent more or 5 percent less over fixed pay); and (b) the preference for next pay increase as all fixed wages, a mixture of fixed and performance-based, or all performance-based pay.

Summative outcomes (behaviors) variable—measures (a) whether the worker is looking hard for a job with another company in the next year (reverse scored); (b) the extent of their loyalty to their company; (c) whether they will work hard for the company; (d) whether they plan to stay with their company for a long time; and (e) whether they see their current job as part of a long-term career.

We will review these findings in some detail. The findings show that as the economic insecurity score increases, workers with increased economic insecurity respond with more negative attitudes about company ownership (lines 1 to 16), weaker preferences for additional shared incentives in their company (lines 17 to 28), and worse workplace outcomes (lines 29 to 39). A higher economic insecurity score is associated with very negative responses to shared capitalism just as Adam Smith's views would suggest.

Looking more closely at the individual measures of *attitudes,* as the economic insecurity score increases, workers report that it is less important to them to work for a company that provides stock ownership or stock options to its employees (line 2), that they feel less like owners (line 3), that ownership is less important to them (line 4), that stock options were less important in attracting them to work for the company (line 5), and that the Employee Stock Purchase Plan was less important in attracting them to work for the company (line 6). (Note that the score does not predict that workers in ESOP companies said ESOPs were less likely to have attracted them to work for the company on line 7. This is probably because ESOPs under most circumstances do not require workers to buy the stock with their own capital so ESOPS are less dangerous as long as they do not involve wage or benefit concessions, which are uncommon in most ESOPs.) As one would expect, as the economic insecurity score increases workers are more likely to say that a less speculative cash incentive (line 8), cash bonus (line 13), or fixed wage increase (line 14) will increase their motivation to improve the business success of the company. As the economic insecurity score increases, workers are less likely to be motivated to improve the business success of the company through more adventuresome incentive practices such as open market purchases of company stock (line 9), stock options (line 10), an Employee Stock Purchase

Plan (line 11), a 401(k) plan company stock match (line 15), a company-wide profit-sharing plan (line 16), or even a less exposed ESOP (line 12).

Regarding individual measures of *preferences* for additional shared incentives, as the economic insecurity score increases, workers are less willing to make a bet that runs the chance of losing 25 percent of fixed pay for a 50/50 chance of making 50 percent more in variable pay (line 19), wish their next pay increase to comprise fixed wages rather than a mixture of fixed/performance-based pay or all performance-based pay (line 20), are unwilling to get company stock or stock options over cash incentives as part of their compensation (line 21), and are unwilling to accept variable pay over fixed pay (line 22). As the economic insecurity score increases, the percentage of fixed pay that they are willing to sacrifice for the chance of getting a possible 10 percent rise in variable pay goes down (line 23). As the economic insecurity score increases, when asked to rank fixed pay, cash profit sharing, company stock, or stock options as the preferred compensation mechanism for their next pay increase, workers rank less vulnerable fixed pay higher and more perilous company stock lower.

Regarding individual measures of workplace *outcomes (behaviors),* as the economic insecurity score increases, workers say they are more likely to: be looking for a job elsewhere in the next six months (line 30), feel less loyalty to the company (line 31), not see themselves working at the company for a long time (line 32), and not see the company as part of a longtime career (line 33). A higher economic insecurity score means more days absent in the last six months (line 35). On other outcome measures reflecting contributing to the company, they say that they are *less* likely to: work harder for the company (line 34) or have participated in teams or meetings where they offer suggestions to superiors on improving the company (line 38).

Two related analyses available from the authors extend these findings. In one analysis we demonstrate that the results hold true for the typical combinations of shared capitalist practices that workers actually experience in the economy as identified by the University of Chicago's General Social Survey. So, for example, these results hold true for workers holding only company stock, for workers holding a combination of company stock, profit sharing, and broad-based stock options, and so forth. In another analysis we focus only on workers who own stock in 401(k) plans by measuring the percent of annual pay invested in company stock. We find that workers with high economic insecurity scores have more turnover, less loyalty, and less willingness to work hard at all levels of pay invested in company stock, not just at low levels of pay invested in company stock. The economic insecurity status appears to be the key to this subjective response.[2] These tables are available from the authors.

2. In a discussion of these findings with Daniel Kahneman, he has raised the issue whether the (different) ideas of an irrelevant gift (one that does not respond to an immediate need) or of a gift that involves costs to the recipient, have anything to do with what we found. (Personal communication, October 26, 2007).

HYPOTHESIS TWO: *Lack of empowerment and poor employee relations help explain the negative relationship between the economic insecurity score and attitudes toward shared capitalism, preferences for variable pay, and behavioral outcomes under shared rewards.*

The measurement of empowerment is the Lack of Empowerment Score. It is an additive index of each worker's participation in employee involvement teams, satisfaction with his or her work life influence overall, and satisfaction with influence in the job, department, and company as a whole. The measurement of employee relations is the Poor Employee Relations Score. It is an additive index of each worker's A-F school grades of their company regarding its trustworthiness in keeping its promises, overall employment relations, fairness, and ability to create a sense of common purpose in the company. (Both are reverse scored so that higher scores represent lower empowerment and worse employee relations. See appendix, variables 21 to 31.)

A first look at this issue is provided in table 3.3 where worker reports of their expected turnover are compared to their scores on economic insecurity, empowerment, and employee relations. For ease of presentation, workers are divided into whether they are above or below the median on these three variables, and expected turnover is presented for the eight permutations. The highest likely turnover (23.7 percent) is among those reporting high eco-

Table 3.3 **Bad versus good corporate culture in the economic insecurity score's impact on workplace outcomes**

	Percent very likely to look hard for a job in the next 12 months or already looking
High economic insecurity/poor empowerment/poor employee relations	23.7
Low economic insecurity/poor empowerment/poor employee relations	21.2
High economic insecurity/good empowerment/poor employee relations	13.2
Low economic insecurity/good empowerment/poor employee relations	10.8
High economic insecurity/poor empowerment/good employee relations	9.8
Low economic insecurity/poor empowerment/good employee relations	8.8
High economic insecurity/good empowerment/good employee relations	4.5
Low economic insecurity/good empowerment/good employee relations	3.9

Notes: In this table high and low economic insecurity refers, respectively, to scores above the median, and at or below the median. The empowerment and employee relations scores are similarly divided at the median.

nomic insecurity, poor empowerment, and poor employee relations, while the lowest (3.9 percent) is among those in the opposite categories on all three variables. Overall, good employee relations appear most important, since workers report good employee relations in the four categories with the lowest likely turnover. In effect, more vulnerable workers may respond less to this uncertainty in better workplaces. Other tables available from the authors demonstrate the same pattern for loyalty and willingness to work hard.

Turning to the regressions in table 3.4, the findings also show that a good corporate culture—the ability to have a say at work and be treated fairly in employment relations—plays a critical role in the relationship between the economic insecurity score and the attitude and behavioral outcomes. When lack of empowerment and poor employee relations are added as predictors of the summative attitudes measure, the economic insecurity coefficient goes down by almost 50 percent (columns [1] and [2]), and when they are added as predictors of the summative outcomes measure, the economic insecurity coefficient goes down by 70 percent (columns [7] and [8]). Lack of empowerment is also a significant predictor of the summative measure of preferences over variable pay, although the economic insecurity measure is not a significant predictor either before or after adding lack of empowerment as a control.

The two key implications of these findings are that: (a) a substantial portion of the negative attitudes toward shared capitalism and the poor behavioral outcomes among the economically insecure is not due to economic insecurity per se, but to corporate cultures that provide little empowerment and poor employee relations; and (b) the negative effects of economic insecurity can be counteracted by policies that increase employment and improve employee relations. Regarding the latter point, the magnitudes indicate that a one standard deviation improvement in either empowerment or employee relations would easily outweigh (by a multiple of two to six) a one standard deviation increase in economic insecurity in predicting the attitude and behavioral outcome index scores.[3] These results paint a picture of potential worker liability in these situations that suggests that a bad and unfair corporate culture is itself seen as a hazard by workers (for more on the issue of unfairness, see Kahneman, Knetsch, and Thaler [1986a, 1986b]).

HYPOTHESIS THREE: *The presence or absence of high performance work practices helps explain the negative effect of high economic insecurity scores on attitudes toward shared capitalism, preferences for variable pay, and behavioral outcomes under shared rewards.*

3. In predicting the summative attitudes measure (column [2]), the effect of a one standard deviation change in the empowerment score (employee relations score) on the ordered probit index would be 2.14 (2.91) times larger than the effect of a one standard deviation change in the insecurity score. In predicting the behavioral outcomes measure (column [8]), the similar multiples would, respectively, be 4.03 and 6.59.

Table 3.4 **Empowerment, employee relations, and high performance work systems as predictors of attitudes, preferences, and behavioral outcomes**

	Summative attitudes measure			Summative preferences measure			Summative outcomes measure		
Dependent variable	(1)	(2)	(3)	(4)	(5)	(6)	(7)	(8)	(9)
Economic insecurity	**–0.109**	**–0.058**	**–0.029**	–0.012	–0.002	–0.004	**–0.109**	**–0.033**	**–0.032**
	(0.005)	(0.006)	(0.006)	(0.007)	(0.008)	(0.008)	(0.005)	(0.006)	(0.007)
Lack of empowerment		**–0.095**	**–0.072**		**–0.027**	**–0.023**		**–0.132**	**–0.094**
		(0.004)	(0.005)		(0.005)	(0.006)		(0.004)	(0.005)
Poor employee relations		**–0.082**	**–0.05**		–0.003	0.005		**–0.139**	**–0.131**
		(0.002)	(0.003)		(0.003)	(0.004)		(0.003)	(0.004)
HPWS			**0.069**			**0.018**			**0.073**
			(0.004)			(0.005)			(0.004)
n	17,922	17,251	11,268	10,707	10,252	9,977	17,469	16,859	10,965
R^2	0.044	0.076	0.049	0.037	0.039	0.04	0.033	0.125	0.137

Notes: Standard errors in parentheses. Coefficients in bold are significant at 95 percent level. Regressions include only workers who said they participated in at least one shared capitalist practice (owning company stock through open market purchases, an Employee Stock Purchase Plan, a 401(k) plan, the exercise of stock options, or an ESOP, participating in a profit-sharing or gain-sharing plan, currently holding or receiving company stock options in the past year). Control variables include age, sex, marital status, children, family size, disability status, education, occupation, full-time status, payment on an hourly rate, hours worked per week, tenure, supervisory status, and log of fixed annual pay.

The score for a high performance work system (HPWS) is based on the following summative index described in detail in the appendix, variables 32 to 38. It captures elements of training intensity, company communication and information, employee buy-in to corporate strategy, and structuring of the company's culture and work organization to support the overall company plan. A recent survey of the high performance work practices literature confirms the relevance of the components used (Blasi and Kruse 2006).

The method is to examine whether the negative coefficient on the economic insecurity score is reduced by the addition of HPWS as a control. As noted earlier, we contend that a more engaging work system will buffer worker response to economic insecurity. The results are in table 3.4, columns (3), (6), and (9). The HPWS measure is a strong and significant predictor of all three summative measures. Controlling for HPWS, the negative coefficient of the economic insecurity score for the attitudes measure (column [3]) is reduced by 50 percent relative to column (2), and the coefficient is only one-fourth as large as it was before controlling for lack of empowerment, poor employee relations, and HPWS (column [1]). It appears that workers have more willingness to have a profit or stock share in their company if they perceive that the company invests more in their performance abilities through a high performance work system. Adding HPWS as a predictor of the summative outcomes measure (column [9]) reduces the economic insecurity coefficient by only a small amount relative to column (8), but the fact that HPWS is closely related to lack of empowerment and poor employee relations (reducing the coefficients on those variables when it is added in column [9]) indicates that HPWS is a key factor in reducing the economic insecurity effect found in column (7). The results strongly suggest that highly economically vulnerable workers moderate their responses to this exposure when the work system is more progressive.

It has been demonstrated that as economic insecurity of workers rises, this is associated with worse worker attitudes toward shared capitalism, preferences for variable pay, and behavioral outcomes under shared capitalist arrangements. Not only do workers make some bad portfolio decisions under shared capitalism as the research literature reviewed in the beginning of this study has shown, but our results indicate that their level of economic insecurity also influences how well they actually respond to shared capitalist arrangements such as employee ownership in their workplace. Insecure workers may moderate their responses in better workplaces. One implication is that employee ownership and shared capitalist plans may need to be designed more carefully when they involve workers with high economic insecurity. Employers with shared capitalist arrangements that are structured to take into account worker responses to their economic insecurity and employment culture would likely, as a result, have better worker attitudes, better workplace outcomes, and a greater willingness of workers to prefer such arrangements. This means, for example, that pushing low paid workers with little wealth who perceive that they are paid noncompetitive wages to buy company stock in 401(k) plans with their savings does not make economic sense for the workers, the firms, the shareholders, or the economy as a whole, because asking workers with little capital to take a flyer on their personal capital is associated with a bad worker response to shared capitalism.

3.5 Is Shared Capitalism Consistent with Proper Diversification?

Does the portfolio diversification problem go away now that we know that workers tend to subjectively respond poorly to excessive economic insecurity under shared capitalist arrangements? The answer is clearly no, it does not go away. Our results only show that workers are subjectively sensitive to the economic gamble under shared capitalism, and manage to respond to it in their own way. However, these results do not mean that workers' investment portfolios always properly diversify risk. Indeed, the irony of our results is that, while workers evidently respond to their subjective risk, the problem of objective risk in their portfolios remains. The fact that workers in the more progressive workplaces respond less to economic insecurity, only increases the importance of solving the objective exposure problem.

The concerns of economists about an objective lack of diversification in workers' portfolios thus needs to be considered more carefully. In the NBER sample the median percent of net wealth in company stock is 5 percent and the mean is 14 percent. While only 0.6 percent of workers have 100 percent of their net wealth in company stock (i.e., Muelbroek's scenario), 4.7 percent of NBER sample workers do have more than 50 percent of their net wealth in company stock, and 15.6 percent have more than twice the mean percent of net wealth in company stock; that is, have *over 28 percent of their net wealth invested in company stock.* Thus, it is likely that at least these three groups—in total, 20.9 percent of the workers in the NBER employee survey sample—may have excessive amounts of company stock in their overall portfolios. We can consider these groups to be approximately the workers for whom employee ownership plays a critical role in lack of diversification.

The remainder of this section explores the question of how much investment in company stock is "too much." The question is oft raised in discussions of employee stock ownership and shared capitalism but it has never been empirically resolved. We provide a mathematical presentation that answers this critical question. Briefly, we show that the optimal portion of an otherwise diversified portfolio that could conceivably be in company stock is 8.33 percent, while 10 to 15 percent would have a small effect on the volatility of the employee portfolio. The implications of this result are discussed in the conclusion.

3.6 Mathematical Presentation

The theory of rational behavior under uncertainty, as developed by Leonard J. Savage (1954), asserts that the rational decision maker maximizes expected utility using probability beliefs where objective probabilities are not known. Levy and Markowitz (1979) show that, for a wide variety of risk-averse utility functions and historical return distributions, mean-variance approximations provide almost maximum expected utility. (See also Markowitz [1959, chapters 6 and 13]; Dexter, Yu, and Ziemba [1980]; Ederington [1986]; Hlawitschka [1994]; Kroll, Levy, and Markowitz [1984]; Markowitz, Reid, and Tew [1994]; Pulley [1981, 1983]; and Simaan [1993].) Thus the justification for the use of mean-variance, according to Markowitz (1959) and others, is not that probability distributions are Gaussian or that utility is quadratic (as asserted as requirements in Tobin [1958] and frequently incorrectly attributed to Markowitz), but as an approximation to expected utility.

The mean-variance approximation to expected utility typically takes the form

$$EU \cong E - \frac{1}{2} kV, \tag{1}$$

where E is the expected and V the variance of returns on the portfolio-as-a-whole, and $k > 0$ is a risk-aversion parameter. For example, following Kelly (1956) and Latané (1959), most financial analysts believe that action for the long run involves maximizing the expected value of the log of 1.0 + return. Levy and Markowitz show that this is closely approximated by equation (1) with $k = 1.0$. In continuous time models, "Ito's Lemma" asserts that this relationship is exact quite generally.

If X is the fraction of an employee's financial assets held "explicitly" in company stock and $(1 - X)$ is the fraction in all other financial assets (including, e.g., an index fund that "implicitly" owns the company stock) then

$$\begin{aligned} E &= m_1 X + m_2(1 - X) \\ V &= V_1 X^2 + V_2(1 - X)^2 + 2X(1 - X)\sigma_{12}, \end{aligned} \tag{2}$$

where m_1 and m_2 are the expected (or mean) returns on the two "investments," V_1 and V_2 their variances, and σ_{12} their covariance. The latter includes the covariance between the company stock held explicitly and that held implicitly. Inserting equation (2) into (1) we have

$$\begin{aligned} EU \cong\ & m_1 X + m_2(1 - X) \\ & - \frac{1}{2} k\{V_1 X^2 + V_2(1 - X)^2 + 2\sigma_{12} X(1 - X)\}. \end{aligned} \tag{3}$$

The optimum value of X is found by setting the derivative of EU to zero, from which emerges that $\hat{X}$, the optimum X, satisfies

(4) $$\hat{X}(V_1 + V_2 - 2\sigma_{12}) + V_2 - \sigma_{12} = \frac{(m_1 - m_2)}{k}.$$

The analysis simplifies considerably if we assume that $\hat{X} = 0$, and $m_1 = m_2$, absent any stock incentive plan. The first equality is plausible; since "other investments" may include the company's stock, we may assume that it includes the ideal amount of this stock, in which case indeed $\hat{X} = 0$. Later we discuss the assumption that $m_1 = m_2$. Given these two assumptions, equation (4) implies that

(5) $$\sigma_{12} = V_2.$$

From this follows that equation (3) may be written as

(6) $$EU \cong m + (\Delta m_1)X - \frac{1}{2}k\{V_1X^2 + V_2(1 - X^2)\}.$$

with $m = m_1 = m_2$ and $\Delta m_1 = 0$.

We are interested here in the tradeoff between increased m_1 (keeping m_2 constant) and increased X, moving the investor's allocation from the optimum at $X = 0$. As $m_1 = m + \Delta m_1$ increases $\hat{X}$, the optimum X increases as well. Specifically, differentiating equation (6) with respect to X, and setting dEU / dX to zero, we find

(7) $$\hat{X} = \frac{\Delta m_1}{k(V_1 - V_2)}.$$

The term $(V_1 - V_2)$ in the denominator of equation (7) may seem strange. For example, if $V_1 = V_2$, the formula implies infinite $\hat{X}$. But equation (5) implies

(8) $$V_2 = \sigma_2^2$$
$$= \rho_1\sigma_1\sigma_2,$$

therefore

$$\sigma_2 = \rho\sigma_1.$$

Thus, $V_2 < V_1$ unless the two "investments" are perfectly correlated.

The assumption that $m_1 = m_2$ may be plausible if $(1 - X)$ represents investment in other equities, but not if it includes substantial investment in money market funds or short-term bonds. Then we would expect $m_2 < m_2$. A standard and very convenient assumption is that X and $1 - X$ represent investments in risky "securities" and, additionally, the investor's risk level is adjusted by holding cash with interest rate r_0. In this case, the Tobin Separation Theorem is applicable. If the investor can borrow as well as lend at the rate r_0, as Sharpe (1964) assumes, then the investor will hold the risky portfolio that maximizes the Sharpe ratio

$$\frac{E - r_0}{\sigma}, \tag{9}$$

where σ is the standard deviation of portfolio return. If the investor can only lend, not borrow, at the rate r_0, as Tobin (1958) assumes, *and* "cash" is part of the investor's portfolio then, again, the investor holds the risky portfolio that maximizes the Sharpe ratio and combines it with lending (i.e., the holding of cash).

In general in this case, the optimum risky portfolio satisfies

$$CY = bv, \tag{10}$$

where C is the covariance matrix among risky securities, Y is the portfolio of risky securities, v is a vector of excess returns (i.e., expected returns minus the risk-free rate), and b is a number (as distinguished from a vector or matrix). In our case equation (10) specializes to

$$\begin{pmatrix} V_1 & \rho^2 V_1 \\ \rho^2 V_1 & \rho^2 V_1 \end{pmatrix} \begin{pmatrix} X_1 \\ X_2 \end{pmatrix} = b \begin{pmatrix} v_1 \\ v_1 \end{pmatrix}, \tag{11}$$

where we write X_1 and X_2 for X and $1 - X$, respectively. Solving equation (11) gives us

$$X_1 = \frac{b(v_1 - v_2)}{(1 - \rho^2)V_1} \tag{12}$$

$$X_2 = \frac{b(v_2 - \rho^2 v_1)}{\rho^2(1 - \rho^2)V_1}.$$

If $b = \rho^2 V_1/v_2 = V_2/v_2$ then $X_1 + X_2 = 1$. A smaller b implies that "cash" equal $1 - X_1 - X_2$ is held.

A plausible example might have $\sigma_2 = 0.2, \sigma_1 = 0.4$. (The former is approximately the standard deviation of the S&P 500 Index; the latter then would follow from a one-factor model

$$r_1 = \alpha + \beta r + u$$

with r_1 representing the return on company stock; r that on an underlying factor with the same variance as the S&P 500; $\beta = 1$ and the variance of the idiosyncratic term u equal three times that to the variance of r.) Then equation (8) implies $\rho = 1/2$.

Solving for $X = X_1$ in equation (12) with these parameters yields

$$3X = \frac{v_1 - v_2}{v_2}. \tag{13}$$

For example, if $(1 - X)$ supplied 4 percentage points of excess return and X supplied 5, then

$$\hat{X} = 0.0833.$$

A higher X, in the neighborhood of 10 or even 15 percent, would not be imprudent. Because the relationship between V and X is quadratic, small deviations from zero, the optimum if $m_1 = m_2$, do not increase V or reduce EU much, even if $m_1 = m_2$. Specifically, equation (6) implies

$$(14) \qquad V = V_2 + (V_1 - V_2)X^2$$

and

$$(15) \qquad \frac{dV}{dX} = 2(V_1 - V_2)X.$$

Thus, at $X = 0$, $dV/dX = 0$. A small increase in X has virtually no effect on V.

Table 3.5 shows the values of portfolio V and σ for various values of X for the parameters of our example. Figure 3.1 plots the relationship between σ and X. These reinforce the observation that X around 10 or 15 percent has small effect of the volatility of the employee's portfolio. For example, a 10 percent investment in company stock has a standard deviation of 20.3

Table 3.5 **Values of V and σ for various values of X**

X	$1 - X$	V	σ
0.00	1.00	0.0400	0.200
0.05	0.95	0.0403	0.201
0.10	0.90	0.0412	0.203
0.15	0.85	0.0427	0.207
0.20	0.80	0.0448	0.212
0.25	0.75	0.0475	0.218
0.30	0.70	0.0508	0.225
0.35	0.65	0.0547	0.234
0.40	0.60	0.0592	0.243
0.45	0.55	0.0643	0.254
0.50	0.50	0.0700	0.265
0.55	0.45	0.0763	0.276
0.60	0.40	0.0832	0.288
0.65	0.35	0.0907	0.301
0.70	0.30	0.0988	0.314
0.75	0.25	0.1075	0.328
0.80	0.20	0.1168	0.342
0.85	0.15	0.1267	0.356
0.90	0.10	0.1372	0.370
0.95	0.05	0.1483	0.385
1.00	0.00	0.1600	0.400

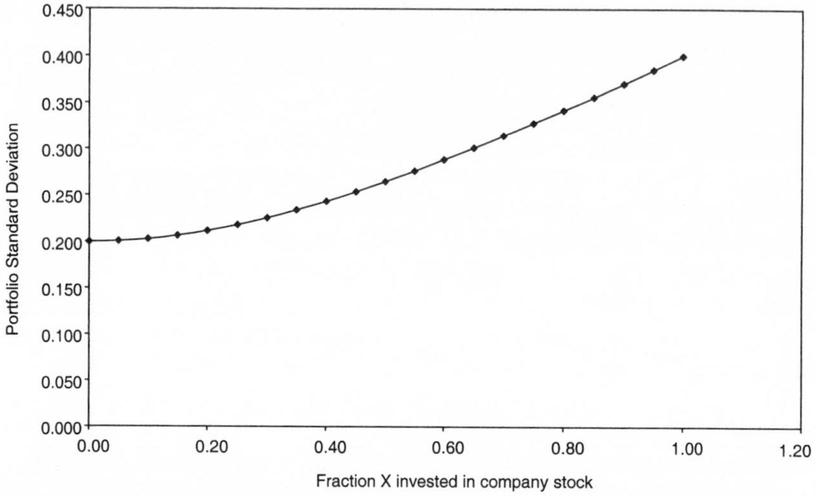

Fig. 3.1 Portfolio standard deviation as a function of investment in company stock

percent, whereas a 15 percent investment in company stock has a standard deviation of return of 20.7 percent, up slightly from 20.0 percent for no company stock as compared to 40.0 percent for all company stock.

The difference between the 8 1/3 percent, which is optimal in this example, and the 10 or 15 percent that is not too imprudent, suggests a possible "free-rider" problem. From the individual employee's point of view, ideally he or she would like everyone else to have 10 or 15 percent invested and have 8 1/3 invested himself or herself.

Variables V, σ, and EU are continuous functions of the input parameters; thus small changes in the assumptions of this example cause small changes in the table and the figure. Thus it seems likely that any reasonable estimates will leave our general conclusion intact. A small but meaningful employee stock ownership level will not significantly deteriorate the diversification of employee portfolios.

3.7 Conclusion

These exploratory insights on the role of risk in properly structuring shared capitalist arrangements have been developed by studying how workers themselves would confront and resolve the issue of such hazard and further examining the implications of portfolio theory. The main revision to the previous empirical research on the economics of employee ownership is that a high level of vulnerability is not a requirement of making shared capitalism work best. The results show clearly that excessive worker exposure based on a worker's level of economic insecurity has the capability of reversing every single positive individual and workplace outcome documented in decades of research on shared capitalism and the other studies in this volume. Lack of empowerment and poor employee relations play key roles in driving the negative impact of this jeopardy. Ironically, workers in corporations with the most progressive work practices may not pay as much attention to their potential liability as their objective economic situation requires.

This finding may partly explain why empirical results on the impact of employee ownership on firm performance are not always uniformly positive and sometimes show dispersion, why some of the most progressive corporations ignore these issues, and why some very large and very speculative employee ownership experiments have failed miserably. The most notable failure is the United Airlines employee buyout where endangering the capital of individual workers, wage substitution, lack of empowerment, and poor employee relations all played a large role consistent with our analysis. Indeed, the implementation and to some extent the design of the United Airlines employee ownership plan appears to have violated every finding of this study. Moreover, many United workers may have also had undiversified portfolios. Worker economic insecurity has been an unmeasured variable in past research. Two clear implications are that: (a) the structure of employee ownership and profit-sharing plans needs to be "fit" to the economic insecurity or economic security profile of the workers; and (b) portfolio diversification can be generally consistent with shared capitalism.

Eliminating shared capitalism from capitalist societies is not the answer to the problem of objective economic hazard. Remember that Adam Smith emphasizes the incentive effect of capitalism and its superiority to feudal systems and expected shared capitalism to be a positive motivator. Portfolio theory suggests how a wide range of workers could have employee ownership and diversification at the same time. Portfolio theory's implications for this discussion is sometimes reduced in the popular mind to the quick summary "buy an index of the entire market" but, as we have seen, this is not precisely what portfolio theory says. Portfolio theory does not propose that all risk be banned so that every global citizen should own a completely diversified basket of securitized assets worldwide. In such a world there would be no home ownership, no individual asset ownership, no sole proprietorships, no small businesspeople, no entrepreneurs, no high tech start-ups, no owners who are "principals" in corporations, no room for workers to have shares in their company; indeed, no shared capitalism. There would, in short, be no capitalism in the individual incentive sense. Nevertheless, as noted in chapter 11, looking at the economy as a whole workers who own company stock report it represents 20 percent of personal wealth in the General Social Survey. This suggests that there are extremes of employee stock holding in the economy but it is most likely concentrated in a minority of employees, as the NBER data suggest.

One limitation of this analysis is that it does not address the additional chance of losing one's job or firm-specific capital at the same time that one can potentially lose one's investment in the stock of the company. If the company closes, both the job and an undiversified portfolio are in danger. Our approach has been to address the exposure in the investment portfolio.

Research on employee ownership and shared capitalism often ignores or minimizes both subjective and objective risk. This disregard has taken place for decades despite the fact that excessive lack of diversification has been the principal objection by some economists, other social scientists, and policy-makers to the idea of broadened shared incentives and employee ownership. The goal of this chapter has been to confront these objections head-on and attempt through fine-tuned empirical analysis and careful mathematical explication to understand them better. As national wage systems evolve in the twenty-first century and inflation-adjusted wage increases flatten, the additional income workers can get from capital income (shares of profits and stock and capital appreciation in their firms), may constitute a potential future component of worker wealth. Risk is not the enemy of shared capitalism, but the elements of it must be directly confronted, empirically understood, and theoretically considered in a sound manner.

Appendix

Variable Definitions and Descriptive Statistics

Dependent Variables

Risk Aversion and Risk Seeking

1. Attitude toward risk: "Some people like to take risks and others dislike taking risks. Where would you place yourself on a scale of how much you like or dislike taking risks, where 0 is hating to take any kind of risk and 10 is loving to take risks?" (0–10 scale, 0 = Hate to take risks, 10 = Love to take risks). Mean = 5.61, s.d. = 2.38, n = 34,794.

2. Highest price paid for a bet: "You are offered a bet. You have a 10 percent chance of winning \$1,000. Would you take the bet if it cost you: (mark highest price you would pay: \$0, \$1, \$10, \$20, \$50, \$100, \$150)?" Mean = \$23.37, s.d. = 32.40, n = 34,751.

Outcomes

3. Planning to stay with employer versus looking to turnover: "How likely is it that you will decide to look hard for a job with another organization within the next twelve months?" (0–3 scale, 0 = Already looking; 1 = Very

likely; 2 = Somewhat likely; 2 = Not at all likely). Mean = 2.45, s.d. = .81, n = 35,080.

4. Extent of loyalty to current employer: "How much loyalty would you say you feel toward the company you work for as a whole?" (0–3 scale, 0 = No loyalty at all; 1 = Only a little; 2 = Some; 3 = A lot). Mean = 2.37, s.d. = .78, n = 34,555.

5. Willingness to work harder to help company succeed: "To what extent do you agree or disagree with this statement? "I am willing to work harder than I have to in order to help the company I work for succeed." (0–4 scale, 0 = Strongly disagree; 1 = Disagree; 2 = Neither agree nor disagree; 3 = Agree; 4 = Strongly agree). Mean = 3.04, s.d. = 0.89; n = 35,091.

6. Whether worker expects to stay with employer for the foreseeable future: "Which ONE of the following statements best describes how you think of your current employer? 1 = I see myself working here for the foreseeable future (a long time). 0 = I do not see myself working here very long." (0–1 scale). Mean = 0.83; s.d. = 0.37; n = 34,794.

7. Whether worker sees current job as part of long-term career: "Thinking about your current job (rather than your employer), do you look upon it as part of your long-term career, or a position that is not part of your long-term career? 1 = Part of my long-term career; 0 = A position that is not part of my long term career." (0–1 scale). Mean = 0.78, s.d. = 0.42, n = 34,991.

8. Summative outcomes variable: Additive index of variables 3–7 above. (0–12 scale). Mean = 9.49, s.d. = 2.26, n = 33,467.

Attitudes

9. Importance of employee ownership: "How important is it to you to work in a company that provides stock ownership to its employees? Please rate on a scale of 0 to 10." (0–10 scale, 0 = Not important, 10 = Highly important). Mean = 7.44, s.d. = 2.68, n = 34,729.

10. Feeling like an owner of the company: "How much do you feel like an owner of this company?" (1–10 scale, 1 = Not important—A moderate degree—10 = Very much). Mean = 4.81, s.d. = 3.02, n = 34,910.

11. Summative attitudes variable: Additive index of variables 9–10 above. (0–20 scale). Mean = 12.24, s.d. = 4.93, n = 34,525.

Preferences

12. Preference regarding a small variable pay risk: "We would like to ask about your attitude toward variable pay in two imaginary jobs. Job A and Job B are identical except for the fact that Job A pays a fixed amount and Job B pays an amount that varies. Based on the following information, which one would you choose? Job A, which guarantees an amount equal to your current pay, or Job B, which each year has a 50/50 chance that you would make 10 percent MORE than your current pay and a 50/50 chance that you

would make 5 percent LESS than your current pay?" (Scale: 0 = Job A, 1 = Job B). Mean = 0.40 s.d. = 0.49, n = 28,700.

13. Preference regarding variable or fixed pay for next pay increase: "For your next pay increase, would you prefer that it come in the form of: 1.) All fixed wages, with no profit sharing or company stock. 2.) Split between fixed wages and profit sharing or company stock. 3.) All in the form of profit sharing or company stock." (1–3 scale, textual responses as shown.) Mean = 1.84, s.d. = .60, n = 22,623.

14. Summative preferences variable: Additive index of variables 12–13 above. (0–4 scale) Mean = 2.22, s.d. = 0.81, n = 21,040.

15. Incentive threshold point: "Some people think that basing pay on company performance will encourage employees to take an active role in promoting the company's success. At your company, how much of their pay would most employees have to get in performance-based pay to motivate them to take more responsibility for the success of the company? _5%, _10%, _20%, _30%, _40%, _50%, _60%, _70%, _80%, _90%, _100%, _Performance-based pay would not make a difference." (0–100 percent scale). Mean = 31.7, s.d. = 24.6, n = 25,435.

16. Percent of worker's wealth in equities overall: "About what percent of your total wealth is in stocks overall? ________% (1–100 percent scale). Mean = 29.2, s.d. = 26.6; n = 25,715.

Independent Variables

17. Economic insecurity score. Measure of the economic status quo of each worker denoting increasing economic insecurity. Summative measure of questions 18–20 below including:

Quartiles representing highest to lowest annual fixed pay plus overtime (Score: 0–3)
Quartiles representing highest to lowest total wealth divided by fixed pay (Score: 0–3)
Five categories representing highest to lowest competitiveness of fixed pay (Score: 0–4)

Mean = 5.28, s.d. = 2.12; n = 22,980. Minimum 0; Maximum 10.

18. Annual fixed pay plus overtime: "What was your annual base pay last year (excluding any overtime, bonuses, and commissions) BEFORE taxes and deductions? If you receive overtime pay, how much did you earn in overtime last year?" Mean = 60,035, s.d. = 42,092, n = 28,365.

For first component of the economic insecurity score, answers were recoded by quartile: 0: >\$80,000; 1: >\$50,000 and ≤\$80,000; 2: >\$33,000 and ≤\$50,000; 3: <\$33,000.

19. Total wealth (minus debts) with spouse/partner: "People have var-

ious assets that constitute their wealth. These include the value of their house minus the mortgage, plus their vehicles, stocks and mutual funds, cash, checking accounts, retirement accounts including 401(k) and pension assets, and so forth. Taking account of all of these things would you say that the WEALTH of you and your spouse/partner is: Less than $5,000; $5,000 to $20,000; $20,000 to $40,000; $40,000 to $75,000; $75,000 to $100,000; $100,000 to $150,000; $150,000 to $250,000; $250,000 to $500,000; $500,000 to $1 million; Over $1 million." For analytical purposes, each worker was assigned the midpoint of each category as their assumed wealth. Mean = 312,020, s.d. = 613,975, n = 28,920.

For second component of the economic insecurity score, answers were divided by fixed pay plus overtime, and recoded into quartiles: 0: >6.37; 1: >3.09 and ≤6.37; 2: >1.28 and ≤3.09 3: <1.28.

20. Competitiveness of annual fixed pay: "Do you believe your fixed annual wages last year were higher or lower than those of employees with similar experience and job descriptions in other companies in your region? Please circle a number from 1 to 5." Mean = 2.67, s.d. = 1.00, n = 31.091.

For third component of the economic insecurity score, answers were subtracted from 5 for a range of 0 to 4.

Other Variables

21. Lack of empowerment score: Summative measure of 22–26 below (reverse scored from format used in survey):

Overall satisfaction with job-related influence (Score: 0–3)
Worker influence at the job level (Score: 0–3)
Worker influence at the work group or department level (Score: 0–3)
Worker influence at the company level (Score: 0–3)
Worker involvement in a team, committee, or task force (Score: 0–1)

Mean = 6.07, s.d. = 2.66, n = 33,855; Minimum 0; Maximum 13.

22. Overall satisfaction with job-related influence. "Overall, how satisfied are you with the influence you have in company decisions that affect your job and work life?" (Scale: 0–3, 0 = very satisfied, 1 = somewhat satisfied, 2 = not too satisfied, 3 = not at all satisfied). Mean = 1.36; s.d. = 0.84, n = 34,981.

23. Worker influence at the job level. "How much involvement and direct influence do YOU have in: A. Deciding how to do your job and organize the work." (Scale: 0–3, 0 = A lot, 1 = Some, 2 = Only a little, 3 = None). Mean = 0.69, s.d. = 0.86, n = 35,109.

24. Worker influence at the work group or department level. "How much involvement and direct influence do YOU have in: B. Setting goals for your

work group or department." (Scale: 0–3, 0 = A lot, 1 = Some, 2 = Only a little, 3 = None). Mean = 1.38, s.d. = 1.03, n = 35,015.

25. Worker influence at the company level. "How much involvement and direct influence do YOU have in: C. Overall company decisions." (Scale: 0–3, 0 = A lot, 1 = Some, 2 = Only a little, 3 = None). Mean = 2.28, s.d. = 0.86, n = 34,978.

26. Worker involvement in a team, committee, or task force: "Some companies have organized workplace decision-making in ways to get more employee input and involvement. Are you personally involved in any team, committee, or task force that addresses issues such as product quality, cost cutting, productivity, health and safety, or other workplace issues?" (Scale: 0 = yes; 1 = no). Mean = 0.37, s.d. = 0.48, n = 34,722.

27. Poor employee relations score: Summative measure of 28–31 below (reverse scored from format used in survey):

> Company grade for trustworthiness in keeping its promises (Score: 0–4)
> Company grade for overall employment relations (Score: 0–4)
> Company grade for fairness (Score: 0–6)
> Company grade for creating a sense of common purpose in the company (Score: 0–4)

Mean = 6.75, s.d. = 4.14, n = 34,199; Minimum 0; Maximum 18.

28. Worker's grade of company for trustworthiness: "If you were to rate how well this company takes care of workers on a scale similar to school grades, what grade would you give in these areas? (C is an average grade.) Trustworthiness in keeping its promises." (Scale: A = 0; B = 1; C = 2; D = 3; F = 4). Mean = 1.62, s.d. = 1.14, n = 34,850.

29. Worker's grade of company for fairness: "Overall, this company is fair to its employees." (Scale: Strongly agree = 0, Strongly disagree = 6). Mean = 2.14, s.d. = 1.67, n = 35,031.

30. Worker's grade of company for overall employment relations: "If you were to rate how well this company takes care of workers on a scale similar to school grades, what grade would you give in these areas? (C is an average grade.) Overall relations with employees." (Scale: A = 0; B = 1; C = 2; D = 3; F = 4). Mean = 1.51, s.d. = 1.05, n = 34,928.

31. Worker's grade of company for creating a sense of common purpose: "If you were to rate how well this company takes care of workers on a scale similar to school grades, what grade would you give in these areas? (C is an average grade.) Creating a sense of common purpose in the company." (Scale: A = 0; B = 1; C = 2; D = 3; F = 4). Mean = 1.50, s.d. = 1.04, n = 34,916.

32. High performance work system: Summative measure of 33–38 below:

> Whether workers have received formal training from their employer in the last twelve months.

The number of hours of this training measured by four increasing categories of investment by the firm.
Whether workers say they understand their company's overall plan for being successful.
Whether workers say that they agree with this plan.
Whether workers say that the company is providing them with the information, training, and resources necessary to help achieve the goals of this plan.
Whether workers feel that the company's culture encourages you to share your ideas about how to achieve the goals of this plan.

Mean = 13.35, s.d. = 3.31, n = 23,714.

33. Whether worker received formal training by employer. "In the last twelve months have you received any formal training from your current employer, such as in classes or seminars sponsored by the employer?" (Score: 0 = No; 1 = Yes). Mean = 0.59, s.d. = 0.49, n = 34,913.

34. Hours of formal training in last twelve months: "About how many hours of formal training have you received in the last twelve months?" (Scale: actual number of hours). Mean = 18.88, s.d. = 41.57, n = 34,154.

Recoding for training hours variable into four ascending categories:

	Percent of sample with this score
0: 0 hours	41.0
1: >0 and ≤11 hours	17.6
2: >11 and ≤33 hours	18.5
3: >33 and <1,680 hours	22.8

35. Whether worker says he/she understands company's overall plan: "To what extent do you: Understand your company's overall plan for being successful?" (Scale: 1–4, 1 = not at all, 2 = very little, 3 = to some extent, 4 = to a great extent). Mean = 3.18, s.d. = 0.72, n = 25,046.

36. Whether worker says she/he agrees with company's overall plan: "To what extent do you: Personally agree with this plan?" (Scale: 1–4, 1 = not at all, 2 = very little, 3 = to some extent, 4 = to a great extent). Mean = 3.02, s.d. = –.73, n = 24,515.

37. Whether worker says he/she has info, training, and resources to achieve the company's overall plan. "To what extent do you: Feel that the company is providing you with the information, training, and resources necessary to help achieve the goals of this plan?" (Scale: 1–4, 1 = not at all, 2 = very little, 3 = to some extent, 4 = to a great extent). Mean = 2.84, s.d. = 0.83, n = 24,906.

38. Whether worker feels company culture encourages sharing of ideas about achieving plan's goals. "To what extent do you: Feel that your com-

pany's culture encourages you to share your ideas about how to achieve the goals of this plan?" (Scale: 1–4, 1 = not at all, 2 = very little, 3 = to some extent, 4 = to a great extent). Mean = 2.74, s.d. = 0.91, n = 24,841.

39. Percent of wealth in company stock: "About what percent of your wealth is in your employer's stock?" (Scale: 0–100 percent). Mean = 16.9, s.d. = 21.2, n = 26,818.

References

Akerlof, G. A. 1979. The case against conservative macroeconomics: An inaugural lecture. *Economica* 46 (August): 219–37.

Appelbaum, E., T. Bailey, P. Berg, and A. L. Kalleberg. 2000. *Manufacturing advantage: Why high performance work systems pay off.* Ithaca, NY: Cornell University Press/ILR Press.

Arrow, K. 1973. Social responsibility and economic efficiency. *Public Policy* 21 (Summer): 303–317.

Bartholomew, D., J. Galbraith, I. Moustkaki, F. Steele. 2002. *The analysis and interpretation of multivariate data for social scientists.* Boca Raton, FL: Chapman and Hall/CRC.

Becker, B. E., M. A. Huselid, and D. Ulrich. 2001. *The HR scorecard: Linking people, strategy, and performance.* Cambridge, MA: Harvard Business School Press.

Benartzi, S. 2001. Excessive extrapolation and the allocation of company stock to retirement accounts. *Journal of Finance* 56 (5): 1747–64.

Benartzi, S., and R. Thaler. 2001. Naïve diversification strategies in defined contribution savings plans. *American Economic Review* 91 (1): 79–98.

Bernstein, P. L. 1992. *Capital ideas: The improbable origins of modern Wall Street.* New York: The Free Press.

Blasi, J., and D. Kruse. 2006. High performance work practices at century's end. *Industrial Relations* 45 (4): 547–78.

Blasi, J., R. Freeman, C. Mackin, and D. Kruse. 2008. Creating a bigger pie? The effects of employee ownership, profit sharing, and stock options on workplace performance. Paper presented at NBER/Russell Sage Foundation conference. October, New York.

Cappelli, P., and D. Neumark. 2001. Do "high-performance" work practices improve establishment-level outcomes? *Industrial and Labor Relations Review* 54 (4): 737–75.

Dexter, A. S., J. N. W. Yu, and W. T. Ziemba. 1980. Portfolio selection in a lognormal market when the investor has a power utility function: Computational results. In *Stochastic programming,* ed. M. A. H. Dempster, 507–23. New York: Academic Press.

Ederington, L. H. 1986. Mean-variance as an approximation to expected utility maximization. Working Paper no. 86-5, School of Business Administration, Washington University. St. Louis, Missouri.

Freeman, R., D. Kruse, and J. Blasi. 2008. Worker responses to shirking under shared capitalism. Paper presented at NBER/Russell Sage Foundation conference. October, New York.

Harden, E., D. Kruse, and J. Blasi. 2008. Who has a better idea: Innovation, shared capitalism, and human resource policies. Paper presented at NBER/Russell Sage Foundation conference. October, New York.

Hlawitschka, W. 1994. The empirical nature of Taylor-Series approximations to expected utility. *The American Economic Review* 84 (3): 713–19.

Ichniowski, C., K. Shaw, and G. Prennushi. 1995. *The effects of human resource management practices on productivity.* NBER Working Paper no. 5333. Cambridge, MA: National Bureau of Economic Research, November.

Kahneman, D., J. L. Knetsch, and R. Thaler. 1986a. Fairness and the assumptions of economics. *Journal of Business* 59 (4): S285–S300.

Kahneman, D., J. L. Knetsch, and R. Thaler. 1986. Fairness as a constraint on profit seeking: Entitlements in the market. *American Economic Review* 76 (4): 728–41.

Kahneman, D., and A. Tversky. 1979. Prespect theory: An analysis of decisions under risk. *Econometrica* 47 (2): 313–27.

———. 2000. *Choices, values, and frames.* New York: Cambridge University Press.

Kelly, J. L., Jr. 1956. A new interpretation of information rate. *Bell System Technical Journal* 35 (July): 917–26.

Keynes, J. M. 1983. Letter to F. C. Scott, February 6, 1942. In *The collected writings of John Maynard Keynes*, vol. XII, ed. Donald Moggridge, 81–83. New York: Cambridge University Press.

Kroll, Y., H. Levy, and H. M. Markowitz. 1984. Mean-variance versus direct utility maximization. *Journal of Finance* 39 (1): 47–61.

Kruse, D., J. Blasi, and R. Park. 2008. Shared capitalism in the US Economy: Prevalence, characteristics, and employee views of financial participation in enterprises. Paper presented at NBER/Russell Sage Foundation conference. October, New York.

Laffont, J.-J., and D. Martimort. 2002. *The theory of incentives: The principal-agent model.* Princeton, NJ: Princeton University Press.

Latané, H. A. 1959. Criteria for choice among risky ventures. *Journal of Political Economy* 67 (2): 144–55.

Levy, H., and H. M. Markowitz. 1979. Approximating expected utility by a function of mean and variance. *American Economic Review* 69 (3): 308–17.

Markowitz, H. M. 1959. *Portfolio selection: Efficient diversification of investments.* New York: John Wiley & Sons.

———. 1991. *Portfolio selection: Efficient diversification of investments.* Oxford: Basil Blackwell.

Markowitz, H. M., D. W. Reid, and B. V. Tew. 1994. The value of a blank check. *The Journal of Portfolio Management* 20 (4): 82–91.

Muelbroek, L. 2002. *Company stock in pension plans: How costly is it?* Harvard Business School Working Paper no. 02-025.

Pulley, L. M. 1981. A General mean-variance approximation to expected utility for short holding periods. *Journal of Financial and Quantitative Analysis* 16 (3): 361–73.

———. 1983. Mean-variance approximations to expected logarithmic utility. *Operations Research* 31 (4): 685–96.

Rousseau, D. M., and Z. Shperling. 2003. Pieces of the action: Ownership and the changing employment relationship. *Academy of Management Review* 28 (4): 553–70.

Savage, L. J. 1954. *The foundations of statistics,* 2nd revised ed. New York: Wiley.

Sharpe, W. F. 1964. Capital asset prices: A theory of market equilibrium under conditions of risk. *Journal of Finance* 19 (3): 425–42.

Simaan, Y. 1993. What is the opportunity cost of mean-variance investment strategies? *Management Science* 39 (5): 578–87.

Smith, A. 1776. *The wealth of nations.* New York: The Modern Library.
Tobin, J. 1958. Liquidity preference as behavior towards risk. *The Review of Economic Statistics* 67 (February): 65–86.
Tversky, A., and D. Kahneman. 1981. The framing of decisions and the psychology of choice. *Science* 211 (4481): 453–58.

II
Firm Performance

4

Creating a Bigger Pie? The Effects of Employee Ownership, Profit Sharing, and Stock Options on Workplace Performance

Joseph R. Blasi, Richard B. Freeman, Christopher Mackin, and Douglas L. Kruse

> Cooperation aims to increase the margin from which the increment of gain is to be drawn. It makes industry more productive; it gives the employer somewhat more, and to the laborer much more than they now receive. . . . All the workmen with their employers constitute collectively an exceptionally good entrepreneur. . . . The survival of full cooperation in the long rivalry of systems depends on its power to excel other systems. . . . If in the comparison with other systems, it is shown that it ought to survive, it will do so, and that regardless of initial failures.
>
> —John Bates Clark, *The Philosophy of Wealth,* 1886

One-hundred and twenty years ago John Bates Clark, one of the founders of the American Economic Association, developer of marginal productivity theory, and the person for whom the prestigious Bates Clark Award is

Joseph R. Blasi is a professor of human resource management and labor studies and employment relations at the Rutgers School of Management and Labor Relations, and a research associate of the National Bureau of Economic Research. Richard B. Freeman holds the Herbert Ascherman Chair in Economics at Harvard University and is a research associate of the National Bureau of Economic Research. Christopher Mackin is the founder and president of Ownership Associates, Inc. and is a member of the core faculty of the Harvard Trade Union Program. Douglas L. Kruse is a professor of human resource management and labor studies and employment relations at the Rutgers School of Management and Labor Relations, and a research associate of the National Bureau of Economic Research.

This chapter was presented at the Russell Sage/NBER conference in New York City, October 2006, and benefited from comments by Casey Ichniowski and other participants. An earlier version was presented at the Labor and Employment Relations conference, Boston, Massachusetts, January 5–8, 2006. This research is supported by a grant from the Russell Sage Foundation and the Rockefeller Foundation. The National Opinion Research Center at the University of named, developed a vision of shared capitalism—the cooperative plan—and laid out a key test for this form of capitalist enterprise, its ability to survive in competition with other forms. In his 1886 book *The Philosophy of Wealth,* Clark said that he wanted "to take the workman permanently out of the position in which his gain is his employer's loss" through profit sharing and stock ownership by the workers. His solution to workers' risk aversion and lack of credit and personal funds to invest in capital was that the firm would pay profit shares to workers in the form of stock, which would make profit sharing a gradual vehicle for employee ownership.[1] Clark underlined the need for skilled management and committed investors and stressed that access to new capital investment was critical to the success of such enterprises. He also noted the need for a cooperative management culture in these corporations. Clark did not envision worker-elected managers nor worker-dominated boards of directors. Clark's views suggest that forms of shared capitalism that combine profit sharing and employee ownership without personal worker financing in a cooperative corporate setting would positively affect workplace performance and company success. Clark's interest in shared capitalism was mirrored in the first volume of the *American Economic Review,* which contained extensive articles on cooperative economic relations in New England and Minneapolis in issues 4 and 5.[2]

This chapter analyzes the relationship of various forms of shared capitalist compensation to six workplace outcomes—turnover, absenteeism, per-

Chicago provided valuable assistance with the US General Social Survey segment that forms the basis for some of the analysis. Refen Koh, Rhokeun Park, Michelle Pinheiro, and Patricia Berhau provided excellent assistance in survey scanning, entry, and verification.

1. Adam Smith (1776) credited the incentive of shared capitalism with improved economic performance for the French Metayers or sharecroppers, where the owner of the land and the sharecropper divided the produce equally after capital investments: "Such tenants, being freemen, are capable of acquiring property, and having a certain proportion of the produce of the land, they have a plain interest that the whole produce should be as great as possible, in order that their own proportion may be so" (quoted in Laffont and Martimort [2002, 10]). He stressed that sharecroppers would not risk their own capital to improve the proprietor's land without offering any resolution to this problem.

2. Issue 4 included a 100-page article "Cooperation in a Western City" by Albert Shaw (1886) about such enterprises in Minneapolis, which examined profit sharing by Charles Pillsbury in his mills and included an interview with Pillsbury. Issue 5 had a 129-page article "Cooperation in the Northeast" by Edward Bemis (1886) on Massachusetts companies. In the 1880s a group of doctoral students was assembled at Johns Hopkins University who divided up the United States into regions and studied forms of profit sharing and employee ownership in these regions. The university published these studies as a book (Adams 1888). John Bates Clark worked closely with this group of researchers, several of whose articles appeared in the new journal of the American Economic Association. Clark's views were similar to those of another prominent nineteenth-century economist, John Stuart Mill, who said "The form of association which if mankind continues to improve must be expected in the end to predominate is not that which can exist between a capitalist as chief and workpeople without a voice in the management but the association of the labourers themselves on terms of equality, collectively owning the capital with which they carry on their operations, and working under managers elected and removable by themselves" (John Stuart Mill, *Principles of Political Economy,* Books III-V and Appendices [1848], in J. M. Robson, ed., *Collective Works of John Stuart Mill, Vol. 3.* Toronto: University of Toronto Press, 1965, 775).

ceived effort of co-workers, loyalty to the firm, willingness to work hard, and frequency of worker suggestions to improve productivity—from the perspective of the "John Bates Clark vision" of shared capitalism. We also examine employee responses to questions about their response to shared capitalist incentives. Our analysis uses the General Social Survey (GSS) and NBER data sets (described in the "Studying Shared Capitalism" section of the introduction to this volume).

4.1 The Clark Vision in Modern Eyes

Modern theorists concerned with shared capitalism highlight the potential of corporate culture in helping unify ownership and control with minimal agency costs and enabling shared capitalism to fulfill its potential. In his address to the Industrial Relations Research Association, Joseph Stiglitz defined the goal of shared capitalism as "to increase each worker's involvement in and identification with the firm so that there will be some unification of agent and principal and a resulting tendency for higher effort . . . (in the belief that) a system of high involvement, high rewards, and high levels of skill and information, integrated with a corporate strategy that relies on front-line employees' ideas and creativity, is capable of impressive improvements in organizational performance" (2002). Analogously, in their book on incentives, Laffont and Martimort focus on "how the owners of firms succeed in aligning the objectives of various members, such as workers, supervisors, and managers, with profit maximization" (2002, 2). They emphasize that the decentralized nature of information and the cluster of transactions between the principal and the agent require an interaction of cultural norms and incentives to obtain the best economic institutions. Presaging our analyses of the importance of worker co-monitoring in shared capitalism (chapter 2), they stress that the multitude of tasks performed by the worker means that "a worker is not only involved in productive tasks but also must sometimes monitor his peers." In both cases, as well as in the analyses of others,[3] the implication is that shared capitalist compensation needs an appropriate corporate culture to reduce free rider and moral hazard problems and that low intensity incentives that substitute for wages and increase worker risk would have problematic effects on performance. These questions engage the issue of how much managers should own of the firms in which they work. For example, Morck, Shleifer, and Vishny (1988) show that simply more managerial ownership is not always optimal.

The other issue that theorists have identified as critical to the working of

3. Barnard (1938) defined incentives as involving a package of monetary and nonmonetary items saying material incentives were too weak unless enforced by other incentives. Even the *bête noir* of employee empowerment, Frederick Taylor, argued for paying fair wages along with generous performance-based pay and careful training to keep workers committed to maximum effort, although consultants selling Taylorism dropped this component (Kanigel 1997).

shared capitalism is the allocation of the risk of ownership and the problem of credit barriers keeping workers from becoming real capitalists. Echoing back to Adam Smith, Stiglitz (1974) argued that the key issue in the use of sharecropping, as opposed to having employees renting capital, is the balance between its incentive effects and risk-sharing features. Though the rental system "has greater incentive effects, it forces the worker to bear all the risks, and although the wage system allows the landlord, if he is risk neutral, to absorb all the risk, it may force heavy supervision costs on him." He asserted that the end of sharecropping was best explained by the development of capital markets that allow diversification of risk, capital intensity in production, and a faster rate of technological change. These analyses highlight the other distinct aspect of the John Bates Clark solution to the problem: share ownership arising from profit sharing as a way to allow workers to obtain ownership without taking on risk beyond their means. Akerlof's concept of a gift exchange carries this line of thinking a step further, with the exchange of ownership or profit-sharing above fixed pay for reciprocating effort serving as the risk-reducing mechanism for shared capitalism. Asking workers for an excessively risky personal investment in the firm may defeat the idea and dynamics of a gift exchange. In the United States today, Employee Stock Ownership Plans (ESOPs), stock options, and company stock matches for contributions to retirement savings plans offer workers ways to get equity in their company without buying it with their savings (though there is a small number of cases in which employees use 401(k) assets to create ESOPs or where work rule or wage or benefit concessions are traded for stock as in the 2008 Chrysler restructuring) (see Smiley et al. 2007).

Existing research on shared capitalism has generally found better workplace performance for firms with profit sharing and employee ownership.[4] However, many of these studies were based on large administrative data sets and shed little light on the mechanisms through which shared capitalism functioned "inside the black box." Here we use new data to go inside the black box.

4. Evidence from over 100 studies indicates a positive association on average between shared capitalism programs and company performance, but with substantial dispersion in results. For reviews of the employee ownership literature see Doucouliagos (1995); Kruse and Blasi (1997); Kruse (2002); Kaarsemaker (2006a, 2006b); and Freeman (2007). For subsequent studies see Kramer (2008) and Kim and Ouimet (2008). For detailed looks inside ESOP companies see Logue and Yates (1999) and Logue and Greider (2002). For a review of the broad-based stock option literature see Blasi, Kruse, and Bernstein (2003). For reviews of the profit-sharing and gain-sharing literatures see Weitzman and Kruse (1990); Bullock and Tubbs (1990); Kruse (1993); OECD (1995); Doucialiagos (1995); Welbourne and Mejia (1995); and subsequent studies by Zhuang and Xu (1996); Hansen (1997); Ohkusa and Ohtake (1997); Jones, Kato, and Pliskin (1997); Jones, Klinedinst, and Rock (1998); Collins (1998); McNabb and Whitfield (1998); Arthur and Jelf (1999); Black and Lynch (2000); Knez and Simester (2001); Boning, Ichniowski, and Shaw (2001); Kim (2005); Robinson and Wilson (2006); Peterson and Luthans (2006); and Hassan, Hagen, and Daigs (2006). The average estimated increase in productivity associated with employee ownership and profit sharing is about 4.5 percent, and is maintained when using pre/post comparisons and attempts to control for selection bias.

4.2 Measures of Shared Capitalism

Were Clark to return to the United States today, the first question he would ask about shared capitalism is the extent to which enterprises based on financial sharing and decision-making are found in the market—their "survival . . . in comparison with other systems." The GSS provides the best evidence for answering this question. The overall prevalence of shared capitalist compensation was presented in tables 1.1 and 1.3 of chapter 1. For our purposes here the most important result is that 45 percent of the for-profit private sector employees in the GSS sample report participating in some kind of shared capitalism program (36 percent in profit sharing, 25 percent in gain sharing, 19 percent in employee ownership, and 11 percent in stock options), which gives us good variation for examining the relation of these programs to worker outcomes. The prevalence is of course higher in the NBER sample, since these firms were selected on the basis of having these programs. There is no question that a layer of shared capitalism exists in the US economy. (See also table 4a.1 in the appendix of this chapter.)

As a first step in assessing the relation of shared capitalism to employee outcomes, we constructed a thermometer-style index of shared capitalism, which assigns points based on coverage by shared capitalism programs and the size of the financial stakes. This index helps us assess whether a thick layer of shared capitalism as envisioned by Clark makes any difference. This index is described in appendix B. We also present results breaking out the different forms of shared capitalism types and intensities using the more detailed NBER data.

4.3 Workplace Outcomes

We measure six workplace outcomes: (a) turnover (looking for another job versus staying with the company); (b) absenteeism; (c) workers' perception of the discretionary effort of co-workers; (d) worker loyalty to the firm; (e) workers' willingness to work hard for the firm; (f) the frequency of suggestions to improve efficiency. These outcomes are related to each other—for example, looking for another job predicts increased absenteeism, as does reduced willingness to provide discretionary effort to the company, and lower loyalty. Reduced willingness to provide discretionary effort to the company and lower loyalty relate to looking harder for another job. Increased absenteeism, looking hard for another job, and lower loyalty are linked to less discretionary effort. Because there are large literatures studying most of these outcomes separately, we decided against forming an index of these variables and instead look at each by itself. The summary statistics in appendix A show variation in the measures among respondents in our surveys in the form of large standard deviations. The absenteeism variable is the only one with a "peculiar" distribution since many people report zero absences while there is a long tail of persons absent for different time periods.

We use basic multivariate statistics to assess the link between shared capitalist compensation and the outcomes. We estimate ordinary least squares (OLS) models of the impact of shared capitalist compensation on the workplace outcomes where appropriate, and ordered probit models when the outcomes have several values with a natural ordering (e.g., "not at all true, not very true, somewhat true, and very true"). Because more than half of the values of absenteeism are zero, we use the tobit model to analyze that outcome. We run the regressions with the same independent variables for the national and NBER data sets and then probe our results in the NBER data set by adding measures of other human resource policies that may independently affect the workplace outcomes, such as participation in an employee involvement team, training, and job security.

We interpret the results from the two surveys differently in light of the difference in their sample designs. Since the GSS is a nationally representative survey, it will have few if any workers in the same firm, so that it provides information on workers across firms. The variation in shared capitalist incentives and behavior reflects differences in firm policies. By contrast, the NBER survey covers a representative sample of workers in a nonrepresentative sample of firms. To deal with the nonrepresentative firm problem, we include company fixed effects in most calculations. This focuses on the effect of variation in shared capitalist incentives on attitudes and behavior within companies. However, we analyze some ESOP variables across companies as well as within companies because Employee Retirement Income Security Act (ERISA) rules require virtually all workers in a firm to be covered, so that the cross-firm variation in the data is potentially more informative than within-firm variation, which may reflect peculiarities between groups of workers within the firm.

Table 4.1 summarizes the empirical results of regression analyses of the relationship between the shared capitalism index and outcomes in our data sets. It shows that in both the NBER and GSS surveys, the likelihood of searching for another job is lower the higher is the shared capitalism index. When the controls in the national survey and in the NBER survey are the same, the coefficient on the index is the same. Addition of measures of other human resource policies reduces the coefficient in the shared capitalism variable in the NBER data, but it still remains significant (line 2b). In addition, the NBER asked workers if they would turn down a higher-paying job to stay with their firm. The shared capitalist index raises the likelihood that workers would do so (line 3), which implies that they value these policies either for the additional income they are likely to bring or for the stake they give workers in the company.

The NBER survey asked workers how many days they were absent in the previous six months—a question that was not included on the GSS. Here,

Table 4.1 **Relation of shared capitalism to workplace outcomes**

Dependent variables	Coefficient (s.e.) of shared capitalism index	Controls: Job and demographics	Controls: EI team	Controls: Training	Job security	*N*
	Turnover					
National data						
1 Not likely to search for new job (1–3 scale, ordered probit)	**0.039**** (0.017)	x				1,743
NBER company data						
2a Not likely to search for new job (1–4 scale, ordered probit)	**0.039***** (0.004)	x				39,132
2b	**0.018***** (0.005)	x	x	x	x	35,644
3a Would turn down another job for more pay to stay with	**0.059**** (0.027)	x				1,086
3b this co. (1–5 scale, ordered probit)	**0.062**** (0.028)	x	x	x	x	1,079
	Absenteeism					
NBER company data						
4a Number of days absent in past 6 mos. (tobit)	**0.152***** (0.056)	x				38,069
4b	**0.161***** (0.057)	x	x	x	x	34,834
	Job effort and loyalty					
National data						
5 Co-worker effort (1–10 scale, OLS)	**0.116***** (0.026)	x				1,741
6 Proud to be working for employer (1–4 scale, ordered probit)	**0.056***** (0.014)	x				1,745
NBER company data						
7a Co-worker effort (1–10 scale, OLS)	**0.018**** (0.007)	x				39,252
7b	0.006 (0.008)	x	x	x	x	35,653
8a Co-workers have enough interest in company issues to	**0.027***** (0.005)	x				38,980
8b get involved (1–7 scale, OLS)	**0.014**** (0.006)	x	x	x	x	35,518

(continued)

Table 4.1 (continued)

	Dependent variables	Coefficient (s.e.) of shared capitalism index	Controls: Job and demographics	Controls: EI team	Controls: Training	Job security	*N*
9a	Co-workers generally encourage each other to make	**0.038***** (0.008)	x				12,799
9b	extra effort (0–1, OLS)	**0.029***** (0.009)	x	x	x	x	12,537
10a	Loyalty toward co. (1–4 scale, ordered probit)	**0.041***** (0.004)	x				38,514
10b		**0.021***** (0.005)	x	x	x	x	35,082
11a	Willing to work harder to help co. (1–5 scale, ordered probit)	**0.023***** (0.004)	x				39,159
11b		**0.015***** (0.004)	x	x	x	x	35,595
12a	Frequency of suggestions (1–5 scale, ordered probit)	**0.035***** (0.005)	x				29,965
12b		**0.027***** (0.005)	x	x	x	x	26,860

Notes: Each row represents results of separate regression. See appendix A for variable definitions and descriptive statistics. Job and demographic controls include age, sex, race, tenure, occupation, education, full-time status, and ease of seeing co-workers for all regressions. The national data regressions also include work in a team and ln(yearly earnings), and the NBER regressions also include management level (3 dummies), supervisory status, union membership, disability status, payment on an hourly rate, country effects (21 dummies), closeness of supervision, ln(base pay), and company fixed effects. s.e. = standard error; OLS = ordinary least squares. Coefficients in bold are significant at $p < .05$.

***Significant at the 1 percent level.

**Significant at the 5 percent level.

*Significant at the 10 percent level.

the estimate in line 4 of table 4.1 shows that the shared capitalism index alone—without looking at the impact of the firm's corporate culture—raises absences. This is the only outcome variable that is adversely associated with the index. Why? Reviewing absenteeism and turnover research, Johns (2002) emphasizes that persistent absenteeism signals a break in the psychological contract of trust and deeper problems in the corporate culture. This perspective sees absenteeism as part of a withdrawal continuum involving lateness-absenteeism-lack of loyalty-intended turnover-ultimate withdrawal of membership in the firm. Thus, the finding that shared capitalism has a different effect on absenteeism than on prospective turnover, loyalty, and other factors runs against the basic analysis of absenteeism. Studies of the relation between unionism, which also reduces turnover, however, often also find a positive association with absences. It may be that a greater sense of job security underlies both results. Another possibility is that absenteeism is a form of free riding that avoids co-worker scrutiny and criticism. Yet another possibility, which we explore later, is that the result is related to interactions with other firm policies and corporate culture.

Both the GSS and the NBER surveys ask workers how hard they believe their co-workers work. The estimates show that perceptions of co-worker effort are significantly positively related to the shared capitalism index, though the NBER result is no longer significant after controlling for several human resource policies (lines 5, 7). The NBER survey has two other measures that reflect perceptions of the extent to which co-workers are committed to the firm: the extent to which co-workers have enough interest in company issues to get involved in the firm, and whether co-workers generally encourage each other to make extra efforts. Again, the results show that shared capitalist programs raise the likelihood that workers report positively on these outcomes, both before and after controlling for human resource policies (lines 8–9).

Interpretation of the positive coefficients of a worker's receipt of shared capitalist compensation in predicting their perceptions of the work attitudes of co-workers is not, however, simple in the presence of the company dummy variables. The regressions reflect how workers paid with shared capitalist compensation view their fellow workers (with a glow) rather than how shared capitalism affects the workplace. Since we have many establishments or facilities within firms, they could also be telling us that facilities with greater shared capitalist compensation have workers who are willing to do more for the firm. One way to deal with this issue is to eliminate the company dummies from the regressions. This strengthens the estimated effects. Another way to deal with the problem is to aggregate the data by facilities so that we relate the average shared capitalism index at a workplace to the average perception of co-worker effort within that worksite. This asks the question most relevant to our analysis: whether respondents perceive greater effort in worksites with more shared capitalism, rather than whether workers with greater personal shared capitalist compensation perceive greater effort in their fellow workers. Figures 4.1 to 4.3 display the scatter plot of observations for the site averages and the regression line for them. They show that the shared capitalist index at a worksite is positively associated with workers saying that co-workers give greater effort to the firm.

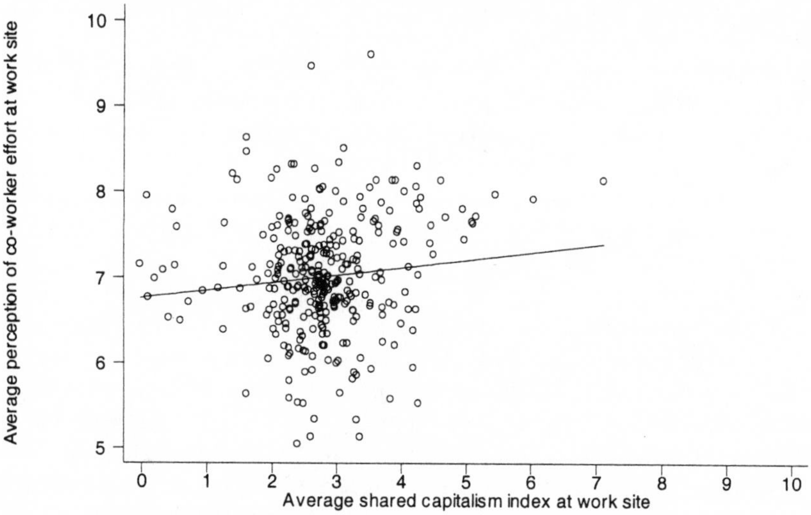

Fig. 4.1 Shared capitalism and worker effort

Note: Co-workers effort (1–10 scale) = 6.765 (.125) + 0.087 (.043) (shared capitalist index).

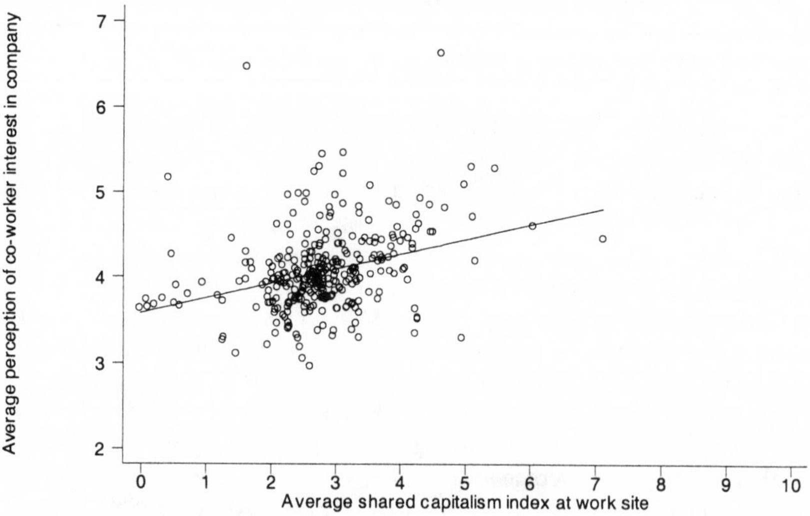

Fig. 4.2 Shared capitalism and co-worker interest in company

Note: Co-workers work interest in firm (1–10 scale) = 3.580 (.082) + 0.173 (.028) (shared capitalist index).

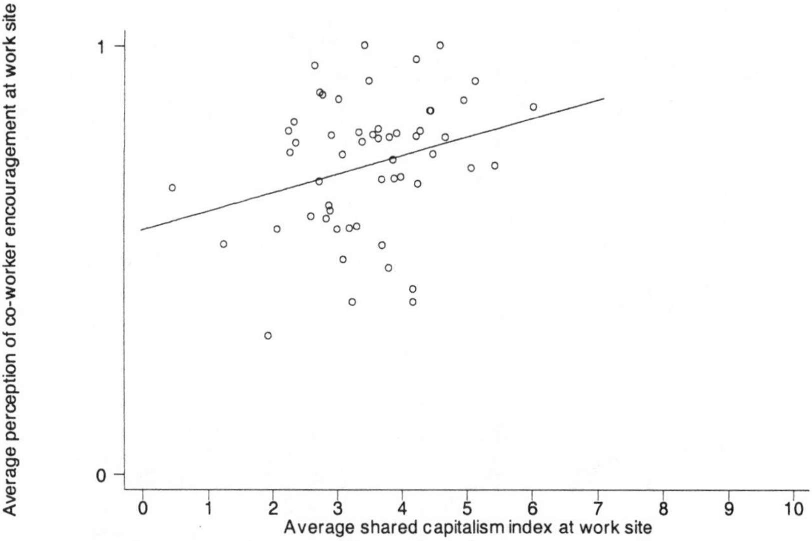

Fig. 4.3 Shared capitalism and worker encouragement

Note: Co-workers encourage others (1–10 scale) = 0.572 (.073) + 0.043 (.020) (shared capitalist index).

Finally, we turn from perceptions of how co-workers behave to questions in which workers report on their own attitudes and behavior and relate these responses to the workers' own shared capitalist compensation. Both surveys asked questions relating to worker loyalty. The GSS asked if workers were proud to be working for their employer: shared capitalism raises positive responses on this item (line 6). The NBER asked about loyalty to the firm: this measure is positively related to the shared capitalism index before and after controlling for high-performance policies in the NBER survey (line 10). The NBER survey also asked how willing workers would be to work harder to help the company, and the frequency with which they make suggestions about improving the workplace. The higher the shared capitalist index the more likely are workers to say that they themselves would work hard for the firm (line 11), and the more likely are workers to say that they make many suggestions (line 12).

4.4 Particular Programs

The NBER survey contains sufficiently detailed information and a large enough sample to allow us to disaggregate the shared capitalist index into its component parts to see which policies or programs contribute more/less to the estimated effects in table 4.1. Table 4.2 gives the results of these calculations for variables in which the individual reports on their own behavior or attitudes. Column (1) shows that the likelihood of not searching for a new

Table 4.2 **Workplace outcomes related to type of shared capitalism plan**

Dependent variable:	Not likely to search for new job (ordered probit) (1)	Absenteeism (Tobit) (2)	Loyalty (ordered probit) (3)	Willing to work harder (ordered probit) (4)	Suggestion frequency (ordered probit) (5)
Bonuses					
Profit sharing	0.096 (0.021)***	0.929 (0.268)***	0.011 (0.021)	0.039 (0.019)**	0.034 (0.023)
Profit sharing bonus as % of base pay	0.175 (0.100)*	0.529 (1.346)	0.546 (0.107)***	0.436 (0.095)***	–0.091 (0.132)
Gain sharing	0.085 (0.028)***	0.489 (0.360)	0.015 (0.028)	0.034 (0.026)	0.021 (0.034)
Gain sharing bonus as % of base pay	0.095 (0.114)	–4.117 (1.559)***	0.203 (0.123)	0.266 (0.109)**	–0.114 (0.199)
Individual bonus	0.082 (0.027)***	–0.975 (0.342)***	0.143 (0.027)***	0.063 (0.025)***	0.004 (0.032)
Individual bonus as % of base pay	0.012 (0.117)	–0.364 (1.602)	–0.100 (0.124)	0.128 (0.111)	0.152 (0.188)
Stock options					
Stock option holding	0.111 (0.059)*	1.583 (0.715)**	–0.140 (0.058)**	–0.085 (0.053)	–0.021 (0.070)
Stock option value as % of base pay	0.010 (0.006)*	0.085 (0.077)	0.003 (0.006)	0.002 (0.006)	–0.037 (0.032)
Rec'd stock option grant last year	–0.074 (0.058)	–0.633 (0.699)	0.187 (0.057)***	0.034 (0.052)	0.028 (0.071)
Stock option grant as % of avg. grant	0.037 (0.014)***	0.175 (0.165)	0.016 (0.014)	0.009 (0.012)	–0.032 (0.020)
Employee ownership					
Any employee ownership	0.072 (0.020)***	0.347 (0.248)	0.065 (0.019)***	0.015 (0.018)	0.166 (0.021)***
Employee-owned stock as % of pay	0.001 (0.010)	–0.171 (0.127)	0.051 (0.010)***	0.008 (0.009)	0.024 (0.014)*
n	37796	36,769	37192	37817	29,292
(pseudo) R^2	0.035	0.018	0.060	0.042	0.074
Cut point 1	–0.826 (0.239)		–0.578 (0.246)	–0.858 (0.226)	1.327 (0.313)
Cut point 2	–0.318 (0.239)		0.226 (0.246)	–0.318 (0.226)	3.560 (0.313)

Cut point 3	0.640 (0.239)		1.381 (0.246)	0.627 (0.226)	4.117 (0.313)
Cut point 4				1.864 (0.226)	4.826 (0.314)
Breakdowns by type of employee ownership[a]					
ESOP	0.097 (0.057)*	–0.539 (0.679)	–0.041 (0.055)	–0.091 (0.052)*	0.304 (0.064)***
ESOP stock as % of pay	–0.022 (0.022)	0.105 (0.265)	0.018 (0.022)	0.053 (0.020)***	0.034 (0.024)
ESPP	–0.013 (0.042)	0.780 (0.518)	0.047 (0.043)	0.058 (0.039)	–0.039 (0.068)
ESPP stock as % of pay	0.063 (0.035)*	–0.519 (0.441)	0.053 (0.036)	0.029 (0.031)	–0.094 (0.114)
401(k) stock	0.105 (0.019)***	0.118 (0.230)	0.111 (0.018)***	0.072 (0.017)***	0.115 (0.020)***
401(k) stock as % of pay	0.031 (0.017)*	–0.180 (0.213)	0.087 (0.016)***	–0.011 (0.015)	–0.003 (0.021)
Stock from options	–0.032 (0.040)	0.810 (0.503)	0.061 (0.043)	–0.002 (0.038)	–0.012 (0.069)
Stock from options as % of pay	–0.040 (0.021)*	–0.176 (0.286)	0.019 (0.024)	–0.001 (0.021)	0.047 (0.073)
Open mkt. stock	–0.018 (0.029)	–1.146 (0.399)***	0.089 (0.031)***	0.072 (0.028)**	0.160 (0.052)***
Open mkt. stock as % of pay	0.010 (0.049)	0.300 (0.625)	–0.031 (0.052)	0.035 (0.048)	–0.515 (0.255)**
ESOP coefficients without fixed effects[a]					
ESOP	0.168 (0.035)***	–0.190 (0.422)	0.186 (0.034)***	–0.001 (0.032)	–0.080 (0.038)**
ESOP stock as % of pay	–0.021 (0.020)	–0.170 (0.242)	0.017 (0.020)	0.051 (0.018)***	0.037 (0.023)

Notes: See appendix A for variable definitions and descriptive statistics. All regressions include controls for occupation (5 dummies), mgt. level (3 dummies), hourly pay status, supervisory status, tenure in years, hours worked per week, union status, age, gender, marital status (2 dummies), family size, college graduate, graduate degree, number of kids, race (4 dummies), disability status, ln(fixed pay), closeness of supervision, ability to observe co-workers, country effects (21 dummies), and company fixed effects. Standard error in parentheses.

[a]The sections labeled "Breakdown by type of employee ownership" and "ESOP coefficients without fixed effects" represent separate regressions that contain all of the bonus and stock option variables listed above, along with the control variables listed below.

***Significant at the 1 percent level.

**Significant at the 5 percent level.

*Significant at the 10 percent level.

job is strongly related to profit-sharing and gain-sharing eligibility, employee ownership, and having a larger stock option grant last year, and that workers who receive individual bonuses are also less likely to look for another job.

Column (2) shows that the aberrant finding that shared capitalism increases absenteeism is higher among those who are eligible for profit sharing and who hold stock options. This goes against the findings of lower absenteeism in profit-sharing companies in UK and French firms (Wilson and Peel 1991; Brown, Fakhfakh, and Sessions 1999) and with a study of US firms that found employee ownership alone did not affect absenteeism (Hammer, Landau, and Stern 1981), though it is consistent with the finding by Brown, Fakhfakh, and Sessions (1999) that absenteeism increased slightly when profit sharing was introduced after employee ownership. The regression finding that absenteeism is lower among those who are eligible for individual bonuses lends some support to the possibility that higher absenteeism among those paid by group incentives reflects free rider behavior.

The next two columns show that loyalty and willingness to work hard are positively related to the size of the profit-sharing and gain-sharing bonuses, and to holding employer stock purchased through a 401(k) plan or on the open market (columns [3] and [4]). Loyalty is also positively linked to receiving a stock option grant last year, while willingness to work hard is linked to the size of one's ESOP stake. The frequency with which workers report making suggestions is, by contrast, significantly related only to employee ownership (column [5]).

Overall, the forms of shared capitalism that appear to have the strongest effects on outcomes are profit sharing and employee ownership.

The bottom panels in table 4.2 disaggregate the ownership variable and report coefficients when the company dummy is removed from the regression. The results for the disaggregation of the ownership variable show that the largest ownership impacts come with 401(k) plans and when workers buy shares on the open market. The sizable 401(k) effect compared to the ESOP ownership effect may reflect the greater individual ownership of the 401(k) (although the company stock match for which workers do not pay with their savings in 401(k) plans is comparable to an ESOP) while the impact of buying shares on the open market may reflect individual's positive assessment of the future of the firm. Finally, the regressions that exclude company dummies to pick up differences in shared capitalist compensation across companies as well as across facilities and individuals within facilities find stronger ESOP effects than the regressions that include the company dummy variables.

4.5 Complementarities → Corporate Culture?

A critical issue in analyzing a distinct organizational or institutional form is whether its impact on behavior and outcomes operates independently of other practices or policies or whether its impact depends interactively on them. The thrust of theoretical analysis of shared capitalist compensation, from Clark to the present, is that changing the monetary incentives by itself is unlikely to occur or work well independent of other policies. Firms that introduce profit sharing or employee ownership must give workers the authority to make decisions that increase performance to change their behavior in ways that raise output and profits.[5] Research on "high performance work systems" have found that they work best as a package of complementary policies regarding recruitment, training/information, performance management/sharing, work redesign, and so on.[6] Recent evidence from the United Kingdom strongly suggests that the effects of shared capitalism are conditioned by complementarities with other policies (Robinson and Wilson 2006). Based on these considerations and evidence we expect that shared capitalist incentives should also work better when combined with certain other firm policies.

To examine the interaction or complementarity of shared capitalist compensation with high-performance workplace policies, we constructed an *index of high-performance work policies* that gives one point each for being in an employee involvement team, receiving formal training in the past twelve months, and having high job security.[7] We interacted this index with the shared capitalism index in regressions for the likelihood of searching for a new job, absenteeism, loyalty to the firm, willingness to work harder, and frequency of suggestions. In addition, we examined the interaction between shared capitalism and a measure of employer *supervision of employees.* Evi-

5. Research often finds an interaction between participation and ownership on output but most data sets contain little information on the mechanisms for this. The US Government Accountability Office (GAO) study (1987), which matched survey data with records on company finances, found an interaction between employee participation in management and employee ownership on productivity, as did the US National Institute of Mental Health study (Rosen, Klein, and Young 1986) and its follow-up study (Rosen and Quarry 1987). Freeman and Dube (chapter 5 of this volume) found that employee involvement had a larger impact on indicators of worker productivity, job satisfaction, and attitudes toward the firm than did participation in financial rewards, but that the highest outcomes occurred when firms combined pay for company/group performance, ownership stake in the firm, and employee involvement committees. Analyzing UK establishments, Conyon and Freeman (2001) found that the companies that adopted profit sharing, employee ownership, and broad stock option schemes had higher productivity and more information and decision sharing practices. Studies of ESOPs and other forms of employee ownership generally find a positive relationship between ownership and performance (Levine 1995, 81) that is strongest with worker participation.

6. Ichniowski et al. (1996); Ichniowski, Shaw, and Prennushi (1997); Huselid, Jackson, and Schuler (1997); Becker and Huselid (1998); and Becker, Huselid, and Ulrich (2001). Cappelli and Neumark found that high performance work practices such as self-directed work teams only significantly predicted increased productivity when combined with profit/gain sharing (2001, 34).

7. We experimented with indices that also included measures of information sharing, job rotation, and rigorous selection, and obtained similar results. We focus on the index based on employee involvement, training, and job security since the sample sizes are smaller for job rotation and rigorous selection, and the grade of the company on sharing information reflects an employee evaluation of the policy's success rather than the existence of a policy.

dence presented in chapter 8 shows that workers covered by more shared capitalist policies are less closely supervised than others, suggesting that shared capitalism substitutes for supervision in motivating workers. Combining shared capitalism with close supervision may reduce the effect of shared capitalism by sending a mixed message to employees: "We want you to work harder and be more committed to the company because of your (profit share/employer stock/stock options), but we're still going to keep a very close eye on you."

Finally, we also examine whether the extent to which shared capitalism substitutes for fixed wages may also be an important determinant of its effects. We expect that employees will react better to shared capitalist compensation when it is a gift-exchange add-on to existing compensation, rather than a substitute for which they sacrifice certain income flows for greater risk in compensation. While we do not have measures of alternative wages available to employees, the NBER survey asked how employees' fixed wages compare to market levels, from which we constructed a dummy variable indicating that the worker feels she or he is *paid at or above market levels.* We interact this variable with the shared capitalist index as well.

Table 4.3 summarizes the results of these calculations. The regression coefficients on the interaction terms show that other firm policies measured by the high performance practice index affects the impact of shared capitalism—representing possible complementarities on most outcome variables—and that supervision intensity and wage relative to market wage also have some interactive effects. Column (1) shows that the positive effect of shared capitalism on not searching for a new job exists only for those who are covered by the high performance policies and reveals a strong negative interaction of shared capitalism with close supervision. While column (2) finds no significant interactions for any of the three new variables with the shared capitalism index in affecting absenteeism, the high performance indicator reduces absences while close supervision raises them. With these variables and interactions the strong positive relation between shared capitalism and absenteeism is weakened and no longer significantly different from zero, suggesting that the effect found in table 4.1 may be masking that of high performance, supervision, and pay relative to market. Columns (3) and (4) show substantial shared capitalism interactions on loyalty and willingness to work hard. These outcomes are enhanced when shared capitalism is combined with high performance policies and fixed pay at or above the market level, and are hurt when shared capitalism is combined with close supervision.

Finally, column (5) shows that shared capitalism has a negative interaction with high performance policies and a positive link to supervision in affecting frequency of suggestions. The positive effect of shared capitalist policies among workers who are not covered by high performance policies might reflect the fact that those in high performance workplaces

Table 4.3 **Interactions between company policies and workplace outcomes**

Dependent variable:	Not likely to search for new job (ordered probit) (1)	Absenteeism (Tobit) (2)	Loyalty (ordered probit) (3)	Willing to work harder (ordered probit) (4)	Suggestion frequency (ordered probit) (5)
Shared capitalism index	0.002 (0.009)	0.064 (0.116)	–0.024 (0.009)***	0.017 (0.008)**	0.035 (0.012)***
High performance policy index	0.058 (0.016)***	–0.642 (0.201)***	0.135 (0.016)***	0.131 (0.015)***	0.253 (0.018)***
× shared capitalism index	0.013 (0.003)***	0.069 (0.042)	0.027 (0.003)***	0.008 (0.003)**	–0.015 (0.005)***
How closely supervised	0.001 (0.005)	0.117 (0.059)**	0.001 (0.004)	0.004 (0.004)	–0.017 (0.005)***
× shared capitalism index	–0.004 (0.001)***	–0.001 (0.014)	–0.005 (0.001)***	–0.007 (0.001)***	0.003 (0.002)**
Fixed pay at or above market	0.373 (0.024)***	–0.268 (0.311)	0.259 (0.024)***	0.147 (0.023)***	–0.073 (0.028)***
× shared capitalism index	0.003 (0.005)	–0.028 (0.069)	0.016 (0.005)***	0.011 (0.005)**	0.006 (0.008)
Selected controls[a]					
Individual bonuses (dummy)	0.087 (0.020)***	–0.782 (0.252)***	0.083 (0.020)***	0.104 (0.018)***	–0.009 (0.022)
Ease of seeing how well co-worker is working	–0.001 (0.003)	0.023 (0.033)	0.017 (0.003)***	0.031 (0.002)***	0.031 (0.003)***
n	31,411	30,706	30,920	31,364	24,936
(pseudo) R^2	0.103	0.017	0.101	0.054	0.081
Cut point 1	0.031 (0.269)		–0.286 (0.275)	–0.817 (0.254)	1.293 (0.291)
Cut point 2	0.595 (0.269)		0.575 (0.275)	–0.267 (0.254)	3.579 (0.291)
Cut point 3	1.682 (0.269)		1.790 (0.275)	0.683 (0.254)	4.167 (0.291)
Cut point 4			1.948 (0.254)	4.917 (0.292)	

Notes: See appendix A for variable definitions and descriptive statistics. All regressions include controls for occupation (5 dummies), mgt. level (3 dummies), hourly pay status, supervisory status, tenure in years, hours worked per week, union status, age, gender, marital status (2 dummies), family size, college graduate, graduate degree, number of kids, race (4 dummies), disability status, ln(fixed pay), closeness of supervision, ability to observe co-workers, country effects (21 dummies), and company fixed effects. Standard errors in parentheses.

***Significant at the 1 percent level.

**Significant at the 5 percent level.

*Significant at the 10 percent level.

already have the means and motivation to provide suggestions. One interpretation of the positive interaction with supervision is that shared capitalism provides motivation to closely supervised workers to try to make changes in their work environment to relieve supervisory intensity. Whether these or other explanations account for the observed interactions, the important point is that the interactions are substantial, implying that analyses that treat shared capitalist compensation as a single innovation will invariably miss some of the ways in which it works and the conditions for it to work successfully.

As a graphic demonstration of the importance of the interactions, we show in figure 4.4 the relation between workers' likelihood of looking to leave the firm with the shared capitalist index contingent on different values of the interacting variables. Each line shows how the potential leaving variable changes with shared capitalism given the specified interaction. What is striking is the fanning out of the lines. Shared capitalism *increases* likely turnover when workers are very closely supervised and are not covered by any high performance policies (top line)—this may reflect workers becoming cynical and wanting to leave when they learn that management espouses a shared capitalism philosophy but still treats them like ordinary employees. In contrast, shared capitalism *decreases* likely turnover when workers are covered by high performance policies, especially as supervision is lowered. The strongest effects of shared capitalism are when it is combined with high performance policies and low levels of supervision, causing likely turnover to be cut from 12.0 percent to 6.6 percent as the shared capitalism index goes from 0 to 10 (bottom line of figure 4.4). The average results shown in table

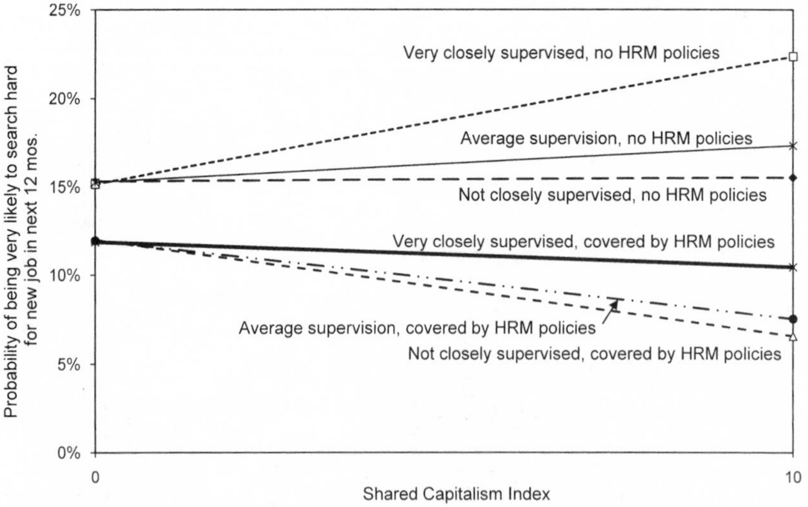

Fig. 4.4 Contingent effects of shared capitalism on likely turnover

4.2 reflect these diverse effects, weighted by the proportion of workers in the various interactive categories.

Finally, we view the interactions shown in table 4.3 and figure 4.4 as suggesting that the concept of "corporate culture" may provide a useful way to understand the relation between shared capitalism and the workplace outcomes. Analysts sometimes use the corporate culture term loosely without any operational measurement/definition that risks making it a catch-all phrase to describe residuals or puzzles. But when interaction or complementary effects are demonstrably important, it seems natural to think that some underlying latent variable—corporate culture—may more usefully describe reality than analyses of separate interacting variables.

4.6 Worker Views

As an alternative way to assess the impacts of shared capitalist incentives and of their interrelation with other aspects of corporate policy/culture, we asked workers the following hypothetical question on the NBER survey:

To what extent would each of the following affect your motivation to improve the business success of the company?[8]
You receive a cash incentive
The company grants you stock options
You receive some stock in the company ESOP
You can buy some company shares in the Employee Stock Purchase Plan (ESPP)
You buy some company shares in the open market

The upper panel of table 4.4 reports the responses to these questions. Close to three-fourths of workers said that their motivation would be improved to a "great" or "very great" extent by receiving a cash incentive (78 percent) or stock options (77 percent), while about two-thirds of workers said the same about receiving ESOP stock (69 percent) or buying shares through an ESPP (63 percent), and less than one-third said this about buying company stock on the open market (30 percent). It is possible that this pattern reflects employees' analysis of risk, with the cash incentive and options and receiving stock in an ESOP being the least risky forms of compensation, and buying shares in the open market placing the workers' capital at greatest risk. This pattern may also partly reflect the immediacy of the reward, with cash incentives and stock options providing the most immediate rewards. Alternatively, the lower responses for buying company stock through an ESPP or on the open market may reflect lower enthusiasm for shared capitalism that the

8. Employees were asked the stock options, ESOP, and ESPP questions only if the company provided these programs, and were asked the open market purchase questions only if they worked in a public company.

Table 4.4 **Employee views of the impact of shared capitalist incentives on their behavior**

	To what extent would each of the following affect your motivation to improve the business success of the company?				
	You receive a cash incentive from the co. (1)	The co. grants you some stock options (2)	You receive some stock in the co. ESOP (3)	You buy some co. shares in the ESPP (4)	You buy some co. shares on the open mkt. (5)
Tabulation of responses					
To a very little extent	2.2%	2.3%	4.4%	5.3%	20.1%
To a little extent	3.0%	3.6%	5.2%	6.7%	17.8%
To some extent	17.2%	17.2%	20.9%	25.2%	32.4%
To a great extent	32.5%	31.7%	28.8%	33.8%	17.5%
To a very great extent	45.1%	45.2%	40.8%	29.0%	12.2%
n	10,389	8,187	3,155	8,151	8,135
Ordered probit coefficients					
High performance policy index	0.022 (0.015)	0.222 (0.018)***	0.130 (0.028)***	0.173 (0.017)***	0.129 (0.017)***
How closely supervised	0.011 (0.006)**	–0.028 (0.006)***	0.010 (0.009)	–0.004 (0.006)	–0.002 (0.006)
Fixed pay at or above market	–0.147 (0.025)***	0.094 (0.028)***	0.045 (0.044)	0.093 (0.027)***	0.077 (0.026)***
Ease of seeing how well co-worker is working	0.019 (0.004)***	0.028 (0.005)***	0.035 (0.008)***	0.023 (0.005)***	0.013 (0.005)***
n	9749	7832	2816	7798	7787
(pseudo) R^2	0.015	0.060	0.053	0.038	0.022
Cut point 1	–2.834 (0.428)	1.859 (0.469)	–0.209 (0.710)	–0.057 (0.422)	–0.201 (0.441)
Cut point 2	–2.436 (0.428)	2.337 (0.468)	0.246 (0.710)	0.428 (0.422)	0.349 (0.441)
Cut point 3	–1.544 (0.428)	3.251 (0.469)	1.106 (0.710)	1.343 (0.422)	1.225 (0.441)
Cut point 4	–0.641 (0.428)	4.196 (0.469)	1.929 (0.711)	2.279 (0.423)	1.881 (0.441)

Note: Standard error in parentheses.

[a]All regressions include controls for occupation (5 dummies), mgt. level (3 dummies), hourly pay status, supervisory status, tenure in years, hours worked per week, union status, age, gender, marital status (2 dummies), family size, college graduate, graduate degree, number of kids, country (21 dummies), race (4 dummies), disability status, ln(fixed pay), and company fixed effects.

***Significant at the 1 percent level.

**Significant at the 5 percent level.

*Significant at the 10 percent level.

worker must pay for, and is therefore not part of a "gift exchange" in which the employer provides shared capitalism on top of standard pay and benefits. It is noteworthy, however, that the small response to buying shares in the open market conflicts with the significant impacts of that activity on some of the outcome variables in table 4.2.

To see whether worker responses to the hypothetical are influenced by other aspects of company policy/practice, we estimated ordered probit regressions using the variables found to have important interactions with the shared capitalism index in table 4.3. The results of these regressions, summarized at the bottom of table 4.4, show positive effects of the high performance policy index in four of the five questions (columns [2] through [5]), supporting the notion of a major complementarity between high performance policies and shared capitalist compensation. Three of the regressions show positive effects of having fixed pay at or above market levels (columns [2], [4], and [5]), likewise supporting a complementarity, but only one regression shows a negative effect of closer supervision (column [2]). The regression that shows a different pattern from all others is the one assessing the effects of receiving a cash incentive (column [1]). In this case, close supervision and perceiving one's pay as below market raises its impact. The positive supervision interaction may be because workers believe that they are more likely to receive the incentive if their supervisor pays close attention to their effort. The stronger effect among those with below-market pay may reflect the view that cash incentives can help make up the perceived pay gap more quickly than by receiving company stock. Finally, we note that the ease of seeing how well co-workers work positively affects each response, supporting the idea that an environment of worker co-monitoring is a component in the effectiveness of shared capitalism plans.

4.7 Additional Issues

Our analysis cannot rule out some potentially different interpretations of the results. As discussed in the "Studying Shared Capitalism" section of the introduction to this volume, the findings may reflect the selectivity of workers into shared capitalist enterprises rather than or in addition to their response to the way those firms operate. Selectivity could affect the analyses of workers in shared capitalist firms versus others in the GSS survey and would limit generalizing the NBER results to workers who do not work in such firms. Even within a firm, moreover, there may be something special about those who choose greater participation in shared capitalism—for instance, by buying stock through an ESPP or 401(k)—or who management places in positions with more shared capitalist incentives. To get some notion of the possible effects of worker selectivity on our results, we examined the sensitivity of the results to two possible factors that might be associated with self-selection of workers into shared capitalism: a measure of self-rated risk aversion, and family wealth. Neither of these variables made noticeable changes in the relationship of the shared capitalism index either alone or with interactions to the outcomes in tables 4.2 and 4.3.

A second problem relates to the selectivity of firms into our NBER sample and the endogeneity of the decision to offer shared capitalist compensation in both the NBER and GSS samples. Since our NBER results hold constant firm policies and characteristics by comparing workers with greater and lesser shared capitalism in the same firm, we doubt that they are seriously affected by selectivity of firms, but there is the selectivity or endogeneity of the specific policies that the firms have chosen, which still makes causal interpretations of the type we have offered open to criticism. In addition, because the NBER sample does not include firms with no shared capitalist arrangements and is based on firms' willingness to participate, we cannot rule out serious selectivity problems along the firm dimension that might interact with other factors. As described in the "Studying Shared Capitalism" section of the introduction, we experimented with specifications to reduce endogeneity but had little luck in finding suitable exogenous variables that would predict the endogenous variables but not directly affect the outcome variables of interest.

Even substantial selectivity among workers or firms, however, does not gainsay the importance of shared capitalist compensation, for it is presumably the interaction between shared capitalist incentives and mode of operating and worker characteristics that underlies the selectivity of workers, and the interaction between other firm policies and their choice of shared capitalist compensation that underlies the selectivity of firms. What selectivity does is weaken our ability to infer what might happen if additional firms adopted shared capitalist arrangements from the successes of existing firms with those practices.

4.8 Conclusion

The principal finding of this chapter is that shared capitalism affects workplace performance. The robustness of the finding is increased by the fact that the results from the NBER sample are broadly similar to the results from the nationally-representative GSS. Shared capitalism is linked to lower turnover and greater loyalty and willingness to work hard, particularly when combined with high-performance policies, low levels of supervision, and fixed pay at or above market levels. Workplaces where workers average more shared capitalist compensation report greater employee effort along several dimensions. The only outcome with which shared capitalist compensation is adversely related is absenteeism, but this result largely disappears when controlling for interactions with high performance policies and closeness of supervision.

Looking at particular programs, the strongest effects of shared capitalism are for profit sharing and employee ownership. The largely positive results are corroborated by worker views: most workers report that cash incentives, stock options, ESOP stock, and ESPP participation motivate them to work harder. The less risky forms of shared capitalist programs—profit sharing, gain sharing, stock options, and ESOPs—have greater effects than the riskier programs in line with concerns about workers being averse to risking their own capital. (For a closer look at the role of objective and subjective risk in shared capitalism programs, see chapter 3.)

Finally, we find important interactions between shared capitalist programs and other aspects of company policies that affect workplace performance. High performance policies are positively linked to good workplace outcomes, and are driven by certain types of shared capitalism. This evidence, combined with chapter 2 (which finds that shared capitalism increases worker monitoring), challenges the critique that the motivations of the average worker interfere with the introduction of basic shared capitalism principles. The interaction of the effects of shared capitalism with other corporate policies suggests that the various shared capitalist and other policies may operate through a latent variable, "corporate culture." Practically speaking, the most important implication of this chapter is that shared capitalism and high performance policies appear to work together, with greater impacts when they are combined than when they are used separately.

Appendix

Table 4A.1 **Prevalence of shared capitalism programs**

	General Social Survey 2002–2006	NBER company data set	Sample sizes	
			GSS	NBER
Bonus eligibility				
Profit sharing	35.9%	71.3%	2,386	41,018
Gain sharing	24.9%	20.7%	2,386	41,023
Size of most recent bonus, if eligible for any				
Mean dollar value	$6,265	$11,329	693	26,113
Median dollar value	$1,500	$2,000	693	26,113
Mean % of pay	8.9%	12.1%	645	22,019
Median % of pay	4.6%	5.7%	645	22,019
Employee ownership				
Own employer stock in any form	19.4%	64.0%	2,406	41,206
Own employer stock through:				
Employee Stock Ownership Plan		8.1%		41,109
Employee Stock Purchase Plan		17.6%		40,990
401(k) plan		33.5%		40,885
Exercising options and keeping stock		5.0%		41,032
Open market purchase		7.3%		41,145
Value of employer stock, if own stock				
Dollar value: Mean	$63,130	$60,078	318	25,447
Dollar value: Median	$10,000	$14,375	318	25,447
% of pay: Mean	81.7%	65.0%	302	22,715
% of pay: Median	23.0%	30.6%	302	22,715
% of wealth: Mean		19.6%		23,141
% of wealth: Median		10.0%		23,141
Stock options				
Currently hold stock options	11.3%	21.9%	2,392	41,166
Ever granted stock options		22.3%		41,166
Granted stock options last year		20.4%		41,158
Value of stock options, if hold options:				
Mean dollar value of unvested options		$112,882		8,390
Mean dollar value of vested options		$143,117		8,497
Total dollar value: Mean		$249,901		8,656
Total dollar value: Median		$75,000		8,656
% of pay: Mean		183.7%		8,403
% of pay: Median		100.0%		8,403
% of wealth: Mean		60.3%		8,104
% of wealth: Median		28.6%		8,104
Any of above programs	44.9%	85.7%	2,430	41,206

Source: Tabulated from GSS and NBER surveys. The GSS sample is limited to private for-profit employees.

References

Adams, H. B. 1888. *History of cooperation in the United States.* Baltimore, MD: Johns Hopkins University and N. Murray.

Arthur, J. B., and G. S. Jelf. 1999. The effects of gainsharing on grievance rates and absenteeism over time. *Journal of Labor Research* 20 (1): 133–45.

Barnard, C. 1938. *The functions of the executive.* Cambridge, MA: Harvard University Press.

Becker, B. E., and M. A. Huselid. 1998. High performance work systems and firm performance: A synthesis of research and managerial implications. In *Research in personnel and human resources,* vol 16, no. 1, ed. G. Ferris, 53–101. Greenwich, CT: JAI Press.

Becker, B. E., and M. A. Huselid, and D. Ulrich. 2001. *The HR scorecard: Linking people, strategy, and performance.* Cambridge, MA: Harvard Business School Press.

Bemis, E. W. 1886. Cooperation in the Northeast. *Publications of the American Economic Association* 1 (5): 7–136.

Black, S. E., and L. N. Lynch. 2000. What's driving the new economy: The benefits of workplace innovation. NBER Working Paper no. W7479. Cambridge, MA: National Bureau of Economic Research, January.

Blasi, J., D. Kruse, and A. Bernstein. 2003. *In the company of owners.* New York: Basic Books.

Boning, B., C. Ichniowski, and K. Shaw. 2001. Opportunity counts: Teams and the effectiveness of production incentives. NBER Working Paper no. 8306. Cambridge, MA: National Bureau of Economic Research, May.

Brown, S., F. Fakhfakh, and J. G. Sessions. 1999. Absenteeism and employee sharing: An empirical analysis based on French panel data, 1981–1991. *Industrial and Labor Relations Review* 52 (2): 234–51.

Bullock, R. J., and M. E. Tubbs. 1990. A case meta-analysis of gainsharing plans as organization development interventions. *Journal of Applied Behavioral Science* 26 (3): 383–404.

Cappelli, P., and D. Neumark. 2001. Do "high-performance" work practices improve establishment-level outcomes? *Industrial and Labor Relations Review* 54 (4): 737–75.

Clark, J. B. 1886. *The philosophy of wealth.* Boston: Ginn and Company.

Collins, D. 1998. *Gainsharing and power: Lessons from six Scanlon plans.* Ithaca, NY and London: Cornell University Press, ILR Press.

Conyon, M., and R. Freeman. 2001. Shared modes of compensation and firm performance: UK evidence. NBER Working Paper no. 8488. Cambridge, MA: National Bureau of Economic Research, August.

Doucouliagos, C. 1995. Worker participation and productivity in labor-managed and participatory capitalist firms: A meta-analysis. *Industrial and Labor Relations Review* 49 (1): 58–77.

Freeman, S. F. 2007. Effects of ESOP adoption and employee ownership: Thirty years of Research and Experience. Working Paper no. 07-01, Organizational Dynamics Programs, University of Pennsylvania.

Hammer, T. H., J. Landau, and R. N. Stern. 1981. Absenteeism when workers have a voice: The case of employee ownership. *Journal of Applied Psychology* 66 (5): 561–73.

Hansen, D. G. 1997. Worker performance and group incentives: A case study. *Industrial and Labor Relations Review* 51 (1): 37–49.

Hassan, M., A. Hagen, and I. Daigs. 2006. Strategic human resources as a strategic weapon for enhancing labor productivity: Empirical evidence. *Academy of Strategic Management Journal,* Annual.

Huselid, M., and S. Jackson, and R. Schuler. 1997. Technical and strategic human resource management effectiveness as determinants of firm performance. *Academy of Management Journal* 40 (1): 171–88.

Ichniowski, C., T. Kochan, D. Levine, C. Olson, and G. Strauss. 1996. What works at work: Overview and assessment. *Industrial Relations* 35 (3): 299–333.

Ichniowski, C., K. Shaw, and G. Prennushi. 1997. The effects of human resource management practices on productivity: A study of steel finishing lines. *American Economic Review* 87 (3): 291–13.

Johns, G. 2002. The psychology of lateness, absenteeism, and turnover. In *Handbook of industrial, work, and organizational psychology,* ed. N. Anderson, D. S. Ones, and H. K. Sinnangil, 232–52. Thousand Oaks, CA: SAGE.

Jones, D., T. Kato, and J. Pliskin. 1997. Profit sharing and gainsharing: A review of theory, incidence, and effects. In *Handbook of human resources,* ed. D. Lewin, D. Mitchell, and M. Zaidi. Greenwich, CT: JAI Press.

Jones, D., M. Klinedinst, and C. Rock. 1998. Productive efficiency during transition: Evidence from Bulgarian panel data. *Journal of Comparative Economics* 26 (3): 446–64.

Kaarsemaker, E. C. A. 2006a. Employee ownership and human resource management: A theoretical and empirical treatise with a digression on the Dutch context. Doctoral Dissertation, Radboud University Nijmegen, Nijmegen, Netherlands.

———. 2006b. Employee ownership and its consequences: Synthesis-generated evidence for the effects of employee ownership and gaps in the research literature. York, UK: University of York.

Kanigel, R. 1997. *The one best way: Frederick Winslow Taylor and the enigma of efficiency.* New York: Viking.

Kim, D.-O. 2005. The benefits and costs of employee suggestions under gainsharing. *Industrial and Labor Relations Review* 58 (4): 631–52.

Kim, E. H., and P. Ouimet. 2008. Employee capitalism or corporate socialism? Broad-based employee stock ownership. Ross School of Business, University of Michigan. Working Paper, October.

Knez, M., and D. Simester. 2001. Firm-wide incentives and mutual monitoring at Continental Airlines. *Journal of Labor Economics* 19 (4): 743–72.

Kramer, B. 2008. Employee ownership and participation effects on firm outcomes. Doctoral Dissertation. Department of Economics, City University of New York.

Kruse, D. 1993. *Profit sharing: Does it make a difference?* Kalamazoo, MI: W. E. Upjohn Institute for Employment Research.

———. 2002. Research evidence on prevalence and effects of employee ownership. Testimony before the Subcommittee on Employer-Employee Relations, Committee on Education and the Workforce, US House of Representatives, February 13.

Kruse, D., and J. Blasi. 1997. Employee ownership, employee attitudes, and firm performance: A review of the evidence. In *Human resources management handbook, part 1,* ed. D. Lewin, D. J. B. Mitchell, and M. A. Zaidi, 131–51. Greenwich, CT: JAI Press.

Laffont, J.-J., and D. Martimort. 2002. *The theory of incentives: The principal-agent model.* Princeton, NJ: Princeton University Press.

Levine, D. I. 1995. *Reinventing the workplace: How business and employees can both win.* Washington, DC: Brooking Institution.

Logue, J., and W. Greider. 2002. *The real world of employee ownership.* Ithaca, NY: ILR Press.

Logue, J., and J. S. Yates. 1999. Worker ownership American style: Pluralism, participation and performance. *Economic and Industrial Democracy* 20 (2): 225–52.
McNabb, R., and K. Whitfield. 1998. The impact of financial participation and employee involvement on financial performance. *Scottish Journal of Political Economy* 45 (2): 171–87.
Morck, R., A. Shleifer, and R. W. Vishny. 1988. Management ownership and market valuation: An empirical analysis. *Journal of Financial Economics* 20 (January–March): 293–315.
Ohkusa, Y., and F. Ohtake. 1997. The productivity effects of information sharing, profit sharing, and ESOPs. *Journal of the Japanese and International Economies* 11 (3): 385–402.
Organization for Economic Cooperation and Development (OECD). 1995. Profit sharing in OECD countries. *OECD Employment Outlook:* 139–69.
Peterson, S. J., and F. Luthans. 2006. The impact of financial and nonfinancial incentives on business-unit outcomes over time. Journal of Applied Psychology 91 (1): 156–65.
Robinson, A., and N. Wilson. 2006. Employee financial participation and productivity: An empirical reappraisal. *British Journal of Industrial Relations* 44 (1): 31–50.
Rosen, C., K. Klein, and K. M. Young. 1986. *Employee ownership in America: The equity solution.* Lexington, MA: D.C. Heath, Lexington Books.
Rosen, C., and M. Quarrey. 1987. How well is employee ownership working. *Harvard Business Review* 65 (September–October): 126–30.
Shaw, A. 1886. Cooperation in a western city. *Publications of the American Economic Association* 1 (4): 7–106.
Smiley, R. W., R. J. Gilbert, D. M. Binns, R. L. Ludwig, and C. M. Mosen. 2007. *Employee stock ownership planc: Business planning, implementation, law and taxation.* LaJolla, CA: The Beyster Institute, University of California, San Diego.
Smith, A. 1776. *The wealth of nations.* New York: The Modern Library.
Stiglitz, J. E. 2002. Democratic developments as the fruits of labor. Keynote Address, Industrial Relations Research Association, Boston.
———. 1974. Incentives and risk sharing in sharecropping. *The Review of Economic Studies* 4 (2): 219–55.
US General Accounting Office (GAO). 1987. *Employee stock ownership plans.* Washington, DC: GAO, October, GAO/PEMD-88-1.
Weitzman, M., and D. Kruse. 1990. Profit sharing and productivity. In *Paying for productivity: A look at the evidence,* ed. A. Blinder, 95–140. Washington, DC: The Brookings Institution.
Welbourne, T. M., and L. R. G. Mejia. 1995. Gainsharing: A critical review and a future research agenda. *Journal of Management* 21 (3): 559–610.
Wilson, N., and M. Peel. 1991. The impact on absenteeism and quits of profit-sharing and other forms of employee participation. *Industrial and Labor Relations Review* 44 (3): 454–68.
Zhuang, J., and C. Xu. 1996. Profit sharing and financial performance in the Chinese state enterprises: Evidence from panel data. *Economics of Planning* 29 (3): 205–22.

5

Complementarity of Shared Compensation and Decision-Making Systems

Evidence from the American Labor Market

Arindrajit Dube and Richard B. Freeman

In the 1990s an increasing proportion of US firms moved toward compensation systems that made part of pay depend on the economic performance of work groups or the firm. They gave profit-sharing bonuses, paid group incentive schemes (gain sharing), developed employee stock ownership programs (ESOPs), awarded stock options, and funded pensions through defined contribution pension plans that put considerable assets in the stock of the firm. Over the same period, firms introduced teams, total quality management, quality circles, employee involvement committees, and other structures that gave employees a greater role in decision making.

How significant are these new forms of compensation and modes of employee involvement? To what extent are the new forms of compensation linked to employee involvement programs? How have they affected employee behavior and attitude?

This chapter examines these questions using the nationally representative 1994–1995 Freeman-Rogers Workplace Representation and Participation Survey (WRPS) for the United States (Freeman and Rogers 1999), and the 2003 California Establishment Survey (CES). The WRPS focuses on employee involvement and work organization but also asks about the mode of compensation so that we can link compensation systems and employee decision making. The CES surveys businesses on compensation and decision-making practices, and has productivity-related outcomes that allows us to examine the relation between firm performance and compensation and decision-making systems. These data provide an independent

Arindrajit Dube is assistant professor of economics at the University of Massachusetts, Amherst. Richard B. Freeman holds the Herbert Ascherman Chair in Economics at Harvard University and is a research associate of the National Bureau of Economic Research.

check on the results from the analysis of the General Social Survey and the NBER Shared Capitalism surveys used in previous chapters.

We find that: (a) new forms of compensation based on pay for group or company performance, or ownership of company shares have increased rapidly; (b) compensation systems that base part of pay on company or group performance are linked with employee participation in decision making, suggesting that these institutions form a complementary package of employee-management relations; (c) together, employee involvement programs and shared compensation improve outcomes such as job satisfaction, attitude toward the firm, and the likelihood of staying with the firm. In the worker survey, involvement programs have an independent effect on outcomes whereas the effect of shared compensation depends on the presence of involvement programs. (d) The highest outcomes occur when firms combine pay for company or group performance with an ownership stake in the firm and employee involvement committees. This supports the notion that these policies form a complementary package of employee-management relations.

The principal weakness in our study is the lack of exogenous variation in the presence of compensation and decision-making systems, which firms choose, presumably for economic reasons. Still, the evidence fits more readily with the hypothesis that shared compensation and decision-making have real economic impact through altering *collective* employee incentives than with the null hypothesis that the results reflect sorting of firms or the impact of a single unobservable variable. We find similar associations in the two data sets and in specifications that control for unobserved factors. We also find complementarity in both the incidence of shared compensation and decision making *and* in their relation to outcomes that suggests that the systems have real effects even though unobservable factors may bias estimated magnitudes.

5.1 The New Forms of Pay

Traditional economic analysis of labor contracts distinguish between: *employment contracts,* whereby a firm buys the time of a worker to do what management views as profitable and pays a time-based wage; and *sales contracts,* where the firms buys a product from the worker (Simon 1957). In the employment contract model, the employer determines the activities that workers undertake at the workplace subject to principal/agent problems when the employer cannot fully monitor employee effort. By contrast, the sales contract is a model of self-employment where the worker decides how much to work and how to produce the product. The classic sales contract in the job market is the piece rate. In cases where pieces can be readily measured, this solves principal agent problems but loses the advantages of coordinating work and of workers sharing knowledge of newly discovered ways to improve productivity.

The *shared compensation and decision-making* arrangements on which we focus fit between these polar cases. Under these arrangements workers share the financial benefits and risks of economic activity and/or decisions about production with the firm. Ideally, giving workers a financial incentive to behave in the interests of the firm and empowering them to make decisions increases the value of the firm and enhances worker well-being.

There are diverse systems of shared compensation. We differentiate between systems that involve *financial ownership,* where the workers' reward depends on share prices, and group or company *profit-sharing or bonus systems* that reward workers on the basis of group or company performance irrespective of share prices. Employee stock ownership plans (ESOPs), majority employee ownership, defined contribution retirement plan money invested in one's own firm, stock purchase plans, and employee stock options all fit under the financial ownership rubric. Gain sharing, profit sharing, bonuses linked to performance, Scanlon plans based on cost-saving, and so on, fit under the profit-sharing rubric.

There are also diverse institutions for *shared decision making.* Employee involvement committees (EI), works councils as in the European Union, quality circles, and team production give workers a say in what happens at their work site. At the corporate level, workers can serve on boards, which Germany legislatively requires but which is uncommon in the United States, and worker-run pension funds can appoint directors.

Our classification arguably exaggerates differences among systems. Almost all employment arrangements have scope for sharing profits and decisions between owners and workers. Most workers paid straight time wages have some control over decisions, and the better they perform, the more likely the firm will give them pay increases, promotions, and other benefits in the future. At the other end, even small partnerships will divide decision making unevenly, while piece rate systems are more complicated than the simple sales contract model indicates, especially when the firm has to update the piece rates regularly due to technological change (Freeman and Kleiner 1999). Still, the differences between traditional employment and sales contracts and modern shared compensation contracts are sufficiently large to make this a useful typology.

The incentive to free ride can create a problem for shared compensation structures. Rationalizing employee stock ownership or company-wide profit sharing is difficult because it is hard to see how these systems can motivate individual workers. Some observers think that it is one thing to pay the CEO of Starbucks or Bank of America stock options or profit-related bonuses, since their decisions can affect the share price and profits; but the clerks at a local store can hardly affect the share price or company-wide profits. Lazear (1999) offers a sorting explanation for variable pay among managers—that compensation linked to long-term financial viability of the company elicits better information from managers about the true state of affairs. But, as he notes, such an explanation does not explain shared compensation for lower level workers. Oyer (2004) argues that options may attract workers optimistic about the firm—which in conjunction with tax benefits from delayed exercise of options can provide an edge to this form of compensation. However, this seems to imply that options are useful mainly when they can fool employees, which is unlikely over a long period of time.

One possible explanation is that variable compensation affects employees by helping create a corporate culture that improves company performance. For instance, if employees share the gains when the company is doing well, they may feel more enthusiastic about putting forth greater effort based on notions of fairness, even if rational calculations favor free riding on the efforts of others. They may self-monitor effort at the workplace, along the lines shown by Freeman, Kruse, and Blasi (chapter 2)

In any case, if shared compensation schemes affect employees' willingness to engage in production issues, it makes sense to couple such schemes with programs that devolve workplace decisions to workers. Firms that give workers financial incentives but that do not empower them to make decisions are unlikely to benefit from the incentive system. Firms that give workers decision-making authority but no financial incentive risk workers making decisions that are not in the firms' interest. Thus, we expect financial sharing systems to be complementary with systems of shared decision making, and for shared compensation and decision making to produce higher outcomes together than they do separately.

5.2 Extent of Shared Compensation and Decision-Making Systems

How extensive are shared compensation and decision-making systems? How has their prevalence changed over time? These basic questions are difficult to answer because until the General Social Survey (GSS) asked about the systems in 2002 and 2006 there was no single nationally representative source of data on the extent of shared capitalism. Most administrative-based or establishment-based compensation surveys cover a single form of pay—such as defined contribution pension funds, 401(k) plans, or profit-sharing—without information on the overlap with other forms of financial sharing. Since workers receive several forms of pay related to performance, simply adding the numbers under each separate category will overstate the total number of workers having shared compensation pay systems. The employment cost index includes bonuses and profit sharing but excludes stock options and related programs and provides no information on pension funds invested in the firm. The Bureau of Labor Statistics (BLS) conducted a national benefit survey in 2000, but this focused primarily on retirement and health benefit plans. The BLS's 1999 survey of the incidence of stock option-based compensation did not ask about other types of shared compensation plans.

Employee-based surveys can resolve the overlap problem but suffer from

Table 5.1 **Percentage of employees/firms with pay related to company/group performance**

Stock ownership programs	25% of nonagricultural workforce
Profit or gain sharing	25% of US workforce
Defined contribution pension funds invested heavily in company stock	11% of US workforce
Total with any form of shared compensation adjusted for overlap	45% of US workforce

Source: For details, see appendix table 5A.1.

Note: If workers were covered by only one form of variable pay, our estimate would be the sum of the estimates for the bold categories in the table: 61 percent, of which 50 percentage points consists of ownership and incentive pay. But there is considerable overlap in coverage. On the basis of the WRPS figures in table 5.2, we estimate that the proportion of workers with any form of performance pay and ownership exceeds the sum of the proportions covered by each form separately by 33 percent = (41.9 + 29.6)/53.8. Thus, we reduce the 50 percent to 38 percent. We do not have data on the overlap with the estimated 11 percent of workers with 401(k) or other plans with sizable amounts of company shares, but anticipate that this will be modest, giving us the 45 percent in the text.

measurement error, particularly of the size and nature of benefit programs. In their study of pensions held by older workers, Gustman and Steinmeier (1999) report that "discrepancies between firm provided and administrative records . . . and respondent reports . . . are large for many respondents." Opinion surveys find that 10 or so percent of workers report that their firm is employee-owned, which far exceeds any plausible estimate from administrative records (Freeman and Rogers 1999). Many workers may interpret having a 401(k) plan that invests in their firm, or individual ownership of shares, as employee ownership when in fact the firm is principally owned by shareholders rather than workers. Still, by piecing together data from several sources, and comparing the results with the GSS, we can get a general picture of the extent and growth of new forms of compensation.

Table 5.1 estimates the proportion of the private sector workforce that had a financial stake in the performance of their firm in the late 1990s from the sources described in appendix table 5A.1. This alternative approach provides a good check on the recent data from the General Social Survey. Approximately 25 percent of the workforce had a stake in their firm through some form of ownership. The main vehicle for employee ownership has been the Employee Stock Ownership Plan (ESOP). The National Center of Employee Ownership (NCEO) estimated that in 1998 some 8,500,000 workers were employed in over 11,400 ESOP and related stock bonus plans with combined assets of around 400 billion.[1] This is about 8 percent of the US private sector workforce. In addition, the NCEO estimates that 7 to 10 mil-

1. More recent figures from NCEO indicate that in 2002, some 8.8 million workers were enrolled in ESOP plans, and around 15 million participated in stock purchase plans.

lion workers receive stock options as part of all employee stock option plans, for another 8 percent or so of the private sector workforce. This estimate contrasts with the employee survey conducted by the BLS, which found that in 1999, 1.7 percent of all employees, or 5.3 percent of employees of publicly-traded companies received options grants in 1999. Some of the divergence is likely due to differences in the timing covered by questions. Since companies may not give out broad-based options each year, the number of employees who "regularly" receive options is greater than those who might receive it in one particular year. An additional 10 percent or so of the workforce received special opportunities to buy company stock.

Profit sharing differs from employee ownership because it depends on accounting profits rather than share values. Employees at Amazon.com would receive nothing in profit shares when the firm has not turned a profit but would have gained from ownership of options, as the share price of the company increased rapidly. Most profit sharing is deferred, with the profit share put into an employee retirement account (Profit Sharing Council of America [PSCA] 1993; BLS 1999). Gain-sharing plans typically tie employee compensation to a group-based operational measure—such as physical output, productivity, quality, safety, customer satisfaction, or costs—rather than to a financial measure such as profitability. We estimate that about 25 percent of American workers are paid in part with some form of group or company financial incentives.

The third major way in which firms pay workers based on firm performance is through non-ESOP defined contribution pension plans, such as 401(k) plans. In 1997 55 percent of full-time employees had 401(k) plans (approximately the same proportion had any form of defined contribution pension). While we lack estimates on the proportion of *workers* with 401(k) or other defined contribution funds invested in their firm, estimates of the proportion of 401(k) *assets* in company stock hover around 20 percent. Absent better information, on the basis of these figures we estimate that roughly 11 percent ($= .55 \times 20$) of workers have their retirement pay depend on company shares to some extent.

Because workers who receive one form of shared compensation may also receive another form, we cannot add these separate estimates together to obtain the proportion of the workforce whose compensation depends on company performance. We must subtract the proportion with an overlap in coverage. Making such an adjustment, we estimate that about 45 percent of workers have a substantial portion of their pay varying with company or group performance. This proportion is almost identical to estimates of shared compensation programs from the 2002 and 2006 General Social Survey.[2]

Figure 5.1 shows that the forms of variable pay have increased rapidly. The

2. http://www.nceo.org/library/gss_2006_tables.html.

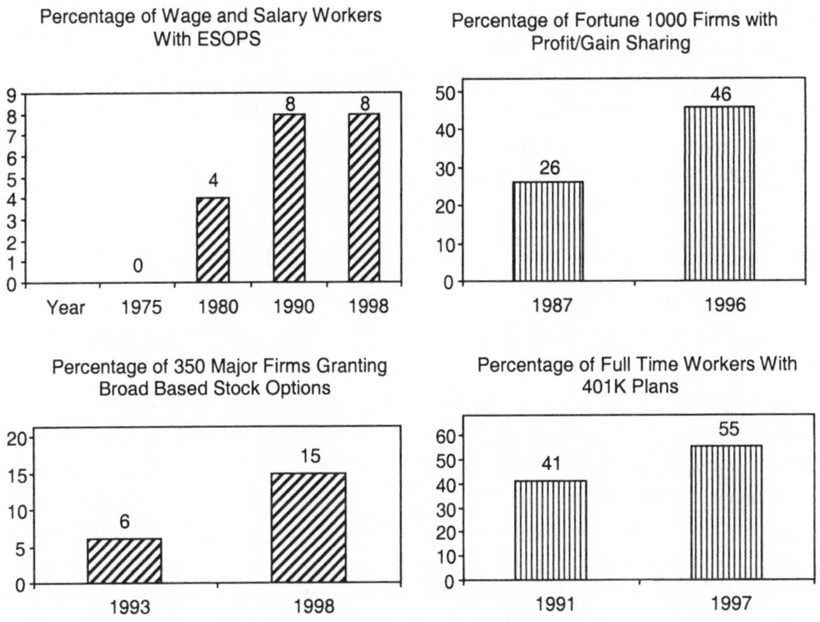

Fig. 5.1 The growth of shared compensation systems

Source: ESOP Employees from NCEO Employee Ownership Report, Jan–Feb.'00, p. 9; Broad Based Stock Options: from Mercer & Co. Executive Compensation Research Topics RT#10—May 26, 1998, p. 5; Fortune 1000 firms with gain-/profit-sharing from employment policy foundation, "US Wage and Productivity Growth," 1998; Workers with 401(K) plans from US Statistical Abstract, 1999, table 622.

proportion of private sector employees with ESOPs rose from 0 percent in 1975 to 4 percent in 1980 to 8 percent in 1990, but then stabilized in the 1990s. By contrast, the proportion receiving stock options rose greatly in the 1990s. A William Mercer company study found that the proportion of firms granting options more than doubled between 1993 and 1998. Figures for large electronics firms show a fourfold increase between 1994 and 1997. In 1999 39 percent of the *Inc.* magazine 500 fastest-growing privately-held firms offered options to workers; in 1998, the figure was 26 percent.[3] A Federal Reserve Board Survey of 125 large firms found that 23 percent had introduced stock option programs for regular employees between 1996 and 1998, while 37 percent had broadened the eligibility of their existing program.[4] Profit-sharing plans or gain-sharing plans increased over the period among large firms. The 45 percent of Fortune 1000 firms that reported profit-gain-sharing systems in 1995 was up from 26 percent in 1987. Finally, fixed contribution pension plans grew in the 1990s as well. Assuming that investment in company stock

3. See NCEO (2000, 10).
4. Lebow et al. (1999), table 3.

fell less rapidly or did not fall at all, more workers had part of their retirement income tied to company performance.

In short, although measures of variable compensation are incomplete, there is no gainsaying that shared compensation mechanisms linking rewards to firm or group economic performance rose in the 1990s and to some extent in the 1980s as well.

5.3 Shared Compensation System and Employee Involvement

Over roughly the same time period that compensation practices were changing, employee involvement committees, teamwork, and other forms of empowering workers became the cutting edge of labor relations in the United States. Freeman, Kleiner, and Ostroff's (2000) analysis of firms found a large increase in the number using various forms of employee involvement activity between 1983 and 1993. Osterman's 1994 survey of establishments found that 55 percent used work teams, 34 percent had Total Quality Management (TQM), and 41 percent had quality circles (QC), with most introduced in the late 1980s/early 1990s. One-third of the workers in the 1995 and 1996 WRPS reported that they served on employee involvement committees, defined broadly to include TQM, QC, and related groups; and 55 percent reported that their firm had such committees (Freeman and Rogers 1999).

Does the data support the prediction that financial sharing and employee involvement are complementary ways of organizing work? For this we use the WRPS, which was a nationally representative survey of 2,408 adults age eighteen or older who were currently employed in private companies or nonprofit organizations in the continental United States with twenty-five or more employees. A total of 2,408 employees responded to the first wave in September and October 1994, and 801 respondents were reinterviewed in a second wave in December 1994 and January 1995 (see Freeman and Rogers [1999] for further detail).

Table 5.2 presents data from the WRPS on modes of compensation and shared decision making through employee involvement committees. With respect to compensation, we asked:

> "On your main job do you . . . Participate in an employee stock ownership or ESOP plan?; Work in an employee-owned company?; Receive any bonuses based on profit sharing?; Receive any bonuses based on meeting workplace goals?"

Because the WRPS did not ask detailed questions about modes of financial sharing—for instance, distinguishing 401(k) plans or stock purchase plans—nor differentiate between gain-sharing and individual bonuses, the data is not ideal. Still, aggregated into broad categories, it gives evidence on the coverage among workers of group incentive pay or ownership plans.

The first column of table 5.2 records the distribution of nonmanagerial

Table 5.2 **Proportion of workers with shared compensation systems, full sample, and by presence of employee involvement (EI)**

	Full sample (%)	With EI (%)	Without EI (%)
Any compensation structure	53.8	66.1	33.9
Performance pay	41.9	53	37
Profit Sharing	28.9	39.9	24.1
Gain sharing	26.2	32.8	23.3
Ownership	29.6	40.2	25
ESOP	23	34.5	18
Employee owned	11.2	13.1	10.4
Employee involvement	29.9	100	0

Source: WRPS Survey, in *What Workers Want.* For exact wording of relevant WRPS questions, see appendix B, table 5A.2.

workers according to their modes of compensation. It shows that 54 percent of the sample reported at least one of the variable forms of compensation, and that the incentive-based systems of pay were more common than the ownership-based systems. The figures for ESOPs and ownership and incentive bonuses are higher than those in table 5.1 (in part perhaps because the WRPS covers larger firms) with the result that the proportion of workers covered by at least one form of shared compensation exceeds the estimate in table 5.1.

The final line in table 5.2 records the proportion of nonmanagerial employees who serve on employee involvement committees: 29.9 percent. Since the WRPS contained a full module on these committees, and asked workers details about how the committees operated and what they thought about them (see Freeman and Rogers [1999, chapter 4]), this is likely to be a reasonably accurate measure, at least for the sample covered.

The second column in table 5.2 gives the percentage of workers on EI committees who are paid with different forms of variable pay, while the third column gives the percentage of workers not on EI committees paid by the same forms. Overall, 66 percent of workers on EI committees have some form of shared compensation, compared to 34 percent of workers who are not on those committees. A similar pattern is found for each of the individual forms of pay. The difference in the distribution of compensation between workers with EI and those without EI are statistically significant in this comparison, and remains so in analyses that control for diverse covariates. Thus, the WRPS confirms the prediction that employee involvement programs will be closely tied to financial sharing arrangements.

Figure 5.2 shows the complementarity among the forms of shared compensation and employee involvement from a different perspective. It contrasts the proportion of workers having various combinations of incentive pay, financial sharing, and shared decision making with the proportion that we would expect if the probability of having the different forms was an

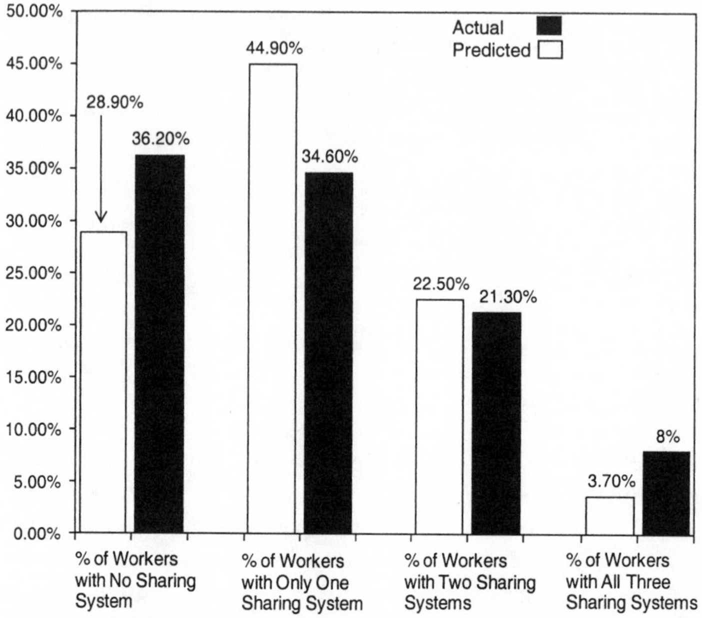

Fig. 5.2 The distribution of shared compensation and decision-making systems
Source: Calculated from WRPS (Workers Representation and Participation Survey).
Notes: The predicted values treat the proportion of workers with each of the shared systems as independent events. Thus, if 1/2 of the workers had an EI system and 1/10th had some ownership, the predicted proportion with both systems would be 1/20th, the predicted proportion with neither system would be 9/20ths and the predicted proportion with only one of the two would be 1/2. The actual proportions are taken directly from the data.

independent draw from separate urns. Over twice as many workers report having all three forms than would occur if they were independent, and more workers have neither financial nor incentive systems nor EI committees than would be expected. The concentration of frequency at the extremes is consistent with the hypothesis that these forms of workplace organization and compensation are complementary.

Table 5.3 examines the characteristics of workers and firms with shared compensation systems and employee involvement activity. It reports the proportion of workers with specified demographic characteristics in the sample and in two polar cases: workers who have an ownership stake, profit/gain sharing, and shared decision making through EI committees; and workers with none of the systems. The pattern is clear. Workers at companies with shared decision-making and compensation systems are better educated, more likely to be in the upper quartile of the wage distribution, more likely to be male, and more than twice as likely to be salaried than workers with none of the shared systems. In addition, the workers with all three forms of sharing are disproportionately professionals, sales workers, and skilled

Table 5.3 **Proportion of persons with specified characteristics, total sample and by extent of shared capitalism**

	Full sample	Nothing	Everything (P, O, EI)
A Demographic, occupational, and industrial characteristics			
College Education	0.26	0.21	0.35
High wage	0.24	0.19	0.38
Male	0.54	0.50	0.64
Salaried	0.31	0.22	0.46
Age	37.81	36.27	38.39
Occupations:			
Professional	0.24	0.20	0.27
Clerical	0.19	0.20	0.14
Sales	0.10	0.07	0.16
Manuf. representative	0.03	0.01	0.04
Service worker	0.10	0.14	0.04
Skilled tradesman	0.15	0.15	0.17
Semi-skilled worker	0.10	0.11	0.10
Laborer	0.09	0.11	0.08
Other	0.01	0.01	0.01
Industries:			
Agriculture/forestry/fishing	0.02	0.02	0.02
Mining	0.01	0.01	0
Construction	0.05	0.06	0.04
Manufacturing	0.27	0.23	0.39
Transport/public utilities/communications	0.09	0.06	0.08
Wholesale trade	0.05	0.04	0.05
Retail trade	0.16	0.18	0.12
FIRE	0.08	0.06	0.16
Health services	0.11	0.13	0.06
Business services/law	0.07	0.07	0.05
Educational, social services/membership orgs.	0.05	0.09	0.01
Hotels	0.01	0.02	0.01
Amusement/recreation services	0.00	0.01	0.00
Personal services	0.01	0.01	0.00
Misc.	0.00	0.00	0.00
Other	0.01	0.01	0.01
No answer	0.02	0.02	0.01
B Firm characteristics			
Firm size:			
< 25	0.00	0.00	0.00
25–99	0.21	0.27	0.09
100–499	0.25	0.27	0.21
500–999	0.11	0.10	0.09
> 1,000	0.44	0.36	0.60
Personnel dept	0.71	0.61	0.87
Open door policy (individual)	0.87	0.81	0.92
Grievance procedure	0.36	0.34	0.44
Town meeting	0.49	0.34	0.76
Open door policy (groups)	0.66	0.56	0.83
Employee committee	0.40	0.28	0.61

Sources: Panel A, WRPS, *What Workers Want.* For full distribution, see appendix tables 5A.1 and 5A.2; panel B, WRPS, *What Workers Want.* For full distribution, see table 3.9.

trades persons, and are disproportionately employed in manufacturing and finance, insurance, and real estate, and are twice as likely to be in firms with over 1,000 employees than those without any of these programs. The bottom part of table 5.3 shows that firms that share financial rewards with employees and who have EI committees also have other "good" labor practices: personnel policies, open door policies, town meetings, and employee committees beyond EI committees.

5.4 Relation to Outcomes

To see whether shared compensation practices and employee involvement activities affect worker attitudes and behavior, we examine seven measures of attitudes and behavior from the main body of the WRPS and two measures from the second wave of the survey[5] that fit broadly into four areas: productivity, satisfaction with workplace relations, attitudes toward the company, and worker retention.

The measures relating to productivity are the most problematic because the WRPS contains worker reports on productivity-enhancing activity but not on actual productivity. The survey asked workers how often they made productivity-related suggestions and how often management heeded them, coded on a four-point scale from least (1) to most (4). We took the product of these two responses as the first measure of productivity-enhancing activity, which gives a variable that ranges from 1 to 16. The survey also asked workers how much influence they exercise over workplace practices. This is our second measure of productivity-related activity. Our third measure, from the second wave of the survey, asked workers to rate fellow employees on their concern for the success of the company and willingness to take on new responsibilities and to work hard using a school grade scale from A to E, which we coded as a rating from 1 to 5. These three measures are broadly informative about the extent to which workers engage in productivity-enhancing activities at their workplace.

To determine how workers feel about their job, we selected four variables: whether workers looked forward to going to work in the morning versus wishing they did not have to go; how they rated labor-management relations at their firm; their satisfaction with the influence they had at their workplace; and how they graded management's treatment of employees using the school grade scheme. We chose these variables to investigate whether shared compensation and decision-making create a work atmosphere where workers feel that their voice is heard and where management treats them fairly.

To measure the general attitude that workers have toward their firm, we took a question on the loyalty workers felt toward the firm and another on

5. One-third of the WRPS respondents were asked a short follow-up set of questions, constituting a smaller second wave sample. See Freeman and Rogers (1999).

the degree of trust they had that the firm would carry out its promises to workers. For worker retention, we use a question that asks how likely an employee will remain at the same company.

Finally, as a broad summary statistic of worker attitudes and possible behavior, we constructed an average outcome measure that includes the productivity indicators, workplace satisfaction, and attitude toward the firm, and likelihood of staying with the company, with the variables given equal weight.[6]

What does the data show about the relation between shared compensation and shared decision-making practices and these outcomes?

Row 1 of table 5.4 reports the coefficients from a regression of our overall outcome measure on the forms of compensation and employee involvement, and on an extensive set of covariates that include the characteristics of workers (age, gender, etc.) and of their firm (size, industry) as described in the table footnote. In addition, the covariates include measures of labor relations policies toward workers as groups and as individuals beyond shared capitalism and employee involvement. These measures are based on the presence of particular policies at the firm and on workers' assessment of their effectiveness, as reported on the WRPS.[7] We give the highest score when firms have many practices that workers view as effective and lower scores when firms have few practices or when workers view their practices as less effective. With these measures of human resource practices in the equation, our estimates attribute to the shared compensation and decision-making variables only the portion of the outcomes above and beyond those associated with these other attributes of firms.

Line 1 of the table shows that performance pay (PP), employee involvement (EI), and ownership stake (OS) variables have statistically significant effects on the average outcome. The table also shows that while shared decision-making structures have an *independent* effect on outcomes, the impact of compensation practices appears to be *contingent* on such decision-making structures. The firm has to empower workers to make decisions if it expects to gain from shared compensation and ownership structures, consistent with the hypothesis that such shared compensation schemes actually have incentive effects.

We tested for complementarities by including interaction terms in the regressions—that is, a term for the presence both of an ownership stake and employee involvement committee, a term for ownership and profit/gain sharing, and so forth. Statistical tests reject the null hypothesis that there is no added effect on outcome from complementarity between PP and EI at the 6 percent level and reject the null of no interaction effects between PP and

6. Since all other variables here are in a 1 to 4 scale, we multiply the likelihood by 4 in terms of the overall outcome measure to ensure all variables get roughly an equal weight.

7. Questions on the labor relations policies can be found in Freeman and Rogers (1999).

Table 5.4 **Regression coefficients and robust standard errors for the relation between EI, performance pay and ownership combinations and outcomes in the WRPS**

	EI	P	O	P,O	P,EI	O,EI	P,O,EI
1. Average, all outcomes	0.09**	0.11***	0.07**				
	(0.04)	(0.03)	(0.04)				
2. Average, all outcomes	0.28***	0.11**	0.01	0.18***	0.26***	0.26***	0.42***
	(0.06)	(0.05)	(0.07)	(0.06)	(0.07)	(0.07)	(0.06)
Productivity related outcomes							
3. Average	0.44***	0.09	0.01	0.01	0.38***	0.42***	0.57***
	(0.07)	(0.06)	(0.08)	(0.07)	(0.08)	(0.08)	(0.07)
4. Productive suggestions	0.55***	0.15*	–0.02	–0.04	0.46***	0.53***	0.77***
	(0.09)	(0.08)	(0.09)	(0.09)	(0.10)	(0.11)	(0.10)
5. Overall influence at job	0.35***	0.03	0.04	0.09	0.32***	0.32***	0.39***
	(0.07)	(0.07)	(0.09)	(0.09)	(0.09)	(0.09)	(0.08)
5. Effort of fellow employees[a]	0.07	0.09	0.01	0.05	0.06	0.12	0.35***
	(0.10)	(0.09)	(0.10)	(0.15)	(0.12)	(0.17)	(0.11)
Worker satisfaction related outcomes							
6. Average	0.19***	0.06	0.06	0.09	0.17***	0.19**	0.33***
	(0.06)	(0.05)	(0.07)	(0.06)	(0.06)	(0.08)	(0.06)
7. Overall satisfaction with workplace influence	0.26***	0.07	0.04	0.11	0.26***	0.18	0.35***
	(0.07)	(0.07)	(0.09)	(0.08)	(0.08)	(0.11)	(0.08)
8. Overall job satisfaction	0.14*	0.07	0.04	0.14*	0.05	0.23**	0.24**
	(0.08)	(0.07)	(0.10)	(0.08)	(0.09)	(0.11)	(0.09)

9. Management-employee relations	0.17*	0.02	0.09	0.02	0.19*	0.13	0.38***
	(0.09)	(0.07)	(0.09)	(0.09)	(0.10)	(0.13)	(0.10)
10. Composite "grade" for management[a]	0.16	0.09	0.11	0.09	0.21	0.36**	0.40***
	(0.12)	(0.11)	(0.14)	(0.15)	(0.13)	(0.17)	(0.13)
Attitudes toward company:							
11. Reported loyalty toward company	0.17**	0.07	0.08	0.17**	0.24***	0.11	0.29***
	(0.08)	(0.06)	(0.09)	(0.08)	(0.08)	(0.11)	(0.08)
12. Reported trust toward company	0.30**	0.11	0.24*	0.21*	0.23*	0.20	0.34**
	(0.11)	(0.10)	(0.13)	(0.12)	(0.12)	(0.16)	(0.13)
13. Likely to keep working in company	0.10**	0.11***	–0.02	0.21***	0.14**	0.13**	0.18***
	(0.04)	(0.04)	(0.05)	(0.04)	(0.05)	(0.06)	(0.05)

Source: WRPS waves 1 and 2.

Notes: All regressions include controls for: age, education, sex, race, experience, union membership, tenure, firm size, occupation (nine categories); industry (fifteen categories); salaried/nonsalaried status, as well as individual and group-based human resource practices. "Average" productivity is a composite based on "productive suggestions" and "overall influence at job," and "average" satisfaction is a composite based on "Overall satisfaction with workplace influence," "Overall job satisfaction," and "Management employee relations."

[a]Other variables not used for the "Averages" if they were from the smaller wave 2 subsample.

***Significant at the 1 percent level.

**Significant at the 5 percent level.

*Significant at the 10 percent level.

OS and EI and OS at weaker levels (15 to 21 percent). Thus, the data support a complementary relation of the impact of the shared systems variables on the average outcome.

To examine the interactive effects of variables on outcomes more directly we replaced the measures of each separate policy with mutually exclusive variables representing each possible combination of practices, and regressed outcome variables on this new set of independent variables. Rows 2 through 13 of table 5.4 gives the regression coefficients on dummy variables representing all the combinations of EI, Ownership, and Performance Pay. Here, EI means "EI only," "P" means "Performance Pay only," "P,EI" means "Performance Pay and EI" and so on. Row 2 gives the coefficients on these variables on our overall outcome measure. Succeeding lines give coefficients on separate outcomes grouped into our three categories.

These calculations show that EI has a substantial and statistically significant link to all outcomes, whereas the compensation variables by themselves have limited importance. But the threefold combination of EI, ownership, and performance pay is *always* statistically significant and represents the numerically largest value in the overall outcome regression and in all of the regressions for separate outcomes save one. To give a sense of the magnitudes of the effect, we note that the standard deviation in the average outcome (row 1) is around 0.64 (see appendix B). The presence of EI by itself is associated with a 0.43 standard deviation gain, while the presence of EI, O, and P are associated with a gain of 0.66 standard deviation—as compared to companies without any of the shared compensation and decision-making schemes. The average productivity variable shows a gain of 0.59 standard deviations for EI only and a gain of 0.76 standard deviations for the EI/P/O combination.

Looking at the underlying variables, the table shows that EI is critical for practices to affect productivity-related measures. Complementary compensation variables boost the productivity indicators (productivity related suggestions, peer rating of effort, and the extent of influence in productivity decisions) only when coupled with EI decision-making structure. In contrast, attitudes toward companies are affected by shared compensation structures that include *both ownership and performance pay* separately from EI. Finally, for the measures of worker satisfaction EI always matters while compensation structures matter independently for some but not all variables. In all cases, the combination of EI, ownership, and performance pay is significant and quantitatively greater than individual effects and often greater than the sum thereof.

The human resource policy variables enter significantly in our regressions, so that our results on shared compensation and decision-making systems are an "add on" effect. The regressions in table 5.5 show that the efficacy of the human resource policies themselves is related to the shared compensation and decision-making systems. The WRPS asked workers about the effectiveness of our group-based HR policies: town meetings, open door

Table 5.5 **Impact on effectiveness of other human resource practices**

	EI	P	O	P,O	P,EI	O,EI	P,O,EI
Effectiveness of group-based HR policies							
"Town meetings"	0.10	0.05	0.11	0.16	0.22**	0.22	0.36***
	(0.10)	(0.10)	(0.13)***	(0.10)	(0.10)	(0.14)	(0.10)
Open door policies for groups	0.14*	0.06	0.02	0.12	0.19**	0.36***	0.41***
	(0.08)	(0.08)	(0.11)	(0.09)	(0.08)	(0.11)	(0.08)
Employee committees	0.32***	0.17	0.17	0.20	0.15	0.27**	0.42***
	(0.11)	(0.11)	(0.13)	(0.12)	(0.12)	(0.13)	(0.12)
Effectiveness of individual-based HR policies	0.32***	0.17	0.17	0.20	0.15	0.27**	0.42***
	(0.11)	(0.11)	(0.13)	(0.12)	(0.12)	(0.13)	(0.12)

Source: WRPS wave 1.

Notes: Controls include age, education, sex, race, experience, union membership, tenure, firm size, plant size, occupation (nine categories), industry (fifteen categories), and salaried/nonsalaried status. Robust standard errors are within parentheses. All regressions use WRPS sample weights.

***Significant at the 1 percent level.

**Significant at the 5 percent level.

*Significant at the 10 percent level.

policies, employee committees independent of EI, and about HR policies toward individuals as a group. We regressed workers' assessment of the effectiveness of these programs on our shared compensation and decision-making variables and a full set of demographic and company controls. The regressions show that the efficacy of the human resource policies is higher in the presence of shared compensation and decision-making systems with a pattern quite similar to that found in table 5.4. Since our measure of HR policies in those regressions included a weighting of the variables by their effectiveness, at least part of the effect credited to HR policies might be due to compensation and decision-making structures increasing their effectiveness.

5.5 Probing the Results

Even in the presence of the proxies for human resource and personnel policies, the regression results could reflect an unobservable latent variable that is correlated with the EI and compensation policies, which would bias upwards the estimated impact of shared compensation and decision-making on outcomes. "Good" firms, in particular, are likely to have both worker-friendly practices and policies and have workers who are reasonably satisfied with conditions, and may be more likely to attract and retain more productive workers as well.[8] Absent good exclusion restrictions (variables

8. The term "good" is only being used as a shortcut for a firm having a set of practices that tend to produce a higher level of outcome in terms of worker satisfaction and participation.

that impact the incidence of the policies without directly impacting outcome) we probe this possibility by exploiting the multiple outcomes that the WRPS obtained for each person. We focus on the productivity variables on the grounds that they are the most problematic measures and thus more likely to fail to stand up to probing than some of the others. We use a two-equation model to estimate the effect of the policy variables on productivity *net of the composite worker satisfaction variable*. To the extent we expect the general or attitudinal outcomes (such as company loyalty, job satisfaction, and worker-management relations) to reflect an omitted "company effect," using those variables as controls better isolates the impact of EI and compensation structures on the productivity outcomes.

However, simply including the attitudinal outcomes as independent variables in regressions does not recover a lower bound on the effect of shared compensation and decision making on productivity because the measures of attitudes will be correlated with the error term in the regression for productivity. To see this, let Y_{1i} measure productivity, and Y_{2i} be worker satisfaction; a_i is the latent company effect; X_i is the vector of controls. Consider two equations:

$$(1) \qquad Y_{1i} = b_1(X_i) + g_1 D_i + (c_1 a_i + e_{1i}),$$

$$(2) \qquad Y_{2i} = b_2(X_i) + g_2 D_i + (c_2 a_i + e_{2i}).$$

Our model allows $F(a_i, X_i)$, $F(a_i, D_i)$, $F(e_{1i}, e_{2i})$ to be arbitrary. We assume that there is a single unobservable factor a_i correlated with the treatment status, D_i, while the error e is uncorrelated with treatment status. Moreover, the joint distribution of the error e and the covariates X_i is independent of the treatment status.

Substituting the second equation into the first gives the following:

$$(3) \quad Y_{1i} = \left(b_1 - \left(\frac{c_1}{c_2}\right)b_2\right)X_i + \left(\frac{c_1}{c_2}\right)Y_{2i}\left(g_1 - \left(\frac{c_1}{c_2}\right)g_2\right)D_i + \left(e_1 - \left(\frac{c_1}{c_2}\right)e_2\right).$$

But if we regress Y_1 on X, Y_2, and D, we would not recover the desired lower bound $g_1 - (c_1/c_2)g_2$ because our regressor Y_2 is correlated with the error term $e_1 - (c_1/c_2)e_2$.

Netting the productivity measures of the overall job satisfaction involves a two-step procedure. The first step uses moment restrictions implicit in the single factor model to identify the relative importance of the latent factor on the various outcomes. The second step uses this to "net out" the latent factor. The formal derivation of this is in Dube (2003). Here we describe the method. First we note that if we knew c_1/c_2, the following regression would recover the lower bound on b_1, $g_1 - (c_1/c_2)g_2$:

$$(4) \quad Y_{1i} - \left(\frac{c_1}{c_2}\right)Y_{2i} = \left(b_1 - \left(\frac{c_1}{c_2}\right)b_2\right)X_i + \left(g_1 - \left(\frac{c_1}{c_2}\right)g_2\right)D_i + \left(e_1 - \left(\frac{c_1}{c_2}\right)e_2\right).$$

However, since we do not know (c_1/c_2), we must estimate it in another step. Under the assumptions about the covariance structure invoked before, it can be shown that:

$$(5)\qquad \left(\frac{c_1}{c_2}\right)=\left(\frac{V(Y_{1i}|X,D=1)-V(Y_{1i}|X,D=0)}{V(Y_{2i}|X,D=1)-V(Y_{2i}|X,D=0)}\right)^{1/2}.$$

We estimate the previous equation to recover (c_1/c_2) in step one, which is then used to estimate the primary regression to recover a lower bound on b_1; that is, $(b_1-(c_1/c_2)b_2)$. Because (c_1/c_2) is estimated, the ordinary least squares (OLS) standard errors in the primary regression are not valid. Therefore, we use bootstrapped standard errors for this estimation.

Table 5.6 gives the coefficients from this exercise using the average of our productivity variables as the dependent variable and the average of our satisfaction variables as the control for the firm being "good." The results show that even attributing all of the link between job satisfaction and shared compensation variables to a latent variable does not eliminate the effect of EI and the EI, P, O combination of policies on productivity outcomes. Moreover, the effects of the EI, P, O combination continue to be larger than

Table 5.6 **Regression estimates of the impacts of shared compensation and EI on productivity after controlling for their impacts on average satisfaction; and regression estimates of impacts using propensity score matching**

	EI	P	O	P, O	P, EI	O, EI	P, O, EI	Controls for "company effect"
				OLS estimates				
1. Average productivity	0.41***	0.08	0.02	0.03	0.4***	0.43***	0.56***	*N*
	(0.07)	(0.05)	(0.07)	(0.07)	(0.08)	(0.09)	(0.07)	
2. Average productivity (after subtracting weighted "average satisfaction")	0.24***	0.02	0.06	–0.05	0.26***	0.26***	0.3***	*Y*
	(0.07)	(0.06)	(0.07)	(0.07)	(0.08)	(0.09)	(0.08)	
				Propensity score matching estimates				
3. Average productivity	0.38***			0.01			0.62***	*N*
	(0.08)			(0.08)			(0.12)	
4. Average productivity (after subtracting weighted "average satisfaction")	0.26***			–0.05			0.35**	*Y*
	(0.06)			(0.08)			(0.14)	

Source: WRPS wave 1.

Note: Controls include age, education, sex, race, experience, union membership, tenure, firm size, plant size, occupation (nine categories), industry (fifteen categories), and salaried/nonsalaried status. Bootstrapped standard errors are within parentheses. "Average productivity" is a composite variable based on "productive suggestions" and "overall influence at job"; "Average satisfaction" is a composite variable based on "Overall satisfaction with workplace influence," "Overall job satisfaction," and "Management employee relations." (see table 5.5).

***Significant at the 1 percent level.

**Significant at the 5 percent level.

*Significant at the 10 percent level.

those of EI in isolation, supporting the assertion that the compensation variables matter in conjunction with EI. While this single omitted factor model cannot provide the confidence of an experiment, it is the toughest hurdle that we could set up using unobservables and the main results pass it. At the minimum, it shows that the policies impact productivity beyond their impact on worker satisfaction.

5.6 Propensity Score Test

We also probe our results using propensity scores that relate having the relevant policies to covariates and then comparing outcome variables within groups with similar propensity scores. Estimation involves collapsing the covariates into a single function—the propensity score, which is the probability of treatment given the covariates. As demonstrated in Rosenbaum and Rubin (1983), the outcome conditional on the propensity score is stochastically independent of the covariates.[9] If within the groups that have similar probabilities of EI and shared compensation chance determines which workers have EI and shared compensation and which do not, the propensity score technique identifies the effect of the policies on the outcomes.

Propensity score analysis can illuminate the patterns in the data in another way. Propensity score techniques enable us to see whether there is enough overlap in observations with respect to propensity scores (and hence the covariates) to make this analysis credible. Since the estimator is a weighted average of within-propensity-score differences in mean outcomes, it compares "similar companies" in coming up with the treatment effect estimate. Say that the covariates X_i that predict whether or not a worker has EI or receives shared compensation pay are completely nonoverlapping between workers with those policies and those without the policies. Then identification of the treatment effect relies on extrapolation of the data to cover the range of the covariates, and should be viewed with suspicion.

We use a probit to estimate the propensity score for each of the following "treatment" variables—EI only, P, O only, and EI, P, O. For each of these cases, propensity score strata are created, and we check to see if the covariates are balanced (which they are). We then use propensity-score matching to pick with replacement the closest untreated company for each treated one. Table 5.6 reports the propensity score estimates of three of the policy categories—EI only and EI, P, O. We find that the propensity score-based coefficients are quite similar to the coefficients using OLS, and are statistically significant at the 10 percent level for EI and EI, P, O combinations. The

9. Formally, let D measure the presence of the policies of interest, X be the covariates, and Y be the outcome variable and $p(X)$ be the probability that an observation has the policies, then $\Sigma_{p(X)} (E(Y_{1i} \mid p(X), D = 1) - E(Y_{1i} \mid p(X), D = 0))w(p(X)) = \Sigma_{p(X)} (b_1(X_i, D_{i=1}) - b_1(X_i, D_{i=0}) + g_1)$ $w(p(X)) = g_1 + E_X(b_1(X_i, D_{i=1}) - b_1(X_i, D_{i=0}))$.

results continue to hold when we look at differences between similar groups of companies—all of which increases our confidence that shared compensation and decision-making policies have real impacts on worker contributions to company performance.

5.7 Establishment Data

As noted, the measures of productivity in the WRPS are based on worker responses about activity rather than on measured productivity for their establishment or workplace. To obtain an alternative view of the link between shared compensation and decision-making on outcomes at the establishment level, we examine data from the 2003 California Establishment Survey (CES). This survey provides information on 1,080 establishments in 2003.[10] It asked about the use of shared stock ownership (ESOP and stock options) and profit sharing and about organizational (including the use of "employee involvement") programs such as quality circles and quality management programs. The CES asks about stock options besides ESOPs but not whether the companies are employee-owned; and about profit sharing but not about gain sharing or bonuses. With respect to output measures, the CES includes managements' assessments on the extent of employee decision making, product/service quality, and financial performance, given on a 1 to 4 scale and employee retention, defined as 1 minus the annual turnover rate.

Table 5.7 shows the distribution of profit-sharing and stock ownership in the CES, with the summary statistics weighted by firm size to give estimates of the proportion of overall workforce in these programs. The incidence of EI is somewhat larger in the CES than in the WRPS, while the shared compensation figures are somewhat lower—though they are similar to other establishment-level sources. But the incidence of EI by profit sharing and ownership (not shown in the table) has a pattern comparable to that in the WRPS. Appendix table 5A.2 gives the means and standard deviations of the outcome measures for the CES.

The CES allows us to test whether the shared compensation and decision making are associated with better establishment outcomes. To assess the impact of compensation and decision making on establishment-level outcomes, we regressed the management-reported measures of outcome on the same set of disaggregated combinations of EI, ESOP, or stock option

10. This is a data set of private sector businesses designed by the UC Berkeley Institute of Industrial Relations, and conducted by the UC Berkeley Survey Research Center between May and October of 2003. The sample included private and nonprofit establishments with five or more employees in California and excluded government agencies, public schools or universities, and agriculture, forestry, and fishing. The unit of observation was an establishment (i.e., a single physical location at which employees work and business is conducted). A total of 2,806 establishments were sampled, with 2,200 meeting the eligibility criteria. The response rate was 49.1 percent, giving the sample of 1,080 establishments.

Table 5.7 **Extent of participation in employee involvement and shared compensation in establishment-level data**

	Proportion of Workers Participation in			
	EI	Stock ownership	Profit sharing	Stock options
None	64.15%	89.26%	78.32%	88.97%
Under 25%	6.79%	5.11%	4.68%	4.39%
25% to 49%	6.47%	1.36%	2.68%	1.29%
50% to 74%	2.20%	1.18%	1.71%	0.64%
75% to 99%	1.65%	0.92%	1.23%	0.46%
All	18.74%	2.17%	11.39%	4.25%
Some	35.85%	10.74%	21.68%	11.03%

Source: California Establishment Survey, 2003.

ownership, and profit-sharing variables used in the table 5.4 analysis of the WRPS. The regressions include controls on firm size, age of establishment, two-digit level industry dummies, four-part occupational distribution (share of workforce that is managerial, clerical, sales, or blue-collar), share of workforce with college degrees, and share with collective bargaining contracts. We also estimate the impact of the shared compensation and decision-making variables on a summary outcome, which is simply the average of the four variables.

Table 5.8 reports the results. Row 1 shows a pattern of regression coefficients for the impact of the shared compensation and decision-making variable on the average of all outcomes in the CES data that resembles closely that found for their impacts on the average of all outcomes in the WRPS data. By itself, EI has a positive statistically significant effect; but the combination of EI, P, and O has an impact two times that of EI by itself. This corresponds to a 0.58 standard deviation gain—similar to the findings in WRPS. Row 2 shows that a formal EI program is associated with managers reporting greater employee decision making, but the combination of performance pay, ownership, and formal EI program registers the highest mark on worker decision making, though its difference from EI by itself is numerically small. Row 3 of the table shows that the combination of EI and some type of shared compensation leads to the largest and statistically significant effects on quality and financial performance. Finally, the fourth row shows that EI increases employee retention; and that the combination of ownership, performance pay, and EI is associated with greater retention than other configurations.

In sum, the results from the establishment survey support the finding from the WRPS that shared compensation and decision-making systems are complementary ways to increase participation and productivity at the workplace.

Table 5.8 **Regression coefficients and standard errors for the effects of EI, performance pay, and ownership combinations in establishment-level data**

	EI	P	O	P, O	P, EI	O, EI	P, O, EI
1. Average Outcome	0.12**	0.01	0.09	–0.09	0.14**	0.22***	0.23***
	(0.05)	(0.07)	(0.06)	(0.08)	(0.06)	(0.06)	(0.07)
2. Extent of participation in decision making	0.28***	0.15*	0.13**	0.13	0.23***	0.24***	0.36***
	(0.05)	(0.08)	(0.07)	(0.09)	(0.07)	(0.08)	(0.08)
3. Quality performance	0.12	0.03	0.08	–0.03	0.22**	0.35**	0.27*
	(0.09)	(0.12)	(0.11)	(0.17)	(0.11)	(0.13)	(0.14)
4. Financial performance	0.13	–0.04	0.15	–0.31	0.21	0.33**	0.32*
	(0.11)	(0.25)	(0.13)	(0.19)	(0.13)	(0.14)	(0.17)
5. Employee retention	0.06	0.05	0.10*	0.07	0.06	0.08	0.14**
	(0.04)	(0.07)	(0.05)	(0.07)	(0.05)	(0.07)	(0.06)

Source: California Establishment Survey, 2003.

Notes: Controls include firm-size (5 categories), 2-digit industries, percent of workforce with college degrees, percent of workforce managerial/clerical/sales/blue-collar, percent of workforce unionized, and age of establishment. Robust standard errors are within parentheses. Average outcome.

***Significant at the 1 percent level.

**Significant at the 5 percent level.

*Significant at the 10 percent level.

5.8 Conclusion

This chapter has shown that shared compensation is positively associated with shared decision making, and that combining shared compensation systems and employee involvement has greater impacts on outcomes than the systems separately. It has found comparable results in two very different data sets: the worker-based nationally representative WRPS and the establishment-based CES focusing on one state, California. In both cases shared decision making and compensation are more likely to be found together than if firms chose them independently and have larger impacts on outcomes than they have separately. Although our results are based on correlations rather than experimental variation, they are robust to some statistical tests for unobserved "firm effects." Since it is hard to square the effects of shared compensation systems with theories of individual behavior in which free-riding is important, our findings point to possible importance of corporate culture and related behavioral economic factors in determining employee activity.

Appendix A

Table 5A.1 Calculating the percentage of employees/firms with pay related to company/group performance

Stock ownership programs (about 25% of nonagricultural workforce)

1. Employee Stock Ownership Plans (ESOPS) and Stock Bonus Plans (1998)(8.5 million workers) — 8% of nonag empl
2. All Employee Stock Option Plans (1999) (7.0–10.0 million workers) — 8% of nonag empl
3. Receive stock options or opportunity to buy company stock (1999) — 26% of workforce
4. Workers eligible for options from 1,352 large firms, 1999 — 19% of covered
5. Firms offering stock-based compensation, ACA Compensation Survey 1999–2000

	Nonexempt		Exempt	
	Hourly nonunion	Salaried	Salaried	officers/execs
Stock Option	22	26	66	94
Co Stock Purchase	57	56	63	64
Stock Grant	6	6	22	48
Phantom Stock	1	1	5	16
Co Stock via 401(k)	68	72	73	72

6. Fortune 1000 companies offering options to 60% or more workers — 13%

Profit/gain sharing (around 25% of US workforce)

7. Workers in medium and large establishments with deferred profit sharing, 1997 — 19% of workforce
8. Profit/gain sharing in Fortune 1000 (1996) — 45% of firms
9. Firms with some profit sharing, 1993–1998 — 33%–40% of firms
10. Receive bonus based on own performance or company performance — 43% of workforce

Defined contribution pension funds invested in company stock (11% of workforce)

11. Employees with 401(k) plans — 55% of full-time workers in priv. nonfarm estab.
12. Estimated proportion of 401(k) assets in company stock
    - a) EBRI estimate, 1998 — 17.7%
    - b) Hewitt estimate, 1999 — 23.3%
13. Savings and thrift plans, % of workers in plans that allow for investment in company stock
    - Firm contribution — 42%
    - Worker contribution — 46%

Overall variable pay practices, FRB survey

14. Percentage of 125 Major Corporations (1999)

	All workers	Managers	Professionals
Any type	88%	85%	69%
Stock options	34%	33%	7%
Profit sharing	50%	48%	44%
Performance bonus	75%	69%	41%

Sources: Line 1: National Center for Employee Ownership, Employee Ownership Report, Jan/Feb 2000, p. 9.

Line 2: National Center for Employee Ownership, private communication.

Line 3: *Newsweek* Poll, June 24–25, 1999, www.pollingreport.come/workplay.htm.

Line 4: Watson Wyatt (2000) Survey of Top Management Compensation, www.watsonwyatt.com/homepage/us/new/pres_rel/Jan00/execpay_2.htm.

Table 5A.1 (continued)

Line 5: ACA (2000) Compensation Survey, of 2,683 US companies; 208 Canadian companies. See www.acaonline.org/resources/generic/html/aca-salarysurvey-99-2000.html. Number of responding firms ranged from 516 to 896.

Line 6: Association for Quality and Participation Survey, cited by NCEO.org/library/optionfact.html, "The rise of broadly granted employee stock options."

Line 7: US Bureau of Labor Statistics, Employee Benefits in Medium and Large Establishments, 1997, table 1; sum of percent reported deferred profit sharing in various forms.

Line 8: Economic Policy Foundation "US Wage and Productivity Growth" Washington, April 16, 1998.

Line 9: US Chamber of Commerce (1988); Doug Kruse, 1993, pp. 8–10.

Line 10: *Newsweek* Poll, June 24–25, 1999, www.pollingreport.come/workplay.htm.

Line 11: US Bureau of the Census, *Statistical Abstract* 1999, table 622.

Line 12: Economic Benefit Research Institute, EBRI Issue Brief Number 218, February 2000. Hewitt Resources: The Hewitt 401k Index observations, p. 2, www.hewitt.com/resc/resc055.htm.

Line 13: US Bureau of Labor Statistics, Employee Benefits in Medium and Large Establishments, 1997, table 155.

Line 14: Survey by FRB, Lebow et al. (1999), table 1.

Appendix B

Table 5A.2 **Means and standard deviations of outcome measures in WRPS and CES**

	Mean	Standard deviation
WRPS outcomes		
Average outcome	2.84	0.64
Productivity AVERAGE	2.65	0.74
Productive suggestions	2.45	0.96
Overall influence in job	2.87	0.85
Effort of fellow employees	2.34	0.60
Satisfaction AVERAGE	2.74	0.63
Overall satisfaction with workplace influence	2.92	0.85
Overall job satisfaction	2.42	0.86
Management-employee relations	2.87	0.94
Composite "grade" for management	1.88	0.79
Reported loyalty toward company	3.34	0.82
Reported trust toward company	3.10	0.90
Likely to keep working in company	0.58	0.49
Effectiveness of		
Town meetings	3.01	0.77
Open door policies for groups	3.18	0.72
Employee committees	3.15	0.68
Individual-based HR policies	3.00	0.82
CES outcomes		
Average outcome	1.85	0.40
Extent of participation in decision making	0.53	0.40
Quality performance	3.36	0.65
Financial performance	2.79	0.89
Employee retention	0.71	0.67

Appendix C

Table C1: Relevant WRPS questions for table 5.2

For compensation practices, the following question was asked:

D16. On your (main) job, do you . . . **(READ ITEMS, IN ORDER) (answer yes/know/don't know)**

d16a. Receive any bonuses based on profit sharing?
d16b. Receive any bonuses based on meeting workplace goals?
d16c. Participate in an employee stock ownership or ESOP plan?
d16d. Work in an employee-owned (company/organization)?

For Employee Involvement, the following two questions were asked. Only those answering yes to q24 were coded as being in EI programs.

q23. Some companies are organizing workplace decision-making in new ways to get employees more involved—using things like self-directed work teams, total quality management, quality circles, or other employee involvement programs. Is anything like this now being done in your (company/organization)?

1 Yes **(GO TO Q24)**
2 No
9 Don't know/refused

q24 **(ASK ONLY IF RESPONSE TO Q23 = 1)** Are you personally involved in any of these programs at work?

1 Yes
2 No **(GO TO Q27)**
9 Don't know/refused **(GO TO Q27)**

Table C2: Relevant WRPS questions for tables 5.4, 5.5, 5.6

Questions asked to respondents, and definitions of various indices:

All the four-point outcome variables were reordered (so that more is better) for the regressions. Below we report the actual questions used in the Survey, as well as different weighting schemes when appropriate. Unless otherwise reported, all "don't know" responses are coded as missing data.

Outcome variables:

1) "Loyalty to Company":

q9c. And, how much loyalty would you say you feel toward the (company/organization) you work for as a whole—a lot, some, only a little, or no loyalty at all?

1 A lot of loyalty
2 Some loyalty

3 Only a little loyalty
4 No loyalty at all

2) "Trust towards Company":
q10a. **(ASK OF FORM A ONLY)** In general, how much do you trust your (company/organization) to keep its promises to you and other employees? Would you say you trust your (company/organization)? **(READ)**
1 A lot
2 Somewhat
3 Only a little
4 Not at all
9 Don't know/refused **(DO NOT READ)**

3) "Index Rating of Management": This was constructed by taking the summated ratings (where A = 5, . . . , F = 0) on the following three questions, and then scaling by 4/15 to make the final outcome on a 1–4 scale:

16A. If you were to rate the performance of management in your company on a scale similar to school grades (A for excellent, B for good, C for Fair, D for Poor, and F for failure) what grade would you give MANAGEMENT in the following areas? (ROTATE ITEMS)

- Concern for employees
- Giving fair pay increases and benefits
- Willingness to share power and authority

4) "Management Employee Relations"
q11. Do you think relations between employees and management at your (company/organization) are BETTER than average, WORSE than average, or about the SAME as in other places?
1 Better
2 Worse
3 About the same
9 Don't know/Refused

5) "Job Satisfaction": (This was coded as follows, "1" was coded as 4, "8" as 2.5, and "2" as 1.)
q8. On an average day, what best describes your feeling about going to work? Would you say you usually . . . **(READ AND ROTATE CATEGORIES 1 AND 2)**
1 Look forward to it
2 Wish you didn't have to go
8 Don't care one way or the other/mixed feelings **(VOLUNTEERED)**
9 Don't know/refused

6) "Overall Reported Satisfaction with Influence"
q14_1,2,3,4. Now I want to ask about your involvement in decisions on the job. Overall, how satisfied are you with the influence you have in com-

pany decisions that affect your job or work life? Would you say you are . . . **(READ)**

1 Very satisfied
2 Somewhat satisfied
3 Not too satisfied
4 Not satisfied at all
9 Don't know/refused **(READ)**

7) "Effort of Fellow Employees" (Wave 2): This was constructed by taking the summated ratings (where A = 5, . . . , F = 0) on the following questions and then scaling by 4/15 to make the final outcome on a 1–4 scale:

16B. If you were to rate the performance of employees in your company on a scale similar to school grades (A for excellent, B for good, C for Fair, D for Poor, and F for failure) what grade would you give EMPLOYEES in the following areas? (ROTATE ITEMS)

*Willingness to work hard; *Concern for the success of the company; *Willingness to take on new responsibilities

8) "Overall Influence at Job:" This is a summated rating of 3 questions. But there are two versions asked depending of the 1st of second random half of form A.

q12a. **(ASK OF FORM A ONLY)** (Now I want to ask about your involvement in different decisions on the job.) How much direct involvement and influence do YOU have in **(ITEM)**? (A lot, Some, Only a little, No) direct involvement and influence at all? **(ASK ITEMS a–d ONLY OF THE FIRST HALF OF THE FORM AND ITEMS e–h ONLY OF THE SECOND HALF OF THE FORM).** (Responses: 1 A lot of direct involvement and influence, 2 Some direct involvement and influence, 3 Only a little direct involvement and influence, 4 No direct involvement and influence, 5 Does not apply **[VOLUNTEERED]**, 9 Don't know/refused)

q12aa. Deciding HOW to do your job and organize the work

q12ab. Deciding what TRAINING is needed for people in your work group or department

q12ad. Deciding how much of a RAISE in pay the people in your work group should get

q12ae. Setting GOALS for your work group or department

9) "Suggestions": This is a weighted summated rating index. The primary question is:

q17. **(IF S6 = 4)** How often, if ever, do YOU make suggestions to your supervisor or to management about how to improve quality or productivity? Would you say you make such suggestions . . . **(READ)**

1 Often
2 Sometimes

3 Hardly ever
4 Never
9 Don't know/refused **(DO NOT READ)**

This was weighted by the perception of how often these suggestions are listened to. The question is:

q18. **(IF S6 = 4)** When you, or other employees like you, make suggestions about improving quality or productivity, how often does management take them seriously? Would you say management . . . **(READ)**

1 Almost always
2 Sometimes
3 Hardly ever
4 Never . . . takes them seriously?
9 Don't know/refused **(DO NOT READ)**

10) "Worker Retention" is a variable that takes on 0 or 1 depending on whether the respondent says s/he is likely to remain with the company (i.e., responses 1 and 2) to the following question:

q7. Which ONE of the following four statements best describes how you think of your CURRENT job? Is it . . .

1 A LONG-TERM job you will stay in?
2 An opportunity for ADVANCEMENT in this SAME (company/organization)?
3 Part of a CAREER or profession that will probably take you to DIFFERENT companies?
4 A job you will probably LEAVE that is NOT part of a career?
5 Other
9 Don't know/refused

11) "Overall Outcome" is an averaged rating of all the previous variables (scaled to a 1–4 scale) with the following caveats. (9) and (7) were asked of different people so we combined them to make a single question about influence. Also, (3) and (8) were asked of a subsample, so these were not included. (However, we did construct the same variable including [3] and [8] for the subsample: results were similar).

12) The effectiveness of various HR programs came from the following questions:

Individual:

q29. On a different subject, I want to ask how problems involving INDIVIDUAL EMPLOYEES are solved at your workplace. Which of the following, if any, does your (company/organization) have? **(READ AND ROTATE)** **(Responses: 1 Yes, 2 No, 9 Don't know/refused)**

q29a. A PERSONNEL or human resources department

q29b. An OPEN DOOR policy so employees can tell upper management about problems with their immediate supervisors q29c. A GRIEVANCE procedure that uses an outside referee or arbitrator to settle disputes

q32. OVERALL, how effective is your (company's/organization's) system for resolving the problems INDIVIDUAL employees have at work? Would you say it is . . . **(READ)**

1 Very effective
2 Somewhat effective
3 Not too effective
4 Not effective at all
9 Don't know/refused **(DO NOT READ)**

The HR_Individual control variable for the outcomes regression was constructed by summing over q29a through q29c, and multiplying the sum by q32.

Group:

q36. Now let's talk about company policies regarding wages, benefits, and other things affecting employees as a GROUP. Which of the following, if any, does your (company/organization) have to deal with issues that affect employees as a group? (First,) (is/are) there . . . **(READ)(Responses: 1 Yes, 2 No, 9 Don't Know/Refused to Answer)**

q36a. Regular "town" meetings with employees, called by management

q36b. An open door policy for GROUPS of employees to raise issues about policies with upper management

q36c. A committee of employees that discusses problems with management on a regular basis

q37. **(ASK FOR EACH ITEM WHERE Q36 = 1)** How effective (has/have) **(ITEM)** been in resolving group problems or concerns—very effective, somewhat effective, not too effective, not effective at all? (Responses: 1 Very effective, 2 Somewhat effective, 3 Not too effective, 4 Not effective at all, 9 Don't know/Refused to answer)

q37a. The "town" meetings

q37b. The open door policy

q37c. The employee committee

The HR_Grp control variable for the outcomes regression was created by summing up the (weighted) incidences of the various group-based HR policies; that is, q37a*q36a + . . . + q37c*q36c.

Table C3: Questions from CES (for table 5.8)

QL5a: What percentage of **NON-MANAGERIAL AND NON-SUPERVISORY** workers are involved in regularly scheduled meetings to discuss work-related problems:

- None of them
- Less than

- More than 75% but less than all of them
- All of them? %

QL2a: How about the quality of product or service? Would you assess this quality at your workplace as:

- A lot better than average
- Better than average
- Average
- Below average
- A lot below average

QL2b: How about financial performance? Would you assess this quality at your workplace as:

- A lot better than average
- Better than average
- Average
- Below average
- A lot below average

QD3:

How many employees at this location left the worksite in the past year? (We divided this by the number of employees to get the attrition rate, and took 1-attrition rate to be the "retention rate.")

References

Akerlof, G., and J. Yellen. 1990. The fair wage-effort hypothesis and unemployment. *Quarterly Journal of Economics* 105 (2): 255–83.

American Compensation Association. 2000. Compensation survey. Available at: www.acaonline.org/resources/generic/html/aca-salarysurvey-99-2000.html.

Association for Quality and Participation Survey. 1998. The rise of broadly granted employee stock options. NCEO.org/library/option fact.html.

Black, S. E., and L. M. Lynch. 1997. How to compete: The impact of workplace practices and information technology on productivity. NBER Working Paper no. 6120. Cambridge, MA: National Bureau of Economic Research, August.

Blasi, J., and D. Kruse. 1991. *The new owners: The mass emergence of employee ownership in public companies and what it means to American business.* New York: Harper Business.

Brickley, J. A., and K. T. Hevert. 1991. Direct employee stock ownership: An empirical investigation. *Financial Management* 20 (2): 70–84.

Capelli, P., and D. Neumark. 1999. Do "high performance" work practices improve establishment-level outcomes? NBER Working Paper no. 7374. Cambridge, MA: National Bureau of Economic Research, October.

Chandler, A. 1977. *The visible hand.* Cambridge, MA: Bellknap Press.

Collins, D. 1998. *Gainsharing and power: Lessons from six Scanlon plans.* Ithaca, NY and London: Cornell University Press, ILR Press.

Dube, A. 2003. Identifying a lower bound on the Treatment Effect with Multiple Outcomes. Mimeo, University of Massachusetts, Amherst.

Economic Benefit Research Institute (EBRI). 2000. EBRI issue brief no. 218, February.

Economic Policy Foundation. 1998. US wage and productivity growth. Washington, DC, April 16.

Freeman, R., and M. Kleiner. 1998. The last American shoe manufacturers: Changing the method of pay to survive foreign competition. NBER Working Paper no. 6750. Cambridge, MA: National Bureau of Economic Research, October.

Freeman, R., M. Kleiner, and S. Ostroff. 2000. The anatomy and growth of employer involvement programs. NBER Working Paper no. w8050. Cambridge, MA: National Bureau of Economic Research, December.

Freeman, R., and J. Rogers. 1999. *What workers want.* New York: Russell Sage and Cornell University Press.

Gustman, A. L., and T. L. Steinmeier. 1999. What people don't know about their pensions and Social Security: An analysis using linked data from the Health and Retirement Study. NBER Working Paper no. 7368. Cambridge, MA: National Bureau of Economic Research, September.

Hewitt Resources. The Hewitt 401k Index observations. Available at: www.hewitt.com/resc/resc055.htm.

Ichniowski, C., K. Shaw, and G. Prennushi. 1997. The effects of human resource management practices on productivity: A study of steel finishing lines. *American Economic Review,* 87 (3): 291–313.

Kardas, P., A. L. Scharf, and J. Keogh. 1998. Wealth and income consequences of employee ownership: A comparative study from Washington state. Draft, Washington State Department of Community, Trade, and Economic Development.

Kato, T. 2000. The recent transformation of participatory employment practices in Japan. NBER Working Paper no. 7965. Cambridge, MA: National Bureau of Economic Research, October.

Kruse, D. 1993. *Profit sharing: Does it make a difference?* Kalamazoo, MI: W.E. Upjohn Institute for Employment Research.

Lawler, E. E., S. A. Mohrman, and G. E. Ledford. 1995. *Creating high performance organizations.* San Francisco: Jossey-Bass.

Lazear, E. 1999. Output-based pay: Incentives or sorting? NBER Working Paper no. 7419. Cambridge, MA: National Bureau of Economic Research, November.

Lebow, D., L. Sheiner, L. Slifman, and M. Star-McCluer. 1999. Recent trends in compensation practices. Federal Reserve Bank, July 15.

National Center for Employee Ownership (NCEO). 2000. Employee Ownership Report, Jan/Feb.

Newsweek. 1999. Newsweek Poll, June 24–25. Available at: www.pollingreport.come/workplay.htm.

Osterman, P. 1994. How common is workplace transformation and who adopts it? *Industrial and Labor Relations Review* 47 (2): 173–88.

Oyer, P. 2004. Why do firms use incentives that have no incentive effects? *Journal of Finance* 59:1619–40.

Profit Sharing Council of America (PSCA). 1993. *36th annual survey of profit sharing and 401(k) plans.* Chicago: PSCA.

Rosenbaum, P. R., and D. B. Rubin. 1983. The central role of the propensity score in observational studies for causal effects. *Biometrika* 70:41–55.

Schaller, W. L. 2001. Jumping ship: Legal issues relating to employee mobility in high technology industries. *Labor Lawyer* 17 (1): 25.

Simon, H. 1957. A formal theory of the employment relation. In *Models of man: Social and rational,* chapter 11. New York: John Wiley and Sons.

US Bureau of Labor Statistics. 1999. Employee benefits in medium and large establishments, 1997. Press Release USDL-99-02, January 7.

———. 1997. Employee benefits in medium and large establishments. Available at: http://www.allcountries.org/ucensus/703_employee_benefits_in-medium_and_large.html.

US Chamber of Commerce. 1998. *Employee benefits: 1997 edition.* Washington, DC: GPO.

US Department of Commerce, Bureau of the Census. 1999. *Statistical abstract 1999,* table 622.

Watson Wyatt. 2000. Survey of top management compensation. Available at: www.watsonwyatt.com/homepage/us/new/pres_rel/Jan00/execpay_2.htm.

6

How Does Shared Capitalism Affect Economic Performance in the United Kingdom?

Alex Bryson and Richard B. Freeman

There are three reasons for exploring the impact of shared capitalism—employee shared ownership, payment via stock options, and profit sharing and related group incentive pay—on economic outcomes in the United Kingdom.

The first is that shared capitalism is widespread. Table 6.1 shows the incidence and coverage of the major shared capitalist modes of pay in Britain for private sector workplaces with five or more employees in the 2004 Workplace Employment Relations Survey. Around one-fifth of workplaces had some form of *employee share ownership* scheme. This is comparable to US figures as discussed in chapter 1. These schemes include the Save as You Earn (SAYE)—an all-employee plan that gives workers tax breaks when they save to purchase their employer's shares but that does not require that they purchase the shares; the share incentive plan (SIP)—an all-employee scheme that offers tax breaks for employees holding shares in the company for which they work; and the Company Share Option Plan (CSOP)—where companies can grant chosen employees or directors up to £30,000 of tax and national insurance advantaged share options. The majority of the stock

Alex Bryson is a director of employment relations research at the National Institute of Economic and Social Research and Visiting Research Fellow at the Centre for Economic Performance, London School of Economics. Richard B. Freeman holds the Herbert Ascherman Chair in Economics at Harvard University and is a research associate of the National Bureau of Economic Research.

The authors would like to thank the Department for Business, Innovation and Skills Reform for financial assistance and the sponsors of WERS (BERR, ACAS, ESRC, and PSI) and the ESRC Data Archive for access to the data. Thanks also to Wayne Gray, John Addison, Nick Bloom, and participants at the NBER Productivity Lunch, the NBER Share Capitalism Conference, the 2007 American Economic Association Conference in Chicago, the 2006 Comparative Analysis of Enterprise Data Conference in Chicago, and the DTI WERS Conference for their comments on earlier versions of this chapter.

Table 6.1 Percentage of workplaces and employees covered by shared capitalism in the United Kingdom, 2004

	Workplaces (%)	Employees (%)
1. Stock ownership	20	32
Share schemes		
SIP	7	11
SAYE	12	21
CSOP	6	11
Others, including EMI	3	6
Coverage of schemes		
Managers only	3	4
1–99% nonmanagerial	3	6
100% nonmanagerial	14	22
2. Group-based payment by results	26	30
3. Profit-related pay		
Some	23	29
1–99% nonmanagerial	7	12
100% nonmanagerial	16	18
4. Number of schemes		
0	50	38
1	27	30
2	17	24
3	6	9
5. Individual variable pay		
Pay for individual PBR	34	43
Merit pay	16	26

Notes: Source Workplace Employment Relations Surveys. 2004 data relate to workplaces with 5+ employees. Details of the pay schemes are presented in the appendix.

ownership plans are open to all nonmanagerial employees in part because the tax code usually requires such coverage to obtain tax breaks.

Turning to profit sharing and related group incentive pay, one-quarter of workplaces had some form of *profit-related pay* for nonmanagerial employees, and one-quarter had some form of *group-based payment by results,* which is akin to gain sharing in the United States. This incidence is also comparable to the United States as discussed in chapter 1. The vast majority of share ownership schemes and over two-thirds of profit-related pay schemes cover all nonmanagerial employees. The percentage of employees with these schemes exceeds the percentage of workplaces with the schemes because larger workplaces are more likely to choose to pay workers in these ways.

The fourth row in the table combines the three group-level performance pay methods into an additive scale that takes the value 0 if the firm has none of these methods, 1 if it has one, 2 if it has two, and 3 if it has all three methods. It shows that half the firms have at least one scheme and that 62 percent of workers are covered by at least one scheme. Shared capitalism is, from this metric, as much part and parcel of the British capitalist economy as it is of the American economy, where almost half of workers are covered by at least one scheme (chapter 1).

The last row of the table gives the proportion of workplaces and employees who receive variable pay as individuals either through pay for performance or through merit pay. We treat these modes of payment separately because the "sharing" is related to individual performance as opposed to group performance and is thus more akin to piece rate pay than profit sharing.[1]

The second reason for examining shared capitalism in the United Kingdom is that the amount and nature of shared capitalist arrangements have changed over time. Profit-related pay and share-ownership schemes grew in the 1980s, spurred by government tax incentives. Data from Pendleton, Whitfield, and Bryson (2009, tables 5 and 6) on workplaces with twenty-five employees or more show that the proportion of private sector workplaces with some shared capitalist scheme increased from 40 percent in 1984 to 63 percent in 2004. The proportion of firms having profit-related pay increased from 19 percent to 44 percent, the proportion having group pay for performance increased from 15 percent to 25 percent, and the proportion having employee ownership increased from 22 percent to 28 percent.

The third reason is that the UK government has encouraged shared capitalist modes of pay with favorable tax treatment over time. In the 1980s the Conservative government gave tax advantages to profit-related pay. Since 1997 the Labour government has given tax advantages to share ownership schemes at the expense of profit-related pay schemes, which became fully taxable.[2] Unlike the United States, which gives tax breaks for collective ownership of shares through Employee Share Ownership Plans (ESOPs), the United Kingdom gives breaks for individual share ownership. The HM Revenue and Customs estimates that for 2002 and 2003 the Treasury spent about £800 million in tax relief per annum on these schemes (Oxera 2007a, 3). To see whether this is justifiable the Treasury commissioned an extensive econometric study of the impacts of shared capitalism on productivity (Oxera 2007a, 2007b), whose findings we compare with ours shortly.

Our analyses use linked employer-employee data from the British 2004 Workplace Employment Relations Survey (WERS)[3] to estimate the impact of shared capitalism on productivity and to assess some of the mechanisms by which it produces different outcomes at different workplaces. The 2004 WERS provides cross-sectional information on some 1,500 private sector workplaces obtained from HR managers and from employees work-

1. Factor analyses of the five types of performance pay—individual payments-by-results, merit pay, group payments-by-results, share ownership, and profit-related pay—identified two factors with eigenvalues above 1. Share ownership and profit-related pay load together, as do individual payments-by-results and merit pay. Group-level payments-by-results had a lower loading, which was pretty similar across the two factors.

2. For details: http://www.hmrc.gov.uk/stats/emp_share_schemes/menu.htm.

3. For full details of the survey see Kersley et al. (2006) and Chaplin et al. (2005).

ing in those workplaces. With the survey weights used throughout results are nationally representative of workplaces with five or more employees in Britain. These data provide an independent check on the results from the analysis of the General Social Survey and the NBER Shared Capitalism surveys used in previous chapters.

We find that:

1. Different forms of shared capitalist pay complement each other in the sense that firms are more likely to have them in combinations than if they chose forms of pay independently.

2. Firms change modes of compensation frequently, with some adopting schemes and others eliminating them so that the gross changes in schemes are far more numerous than the net changes.

3. Shared capitalist pay is positively associated with other forms of pay and workplace arrangements: individual payment by results, employer reports of devolving decision making to employees, using subjective appraisals of worker performance, monitoring of outputs, and reduced monitoring of workers.

4. Firms with shared capitalist pay, particularly with share ownership schemes, have higher labor productivity than firms without such forms of pay. The impacts of shared capitalism on productivity are larger when the firm combines several schemes.

6.1 Conceptual Issues

The traditional rationale for shared capitalist pay is that it aligns worker and employer objectives in maximizing output. To do this, shared capitalism must overcome free-rider problems associated with any group incentive system and deal with the fact that virtually any contingent pay, including piece rates for individuals, gives incentives for some forms of desirable behavior but not for other forms.[4] Principal/agent problems are ubiquitous in a world where contracts are necessarily incomplete. These issues are addressed in chapter 2 in the discussion of anti-shirking behavior.

Shared capitalism is normally associated with certain modes of work organization. Since firms that pay workers on the basis of firm or group performance do so in the hope of inducing them to take actions that improve firm performance, they are also likely to empower workers to make decisions that affect performance, particularly where the employee has private information about the production process. Group incentive pay may also be

4. Annual profit-sharing bonuses may, for example, induce workers to try hard in the short run but to neglect activities that benefit the firm over a longer horizon. Worker ownership whose benefits do not reach workers until they retire may fail to induce workers to try hard in the present. Piece rates or tournaments can reduce cooperation and the sharing of knowledge at workplaces and even induce one worker to sabotage a rival.

used as an incentive for workers to share their knowledge about the production process with other workers and the employer (Levine and Tyson 1990; Jones 1987).

By contrast, giving workers greater decision-making power absent financial incentives might adversely affect motivation (Ben-Avner and Jones 1995): "they want me to do more without paying me more." And giving shared capitalist pay without greater decision-making power may also fail to affect productivity: "they are making my income risky by varying my pay with performance without giving me autonomy to raise performance."

Shared capitalist modes of pay should also be associated with a shift in management monitoring from watching what workers do to monitoring their final products. When the firm cannot readily observe effort but can monitor outputs, incentive pay related to outputs will motivate effort, substituting for monitoring effort. Shared capitalism may provide workers an opportunity for extra pay by substituting for costly monitoring in situations where it is *especially* difficult to monitor, which is consistent with gift exchange versions of efficiency wage theory. By contrast, when the firm finds it easier to monitor workers than to monitor output, we would expect the firm to use straight-time pay.[5] Indeed, Frederick Taylor viewed output-based pay as a mechanism for the avoidance of shirking.[6] The advent of information and communication technologies (ICT)-based monitoring, including on-line monitoring, electronic point-of-sale equipment, and electronic time recording gave management new tools to monitor previously difficult-to-monitor jobs and output, potentially making this interaction more important than in the past.[7]

Some analysts view individual pay for performance as the polar opposite of group incentive pay. Individual pay for performance is a form of piece rate that induces employees to improve their personal output (and maybe to sabotage the output of others if that might improve their chances for a promotion), whereas group pay induces them to work cooperatively with others. Either you work for yourself or you work for the group. Under some conditions, the two forms of pay may indeed be antithetical but under others individual pay for performance can complement group incentive pay. Consider a situation in which maximizing output and profits requires that workers do their own work *and* also help others. In this case management will need two instruments to induce workers to spend some time working on

5. Daniel and Millward (1983) argue "Traditionally the purpose of PBR systems of pay has been to encourage workers to increase effort and output. . . . In practice . . . there has been a tendency for PBR to become more an instrument of management control designed to ensure consistency of output" (205).

6. Gallie, Felstead, and Green (1998) show that control of workers through close supervision, pay incentives, and appraisal systems all grew in Britain in the late 1980s and early 1990s.

7. White et al. (2004, 100) estimated that in 2002 ICT-based monitoring systems were "already covering around half the workforce and appear to be spreading rapidly." Half of the workplaces with ICT monitoring were using it to evaluate individuals (96).

their own and some time working cooperatively. Just as profit-seeking managements mix imperfect objective measures of performance with subjective evaluation (Baker, Gibbons, Murphy 1994), management could mix pay for individual performance and pay for group performance to induce workers to undertake both activities. Management could even use individual pay for performance as a tool against the temptation to free-ride on the group.

The most far-reaching hypothesis in recent analyses of the effect of human resource management on productivity and labor practices is the "complementarities thesis" that advanced labor practices work most effectively when bundled together into a consistent high-performance workplace (Ichniowski et al. 1996; Pil and MacDuffie 1996). This hypothesis implies that firms should adopt shared capitalist modes of pay and complementary forms of work organization as a package rather than introducing them individually. Some analysts go further and link shared capitalism with the firm's competitive strategy (Huselid 1995; Schuler and Jackson 1987). They argue that firms that compete on the basis of the quality of output should be more attuned to group incentives than firms that compete on the basis of low cost of generic output, where piece rates might be more effective.

We examine the notion that shared capitalist modes of pay and work organization has important complementarities in two ways.

First, we test whether firms choose combinations of pay schemes in proportions that diverge from what we would expect had they chosen them as independent draws from separate urns. Under the null hypothesis, if 50 percent of firms have profit sharing and 50 percent have employee share ownership, the proportion of firms with both profit sharing and employee ownership would be 25 percent. If the complementary hypothesis is correct, the proportion of firms with both practices would exceed 25 percent, whereas if the forms are substitutes, the proportion with both practices would fall short of 25 percent. Using a regression design, we also examine whether individual pay for results, managerial monitoring, and worker decision making are related to shared capitalist modes of pay, other factors held fixed. If the complementary hypothesis is correct, the shared capitalist practices should have positive effects on worker-friendly practices and negative effects on hierarchical control practices.

Second, we follow the bulk of the complementary literature by estimating production functions that relate output to inputs, including modes of compensation, and test for complementary relations among modes of compensation. If the complementary hypothesis is correct, shared capitalist practices X and Z will have greater effects on output when they operate together than when they operate separately. This implies that the regression coefficient on interaction terms such as their product XZ should be positive.

As with other production function models, without identifiably exogenous variation in input variables—in this case shared capitalist pay as well as capital and labor inputs—the regression results are best interpreted as reflecting associations among endogenous variables. Depending on the heterogeneity among firms, moreover, the associations could be affected by selectivity and thus differ from the associations we would get from randomly assigning compensation and practices among firms. Still, our two-part analysis—looking for complementary links in the combinations of shared capitalist modes of pay and looking for such links in production functions—provides a stronger test of the hypothesized positive effect of shared capitalism on outputs than would analysis of either combinations or production functions separately.

6.2 Combinations of Practices

Figure 6.1 uses a Venn diagram to display the incidence of combinations of profit-related pay, share ownership, and group-based incentives in private sector workplaces with five or more employees in the WERS 2004 data. Our test of complementarity in these data compares those proportions with the proportions that would result if the firm selected practices independently on the basis of the proportion in the entire sample. The bottom part of the figure gives the actual incidence of each element in the diagram and the incidence we would expect from the binomial distribution of independent draws based on the proportion of each mode in the population. Half of the workplaces have no group-based incentive payments, which is statistically significantly different from the 39 percent predicted from the independent hypothesis. Twenty-seven percent had one scheme compared to 43.5 percent predicted to have a single scheme; 17 percent of workplaces had two schemes, which is close to the 15.5 percent predicted to have two schemes, but 6.2 percent had all three schemes, which is over three times the 1.7 percent predicted to have three schemes. Thus, there were more workplaces at the extremes of the distribution than predicted, which is consistent with the idea that these schemes are complementary (although it is possible that managerial preferences or some other dynamic is at work).

Using the 1984 Workplace Industrial Relations Survey, which surveyed workplaces with twenty-five or more employees, we made similar computations for that year. These data show a pattern that is similar to that in 2004, albeit with much lower levels of the use of the various schemes. In 1984, 59.5 percent of workplaces had no form of shared capitalist pay compared to a predicted level of 52.9 percent; 25.3 percent had one form of the pay compared to a predicted 36.6 percent, whereas 13.7 percent had two such forms compared to a predicted 9.2 percent while 1.4 percent had three such forms compared to a predicted 0.7 percent. More workplaces had two or three forms of shared capitalist pay and more had zero forms of shared capitalist pay than predicted. In sum, the calculations for 1984 as well as for 2004 reject the null hypothesis that workplaces select shared capitalist modes of compensation independently in favor of the complementary hypothesis.

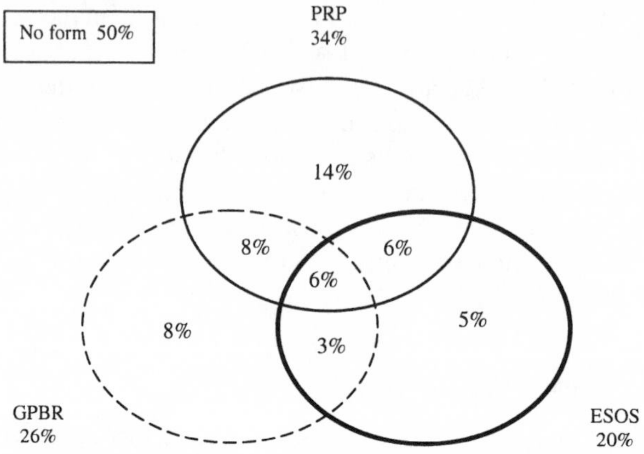

Actual and predicted incidence of Share Capitalism Practices

	Actual	Predicted
PRP	34.5	-
ESOS	19.6	-
GPBR	25.7	-
No scheme	49.7	39.1
Single scheme:	27.0	43.5
PRP	14.4	20.5
ESOS	4.6	9.5
GRPP	8.2	13.5
Two schemes:	17.0	15.5
ESOS & PRP	5.7	5.1
ESOS & GRPP	3.1	3.3
PRP & GRPP	8.2	7.1
Three schemes:	6.2	1.7

Fig. 6.1 Incidence of combinations of shared capitalist pay schemes, WERS 2004 (workplaces with five or more employees)

6.3 Changes in Modes of Pay

The 2004 WERS Panel provides panel data on a random subset of a nationally representative sample of workplaces with ten or more employees that the survey interviewed in 1998. The longitudinal file allows us to examine changes in shared capitalist modes of compensation over time. Rows 1 and 2 of table 6.2 record the incidence of different schemes in the panel data in 1998 and 2004. We differentiate the deferred profit-related pay systems from the others to highlight the fact that the incidence of profit-related pay declined due to the cessation of the tax advantage given to deferred

Table 6.2 **The distribution of shared capitalist forms of pay and proportion of workplaces changing their form of pay, 1998–2004 Panel of private sector workplaces with ten or more employees**

	PRP excluding deferred schemes	All PRP including deferred schemes	Employee share ownership schemes	Any PRP/ESOS	Payments-by-results
Distribution in %					
Distribution of all workplaces in 1998	42	47	20	48	23
Distribution of all workplaces in 2004	42	42	20	49	33
Net change	0	–5	0	1	10
Changes in distribution					
Did not have program in 1998 nor 2004	43	40	71	37	58
Added program between 1998 and 2004	15	18	9	14	9
Had program in 1998 but dropped it by 2004	15	13	10	15	18
Had program in both 1998 and 2004	27	29	11	34	15
Gross change	30	31	19	29	27

Source: Workplace Employment Relations Panel Survey 1998–2004.

profit-related pay schemes. The percentage with other profit-related schemes remained constant at 42 percent; the percentage of workplaces with employee share ownership schemes also remained stable, so that the primary increase in shared capitalist modes of compensation occurred through a 10 percentage point increase in group payments by results. The net change figures in row 3 show rather modest changes in the overall distribution.

But the part of the table labeled "changes in distribution" shows that beneath the stability in the nondeferred performance-related pay (PRP) schemes and in the employee share ownership schemes there is considerable switching among schemes by workplaces. Underlying the 42 percent constant proportion of workplaces with profit-related pay exclusive of the deferred schemes are shifts in nearly one-third of the workplaces: 15 percent of workplaces adopted profit-related pay while 15 percent ended schemes other than the deferred ones that lost tax privileges. Similarly, underlying the 20 percent constant percentage of workplaces with Employee Share Ownership Schemes (ESOS) is a change in 19 percent of workplaces. Even the group payments-by-results, which increased by 10 percentage points from 1998 to 2004, show a gross change of 27 percentage points.

How should we interpret this huge difference between net and gross changes? One interpretation of the high amount of switching is that it reflects experimentation on the part of employers in search of the best arrangements. Another interpretation is that firms change practices because the optimal compensation system changes, perhaps because what matters to employers is the "newness" of a scheme rather than the attributes of a particular payment method. Whichever interpretation is right, it would seem that these changes are not major overhauls in employer practices, implying that the treatments and the inputs required to maintain them are unlikely to be large—that is, switching costs are low.

The substantial amount of switching may create problems for employee expectations. Employee cooperation may be encouraged by stable, well-known plans that create a common understanding of how employees will be rewarded. Shared capitalism can then help to cement long-term bonds between the employer and employees, and dropping or substantially altering these plans may undo the common understanding that underlies better performance. On the other hand, switching plans may be warranted when the plans are not working as initially intended, and a new formula or method is needed to reward the right behaviors. In many cases the switching may not disrupt the perceived commitment of a firm to shared capitalism, but simply reflect experimentation to find the right approach.

To see how the shifts in programs among workplaces might work themselves out in the long run, we have applied Markov chain analysis to the 1998 to 2004 panel data. Specifically, we organized the data into transition matrices whose elements are the probabilities of moving from a given combination of practices to other combinations and, on the assumption that the transition probabilities are constant, estimated the equilibrium or steady state distribution of practices.

Table 6.3 records our results. Panel A defines the state variables simply as the number of shared capitalist pay programs at a workplace. Since there are four possible states, from zero to three programs, the transition matrix is 4 by 4. We raised the matrix to the power 2000 to obtain the steady state distribution. The columns labeled 1998 and 2004 give the proportion of workplaces with the specified numbers of programs in each year, while the column labeled equilibrium is our estimated steady state distribution. It "predicts" that the number of workplaces with two to three programs will rise while the numbers with one program will remain nearly constant, so that shared capitalism will increase gradually over time. Panel B defines the state variables as each of the combinations in our Venn diagram. Since in this case there are eight possible states, the transition matrix is 8 by 8. The calculations here tell a similar but more detailed story about change. The Markov analysis predicts a drop in the proportion of workplaces with only ESOS in contrast to the increase in that proportion from 1998 to 2004 and an increase in the proportion with ESOS and profit-related pay in contrast to the decrease in that proportion from 1998 to 2004.

Consistent with the analysis of the 2004 patterns in figure 6.1, the analysis of the panel data supports the complementarity hypothesis, with the number of workplaces having all three programs and the number expected

Table 6.3 **Markov chain analysis of equilibrium distribution of shared capitalist modes of pay**

	1998	2004	Equilibrium
A Number of shared capitalist pay schemes: esos, prp, group pbr			
0	.499	.474	.438
1	.292	.291	.287
2	.156	.155	.184
3	.053	.080	.090
B Specific combinations of pay schemes			
No shared capitalist pay	.499	.474	.444
Single systems	.292	.291	.281
ESOS only	.035	.054	.047
GRPP only	.049	.044	.040
PRP only	.208	.194	.184
Two systems	.156	.155	.190
ESOS + GRPP	.001	.010	.013
ESOS + PRP	.108	.060	.081
GRPP + PRP	.047	.085	.096
All three	.053	.080	.094

Source: Tabulated from the 1998–2004 WERS panel data file on workplaces.

Notes: Panel A; n = 587 private sector workplaces in WERS panel. All data are survey weighted. Last column based on analyses by James Mitchell, NIESR, for which we are grateful. Transition matrix A (in fact A' to ensure each column sums to unity) is raised to the power 2,000. Since one of A's eigenvalues is unity we have an ergodic Markov chain and the long-run forecast is thus independent of the current state. Panel B; due to rounding, the rows of the transition matrix summed to 1.0001000 so we subtracted 0.0001 to ensure that they sum to unity. GRPP = group payments-by-results; ESOS = employee share ownership schemes; PRP = profit-related pay.

to have more in the future exceeding the number that would be found if firms selected the modes of compensation independently.

6.4 Relation to Other Workplace Practices

To examine the relation between shared capitalism and other workplace policies and practices—individual payment by result, worker autonomy, and managerial monitoring of work activity, outputs, and appraisals—we use a linear regression model. The dependent variables in the regression are the measures of workplace policies and practices. The key independent variables are the forms of shared capitalist compensation.[8] The regressions hold fixed factors such as industry, size of the workplace, size of firm, and the like.

Table 6.4 presents the regression coefficients on dummy variables for employee stock ownership, group payment by results, and profit-related

8. Models were estimated with survey-weighted OLS. Results were not sensitive to the use of probit or ordered probit estimation.

Table 6.4 **Coefficients and *t*-statistics relating other pay and workplace policies to shared capitalist pay schemes**

	INDPBR (1)	INDPBR (2)	Merit (3)	Merit (4)	Decision (5)	Decision (6)	Mon in (7)	Mon in (8)	Mon out (9)	Mon out (10)	Apprais (11)	Apprais (12)
GRPP	0.266		0.006		0.241		0.052		0.289		0.150	
	(6.01)**		(0.18)		(1.13)		(0.66)		(2.74)**		(1.75)	
PRP	0.075		0.089		0.486		–0.051		0.280		0.082	
	(1.91)		(2.71)**		(2.50)*		(0.74)		(2.98)**		(1.06)	
ESOS	0.011		–0.008		–0.138		–0.018		0.503		0.472	
	(0.20)		(0.20)		(0.50)		(0.21)		(3.72)**		(4.90)**	
GRPP + PRP + ESOS		0.432		0.070		0.445		–0.053		1.168		0.675
		(5.53)**		(0.98)		(1.23)		(0.39)		(6.65)**		(4.17)**
ESOS + PRP		0.077		0.124		0.306		–0.101		0.429		0.560
		(0.98)		(1.82)		(0.67)		(0.66)		(2.11)*		(3.72)**
ESOS + GRPP		0.262		0.056		0.412		0.153		1.199		0.617
		(2.31)*		(0.63)		(0.79)		(1.10)		(4.16)**		(2.91)**
ESOS only		–0.046		–0.067		–0.358		–0.170		0.496		0.673
		(0.61)		(1.38)		(0.73)		(1.34)		(2.51)*		(4.88)**
PRP + GRPP		0.242		0.074		0.814		–0.006		0.537		0.249
		(3.52)**		(1.41)		(2.45)*		(0.06)		(3.29)**		(1.76)
GRPP only		0.324		0.025		0.004		–0.057		0.035		0.273
		(4.54)**		(0.50)		(0.01)		(0.39)		(0.23)		(1.89)

PRP only		0.101		0.089		0.519		–0.044		0.333		0.168
		(1.96)		(1.97)*		(1.93)		(0.43)		(2.77)**		(1.60)
Constant	0.271	0.294	0.067	0.081	10.181	10.044	2.012	1.938	1.098	1.168	1.252	1.222
	(1.75)	(1.93)	(0.59)	(0.72)	(16.38)**	(15.81)**	(7.29)**	(6.76)**	(3.39)**	(3.65)**	(4.76)**	(4.65)**
Observations	1,680	1,684	1,680	1,684	1,680	1,684	1,680	1,684	1,680	1,684	1,680	1,684
R^2	0.22	0.23	0.09	0.09	0.20	0.19	0.08	0.08	0.30	0.31	0.28	0.28

Notes: INDPBR (0,1): individual payments-by-results. Merit (0,1): merit pay. Decision (0,12): employer perceptions of employee decision-making autonomy among employees in the workplace's largest occupational group or "core employees." The HR managers were asked: "Using the scale on this card, to what extent would you say that individuals in [Title of the largest occupational group] here have variety in their work, discretion over how they do their work, control over the pace at which they work, involvement in decisions over how their work is organized?" The scale on the card was "a lot, some, a little, none." An additive scale was created running from 0 ("none" on all four items) to 12 ("a lot" on all four items). Mon in (0, 4): additive scale for the monitoring of worker inputs, the workplace scoring a point when the quality of employees' work is monitored by supervisors, if some/all supervisors can dismiss employees for unsatisfactory performance, where 20 percent + of employees are supervisors. A point is deducted if employees monitor the quality of their own work (co-monitoring). Finally a point is added to the scores so they range from 0, 4 rather than –1, 3. Mon out (0, 4): additive scale for monitoring outputs scoring a point when the quality of output is monitored through inspectors located elsewhere, through customer surveys, records of faults/complaints are kept, and there are targets for productivity and records kept. Apprais (0, 3): additive scale for appraisal systems scoring a point when all nonmanagerial staff are appraised, appraisals occur half-yearly or quarterly, and nonmanagerial pay is linked to performance appraisal. All models contain following controls: firm size (three dummies); single-workplace organization (single dummy); industry (twelve dummies); foreign owned (single dummy); workplace aged 25+ year (single dummy); recognizes union for pay bargaining (two dummies); largest occupational group (eight dummies); has many competitors (single dummy); product market is growing (single dummy). In addition, the INDPBR models contain controls for monitoring inputs, outputs, appraisal, and decision making; the decision-making models contain controls for monitoring inputs and outputs and appraisals; and the monitoring and appraisal models contain controls for decision making.

***Significant at the 1 percent level.

**Significant at the 5 percent level.

*Significant at the 10 percent level.

pay; and on dummy variables for the seven independent categories in the Venn diagram.

The dependent variable in columns (1) and (2) is a dichotomous measure of whether workers receive individual payment by results (see appendix). The estimated coefficients show that individual pay by results is more likely in the presence of shared capitalist pay than otherwise. In column (1) the biggest effects occur for group payment by results, indicating that these two forms of compensation are very closely linked. In column (2) the largest coefficient occurs when workplaces have all three forms of shared capitalist pay. These results suggest that, as argued, individual and group payment for results are complements, though we have no reliable way with the WERS data to determine whether firms with the two modes of pay are in fact choosing the optimal levels.

The dependent variable in columns (3) and (4) is merit pay, which is based on a subjective assessment of individual performance by a supervisor or manager. Again, there are indications of a positive association with share capitalism, but in this case it is confined to an association with profit-related pay.

Columns (5) and (6) measure employee autonomy in decision making as reported by human resource managers in response to a question regarding "the extent to which you would say that individuals in the largest occupational group: have variety in their work, discretion over how they do their work, control over the pace at which they work, involvement in decisions over how their work is organized?" The responses have a four-point scale ("a lot, some, a little, none"), from which we formed a summated rating that went from 0 ("none" on all four items) to 12 ("a lot" on all four items).[9] Ten percent of workplaces scored less than 5 on this scale, 47 percent scored 5 to 8, and 44 percent scored 9 or more.

The regression coefficients show modestly greater autonomy for worker decision making in the presence of shared capitalist pay than otherwise, with the primary impact coming through profit-related pay in column (5) and the combination of profit-related pay and group payment for results in column (6). While it is dangerous to compare results from different surveys across countries, the link between shared capitalist pay and employee decision making seems weaker in the United Kingdom than in the United States.[10]

The dependent variable in columns (7) and (8) measures the extent of managerial monitoring of worker *inputs.* It is based on responses to questions about whether workplaces used managers or supervisors to monitor

9. Factor analysis of these items produces a single factor with an eigenvalue of 2.21 and a Cronbach alpha of 0.73, suggesting that the items are aspects of a single construct.

10. As an alternative measure, we also examined employee responses to an analogous question: "In general, how much influence do you have over the following. . . . What tasks you do in your job, the pace at which you work, how you do your work, the order in which you carry out tasks, the time you start or finish your working day?" with responses coded using an additive scale comparable to that used for employers. Because there were five questions the scale ran from (0 to 15). This variable was unrelated to shared capitalist modes of pay.

the quality of work, whether supervisors have the power to dismiss workers, and whether workplaces have a high percentage (20 percent +) of supervisors among their employees, and on whether the firm reports that employees monitor the quality of their own output (in which case a point is deducted from this scale). This variable is scaled from 0 to 4 (see footnote to the table for details). The regression coefficients show that shared capitalism is not significantly associated with managerial monitoring of worker inputs.

The dependent variable in columns (9) and (10) is a measure of employer monitoring of *outputs*. It is based on questions regarding the use of inspectors in separate departments, customer surveys, keeping records of faults and complaints, and the use of records to monitor labor productivity targets. This variable is scaled from 0 to 4. The regression coefficients show that shared capitalist pay is strongly associated with more managerial monitoring of outputs, with employee share schemes having the largest impact in column (9) and the presence of all three schemes or the combination of share schemes and group payments-by-results having the largest impact in column (10).

Finally, columns (11) and (12) examine the relation between employer use of appraisal systems of how workers are doing and shared capitalist pay. The measure of appraisal is an additive scale based on whether the firm appraises all nonmanagerial staff, if appraisals occur half-yearly or quarterly, and if nonmanagerial pay is linked to performance appraisal. This variable is scaled from 0 to 3. The positive regression coefficient on the share ownership dummy variable in column (11) shows that workplaces with shared ownership modes of pay do more appraisal of employees than other workplaces. In column (12) the message is similar, with large coefficients on the interaction relating to workplaces that have stock ownership and on the coefficient on the "only share ownership" dummy variable.

The associations between shared capitalist compensation and the other policies and practices shown in these regressions do not tell us how management coordinates the various pay schemes to form a coherent working environment, but they do support the notion that shared capitalist arrangements work best in conjunction with other innovations in the employment relationship consistent with the model we sketched out earlier.

6.5 Basic Productivity Relations

> "Share ownership offers employees a real stake in their company . . . encourage(s) the new enterprise culture of team work in which everyone contributes and everyone benefits from success. . . . Employee share ownership has a contribution to make towards increasing Britain's productivity." (HM Treasury 1998, 1–2)

To see how shared capitalist modes of pay affect productivity we estimate production functions. We have three measures of productivity. The first measure is an index based on the responses of human resource managers to the question: "Compared with other establishments in the same industry how would you assess your workplace's labor productivity?" Responses are ordered in a five-point scale from "a lot better than average" to "a lot below average". Of the 1,512 human resource managers who answered this question in the 2004 WERS, 6 percent thought their workplace's productivity was either "below" or "a lot below average"[11], 42 percent thought it was "average", 42 percent thought it was "better than average," and 10 percent described it as "a lot above average." Most British studies of the effect of modes of compensation on productivity have used questions of this form in their analyses.[12]

We supplement this measure with two accounting measures collected in the 2004 WERS by a Financial Performance Questionnaire (FPQ): gross output per worker (the ratio of total value of sales of goods and services over the past year to total employment); and gross value added per worker (the ratio of total sales minus the total value of purchases of goods, materials, and services divided by total employment).[13] These measures are correlated with one another at 0.39. But they are not correlated with manager reports of productivity relative to the industry average, suggesting that the financial performance questionnaire and human resource manager reports on productivity contain different information about the workplace.

Given these three measures, our first inclination was to give more weight to the accounting measures in our productivity analysis. The accounting measures underlie standard production function regressions and are more objective than the management reports. But we quickly learned that the accounting measures have problems. Only 47 percent of workplaces participating in WERS responded to the financial performance questions, and some responses were such large outliers that we dropped them from the analysis.[14] After trimming the top and bottom 2.5 percent of values, we had valid data for 586 workplaces for productivity measured as sales per employee and for 524 workplaces for productivity measured as value added per employee.[15] This reduced our sample by about 60 percent. We will give roughly equal weight to the three estimates in our assessment of the effects of shared capitalism on productivity.

Table 6.5 gives the coefficients for the association between the three mea-

11. We collapsed the responses "a lot below" and "below average" into a single category due to the small number of responses in that part of the distribution.

12. Kersley et al. (2006, 287–89) compare alternative productivity measures.

13. The FPQ questionnaire is: www.wers2004.info/wers2004/crosssection.php#fpq. Chaplin et al. (2005) describe the data and administration of the questionnaire.

14. Most of the data relate to an accounting period ending in 2004, with some data relating to a period ending in 2003. Where data did not relate to a full calendar year we adjusted accordingly.

15. The estimation samples are a little lower because we dropped a few observations with missing dependent variables.

Table 6.5 **Coefficients and *t*-statistics relating manager reports of productivity, Ln sales/employee and Ln value added/employee to shared capitalist pay schemes**

	Management view of lab prod (1)	Management View of lab prod (2)	Ln sales/ Em (3)	Ln Sales/ Em (4)	Ln VA/ emp (5)	Ln VA/ emp (6)
GRPP	0.042	0.031	0.001	0.005	0.001	–0.000
	(0.34)	(0.25)	(0.01)	(0.04)	(0.06)	(0.03)
PRP	0.113		–0.040		–0.003	
	(1.09)		(0.33)		(0.31)	
ESOS	0.305		0.436		0.033	
	(2.28)*		(2.90)**		(2.75)**	
PRP (ref: none)						
1–99% covered		–0.149		0.033		0.026
		(0.81)		(0.18)		(1.96)
100% covered		0.269		–0.284		–0.015
		(2.09)*		(1.63)		(1.78)
ESOS (ref: none)						
Managers only		0.180		0.475		–0.001
		(0.95)		(2.05)*		(0.05)
1–99% nonmanagers covered		0.032		0.274		0.009
		(0.11)		(1.43)		(0.47)
100% nonmanagers covered		0.356		0.513		0.045
		(2.36)*		(2.96)**		(3.24)**
Cut 1:Constant	–0.960	–0.983				
	(2.48)*	(2.56)*				
Cut 2:Constant	0.702	0.687				
	(1.77)	(1.75)				
Cut 3:Constant	2.196	2.189				
	(5.43)**	(5.45)**				
Constant			4.523	4.546	6.553	6.551
			(13.93)**	(14.14)**	(227.88)**	(240.53)**
Observations	1,487	1,486	577	577	517	517
R^2			0.54	0.55	0.34	0.37

Notes: Control variables are as per table 6.4 except that the monitoring and appraisal variables were entered separately rather than additive scales and individual PBR and merit pay are included as controls.

***Significant at the 1 percent level.

**Significant at the 5 percent level.

*Significant at the 10 percent level.

sures of productivity and the incidence and intensity of shared capitalist pay in terms of the proportion of workers covered. All models are run with sampling weights that are the inverse of the probability of sample selection. The weights for the models that use the financial performance questionnaire data also adjust for nonresponse, as described in Chaplin et al. (2005). We use a robust estimator to account for heteroskedasticity. The coefficients in models (1) and (2) are from ordered probits for the subjective measure of labor productivity relative to the industry average. The coefficients in models (3) and (4) and in models (5) and (6) are from linear regression models for log sales per employee and log value added per employee, respectively.

The odd-numbered columns give the results for the incidence of shared capitalist forms of pay. They show share ownership schemes are positively associated with labor productivity on all three productivity measures while neither profit-related pay nor group pay for performance have any noticeable relation to productivity. The even-numbered columns give the results when the measure of shared capitalist pay considers the coverage of the pay system—whether it includes all workers or just management and perhaps a select few others. They show that the stock ownership schemes that enlist all employees raise productivity by all three of our measures, while schemes targeted at managers only are positively associated with sales per employee. Again, the other forms of shared capitalism have little relation to the measures of productivity.

6.6 Complementarity in Production

For our production function test of the complementarity of shared capitalist forms of pay, we regressed each of our measures of productivity on dummy variables for the seven independent categories in the Venn diagram. The calculations in table 6.6 summarize the results. There is evidence for complementarity in the effects with each of the measures of productivity, but the particular mixture of pay systems that have the largest impact on productivity differs among the productivity measures.

In the regression for managers' perception of productivity the biggest impacts occur when workplaces have all three forms of pay, or have employee share ownership and profit-related pay or employee ownership and group payments-by-results. This indicates that the positive impact of share ownership found in table 6.5 occurs when share ownership is combined with profit-related pay or group payments-by-results.

By contrast, in the regression in which productivity is measured by sales per worker, the biggest impacts on productivity occur when workplaces have employee share ownership and profit-related pay or employee ownership and group pay for results. Having share ownership by itself does better than having all the schemes together.

The interactions are weakest in the value added regression, with the biggest impacts occurring when workplaces combine employee share ownership with group pay for results followed by combining it with profit-related pay.

Finally, if we simplify the regressions by replacing the share ownership interactions with a single dummy identifying share ownership in combination with group payments-by-results and/or profit-related pay, the dummy is positive and significant for all three productivity measures, confirming that

Table 6.6 **Coefficients and t-statistics for the effects of complementarity among shared capitalist pay and other workplace arrangements on managers' reports of productivity (labrod), Ln sales/employee (lnte) and Ln value added/employee (lngvae)**

	labprod (1)	lnte (2)	lngvae (3)
ESOS + PRP + GRPP	0.505	0.119	0.011
	(2.51)*	(0.46)	(0.57)
ESOS + PRP	0.550	0.647	0.041
	(2.55)*	(2.89)**	(1.77)
ESOS + GRPP	0.480	0.782	0.082
	(1.93)	(2.36)*	(2.38)*
PRP + GRPP	–0.020	0.034	0.002
	(0.10)	(0.19)	(0.20)
ESOS only	0.067	0.301	0.004
	(0.32)	(1.94)	(0.27)
GRPP only	0.212	0.063	–0.018
	(1.14)	(0.30)	(1.56)
PRP only	0.208	–0.003	–0.010
	(1.47)	(0.02)	(1.03)
Cut 1:Constant	–0.919		
	(2.42)*		
Cut 2:Constant	0.750		
	(1.93)		
Cut 3:Constant	2.257		
	(5.70)**		
Constant		4.525	6.552
		(14.19)**	(235.41)**
Observations	1,490	578	518
R^2		0.55	0.36

Note: controls are as per table 6.5.
***Significant at the 1 percent level.
**Significant at the 5 percent level.
*Significant at the 10 percent level.

combinations of shared capitalism systems that include share ownership are positively correlated with productivity, however we measure it.[16]

6.7 Comparison with Prior Literature and Oxera-Treasury

Our production function study follows a long line of UK analyses of the effects of shared capitalism. Many analysts have used earlier waves of

16. The coefficients and *t*-statistics for share capitalist bundles incorporating share ownership are 0.492 (2.96) for managers' assessments of productivity, 0.444 (2.12) for sales per employee, and 0.035 (2.10) for value added per employee.

the WERS to examine the effects of various forms of shared capitalism on manager reports of financial outcomes or labor productivity. Some have used surveys of particular sectors with quantitative measures of productivity such as sales or value added, often within the order of 100 firms. Bryson and Freeman (2007) and Oxera in its analysis for the UK Treasury (Oxera 2007a, appendix 2) summarize this work. The two reviews show that the majority of studies find positive effects of shared capitalist pay on productivity or financial outcomes, while some find negligible effects, and virtually none find negative effects.[17] They also find that the pay schemes that have positive effects vary across studies and sometimes within the same study depending on the measure of outcomes or data under analysis.

After we completed our research, the Treasury released a study that comes as close as we could imagine to giving a definitive analysis of the effects of tax-advantaged modes of shared capitalism on productivity. This study has the largest sample of any done in the United Kingdom—16,844 firms—obtained by matching HM Revenue and Customs' administrative data on Approved Profit Sharing systems, SAYE systems, and CSOP systems to measures of productivity based on sales from the Financial Analysis Made Easy (FAME) data set. In addition, the Oxera-Treasury study obtained measures of productivity for 7,633 companies based on value added from the Annual Respondents Database (ARD) provided by the Office of National Statistics. The Oxera-Treasury study covered enough years and firms to permit a panel analysis with fixed effects as well as cross section comparisons of firms with and without particular schemes.

The results of the Oxera-Treasury study confirm the finding in our study and in the bulk of the earlier literature that shared capitalism raises productivity. When the study measures output by sales "on average, across the whole sample, the effect of tax-advantaged share schemes is significant and increases productivity by 2.5% in the long run" (Oxera 2007a, 3). It also finds important complementarities in the effects that are consistent with our results: "there are further benefits to be gained from operating several types of schemes," with gains accruing primarily to companies that have both tax advantaged and not tax-advantaged schemes; and with large gains for the SAYE share ownership scheme.

With its large sample size and use of panel data as well as cross section data, the Oxera-Treasury analysis has arguably generated the strongest findings thus far on the effects of shared capitalism in the United Kingdom. Surprisingly perhaps given the sample size, the Oxera-Treasury study reports variation in results that resemble those in our study and others using smaller data sets: lower estimated productivity gains when output is measured with

17. A count of the studies in the Oxera report shows that ten of the thirteen that estimated the effects of profit sharing found that it was associated with higher productivity while seven of the ten studies that examined share ownership found that it was associated with higher productivity.

value added than with sales; different estimated effects across sectors; and different estimates of which schemes matter most when output is measured in value added than when output is measured in sales. The study notes that it lacks information on coverage of schemes or on other business practices of firms (as in the WERS) that could cast additional light on the impacts of the schemes.

6.8 Conclusion

In sum, shared capitalism has grown in the United Kingdom, as it has in the United States; firms use various forms of shared capitalist pay together and often accompany them with other labor practices, consistent with the complementary hypothesis. But firms switch among schemes frequently, which suggests that they have trouble optimizing and that the transactions cost of switching are relatively low. Among the single schemes, share ownership has the clearest positive association with productivity, but its impact is largest when firms combine it with other forms of shared capitalist pay. Given that even the large sample Oxera-Treasury study finds sizable variation across groups, schemes, and measures of productivity, additional studies using administrative data or the richer but smaller WERS files are unlikely to greatly advance our knowledge of what makes shared capitalism work in the United Kingdom. To advance our knowledge further would seem to require studies that focus specifically on shared capitalist firms, such as the NBER data set fourteen-firm study used in other chapters of this book, with questions and case analyses directed at particular hypotheses about the detailed operation of shared capitalist programs in corporations.

Appendix

Survey Questions Used to Derive Share Capitalism Variables

The share capitalism measures are derived from the following survey questions.

Payments-by-Results (PBR)

"Do any of the employees in this establishment get paid by results or receive merit pay? On this card is an explanation of what we mean by payment-by-results and merit pay."

Card reads:

1. Payment-by-results

"Payment-by-results" includes any method of payment where the pay is determined by the amount done or its value, rather than just the number of hours worked. It includes commission, and bonuses that are determined by individual, establishment, or organization productivity or performance. It does not include profit-related pay schemes.

2. Merit pay

"Merit pay" is related to a subjective assessment of individual performance by a supervisor or manager.

Follow-up questions establish the occupations covered by PBR and the percentage of nonmanagerial employees covered. In addition, the following question establishes whether PBR is calculated at individual, group, or organization level:

"Thinking just about payment by results, what / What) measures of performance are used to determine the amount that employees receive?"

PROBE: Which others? UNTIL "None".

1. Individual performance/output
2. Group or team performance/output
3. Workplace-based measures
4. Organization-based measures
5. Other measures

Profit-Related Pay

"Do any employees at this workplace receive profit-related payments or profit-related bonuses?"

Follow-up questions establish the occupations covered by PRP, the percentage of nonmanagerial employees covered, and the percentage in receipt of PRP payments. In addition, the following question establishes the organizational level at which PRP is calculated if the workplace is part of a larger organization:

"For what part of your organization is the amount of profit-related pay calculated. . . . Workplace, Division/Subsidiary company, Organization as a whole?"

Share Schemes

"Does this company operate any of the employee share schemes listed on this card for any of the employees at this workplace?"

PROBE: Which others? UNTIL "None."

1. Share Incentive Plan (SIP)
2. Save As You Earn (SAYE or Sharesave)
3. Enterprise Management Incentives (EMI)
4. Company Share Option Plan (CSOP)
5. Other employee share scheme
6. None of these

Card reads:

1. Share Incentive Plan (SIP)—a tax and NIC advantaged plan where employees can purchase shares and companies can give employees free shares or matching shares.
2. Save As You Earn (SAYE or Sharesave) share options scheme—tax advantaged scheme where employees save to purchase their employer's shares.
3. Enterprise Management Incentives (EMI)—where smaller companies can grant up to a total of £3 million of tax and National Insurance Contributions (NIC) advantaged share options to their employees.
4. Company Share Option Plan (CSOP)—where companies can grant each of their employees up to £30,000 of tax and NIC advantaged share options.
5. Other employee share scheme.

Subsequent questions identify the occupations eligible for share ownership schemes and the percentage participating in schemes.

Recent Introduction of Performance-Related Pay

Over the past two years has management here introduced any of the changes listed on this card?

PROBE: Which others? UNTIL "None".

1. Introduction of performance-related pay
2. Introduction or upgrading of computers
3. Introduction or upgrading of other types of new technology
4. Changes in working time arrangements
5. Changes in the organization of work
6. Changes in work techniques or procedures
7. Introduction of initiatives to involve employees
8. Introduction of technologically new or significantly improved product or service
9. None of these

References

Baker, G., R. Gibbons, and K. Murphy. 1994. Subjective performance measures in optimal incentive contracts. *Quarterly Journal of Economics* 109 (4): 1125–56.

Ben-Avner, A., and D.C. Jones. 1995. Employee participation, ownership and productivity: A theoretical framework. *Industrial Relations* 34 (4): 532–54.

Bryson, A., and R. Freeman. 2007. *Doing the right thing? Does fair share capitalism improve workplace performance?* Department of Trade and Industry Employment Relations Research Series Number 81. London: DTI.

Chaplin, J., J. Mangla, S. Purdon, and C. Airey. 2005. *The workplace employment relations survey (WERS) 2004 technical report.* London: National Centre for Social Research.

Daniel, W. W., and N. Millward. 1983. *Workplace industrial relations in Britain.* London: Heinemann.
Gallie, D., A. Felstead, and F. Green. 2004. Changing patterns of task discretion in Britain. *Work, Employment and Society* 18 (2): 243–66.
Gallie, D., M. White, Y. Cheng, and M. Tomlinson. 1998. *Restructuring the employment relationship.* Oxford: Oxford University Press.
HM Treasury. 1998. *Consultation on employee share ownership.* Available at: http://www.hm-treasury.gov.uk/media/B3C/54/2.pdf.
Huselid, M. A. 1995. The impact of human resource management practices on turnover, productivity and corporate financial performance. *Academy of Management Journal* 38 (3): 635–72.
Ichniowski, C., T. A. Kochan, D. Levine, C. Olson, and G. Strauss. 1996. What works at work: Overview and assessment. *Industrial Relations* 35 (3): 299–333.
Jones, D.C. 1987. The productivity effects of worker directors and financial participation by employees in the firm: The case of British retail cooperatives. *Industrial and Labor Relations Review* 41 (1): 79–92.
Kersley, B., C. Alpin, J. Forth, A. Bryson, H. Bewley, G. Dix, and S. Oxenbridge. 2006. *Inside the workplace: Findings from the 2004 workplace employment relations survey.* London: Routledge.
Levine, D. I., and L. D. Tyson. 1990. Participation, productivity and the firm's environment. In *Paying for productivity: Looking at the evidence,* ed. A. S. Blinder, 183–237. Washington DC: Brookings Institute.
Oxera. 2007a. Tax advantaged employee share schemes: Analysis of productivity effects. Report 1: Productivity Measured Using Turnover, January 2007. HM Revenue and Customs Research Report 32.
Oxera. 2007b. Tax advantaged employee share schemes: Analysis of productivity effects Report 2: Productivity Measured Using Gross Value Added, August 2007. HM Revenue and Customs Research Report 33.
Pil, F., and J. P. MacDuffie. 1996. The adoption of high involvement work practices. *Industrial Relations* 35 (3): 423–55.
Pendleton, A., K. Whitfield, and A. Bryson. 2009. The changing use of contingent pay in the modern British workplace. In *The evolution of the modern workplace,* ed. W. Brown, A. Bryson, J. Forth, and K. Whitfield, 256–84. Cambridge: Cambridge University Press.
Schuler, R., and S. Jackson. 1987. Linking competitive strategies with human resource management practices. *Academy of Management Executive* 1 (3): 207–19.
White, M., S. Hill, C. Mills, and D. Smeaton. 2004. *Managing to change? British workplaces and the future of work.* Basingstoke: Palgrave MacMillan.

7

Who Has a Better Idea?
Innovation, Shared Capitalism, and Human Resources Policies

Erika E. Harden, Douglas L. Kruse, and Joseph R. Blasi

7.1 Introduction

Even in today's challenging economic conditions, innovation as a means for organizations to create and maintain a competitive advantage remains a strategic imperative (Mahroum 2008). Organizations that are able to continually generate innovative products and services are better able to retain their current customer base and develop a new customer base.

Unlike the traditional view of innovation as the activity performed by the lone R&D scientist working in isolation, today's organizations embrace the ideas and insights of employees at all levels of the organization. For example, Whirlpool credits their recent successful product innovations not to a couple of departments, such as engineering or marketing. Instead, they contribute their success to the 61,000 employees who have the ability to contribute and develop product, service, or processes innovations (*Business Week* 2006).

Erika E. Harden is with the Rutgers University School of Management and Labor Relations research group. Douglas L. Kruse is a professor of human resource management and labor studies and employment relations at the Rutgers School of Management and Labor Relations, and a research associate of the National Bureau of Economic Research. Joseph R. Blasi is a professor of human resource management and labor studies and employment relations at the Rutgers School of Management and Labor Relations, and a research associate of the National Bureau of Economic Research.

Presented at the Russell Sage/NBER conference in New York City, October 2006. We thank Katherine Klein and other participants for valuable comments. This research is supported by a grant from the Russell Sage Foundation and the Rockefeller Foundation. The National Opinion Research Center at the University of Chicago provided valuable assistance with the General Social Survey segment that forms the basis for some of the analysis. Refen Koh, Rhokeun Park, Michelle Pinheiro, and Patricia Berhau provided excellent assistance in survey scanning, entry, and verification.

Given the new organizational context for innovation, it is important to understand how employees at all levels of the organization can be managed to direct and align their behaviors to achieve innovative outcomes. For example, Annalee Saxenian, in her seminal work on organizational innovation, contrasts two traditional innovation hubs of America: Silicon Valley in California and Route 128 surrounding Boston. Her work indicates that two management practices, organizational structures and rewards, were critical to accounting for differences in innovation output. Silicon Valley spawned innovation through shared capitalism and the use of teams, while innovation in the Boston corridor was stymied by bureaucratic top-down approaches to organizational structure and rewards.

Likewise, in their book *In the Company of Owners,* Blasi, Kruse, and Bernstein (2003) examined in detail one innovation sector, the 100 largest corporations that built, run, and sell on the Internet. They highlight the major role that shared capitalism practices in combination with a participative culture can make in promoting organizational innovation.

Recognizing the importance of innovation for today's organizations, this study will examine the role shared capitalism and high performance work policies play as a means to achieve innovation outcomes. Additionally, we will examine a process mechanism, employee alignment, as one way in which shared capitalism and high performance work policies impact innovation outcomes.

7.2 Literature Review

7.2.1 Can Shared Capitalism Promote Innovation?

Despite the numerous studies on performance effects of shared capitalism, there are only a few studies that discuss or examine the importance of shared capitalism in achieving product, service, or process innovations.

Gamble (2000) finds reduced R&D expenditures in firms where Employee Share Ownership Plans (ESOPs) own larger blocks of stock and argues that this reflects management entrenchment and managerial risk aversion; in contrast, Kruse (1996) finds that R&D expenditures are a strong predictor of the use of a profit-sharing plan, and Sesil et al. (2002) find positive effects of broad-based stock options in high technology knowledge-based industries, noting that "for firms, in which new product development is crucial for success, such as in many knowledge-based industries, broad-based stock options can reduce the agency problem, resulting in greater output" (276). Most recently, and supporting Sesil et al.'s perspective, Lerner and Wulf (2006), using a sample of 300 publicly-traded R&D centralized firms, found that the compensation of corporate R&D heads had dramatically shifted in the 1990s, with a heaver reliance on long-term incentives such as stock options. They find long-term incentives are positively and significantly associated with the number of patent filings, patents' perceived value (patent citations), and patent generality.

While research that examines the role of shared capitalism as a means to achieve innovation outcomes is in its infancy, social and behavior psychologists have actively examined the impact of individual rewards on creative behavior (Amabile 1988; Amabile and Gryskiewicz 1989; Deci and Ryan 1985; Eisenberger and Selbst 1994). Thus, we briefly present empirical evidence and theoretical perspectives from the social and behavioral schools of psychology.

Social-cognitive psychologists assert that creative behavior has defining characteristics that make it distinguishable from other human behavior; in particular, creative behavior is dependent on employees' intrinsic motivation (Amabile 1988; Deci and Ryan 1985). Thus, the aim for social-cognitive psychologists is to uncover the conditions that enhance employee's intrinsic motivation. According to this line of reasoning, extrinsic rewards, such as shared capitalism, will have a detrimental effect on employee's intrinsic motivation and ultimately their creative behavior by directing employee's attention toward the reward itself over the task at hand.

In contrast, behavioral psychologists argue that the effort needed to complete activities is an unpleasant sensation produced by repeated or intense performance of any behavior. Reinforcements, such as rewards, are a means by which organizations can reduce this unpleasant sensation. If an employee is rewarded for putting in a large amount of effort in an activity or behavior (for example, through shared capitalism) it reduces the adverse impact of such behaviors and increases this behavior in the future. In effect, reinforcements work to control employee's creative behavior by decreasing the unpleasant sensations associated with the cognitive effort needed to perform creativity.

Empirically, an abundance of studies in the past thirty years have been conducted to understand if and under what conditions rewards enhance or inhibit creative behavior, with contradictory results and conclusions. Recognizing the conflicting evidence, five meta-analyses aimed to bring cohesion to the divergent results (Rummel and Feinberg 1988; Wiersma 1992, Tang and Hall 1995; Cameron and Pierce 1994; Eisenberger and Cameron 1996; Deci, Koesterner, and Ryan 1999). Of the five, the strongest support for the Cognitive Evolution Theory comes from Deci, Koestner, and Ryan (1999), who combined 128 studies to find that all tangible and intangible rewards undermined intrinsic motivation. However, conclusions from Eisenberger and Cameron's (1996) extensive review indicate that: (a) the detrimental effects of rewards tend to occur in highly restricted, easily avoidable conditions; (b) mechanisms of instrumental and classical conditions are basic for understanding the incremental and detrimental effects of rewards on task motivation; and (c) the positive effects of rewards on performance are easily attainable using procedures derived from behavioral theory.

Taken together, past theory and empirical work on creativity and rewards has failed to provide an understanding of how best, if at all, to reward employees to achieve creative behavior. Additionally, the application of this research to organizational setting is restricted. First, the majority of studies in this field have been conducted outside of organizations and relied heavily on schoolchildren, making the generalizability of these findings limited. Second, organizations are increasingly employing group/team or organizational incentives over individual incentives as a means to encourage cooperation and alignment (Blasi and Kruse 2006). Thus, studies examining individual incentives provide only a limited understanding of the full range of workplace incentives. Third, the sample sizes of the aforementioned studies are generally small. For example, of the 128 studies examined in Deci, Koestner, and Ryan's (1999) meta-analysis the largest sample was 249 employees, with the majority of sample sizes well under 100 employees. While significant effects can often be detected with these sample sizes (depending on the study design), a contribution of this study to the current literature is the large sample size obtained in an organizational setting (more than 25,000 employees in hundreds of work sites) with data on several types of workplace incentives.

7.2.2 Can Employment Practices Promote Innovation?

In contrast to the limited research on organizational incentives, innovation management scholars have actively researched individual human resource management policies that impact innovation outcomes, including job design (Hackman and Oldham 1980), selection (Woodman, Sawyer, and Griffin 1993; Iansiti 1995), training (Wheatley, Anthony, and Maddox 1991), and performance management (Mehr and Schaver 1996). Mumford (2000) reviews an extensive body of literature examining specific human resource management policies that support innovation and creativity. Building on this review, the following sections summarize the management policies that are supportive of innovation and creativity in organizations.

Selection

The consistent development of innovative products, services, and processes requires a workforce with the necessary breadth and depth of technical skills (Amabile and Gryskiewicz 1989; Iansiti 1995), in combination with a constant flow of new ideas and experience (Bontis, Crossan, and Hulland 2002; Jackson and Schuler 2002). Staffing practices work as a means to ensure a consistent flow of technical skills, by identifying and selecting applicants who will add new ideas and experience to the organization. Researchers have examined the employee characteristics supportive of innovation: divergent thinking (Guilford 1950), technical expertise (Amabile and Gryskiewicz 1989; Mumford 2000), and certain personality characteristics (Amabile 1988; King 1990).

Training and Job Rotation

Maintaining employees' current knowledge and skills, while developing new knowledge and skills, is essential to innovative performance (Cohen and Leventhal 1990; Mumford 2000). Two HR policies vital to maintaining and developing employees to achieve innovative outcomes are training and development (Leonard-Barton 1992). A firm's potential to be innovative and creative is enhanced as the new knowledge and abilities are incorporated into the organization (Jackson and Schuler 2002; Cohen and Leventhal 1990). Thus, past research has noted the importance of sabbaticals, subtracting assignments, self-study programs, conferences, external courses, and job rotations as important mechanisms to enhance an organization's ability to innovate (Dougherty 1992; Mumford 2000; Christensen and Raynor 2003; Amabile 1983).

Performance Management

Performance evaluations have been both negatively and positively associated with individual innovation and creativity (Amabile 1979; Shalley 1995). For instance, Amabile (1979) found that individuals who expected their artistic task to be externally evaluated had significantly lower levels of creativity on the task than individuals not being externally evaluated. In contrast, Shalley (1995) conducted two studies with samples of undergraduate students; the results of both studies indicate that expecting an evaluation is not necessarily harmful to people's creativity. The variance in empirical evidence may be explained by the type of performance evaluation. Performance appraisals should not have specific performance objectives or difficult production outcomes (Mumford 2000; Oldham 2003). Instead, appraisals are most conducive to creativity when they consist of broadly defined goals and objectives that allow employees flexibility as to what the final outcome will be (Mumford 2000).

Rewards (Recognition)

As mentioned before, evidence for the impact of individual rewards on creative behavior is mixed. However, for those researchers who support the role of rewards or recognition (both intrinsic and extrinsic) for creativity, other questions remain, such as the skills, behaviors, or outcomes that should be rewarded. For instance, Henderson and Cockburn (1994) in their investigation of the pharmaceutical industry suggest firms that promote researchers according to their standing in the scientific community enjoyed higher productivity levels. Additionally, rewards should not be withheld from employees who step out of established roles or fail to achieve desired outcomes. Instead, a better approach is to reward employees for their effort or progress toward an innovation/creative goal or objective (Mumford 2000). Finally, Dougherty (1992), after extensive field research on product development, suggests that rewards should be provided for the development of expertise, skills, and competencies. Thus, beyond compensation, other forms or rewards and recognition can be used to enhance creative behavior.

Employee Involvement

Empowering employees and utilizing teams are two mechanisms through which employee participation can enhance organizational innovation (Mumford 2000). Christensen and Raynor (2003) in a recent book argue that successful product innovation requires big decisions to be driven down to the lowest level. They reason that decisions about products, services, and processes innovations should be made on the spot, instead of waiting for a response from further up in the organization. Additionally, Jelinek and Schoonhoven (1990) note that employee involvement helps employees to see their part in the innovation process while creating a shared responsibility in the outcome. Supporting this, Leonard-Barton (1992), in her study of innovative projects groups, found that empowerment is most important for innovative capabilities. Those project teams who were empowered felt "exhilarated by the challenges they had created" (117).

Teamwork

The use of team-based work is a popular mechanism for enhancing innovation. Innovations involve different types of tasks and processes, and thus are rarely the creation of one individual or a single department. Team-based work has been argued to increase the speed of product innovation (Hayes, Wheelwright, and Clark 1988), the number of innovations (Dougherty 1992), and the value of the innovation (Ven de Ven 1986). For example, Clark and Fujimoto (1991) conducted a qualitative study where they found that the use of cross-functional teams is central to the product development process. Additionally, effective product development was not housed in solely specialized R&D activities; instead, the most effective product development came from creating linkages between various departments within the organization. Thus, the use of teams enhances product innovation through the diversity of knowledge (Cohen and Levinthal 1990).

Systems Perspective

While the aforementioned policies appear to be valuable for innovation, recent work recognizes the importance of examining Human Resource Management (HRM) policies as a bundle or system of policies as opposed to individual policies in isolation (MacDuffie 1995; Huselid 1995; Ichniowski et al. 1996; Blasi and Kruse 2006). A central tenet of the systems approach is that organizations should create a high degree of internal consistency among their HRM policies (Baird and Meshoulam 1988). Systems of HRM policies that are designed to utilize the knowledge and skills of the workforce have been labeled as "high performance," "high involvement," "high commitment," "HR sophistication," and "HR investment."

Interestingly, there is wide disagreement on what policies constitute "high performance." A recent review by Lepak et al. (2006) highlights the disparate and at times conflicting policies making up high performance systems. While disagreement remains over the policies represented in a "high performance" work system, it is generally agreed that a high performance work system (HPWS) can impact various organizational outcomes. Collectively, twenty years of cumulative research has found HPWS are strongly associated with outcomes including HRM outcomes (i.e., turnover, absenteeism, job satisfaction); organizational outcomes (i.e., productivity, quality, service); financial accounting outcomes (i.e., ROA, profitability); and capital market outcomes (i.e., stock price, growth, returns) (Combs et al. 2006; Becker and Huselid 2006).[1]

As previously noted employee knowledge and skills are critical to achieving innovation outcomes. Thus, it is surprising that the systems approach has had limited application to innovation outcomes. Studies of high performance workplace bundles have so far tended to focus on operational or financial performance without measures of innovation. Given the limited empirical evidence, our study seeks to fill this gap by examining the impact of HPWS on innovation outcomes.

Taken together, the limited empirical work examining the effects of shared capitalism and HPWS on innovation outcomes represents a gap in the literature that needs to be addressed. Our interest is to examine the relationship between shared capitalism, HPWS, and innovative outcomes, in addition to the intervening mechanisms that uncover how these relationships occur. The following theory and hypotheses development provides the rationale for why we expect these relationships to occur.

7.3 Theory and Hypotheses

Laffont and Martimort (2002) describe the principal-agent problem as a fundamental one for the firm: "Indeed, for various reasons the owner of the firm must delegate several tasks to the members of the firm. This necessity raises the problem of managing information flows within the firm. . . . The starting point of incentive theory corresponds to the problem of delegating a task to an agent with private information" (2002, 2–3). For the purposes of this article, one can think of the problem of innovation as how to get the members of the firm interested in working alone or together to use their information to achieve innovation that will profit the owner of the firm. They cite the early work of both Chester Barnard and Charles Babbage in defining the relevance of shared capitalism for the agency problem. For example, Babbage wrote:

1. Despite these positive performance outcomes, bundles of high performance workplace policies appear to have very low incidence among firms (Blasi and Kruse 2006). See Ichniowski et al. (1996) regarding the barriers to adoption of high performance policies.

> "The general principles on which the proposed system is founded, are: 1. That a considerable part of the wages received by each person should depend on the profits made by the establishment; and 2. That *every person* (our emphasis) connected with it should derive more advantage from applying any improvement he might discover than he could by any other course." (Laffont and Martimort 2002, 11 [quoting Babbage 1989, vol 8, 177])

One can readily see that Babbage is specifically addressing both shared capitalism and innovation ("any improvement"). Barnard's views were more explicit and more extreme when he wrote:

> "An essential element of organizations is the willingness of persons to contribute their individual efforts to the cooperative system. . . . Inadequate incentives mean dissolution, or changes in organizational purpose, or failure to cooperate. Hence in all sorts of organizations the affording of adequate incentives becomes the most definitely emphasized task in their existence. It is probably in this aspect of executive work that failure is most pronounced." (Laffont and Martimort 2002, 12 [quoting Barnard 1938, 139])

The research on the effect of individual incentives on innovation is mixed, as previously noted, while the research on teamwork generally shows it to be positively related to innovation efforts. One of the purposes of shared capitalism plans is to enhance teamwork by creating greater cooperation and information sharing among co-workers, and between workers and supervisors/managers. Based on this our first two hypotheses are:

HYPOTHESIS ONE: *Shared capitalism incentives are associated with a workplace culture that is supportive of innovation efforts.*

HYPOTHESIS TWO: *Shared capitalism incentives are associated with a greater willingness of employees to report innovative ideas.*

In line with our interest in exploring the impact of employment culture—specifically high performance work systems—on innovation, past theorists have given some thought to the role of organization design as a complement to incentives.

For example, Barnard virtually defined the high performance work system when he wrote about what Laffont and Mortimort call "nonmonetary incentives" as including: "personal nonmaterial opportunities; ideal benefactions; . . . associational attractiveness; adaptation of conditions to habitual methods and attitudes; opportunity of enlarged participation; [and] the condition of communion." Barnard stressed that what we think of as financial incentives had to be "reinforced by other incentives," specifically referring to these organizational components (Laffont and Martimort 2002, 12 [quoting Barnard 1938, 142]).

In a modern economy where workers are often not manipulating physical objects, much of work itself is inside the mind of the worker and is about collecting, communicating, sharing, manipulating, and combining information in novel and innovative ways. Physical monitoring by supervisors as a solution to the agency problem is very hard in these environments. Many of the features of high performance work systems that theorists like Huselid have defined as essential to innovations are based on information. A number of these high performance policies can create conditions that favor innovation: good wages and benefits can produce high commitment and loyalty; selective recruitment can get the most informed and curious persons into an organization; training can upgrade their informational and cooperative skills; teamwork and job rotation can break down "rigid silos" between them; and employee involvement can bring them closer to the information that both customers and management possess. This is not dissimilar from the classic agency theory notion of the "revelation principle" in which societies have a problem in how to get "informed agents (to) reveal private information to a planner who recommends actions" (Laffont and Martimort 2002, 26–7). One can conceive of a high performance work system as a workplace mechanism to make the revelation principle work.

Based on the theory and research linking high performance work systems to organizational performance, we expect that an HPWS will also contribute to an innovative culture and activity, and will complement shared capitalism plans. Our next four hypotheses are:

HYPOTHESIS THREE: *High performance work systems are associated with a workplace culture that is supportive of innovation efforts.*

HYPOTHESIS FOUR: *High performance work systems are associated with a greater willingness of employees to report innovative ideas.*

HYPOTHESIS FIVE: *Shared capitalism plans have a positive interaction with high performance work systems in predicting a workplace culture that is supportive of innovation efforts.*

HYPOTHESIS SIX: *Shared capitalism plans have a positive interaction with high performance work systems in predicting willingness of employees to report innovative ideas.*

Finally, we expect that if the aforementioned effects exist, they operate in part through greater alignment of employees with the company's strategy. Our final two hypotheses are:

HYPOTHESIS SEVEN: *Individual alignment with company strategy mediates the relationship of shared capitalism and high performance work systems to a workplace culture that is supportive of innovation efforts.*

HYPOTHESIS EIGHT: *Individual alignment with company strategy mediates the relationship of shared capitalism and high performance work systems to the willingness of employees to report innovative ideas.*

7.4 Data and Methods

7.4.1 Data Set

This chapter uses employee surveys from one large company in the NBER data set (described in "Studying Shared Capitalism" in the introduction to this volume). Unique to this company, the survey asked a series of questions about organizational innovation. The survey was administered in 2006 via paper and web-based administration in one firm. A total of 27,825 usable surveys were returned for a response rate of 67.3 percent. Missing data for one or more of the variables reduced the sample to 25,014 respondents who had complete data for all of the variables.

7.4.2 Measures

Human Resource Management

The 5-P model (Schuler 1992) identifies the various ways in which HRM activities can be examined: as philosophies, policies, programs, practices, or processes. This study will examine HRM policies and practices.

Policies, as defined here, are the broadly defined HRM activities. For example, performance-based pay is a broadly defined measure of an HRM activity, but it can be implemented through a number of different practices. By assessing HRM policies, a researcher is able to cast a wide net in understanding the HRM activities within the organization. However, HRM policies limit the detailed information on what specific practices make up a policy.

Alternatively, HRM practices are the specific HRM activities that are employed to implement an HRM policy. For example, under the policy of pay-for-performance there are different HRM practices that can be employed to achieve the pay-for-performance policy. Assessing specific HRM practices provides a level of detail missed by HRM policies. In this study, the primary interest is the impact of shared capitalism, and its various forms, as a means to achieve innovation outcomes. Thus, we examine the individual shared capitalism practices and a combined shared capitalism index that can be utilized to achieve innovation outcomes, discussed in more detail following.

We examine two systems of HRM policies. First, we analyze a *high performance work system* (HPWS), which includes employee participation, training, job rotation or cross-training, selection, job security, and information sharing. The majority of questions (listed in appendix A) ask the respondent to report if she or he is covered by this policy. Second, a high performance work system measure was included that asked employees their perceptions of the *effectiveness* of each high performance policy for their work area or team. This measure thus localizes and focuses the estimation of the high performance practices within the group of workers immediately surrounding the respondent. This is notable, since most HRM scholars do not bring high performance work literature down to the lowest level of the organization (notable exceptions include Allen, Shore, and Griffith [2003] and Zacharatos, Barling, and Iverson [2005]). In particular, this index measures team effectiveness in the following areas: selection, performance goals, training, sharing information, meeting with customers, and rewards. This human resource policy index is referred to as *high performance work system-team* (HPWST).

Shared Capitalism

As noted previously, shared capitalism appears in a variety of forms. This study examines *profit/gain sharing, employee ownership,* and *stock options.* Profit sharing and gain sharing are combined here because this firm has one program combining elements of each: bonus payments are based both on company-wide return on net assets, and on division performance. In addition, we examine the effects of individual incentives. For each incentive plan, the presence of the incentive (yes/no) and the extensiveness of the incentive (as a percent of total fixed annual pay) are examined. Additionally, a thermometer-style *index of shared capitalism* was constructed. The index, described in appendix B, reflects both whether workers have different shared capitalism programs and whether these programs represent a high percentage of the worker's fixed annual pay.

Workplace Outcomes

After consulting with the research literature, two comprehensive measures of innovation were designed. The first is focused on measuring aspects of a firm's *culture for innovation.* According to organizational theory on creativity, employees' innovative behavior can be influenced by the environment or culture an employee encounters (Amabile 1988). Thus, an important outcome to understand is a culture that supports innovative behavior. An extensive review of the literature on cultures that support innovation revealed consistent characteristics across cultures that support innovation. For example, companies can promote innovation by fostering an environment that encourages employees to voice ideas or suggestions, provides the resources to further develop ideas, and recognizes the efforts of employees who do try to innovate (Scott and Bruce 1994). Given the past literature, our study examines the characteristics listed previously. The specific items for the culture of innovation scale are listed in appendix A.

The second measure focuses on individual employee's willingness to marshal their *innovative ideas* and do something about it. Innovative behavior is characterized by a multistage process, with different activities or behaviours necessary at each stage (Scott and Bruce 1994). In this study, we examine an employee's ability and willingness to generate ideas, as opposed to their actual innovative behavior. Specific items developed to assess employee willingness to innovate are listed in appendix A.

Finally, we examine the extent to which employees are aligned with the goals and objectives of the organization (Huselid, Becker, and Beatty 2005). Aligning employees with organizational goals and objectives has become an increasingly important task; especially in organizations where employees' knowledge and skills play a critical role in achieving strategic objectives, such as innovation. It is through alignment that employees are aware of how they can contribute to achieving organizational objectives. Much of the work arguing for the importance of aligning employees behind shared goals and objectives has been at a conceptual level (Wright and McMahan 1992; Boswell and Wright 2002). Thus, this research contributes to the current literature by going beyond the importance of aligning HRM policies to organizational strategy (Huselid 1995). It looks deeper into the organization for how employees, the individuals who implement strategic objectives, recognize and agree with them. Our interest is to examine if and to what extent shared capitalism and high performance work policies are effective means to align a workforce behind organizational objectives. Our measure combines four items representing employee understanding and agreement with the company strategy, and employee views of whether the company provides the resources and culture necessary to implement that strategy.[2]

7.5 Empirical Results

7.5.1 Culture for Innovation

Table 7.1 summarizes the empirical results on the relationship between shared capitalism, high performance work policies, and employees' perception of a culture for innovation.

Shared Capitalism

In models (1), (3), and (5) we examine the impact of the shared capitalism index on employees' perception of a culture for innovation. The results reveal that the shared capitalism index is positively related to employees' perception of a culture for innovation (model [1]). The shared capitalism index remains positively related when HPWST is added to the equation (model [5]), but not when HPWS is added (model [3]), so there is only partial support for hypothesis one.

When the shared capitalism practices are broken out to examine their individual impact on employees' perceptions of a culture for innovation (models [2], [4], and [6]), two shared capitalism practices are consistently related to employees' perceptions of a culture for innovation: the percentage

2. We thank Mark Huselid for insightful comments and suggestions on developing the employee alignment scale.

Table 7.1 **Predicting a culture for innovation**

Independent variables	Model 1	Model 2	Model 3	Model 4	Model 5	Model 6
Shared capitalism index	0.013 (0.003)***		0.000 (0.003)		0.011 (0.003)***	
Bonuses						
Profit/gain sharing		–0.008 (0.013)		–0.038 (0.012)***		0.009 (0.012)
Profit/gain sharing as % of base pay		0.291 (0.070)***		0.174 (0.067)***		0.176 (0.065)***
Individual bonus		0.071 (0.017)***		0.042 (0.017)**		0.037 (0.016)**
Individual bonus as % of base pay		0.007 (0.102)		0.064 (0.098)		0.043 (0.095)
Employee ownership						
Any employee ownership		0.039 (0.012)***		0.023 (0.011)**		0.027 (0.011)**
Employee-owned stock as % of pay		–0.005 (0.010)		–0.010 (0.010)		0.000 (0.010)
Stock options						
Stock option holding		0.031 (0.031)		0.039 (0.029)		0.015 (0.028)
Stock option value as % of base pay		0.045 (0.031)		0.055 (0.029)*		0.038 (0.029)
High performance work policies						
HPWS			0.806 (0.016)***	0.802 (0.016)***		
HPWST					0.180 (0.003)***	0.179 (0.003)***
n	26,364	25,832	26,361	25,830	25,977	25,458
Adjusted R^2	0.054	0.058	0.134	0.137	0.184	0.186

Notes: All regressions include controls for country (twenty-two dummies), occupation (five dummies), mgt. level (three dummies), hourly pay status, supervisory status, tenure in years, hours worked per week, union status, age, gender, marital status (two dummies), family size, college graduate, graduate degree, number of kids, race (four dummies), disability status, ln(fixed pay), and company fixed effects. Standard error in parentheses.

***Significant at the 1 percent level.

**Significant at the 5 percent level.

*Significant at the 10 percent level.

of base pay going to profit/gain sharing, and owning company stock. These results stay strong when adding in either the HPWS or HPWST measure, supporting hypothesis one for these two pay practices.

High Performance Work Policies

A very consistent result in models (3) through (6) is the strong positive association between human resource management policies and employees' perceptions of a culture for innovation. An examination of adjusted R^2 with and without the human resource practices indicates that these practices greatly increase our ability to account for what might create a culture for innovation. These results support hypothesis three and underline the important role high performance policies have in creating and supporting a culture for innovation where employees are encouraged to innovate, are rewarded for this, and are provided the resources to do so.

7.5.2 Innovative Ideas

Table 7.2 summaries the empirical results on the relationship between shared capitalism, high performance work policies, and employees' willingness and ability to innovate.

Shared Capitalism

In models (1), (3), and (5) we report the impact of the shared capitalism index on employees' willingness and ability to contribute innovative ideas to the organization. The results, consistent with those reported for a culture for innovation, find that those employees who reported higher levels of shared capitalism also reported higher willingness and ability to contribute innovative ideas to the organization. These results remained significant after including measures of high performance work policies, supporting hypothesis two.

When the shared capitalism policies are broken out in models (2), (4), and (6), employee ownership is again a significant positive predictor of employees' willingness and ability to contribute innovative ideas to the organization. Unlike the results for culture of innovation, however, profit/gain sharing as a percent of pay is not a significant predictor, and in fact profit/gain sharing eligibility is a negative predictor in two of the models. These latter results contrast strikingly with the positive results for employee ownership, suggesting that profit sharing may focus workers toward short-term outcomes and away from activities with a long-term payoff, while employee ownership helps promote behavior like innovative activity that will have a longer-term payoff.[3] This is because profit sharing in the organization under study

3. This interpretation was supported by several company representatives at the conference where this chapter was initially presented. One person noted that ROI, which stands for return on investment, was sometimes referred to by employees as "repression of innovation" because a focus on short-term profitability discourages investments in innovative activities that have a longer-term payoff.

Table 7.2 Predicting innovative ideas

Independent variable	Model 1	Model 2	Model 3	Model 4	Model 5	Model 6
Shared capitalism index	0.012 (0.003)***		0.006 (0.003)**		0.012 (0.003)***	
Bonuses						
Profit/gain sharing		–0.027 (0.014)*		–0.039 (0.014)***		–0.020 (0.014)
Profit/gain sharing as % of base pay		–0.005 (0.078)		–0.057 (0.078)		–0.032 (0.078)
Individual bonus		0.040 (0.020)**		0.027 (0.019)		0.033 (0.019)*
Individual bonus as % of base pay		0.221 (0.114)*		0.248 (0.114)**		0.224 (0.114)**
Employee ownership						
Any employee ownership		0.072 (0.013)***		0.065 (0.013)***		0.070 (0.013)***
Employee-owned stock as % of pay		0.008 (0.011)		0.005 (0.011)		0.009 (0.011)
Stock options						
Stock option holding		–0.026 (0.034)		–0.022 (0.034)		–0.028 (0.034)
Stock option value as % of base pay		–0.012 (0.034)		–0.009 (0.034)		–0.018 (0.034)
High performance work policies						
HPWS			0.350 (0.019)***	0.347 (0.019)***		
HPWST					0.042 (0.003)***	0.041 (0.003)***
n	26,252	25,728	26,249	25,726	25,875	25,362
Adjusted R^2	0.146	0.148	0.156	0.158	0.149	0.151

Notes: All regressions include controls for country (twenty-two dummies), occupation (five dummies), mgt. level (three dummies), hourly pay status, supervisory status, tenure in years, hours worked per week, union status, age, gender, marital status (two dummies), family size, college graduate, graduate degree, number of kids, race (four dummies), disability status, ln(fixed pay), and company fixed effects. Standard error in parentheses.

***Significant at the 1 percent level.

**Significant at the 5 percent level.

*Significant at the 10 percent level.

specifically rewards employees for productivity and operational achievements (such as on-time customer delivery) of delivering current goods and services, which the organization sees as part of its existing repertoire of offerings. Profit sharing is not, however, tied to ideas or prototypes for future goods and services.

High Performance Work Policies

The impact of high performance work policies on employees' willingness and ability to contribute innovative ideas to the organization is reported in models (3) through (6). The results, across all models, reveal a consistent and significant positive relationship between both high performance work policy indexes and employees' willingness and ability to contribute innovative ideas to the organization. Given these results, support was provided for hypothesis four. Taken together, these results can be interpreted to signify that the use of high performance work policies is one way to increase employees' willingness and ability to contribute innovative ideas to an organization.

An interesting note is that in comparison to the HPWS impact on a culture for innovation, it appears that the HPWS impact is not as substantial for willingness and ability to contribute innovative ideas. We speculate that an employee's ability to contribute innovative ideas may be accounted for by individual differences not captured in this study. For example, divergent thinking (Guilford 1950), openness to new experience (Feist 1998), and internal locus of control (Woodman and Schoenfeldt 1989) have all been related to highly innovative or creative individuals.

7.5.3 Complementarities between Human Resource Policies and Shared Capitalism

An important proposition of the systems perspective is that organizational outcomes will be enhanced to the extent that a firm's human resource management activities fit with and complement one another (Baird and Meshoulam 1988). The underlying rationale is that the more strongly human resources fit together, the more consistent are the signals communicated to employees regarding the behaviors that are valued by the organization (Becker and Huselid 1998). While fit can be tested using various statistical techniques (Venkatraman 1989), we employ a fit-as-moderation hypothesis, testing whether the impacts of shared capitalism on innovation outcomes are dependent on the level of high performance work policies. Stated differently, we expect that the impact of shared capitalism on employees' perceptions of a culture for innovation vary across levels of high performance work policies. To examine this, an interaction term was included in table 7.3 (models [1] and [2]).

The results indicate that shared capitalism does interact positively and significantly with both HPWS and HPWST and provides support for hypothesis five. The fit between shared capitalism and HPWST was positively related to employees' perception of a culture for innovation. Likewise, the

Table 7.3 **Interactions between shared capitalism and high performance work policies in predicting innovation outcomes**

	Culture for innovation		Innovative ideas	
Independent variable	Model 1	Model 2	Model 3	Model 4
Shared capitalism index	–0.007 (0.005)	–0.023 (0.007)***	0.028 (0.006)***	0.032 (0.009)***
HPWS	0.768 (0.027)***		0.463 (0.031)***	
HPWST		0.161 (0.005)***		0.053 (0.006)***
Shared capitalism index				
*HPWS	0.015 (0.009)*		–0.045 (0.010)***	
*HPWST		0.007 (0.002)***		–0.004 (0.002)**
n	26,361	25,977	26,250	25,875
Adjusted R^2	0.134	0.185	0.157	0.149

Notes: All regressions include controls for country (twenty-two dummies), occupation (five dummies), mgt. level (three dummies), hourly pay status, supervisory status, tenure in years, hours worked per week, union status, age, gender, marital status (two dummies), family size, college graduate, graduate degree, number of kids, race (four dummies), disability status, ln(fixed pay), and company fixed effects. Standard error in parentheses.

***Significant at the 1 percent level.

**Significant at the 5 percent level.

*Significant at the 10 percent level.

interaction between shared capitalism and HPWS was positive and marginally significant. To further help with interpretation, the interaction results are portrayed in figure 7.1 (using table 7.3, model [2]). As seen there, shared capitalism has the most positive relationship to innovation culture when HPWST is at high levels, with a mild positive relationship when HPWST is at average levels. The relationship is negative when HPWST are at low levels, indicating that employees may perceive the innovation culture poorly when they are given the incentives, but not the tools, to make a difference—in this case the shared capitalism may be perceived as primarily a shifting of financial risk to employees.

There are very different results, however, in predicting willingness or ability to innovate. As reported in table 7.3 (models [3] and [4]) we find that while the base effects are positive and significant, the interaction between the shared capitalism index and high performance work practices is negative and significant for both HPWS and HPWST. These results indicate that when employees are covered by high performance work practices, the impact of shared capitalism policies on their willingness and ability to innovate for the organization is reduced. Put another way, the positive base effects and negative interaction indicates that these two constructs may substitute for each other: the base effect shows that shared capitalism has a positive effect on innovative activity for those who are not covered by HPWS, but shared capitalism has a much smaller or neutral effect for those who are covered by HPWS. An HPWS appears to provide a strong effect on its own, perhaps making unnecessary the addition of shared capitalism incentives.

To further help with interpretation, the interaction results are portrayed in figure 7.2 (using table 7.3, model [4]). Shared capitalism has a strong positive association with innovative ideas for workers with low values on HPWST, and only a mild positive association when HPWST is at high levels. These illustrate the point made before: high performance work policies and shared capitalist incentives may act somewhat as substitutes here, with shared capitalism providing the strongest incentives for contributing ideas among those who have not been encouraged to contribute ideas through high performance work policies.

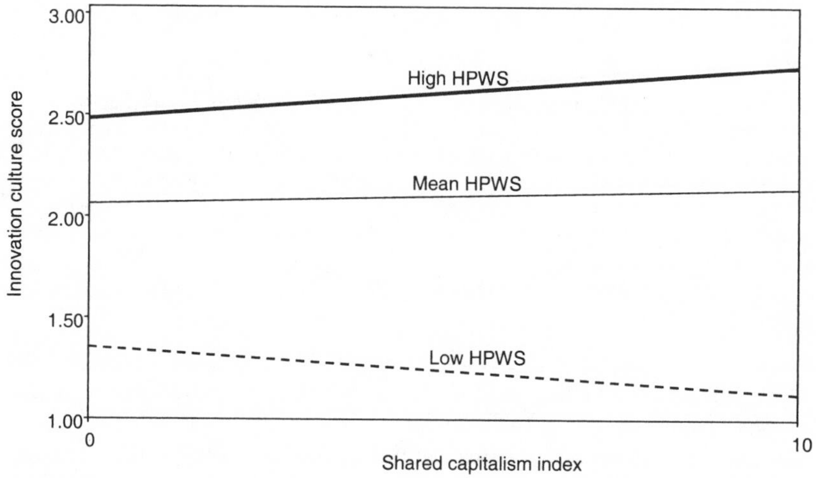

Fig. 7.1 Innovation culture, shared capitalism, and high performance work systems

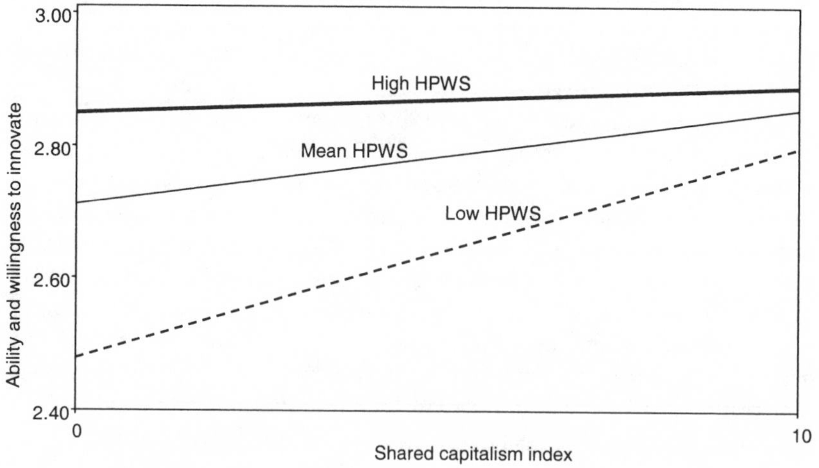

Fig. 7.2 Innovation ideas, shared capitalism, and high performance work systems

7.5.4 Alignment

Table 7.4 summarizes the empirical results on the relationship between shared capitalism, high performance work policies, and organizational alignment.

Shared Capitalism

The results listed in models (1), (3), and (4) indicate that shared capitalism may play a significant and positive role in aligning employees behind the goals and objectives of the organization. Even in the presence of high performance work policies, shared capitalism continues to play a significant and positive role in employee alignment. There are different results when interacting shared capitalism with the two HPWS measures: the base effect of shared capitalism stays strong and the interaction is insignificant in model (3), while the opposite is true in model (6). It is therefore unclear whether shared capitalism operates on its own or only in combination with HPWS in affecting alignment. The results of specific shared capitalism practices on employee alignment are also not consistent between the models controlling for different measures of HPWS. Stock option holding and profit/gain sharing as a percent of pay are predictors when controlling for HPWS, while profit/gain sharing eligibility and employee ownership as a percent of pay are predictors when controlling for HPWST. It is noteworthy that individual bonus eligibility (but not the bonus size) is a strong predictor of alignment, possibly reflecting greater bonus eligibility among high-level managers (not fully captured in the management level controls).

High Performance Work Policies

Consistent with the results for a culture for innovation and innovative ideas, high performance work policies continue to have a strong impact in models (1) to (6) of table 7.4. An interesting finding is the relative impact of the HPWS versus the HPWST on alignment. The adjusted R-square for the models with HPWST accounts for a greater amount of variance in the alignment of employees. This result could indicate that the greater impact on employee alignment is not when employees experience high performance policies (HPWS), but when they perceive these practices as effective (HPWST) in the context of their immediate local work group or team. This finding suggests that the level of measurement of high performance work practices is important.

Complementarities between Human Resource Policies and Shared Capitalism

Once again, using interaction terms we examined the impact of the complementary relationship between human resource management policies and shared capitalism on employee alignment. The only significant result is

Table 7.4 **Predicting employee alignment with company strategy**

Independent variable	Model 1	Model 2	Model 3	Model 4	Model 5	Model 6
Shared capitalism index	0.010 (0.003)***		0.014 (0.005)***	0.024 (0.003)***		0.009 (0.007)
Bonuses						
Profit/gain sharing		0.016 (0.013)			0.075 (0.012)***	
Profit/gain sharing as % of base pay		0.118 (0.070)*			0.139 (0.068)	
Individual bonus		0.053 (0.017)***			0.050 (0.017)**	
Individual bonus as % of base pay		0.058 (0.101)			0.012 (0.097)	
Employee ownership						
Any employee ownership		0.009 (0.012)			0.017 (0.011)	
Employee-owned stock as % of pay		0.011 (0.010)			0.022 (0.010)**	
Stock options						
Stock option holding		0.070 (0.031)**			0.035 (0.030)	
Stock option value as % of base pay		0.021 (0.032)			0.008 (0.031)	
High performance work policies						
HPWS	1.085 (0.017)***	1.081 (0.017)***	1.106 (0.028)***			
HPWST				0.230 (0.003)***	0.230 (0.003)***	0.222 (0.005)***
Shared capitalism index						
× HPWS			–0.008 (0.009)			
× HPWST						0.003 (0.002)**
n	26,787	26,243	26,787	26,348	25,819	26,348
Adjusted R^2	0.220	0.221	0.220	0.275	0.275	0.275

Notes: All regressions include controls for country (twenty-two dummies), occupation (five dummies), mgt. level (three dummies), hourly pay status, supervisory status, tenure in years, hours worked per week, union status, age, gender, marital status (two dummies), family size, college graduate, graduate degree, number of kids, race (four dummies), disability status, ln(fixed pay), and company fixed effects. Standard error in parentheses.

***Significant at the 1 percent level.

**Significant at the 5 percent level.

*Significant at the 10 percent level.

reported in model (6). Here shared capitalism interacts with HPWST and results in a positive effect on employee alignment. This result confirms the importance of ensuring that human resource policies and shared capitalism complement each other in order to achieve maximum benefits. Again, it is interesting to note that the interaction with shared capitalism was only significant with HPWST, which indicates the importance of perceived policy effectiveness in work groups over the mere presence of policies. It appears that such practices need not only to be bundled together but need to be bundled together in a way that is seen as effective within a local work group.

7.5.5 Mediating Role of Alignment

Across the results, a consistent finding is that HRM policies and shared capitalism are related to employees' perception of a culture for innovation and employees' willingness and ability to contribute innovative ideas. However, it is not clear how HRM policies and shared capitalism impact these outcomes (Becker and Gerhart 1996; Ostroff and Bowen 2000). For instance, management scholars have argued that HRM policies impact organizational outcomes through organizational culture (Ostroff and Bowen 2000), organizational commitment (Allen, Shore, and Griffeth 2003), and employee skills, motivation, and opportunities (Lepak et al. 2006).

While the intervening mechanisms previously listed are plausible, our interest is the impact HRM policies have in creating employee alignment. To test for mediation, three models are run to test four conditions (Baron and Kenny 1986). First, the independent variable (HRM policies or shared capitalism index) must significantly impact innovation outcomes. Second, the independent variable must significantly impact the mediator (alignment). Third, with the independent variable in the equation, alignment must impact innovation outcomes. The fourth necessary condition is a decrease in the coefficient between the independent variable and innovation outcomes as alignment is added. Using this technique it is possible to assess if the coefficient between the independent variable and the outcomes decreased with alignment in the equation. The extent of reduction in the coefficient reveals how much of the relationship between the independent variable and dependent is indirectly working through the mediator (alignment). Finally, Sobel's test is employed to ensure that the drop in the coefficient is significantly different from zero (Sobel 1982). Tables 7.5 and 7.6 report the results of the test of mediation.

Shared Capitalism

The results in tables 7.5 and 7.6 reveal that alignment does partially mediate the relationship between shared capitalism and employee's perception of a culture for innovation. This is indicated by the reduction in the shared capitalism coefficient from model (4) to model (6), and a significant value for Sobel's test, in both tables. Combined, these results suggest that one

Table 7.5 **Mediating role of alignment in predicting a culture for innovation**

Independent variable	Innovative environment	Alignment	Innovative environment	Innovative environment	Alignment	Innovative environment
Shared capitalism index	0.000 (0.003)	0.010 (0.003)***	–0.002 (0.002)	0.011 (0.003)***	0.024 (0.003)***	0.005 (0.002)*
High performance work policies						
HPWS	0.806 (0.016)***	1.085 (0.017)***	0.446 (0.017)***			
HPWST				0.180 (0.003)***	0.230 (0.003)***	0.117 (0.003)***
Alignment			0.313 (0.006)***			0.271 (0.006)***
n	26,361	26,787	26,145	25,976	26,347	
Adjusted R^2	0.134	0.220	0.237	0.184	0.275	

Notes: All regressions include controls for country (twenty-two dummies), occupation (five dummies), mgt. level (three dummies), hourly pay status, supervisory status, tenure in years, hours worked per week, union status, age, gender, marital status (two dummies), family size, college graduate, graduate degree, number of kids, race (four dummies), disability status, ln(fixed pay), and company fixed effects. Sobel Test HPWS: 40.39 ($p = .000$); Sobel Test Shared Capitalism: 7.88 ($p = .000$); Sobel Test HPWST: 38.92 ($p = .000$). Standard error in parentheses.

***Significant at the 1 percent level.

**Significant at the 5 percent level.

*Significant at the 10 percent level.

Table 7.6 **Mediating role of alignment in predicting innovative ideas**

Independent variable	Innovative ideas Model 1	Alignment Model 2	Innovative ideas Model 3	Innovative ideas Model 4	Alignment Model 5	Innovative ideas Model 6
Shared capitalism index	0.006 (0.003)**	0.010 (0.003)***	0.006 (0.003)**	0.012 (0.003)***	0.024 (0.003)***	0.011 (0.003)***
High performance work policies						
HPWS	0.350 (0.019)***	1.085 (0.017)***	0.311 (0.020)***			
HPWST				0.042 (0.003)***	0.230 (0.003)***	0.031 (0.004)***
Alignment			0.036 (0.007)***			0.047 (0.007)***
n	26,250	26,786	26,039	25,875	26,347	25,703
Adjusted R^2	0.156	0.220	0.157	0.149	0.275	0.151

Notes: All regressions include controls for country (twenty-two dummies), occupation (five dummies), mgt. level (three dummies), hourly pay status, supervisory status, tenure in years, hours worked per week, union status, age, gender, marital status (two dummies), family size, college graduate, graduate degree, number of kids, race (four dummies), disability status, ln(fixed pay), and company fixed effects. Sobel Test HPWS: 5.13 (p = .000); Sobel Test Shared Capitalism: 5.14 (p = .000); Sobel Test HPWST: 6.69 (p = .000). Standard error in parentheses.

***Significant at the 1 percent level.

**Significant at the 5 percent level.

*Significant at the 10 percent level.

way in which shared capitalism impacts innovation outcomes is by aligning the workforce behind the goals and strategic objectives of the organization. However, the shared capitalism coefficient was not reduced to zero for either outcome, implying other mechanisms are working between shared capitalism and innovation outcomes. These findings indicate that the overall corporate culture that binds employees together (understanding and agreeing with common goals, having the tools and involvement to advance those goals, and believing the culture is right to achieve these goals) does play a key role in determining how shared capitalism incentives relate to innovation, but that there still exists an independent incentive effect from shared capitalism. This is very similar to Barnard's view concerning the need for a package of monetary and nonmonetary incentives. The sense of common enterprise that results from shared capitalism appears to impact the agency problem by reinforcing a common culture among the members of the firm, yet the pure incentive effect of shared rewards themselves also appears to focus the individual worker (similar to the findings in Freeman, Kruse, and Blasi in chapter 2).

High Performance Work Policies

Also reported in tables 7.5 and 7.6 is the mediating role of alignment with high performance work policies. Specifically, the analysis reveals that alignment partially mediates the relationship that HPWS (models [1] through [3]) and HPWST (Models [4] through [6]) have with employees' perception of a culture for innovation. A similar result is obtained in predicting and employees' willingness and ability to contribute innovative ideas (table 7.6). These results indicate that part of the effect of high performance work policies on innovation outcomes is through aligning the workforce behind shared goals and objectives. However, since the high performance work system coefficients are not reduced to zero, high performance work policies also impact the innovation outcomes through additional means.

7.6 Conclusion

The principal findings of this chapter are that shared capitalism and high performance work policies affect innovation outcomes through direct effects, interactions, and indirect effects. The results of this study contribute to the current literature on shared capitalism and human resource management literature in a number of ways. First, empirical research on the importance of rewards and compensation practices as a means to achieve innovation outcomes is limited. This study adds to and extends the literature by examining multiple forms of shared capitalism and their impact on innovation outcomes. We demonstrate these effects in a population of adult workers in a large sample of respondents in hundreds of work sites, which provides several advantages in relation to past research. Additionally, we were able to identify a possible mediating mechanism between shared capitalism and innovation outcomes. Second, taking a systems perspective, we investigate the impact of two systems of high performance work policies on innovation outcomes. While innovation management scholars have examined the impact of individual human resource management practices on creativity or innovation, a systems approach has, to our knowledge, never been published (Harden 2006).

Organizations seeking to develop a culture of innovation could look to this research as an answer for how this occurs. Specifically, our results reveal that a culture for innovation can be developed and supported through the use of shared capitalism and high performance work practices. We found moderate support for the importance of pairing shared capitalism and high performance work practices together to achieve the greatest impact on a culture for innovation. Additionally, shared capitalism and high performance work practices work in part by aligning employees around the goals and objectives of the organization.

As organizations increasingly depend on all employees to contribute innovative ideas to the organization, this research aims to address the role that shared capitalism and high performance work policies play to achieve these ends. The results of this study indicate that a means to promote employee willingness and ability to contribute innovation ideas is the use of high performance work policies and shared capitalism, both of which had a strong positive relationship with this outcome. However, an interesting finding of this study is that the impact of shared capitalism on innovative ideas varies by the level of high performance work policies the employee experiences in his or her work group. And finally, the indirect effect of high performance work practices and shared capitalism on innovative ideas indicates that an aligned employee is more willing and able to contribute innovative ideas to the organization. Shared capitalism and high performance work practices are one way to align an employee behind the goals and objectives of the organization.

To the extent that innovation can be conceived as a principal-agent problem, we have demonstrated that a system of shared incentives and a shared high performance employment culture at the lowest levels of organizations is important to create both an innovative environment that is fertile ground for innovative ideas, and the willingness to work on innovative ideas. Taken together, these findings indicate that the overall corporate culture that binds employees together does play a key role in determining how shared capitalism incentives relate to innovation, but there still exists an independent incentive effect from shared capitalism. The sense of common enterprise that results from shared capitalism appears to impact the agency problem by reinforcing a common culture among the members of the firm, yet the pure incentive effect of shared rewards themselves also appears to focus the individual worker.

In summary, these findings confirm several of the main themes of agency theory: that the principal-agent problem can be addressed by incentives, and that agency conflicts respond to a cooperative culture between workers that encourages mutual monitoring and opportunities to share information. The results of this study make two unique and nuanced contributions to this perspective: first, that it is the combination of shared incentives, cooperative culture, and mutual monitoring that works best, and second, that high performance workplace systems help resolve agency problems when employees work in teams at the lowest level of the organization that are rich with rigorous selection, training, information sharing, clear goals, and fair rewards.

References

Allen, D. G., L. M. Shore, and R. W. Griffeth. 2003. The role of perceived organizational support and supportive human resource practices in the turnover process. *Journal of Management* 29 (1): 99–118.

Amabile, T. M. 1979. Effects of external evaluation on artistic creativity. *Journal of Personality and Social Psychology* 37 (2): 221–33.

———. 1983. *The social psychology of creativity.* New York: Springer-Verlag New York, Inc.

———. 1988. Poetry in a nonpoetic society. *Contemporary Psychology* 33:65–66.

Amabile, T., and N. D. Gryskiewicz. 1989. The creative environment scales: Work environment inventory. *Creativity Research Journal* 2 (3): 231–53.

Babbage, C. 1989. Martin Campbell-Kelly, ed. *The works of Charles Babbage.* London: William Pickering.

Baird, L., and I. Meshoulam. 1988. Managing two fits of strategic human resource management. *Academy of Management Review* 13 (1): 116–28.

Barnard, C. I. 1938. *The functions of the executive.* Cambridge, MA: Harvard University Press.

Baron, R. M., and D. A. Kenny. 1986. The moderator-mediator variable distinction in social psychological research: Conceptual, strategic and statistical considerations. *Journal of Personality and Social Psychology* 51 (6): 1173–82.

Becker, B. E., and M. A. Huselid. 1998. High performance work systems and firm performance: A synthesis of research and managerial implications. In *Research in personnel and human resource management,* vol. 16, ed. G. Ferris, 53–101. Greenwich, CT: JAI Press.

———. 2006. Strategic human resource management: Where do we go from here? *Journal of Management* 32 (6): 898–925.

Becker, B. E., and B. Gerhart. 1996. The impact of human resource management on organizational performance: Progress and prospects. *Academy of Management Journal* 39:779–801.

Blasi, J., and D. Kruse. 2006. High performance work practices at century's end. *Industrial Relations* 45 (4): 547–78.

Blasi, J., D. Kruse, and A. Bernstein. 2003. *In the company of owners: The truth about stock options (and why every employee should have them).* New York: Basic Books.

Bontis, N., M. M. Crossan, and J. Hulland. 2002. Managing an organizational learning system by aligning stocks and flows. *Journal of Management Studies* 39 (4): 437–69.

Boswell, W., and P. Wright. 2002. Desegregating HRM: A review and synthesis of micro and macro human resource management research. *Journal of Management* 28 (3): 247–76.

Business Week. 2006. How Whirlpool defines innovation. March 6.

Cameron, J., and W. D. Pierce. 1994. Reinforcement, reward and intrinsic motivation: A meta-analysis. *Review of Educational Research* 64 (3): 363–423.

Christensen, C. M., and M. L. Raynor. 2003. *The innovators solution: Creating and sustaining successful growth*. Boston: Harvard Business School Press.

Clark, K. B., and T. Fujimoto. 1991. *Product development performance: Strategy, organization and management in the world auto industry*. Boston: Harvard Business School.

Cohen, W. M., and D. A. Levinthal. 1990. Absorptive capability: A new perspective on learning and innovation. *Administration Science Quarterly* 35 (March): 128–52.

Combs, J., Y. Liu, A. A. Hall, and D. Ketchen. 2006. How much do high-performance work practices matter? A meta-analysis of their effects on organizational performance. *Personnel Psychology* 59 (October): 501–28.

Deci, E. L., R. Koestner, and R. M. Ryan. 1999. A meta-analytic review of experiments examining the effects of extrinsic rewards on intrinsic motivation. *Psychological Bulletin* 125 (6): 627–68.

Deci, E. L., and R. M. Ryan. 1985. *Intrinsic motivation and self-determination in human behavior*. New York: Plenum.

Dougherty, D. 1992. A practice-centered model of organizational renewal through product innovation. *Strategic Management Journal* 13 (51): 77–92.

Eisenberger, R., and J. Cameron. 1996. Detrimental effects of reward: Reality or myth? *American Psychologist* 51 (11): 1153–66.

Eisenberger, R., and M. Selbst. 1994. Does reward increase or decrease creativity? *Journal of Personality and Social Psychology* 66:1116–27.

Feist, G. J. 1998. A meta-analysis of personality in scientific and artistic creativity. *Personality and Social Psychology Review* 2 (4): 290–309.

Gamble, J. E. 2000. Management commitment to innovation and ESOP stock concentration. *Journal of Business Venturing* 15 (5-6): 433–47.

Guilford, J. P. 1950. Creativity. *American Psychologist* 5:444–54.

Hackman, J. R., and G. R. Oldham. 1980. *Work redesign*. Reading, MA: Addison-Wesley.

Harden, E. E. 2006. High performance work practices and firm performance: Assessing the mediating role of innovative capabilities and the moderating role of strategy. Master's Thesis, Rutgers University.

Hayes, R. H., S. C. Wheelwright, and K. B. Clark. 1988. *Dynamic manufacturing*. New York: Free Press.

Henderson, R., and I. Cockburn. 1994. Measuring competence? Exploring firm effects in pharmaceutical research. *Strategic Management Journal* 15 (Winter): 63–84.

Huselid, M. 1995. The impact of human resource management practices on the turnover, productivity, and corporate financial performance. *Academy of Management Journal* 38:635–72.

Huselid, M. A., B. E. Becker, and R. W. Beatty. 2005. *The workforce scorecard: Managing human capital to execute strategy*. Boston: Harvard Business School.

Iansiti, M. 1995. Shooting the rapids: Managing product development in turbulent environments. *California Management Review* 38 (1): 37–58.

Ichniowski, C., T. Kochan, D. Levine, C. Olson, and G. Strauss. 1996. What works at work: Overview and assessment. *Industrial Relations* 35 (3): 299–333.

Jackson, S. E., and R. S. Schuler. 2002. Managing individual performance: An individual perspective. In *Psychological management of individual performance,* ed. S. Sonnentag, 371–90. New York: John Wiley and Sons.

Jelinek, M., and C. B. Schoonhoven. 1990. *Innovation marathon: Lessons from high technology firms.* Oxford: Basil Blackwell.

King, N. 1990. Innovation at work: The research literature. In *Innovation and creativity at work,* ed. M. A. W. J. L. Farr, 15–59. New York: Wiley.

Kruse, D. 1996. Why do firms adopt profit sharing and employee ownership plans? *British Journal of Industrial Relations* 34 (4): 515–38.

Laffont, J., and D. Martimort. 2002. *The theory of incentives: The principal-agent model.* Princeton, NJ: Princeton University Press.

Leonard-Barton, D. 1992. Core capabilities and core rigidities: A paradox in managing new product development. *Strategic Management Journal* 13 (51): 111–25.

Lepak, D. P., H. Liao, Y. Chung, and E. E. Harden. 2006. A conceptual review of high involvement HR systems in strategic HRM research. In *Research in personnel and human resource management,* vol. 25, ed. J. M., 217–71. Greenwich, CT: JAI Press.

Lerner, J., and J. Wulf. 2007. Innovation and incentives: Evidence from corporate R&D. *The Review of Economics and Statistics* 89 (4): 634–44.

MacDuffie, J. P. 1995. Human resource bundles and manufacturing performance: Organizational logic and flexible production systems in the world auto industry. *Industrial and Labor Relations Review* 48 (January): 197–221.

Mahroum, S. 2008. Innovate out of the economic downturn. *Business Week,* October 27. Available at: http://www.businessweek.com.

Mehr, D. G., and P. R. Shaver. 1996. Goal structures in creating motivation. *Journal of Creative Behavior* 30:77–104.

Mumford, M. 2000. Managing creative people: Strategies and tactics for innovation. *Human Resource Management Review* 10 (3): 313–51.

Oldham, G. R. 2003. Stimulating and supporting creativity in organizations. In *Managing knowledge for sustained competitive advantage,* S. E. Jackson, M. A. Hitt, and A. S. DeNisi, 243–73. San Francisco: Jossey-Bass.

Ostroff, C., and D. E. Bowen. 2000. Moving HR to a higher level. In *Multilevel theory, research, and methods in organizations,* ed. K. J. Klein and S. W. Kozlowski, 211–66. San Francisco: Jossey-Bass.

Rummel, A., and R. Feinberg. 1988. Cognitive evaluation theory: A meta-analytic review of the literature. *Social Behavior and Personality* 16 (2): 147–64.

Schuler, R. S. 1992. Strategic human resource management: Linking the people with the strategic needs of the business. *Organizational Dynamics* (Summer):18–32.

Scott, S. G., and R. A. Bruce. 1994. Determinants of innovative behavior: A path model of individual innovation in the workplace. *Academy of Management Journal* 38:1442–65.

Sesil, J., M. Kroumova, J. Blasi, and D. Kruse. 2002. Broad-based employee stock options in US new economy firms. *British Journal of Industrial Relations* 4 (2): 273–94.

Shalley, C. E. 1995. Effects of coaction, expected evaluation, and goal setting on creativity and productivity. *Academy of Management Journal* 38 (2): 483–503.

Sobel, M. E. 1982. Asymptotic intervals for indirect effects in structural equations models. In *Sociological methodology,* ed. S. Leinhart, 290–312. San Francisco: Jossey-Bass.

Tang, S. H., and V. C. Hall. 1995. The overjustification effect: A meta-analysis. *Applied Cognitive Psychology* 9 (5): 365–404.
Van de Ven, A. H. 1986. Central problems in the management of innovation. *Management Science* 32 (5): 590–607.
Venkatraman, N. 1989. The concept of fit in strategy research: Toward verbal and statistical correspondence. *Academy of Management Review* 14 (3): 423–44.
Wheatley, W. J., W. P. Anthony, and E. N. Maddox. 1991. Selecting and training strategic planners with imagination and creativity. *Journal of Creative Behavior* 25 (1): 52–60.
Wiersma, U. J. 1992. The effects of extrinsic rewards on intrinsic motivation: A meta-analysis. *Journal of Occupational and Organizational Psychology* 65 (2): 101–14.
Woodman, R. W., J. E. Sawyer, and R. W. Griffen. 1993. Toward a theory of organizational creativity. *Academy of Management Review* 18 (2): 293–321.
Woodman, R. W., and L. F. Schoenfeldt. 1989. Individual differences in creativity: An interactionist perspective. In *Handbook of creativity,* ed. J. A. Glover, R. R. Ronning, and C. R. Reynolds, 77–92. New York: Plenum.
Wright, P. M., and G. C. McMahan. 1992. Theoretical perspectives for strategic human resource management. *Journal of Management* 18 (2): 295–320.
Zacharatos, A., J. Barling, and R. D. Iverson. 2005. High-performance work systems and occupational safety. *Journal of Applied Psychology* 90 (11): 77–93.

III

Worker Well-Being

8

Do Workers Gain by Sharing?
Employee Outcomes under Employee Ownership, Profit Sharing, and Broad-Based Stock Options

Douglas L. Kruse, Richard B. Freeman, and Joseph R. Blasi

Today, more employees than ever before have ownership stakes in their firms through Employee Stock Ownership Plans (ESOPs) and firm-based stock ownership plans, receive stock options once limited to top executives, and are covered by profit-sharing plans. The media has publicized both the rewards and dangers of tying worker pay and wealth to company performance. The 1990s produced many stories of regular employees becoming millionaires by working in Silicon Valley firms with broad-based options that paid off handsomely. The early 2000s produced stories about Enron employees losing their retirement moneys in a 401(k) plan that was heavily concentrated in company stock. Apart from the extreme cases that get publicized, are these programs generally good or bad for workers?

This chapter uses the General Social Survey (GSS) and NBER data sets to analyze the relationship of shared capitalism programs to a range of employee outcomes: participation in decisions, supervision, training, company treatment of employees, pay, job security, and job satisfaction.

8.1 What We Expect

On the basis of incentive and organization theory and previous empirical work, we expect that linking employee pay to company performance will impact workers in several ways.

Douglas L. Kruse is a professor of human resource management and labor studies and employment relations at the Rutgers School of Management and Labor Relations, and a research associate of the National Bureau of Economic Research. Richard B. Freeman holds the Herbert Ascherman Chair in Economics at Harvard University and is a research associate of the National Bureau of Economic Research. Joseph R. Blasi is a professor of human resource management and labor studies and employment relations at the Rutgers School of Management and Labor Relations, and a research associate of the National Bureau of Economic Research.

8.1.1 Employee Participation in Decision Making

Shared capitalist compensation systems should be associated with greater freedom for workers to make decisions at their workplace. It is difficult to imagine a firm devolving decisions to workers without developing some pecuniary mechanism for motivating them to make decisions in the firm's interest, be it profit sharing, gain sharing, stock options, or share ownership. Indeed, one common reason for firms to institute compensation systems relating employee pay to company performance is to induce workers to make decisions that improve firm performance (assessed in chapter 4).

Two national surveys of workers have found the expected relation. For the United States, Dube and Freeman (2001) found a positive relation between shared capitalist compensation systems and employee decision making in Freeman and Rogers' (2006) Worker Representation and Participation Survey, with strong results for profit sharing but weak results for employee ownership. For the United Kingdom, Conyon and Freeman (2004) found a positive link between changes in variable pay and changes in decision making in the Workplace Employment Relations Survey. However, firm-based studies of *employee ownership* find only a weak pattern between perceived or desired participation in decision making and employee ownership. Half of the ten studies reviewed by Kruse and Blasi (1997) found participation levels higher with employee ownership while half found no difference in participation. None of the studies found a connection between participation in decisions and the size of one's ownership stake. Two of the studies that asked about *desired* participation found no difference between employee-owners and nonowners, while a third study found a decline in desired worker participation after an employee buyout, which the author attributes to wariness by employees about the commitment levels of new employees and trust in management (Long 1981, 1982).

8.1.2 Supervision, Training, and Workplace Relations

Any shared compensation system must overcome potential free rider problems. The larger the number of people who share in the rewards of the firm or group, the lower is the incentive for the individual to work hard and the greater the reward to shirking. In chapter 2, we find that worker monitoring of the group is an important mode for overcoming the free rider problem. Firms cannot force workers to self-monitor but they can provide supportive supervision, training, and a workplace climate that encourages group norms to sustain a self-monitoring equilibrium.

Few studies have examined the relation of shared capitalism programs to supervision, training, and workplace climate. Regarding supervision, Pendleton (2006) finds greater employee discretion in establishments with broad-based employee ownership plans. Brown and Sessions (2003) report that employees in performance-related pay plans have more positive views about management-employee relations and how the workplace is run. Consistent with the idea of improved management-employee relations, the probability of a strike goes down after a unionized firm adopts an ESOP (Cramton, Mehran, and Tracy 2008). Two studies have found that employees in profit-sharing plans are more likely to receive employer-provided training (Azfar and Danninger 2001; Robinson and Zhang 2005). One study found mixed effects of profit sharing on relations among co-workers, with profit sharing increasing cooperation for nonsupervisory personnel but decreasing it for supervisors, and having no effect for those who highly value cooperation on the job (Heywood, Jirjahn, and Tsertsvadze 2005b). A companion study found that profit sharing reduces worker-management conflict for nonsupervisory workers in excellent health, but not for supervisors or those not in excellent health (Heywood, Jirjahn, and Tsertsvadze 2005a).

Two studies have examined whether workplaces are safer under shared employee ownership. Rooney (1992) found fewer OSHA injuries in employee ownership companies with greater worker participation in decisions, but otherwise found mixed results for ownership without participation. Rhodes and Steers (1981) found that accidents were no lower in a plywood cooperative compared to a standard plywood company.

8.1.3 Pay and Benefits

There are two reasons for expecting shared capitalist compensation systems to be associated with higher pay and benefits.

First, shared capitalist systems could operate in part as a "gift exchange" between the worker and the firm, in which the higher pay increases worker effort, decreases turnover, and increases worker loyalty (Akerlof 1982). By encouraging employee cooperation, shared capitalism programs could increase output, some of which would go to workers as their share of profits and some as higher base wages or benefits. The sharing system would be a key component of a mutual-gains or high-commitment system where both workers and the firms come out ahead (Handel and Levine 2004, 5). While employers may get some gift exchange benefits simply by raising levels of fixed pay, the provision of this higher compensation in the form of shared capitalist pay may further help to create and reinforce a sense of common interests and incentives for discouraging free riding. Second, since shared capitalism increases risk to workers, compensating differential theory predicts that workers will want higher overall compensation. Whether this compensation takes the form of fixed pay and benefits or shows up in a larger share in profits and ownership is unclear. Again, what creates the potential for higher income to workers is the higher productivity generated by the system. If the higher compensation is only enough to compensate for the added risk, then we might see some greater effort by employees to justify the higher compensation, but would not expect other changes in attitudes and behavior associated with a gift exchange (higher commitment and loyalty, reduced turnover, etc.). If the higher compensation also provides a gift on top of the risk premium to help change attitudes and behaviors, shared capitalism will need to pay for itself through large productivity improvements, both to cover the risk premium and the extra gift.

Despite some well-publicized examples of wage concessions when workers buy out their companies or accept large ownership stakes (which make up a very small percentage of the employee ownership landscape), workers in employee ownership plans tend to have comparable or higher wages or compensation than other workers. In a pre/post study of ESOPs adopted by public companies between 1980 and 2004, Kim and Ouimet (2008) find significant increases in employee compensation following the adoption of ESOPs, particularly for ESOPs owning more than 5 percent of a company where the long-term increase in compensation is 4.5 percent. A similar method used on German firms adopting profit-sharing plans also concluded that profit sharing supplemented rather than substituted for standard compensation (Ugarkovi 2007). Blasi, Conte, and Kruse (1996) found that US public companies with broad-based employee ownership plans had 8 percent higher average compensation levels than other comparable public companies, and compensation increased with the percentage of stock held by employees. Studies of pay and benefits in ESOP and non-ESOP firms in Massachusetts and Washington state also found that the levels of pay and other benefits were similar between these two types of firms, so that ESOPs appear to come on top of other worker pay and benefits (Kardas, Scharf, and Keogh 1998; Scharf and Mackin 2000). With regard to other forms of ownership, Renaud, St-Onge, and Magnan (2004) found that stock purchase plan participation was associated with subsequent pay increases for employees, and employer stock held in 401(k) plans appears to come largely on top of other pension assets (Kroumova 2000). Seven studies from the United States, Great Britain, and Germany find that profit-sharing firms also have generally higher average compensation than otherwise-comparable firms (Kruse 1993, 113–14; Handel and Gittleman 2004).

Still, it is possible that the higher pay levels associated with shared capitalist compensation reflect higher unmeasured worker quality, and that workers in fact take a cut in compensation to link their pay to company performance. But the evidence runs against these possibilities. Kruse (1998) found that average base pay levels and other benefits increase as young workers join profit-sharing firms and decrease as they leave such firms, so worker selectivity cannot dominate the cross-section relation. Similarly, Azfar and Danninger (2001) found that employees in profit-sharing plans receive higher annual raises in base pay than employees in other firms, connected in part to the greater training noted earlier. Other studies find that neither wages nor total labor costs exclusive of the sharing component fall significantly in pre/post comparisons of firms that adopt profit sharing (Black, Lynch, and Krivelyova [2004] for wages; Cappelli and Neumark [2004] for total labor costs). The implication is that trade-offs between base pay and shared capitalist compensation are minimal and that profit sharing may be used in conjunction with higher base pay levels as part of an efficiency wage strategy.

Another possibility is that the higher monetary compensation associated with shared capitalist systems may come at the cost of greater effort, stress, workplace danger, or other disamenities at work. Some analysts view the systems as a bit of a sham, designed to elicit greater worker effort and to shift risk to workers, without increasing the pay or quality of jobs. This is "'management by stress' . . . which believes that [employee involvement] is simply a method of sweating the workforce and curbing worker power and influence" (Handel and Levine 2004, 6).

Our data allows us to compare compensation for workers covered and not covered by the shared capitalist compensation and to compare compensation for workers by the intensity of their shared compensation arrangements.

8.1.4 Job Security

Traditional theoretical analysis of hypothetical labor-run firms predicts that they have lower employment than in management-run firms, and respond perversely to demand shocks, lowering employment when output prices increase (reviewed in Bonin and Putterman [1987]). Most empirical studies show that employee ownership firms tend to have more stable employment than other firms, and do not respond perversely to demand shocks (Craig and Pencavel 1992, 1993; Blair, Kruse, and Blasi 2000). Two studies report that employment grew faster in firms following the adoption of ESOPs, particularly if they had greater employee participation in decision making (Quarrey and Rosen 1993; Winther and Marens 1997). In addition, public firms with substantial employee ownership are more likely than other comparable firms to survive over time (Blair, Kruse, and Blasi 2000; Park, Kruse, and Sesil 2004). French worker cooperatives also have high rates of survival (Estrin and Jones 1992).

Profit sharing, in contrast, should create excess demand for employment and thus provide substantial job security (Weitzman 1984). Nineteen studies have examined Weitzman's predictions that profit sharing should stabilize firm employment (Kruse 1998, 109–13). A majority found that firms view profit sharing differently from fixed wages in making employment decisions. Of the twelve studies directly examining employment stability, six found greater employment stability under profit sharing; four showed greater stability in some but not all samples; while two have little or no support for the stabilizing effects of profit sharing.

8.1.5 Job Satisfaction

If shared capitalism is associated with greater participation and decision making at the workplace, better supervision, more training, more job security, and higher total compensation, these modes of pay ought to raise job satisfaction. But the twelve existing studies on job satisfaction under employee ownership yield no clear generalization.[1] Several studies show higher satisfaction; several show no relationship; and one study shows lower satisfaction among employee-owners where the union had lost a bitter strike the year before.[2] Participation in decisions seems to be important: one longitudinal study found that satisfaction went up only among those who perceived increased participation in decisions after an employee buyout (Long 1982). Our data provide the largest sample for assessing these inconclusive findings.

In sum, prior research on employee outcomes under shared capitalism has yielded generally positive results, though there is sufficient variability in some results to suggest that they depend on the context in which they are implemented. By addressing all of the employee outcomes with the GSS and the NBER data sets, and providing more robust measures of the employment context inside these firms, we should be better able to provide a more consistent generalization than the existing work. These studies span a period of a quarter century. It must be recognized, for example, that the phenomenon of employee decision making and shared capitalism may have been evolving over this period. (For an example of evolution in Silicon Valley, see Blasi, Kruse, and Bernstein [2003].)

8.2 Data and Analysis

This chapter uses the GSS and NBER data sets (described in the "Studying Shared Capitalism" section of the introduction to this volume). Our key independent variable of interest is the thermometer-style index of shared capitalism, which assigns points based on coverage by shared capitalism programs and the size of the financial stakes. This index is described in appendix B. We also present results breaking out the different forms of shared capitalism types and intensities using the NBER data.

We have organized employee outcomes into eight areas: participation in decisions, company treatment of employees, supervision, training, pay and benefits, co-worker relations, job security, and job satisfaction. These outcomes are related to each other—for example, training generally leads to higher pay; participation in decisions, training, job security, and supervision are likely to affect perceptions of how the company treats employees; and so on. We lack instruments to identify causality, so we do not try to tease

1. This is based on nine studies on job satisfaction in Kruse and Blasi (1997); plus Pendleton, Wilson, and Wright (1998); Keef (1998); and Bakan et al. (2004). The studies were selected if they used systematic data collection from representative samples of employees, and used statistical techniques to rule out sampling error. Many used multivariate analysis to hold constant the effect of other factors on employee attitudes or behavior.

2. Reminders by management that the strike would hurt ESOP account values brought the response "We don't vote; we don't control the company; we don't care" (Kruse 1984, 51).

out possible causal links among the outcomes. Rather, we test for the reduced form relationship between shared capitalism and each of the individual outcomes conditional on demographic and job characteristics, and in some cases on other outcomes as well—for example, since company training is likely to affect pay, we examine whether shared capitalism is related to pay both before and after controlling for training.

8.3 Empirical Results

We first use the shared capitalist index to predict each of the outcomes (table 8.1), and then probe the impact of different types and intensities of shared capitalist compensation using the NBER data set (tables 8A.1 to 8A.5). We estimate ordinary least squares (OLS) regressions when outcomes are numeric and use ordered probits when the outcomes have three or four values with a natural ordering (e.g., "not at all true, not very true, somewhat true, and very true"). The regression predicting hours of training use a Tobit specification, to account for the censoring at zero. Most of the regressions using the NBER data set include company fixed effects so that coefficients reflect *within-company differences* rather than cross-company differences that might be due to unmeasured differences among the companies. At the bottom of tables 8A.1 to 8A.5, some ESOP coefficients are reported where company fixed effects are not used. Federal Employee Retirement Income Security Act (ERISA) law imposes strict requirements on coverage so that most or all employees are covered by an ESOP within a firm; the small number of excluded employees are thus likely to differ in some particular way from other employees in the same firm. Because of this the ESOP effects are better determined by comparing otherwise-similar ESOP and non-ESOP workers *across firms* in the specifications without fixed effects.

Table 8.1 summarizes our empirical results in terms of the coefficients on the shared capitalism index variable for the eight outcomes under study. In most cases, we examine more than one outcome under the specified domain.

8.3.1 Employee Participation in Decisions

Almost all of the measures of participation in decision making in table 8.1 are positively and significantly related to the shared capitalism index in both the GSS national and NBER data sets. There are two exceptions in the NBER data—the relationships with participation in company decisions and satisfaction with participation in the NBER data, but only after controlling for other outcomes (employee involvement team, training, and job security). This indicates that shared capitalism is strongly correlated with these policies, and the package of these policies may be the most important determinant (which we examine in table 8.2).

When the shared capitalism policies are broken out in appendix table

Table 8.1 Relation of eight employee outcomes to shared capitalist compensation

Dependent variables	Coefficient (standard error) of shared capitalism index	Job and demog.	EI team	Training	Job security	*N*
1. Participation in decisions						
National data						
Lot of say about what happens on job (1–4 scale)	**0.064** *** (0.014)	x				1,677
Take part with others in making decisions (1–4 scale)	**0.100** *** (0.015)	x				1,680
Participate with others in setting way things are done (1–4 scale)	**0.084** *** (0.015)	x				1,679
Lot of freedom to decide how to do work (1–4 scale)	**0.053** *** (0.015)	x				1,680
NBER company data						
Part. in job decisions (1–4 scale)(ordered probit)	**0.039** *** (0.004)	x				39,117
	0.019 *** (0.005)	x	x	x	x	35,596
Part. in group/dept. goals (1–4 scale)(ordered probit)	**0.020** *** (0.004)	x				38,997
	0.004 ** (0.004)	x	x	x	x	35,501
Part. in company decisions (1–4 scale)(ordered probit)	**0.012** *** (0.004)	x				38,942
	–0.002 (0.004)	x	x	x	x	35,462
In employee involvement team (0–1)(linear prob.)	**0.020** *** (0.002)	x				38,576
	0.017 *** (0.002)	x		x	x	35,838
Satisfaction with participation (1–4 scale)(ordered probit)	**0.016** *** (0.004)	x				38,964
	–0.002 (0.004)	x	x	x	x	35,494
2. Company treatment of employees						
National data						
Am treated with respect at work (1–4 scale)(ordered probit)	0.029 * (0.015)	x				1,679
Mgt-employee relations (1–4 scale)(ordered probit)	**0.036** *** (0.014)	x				1,677
Promotions are handled fairly (1–4 scale)(ordered probit)	**0.042** *** (0.014)	x				1,610
Worker safety is high priority with mgt. (1–4 scale)(ordered probit)	**0.067** *** (0.015)	x				1,671
Lack of stress at work (1–4 scale)(ordered probit)	0.008 (0.013)	x				1,681

NBER company data						
When co. does well, ees. share benefits (1–7 scale)(OLS)	**0.126** *** (0.006)	x				39,065
	0.104 *** (0.006)	x	x	x	x	35,592
Co. is fair to ees. (1–7 scale)(OLS)	**0.063** *** (0.006)	x				39,030
	0.038 *** (0.006)	x	x	x	x	35,548
Grade of co. on sharing info (0–4 scale)(OLS)	**0.023** *** (0.004)	x				38,932
	0.008 ** (0.004)	x	x	x	x	35,452
Grade of co. on trustworthiness (0–4 scale)(OLS)	**0.029** *** (0.004)	x				38,821
	0.012 *** (0.004)	x	x	x	x	35,394
Grade of co. on employee relations (0–4 scale)(OLS)	**0.023** *** (0.004)	x				38,884
	0.008 ** (0.004)	x	x	x	x	35,420
3. Supervision						
National data						
Supervisor is helpful to me (1–4 scale)(ordered probit)	**0.038** *** (0.015)	x				1,675
Supervisor cares about welfare of those under him or her (1–4 scale)(ordered probit)	**0.055** *** (0.015)	x				1,667
NBER company data						
Freedom from close supervision (0–10 scale)(OLS)	**0.039** *** (0.009)	x				39,488
	0.034 *** (0.009)	x	x	x	x	35,838
4. Training						
National data						
Have training opportunities I need	**0.045** *** (0.016)	x				1,678
NBER company data						
Formal job training in past 12 mos. (0–1)(OLS)	**0.019** *** (0.002)	x				38,863
	0.015 *** (0.002)	x	x		x	35,838
Hours of training in past 12 mos. (Tobit)	**2.289** *** (0.226)	x				37,905
	1.838 *** (0.236)	x	x		x	34,974
Informal job training from co-workers (1–4 scale)(ordered probit)	**0.022** *** (0.004)	x				39,033
	0.009 *** (0.004)	x	x	x	x	35,597

(continued)

Table 8.1 (continued)

Dependent variables	Coefficient (standard error) of shared capitalism index	Job and demog.	EI team	Training	Job security	*N*
5. Pay and Benefits						
National data						
Yearly earnings (natural logarithm)(OLS)	**0.092** *** (0.009)	x				1,681
Paid what you deserve (1–5 scale)(ordered probit)	**0.059** *** (0.013)	x				1,841
Fringe benefits are good (1–4 scale)(ordered probit)	**0.117** *** (0.014)	x				1,860
NBER company data						
Fixed pay (natural logarithm)(OLS)	**0.023** *** (0.002)	x				30,122
	0.024 *** (0.002)	x	x	x	x	28,324
Fixed pay % diff. from market (OLS)	0.094 (0.067)	x				30,782
	0.051 (0.070)	x	x	x	x	28,152
Total compensation % diff. from market (OLS)	**0.511** *** (0.072)	x				29,569
	0.468 *** (0.075)	x	x	x	x	27,199
Grade of co. on wages (0–4 scale)(OLS)	**0.025** *** (0.004)	x				39,068
	0.018 *** (0.004)	x	x	x	x	35,564
Grade of co. on benefits (0–4 scale)(OLS)	**0.034** *** (0.004)	x				39,011
	0.024 *** (0.004)	x	x	x	x	35,519
6. Co-worker relations						
National data						
Co-workers can be relied on for help	**0.030** ** (0.015)	x				1,680
Co-workers take personal interest in me	**0.047** *** (0.015)	x				1,675
7. Job security						
National data						
Job security (1–4 scale)(ordered probit)	**0.047** *** (0.015)	x				1,676
Not laid off in past year (0–1 dummy)	**0.012** *** (0.003)	x				1,681

NBER company data							
Job security (1–4 scale)(ordered probit)	**0.054** ***	(0.004)	x				37,052
	0.051 ***	(0.004)	x	x	x		35,838
8. Job satisfaction							
National data							
Job satisfaction (1–4 scale)(ordered probit)	0.022	(0.018)	x				1,262
NBER company data							
Job satisfaction (1–7 scale)(OLS)	**0.015** ***	(0.005)	x				39,192
	–0.004	(0.005)	x	x	x	x	35,685

Notes: Each row represents results of separate regression. Job and demographic controls include age, sex, race, tenure, occupation, earnings, full-time status, and ease of seeing co-workers for all regressions, plus work in a team for national regressions, and management level, supervisory status, disability status, closeness of supervision, payment on an hourly rate, and company fixed effects for the NBER company regressions. Earnings controls include ln(yearly earnings) for the national data and ln(base pay) for the NBER company regressions. See appendix A for variable definitions and descriptive statistics. Coefficients in bold are significant at $p < .05$. ees. = employees.

***Significant at the 1 percent level.

**Significant at the 5 percent level.

*Significant at the 10 percent level.

Table 8.2 **Complementarities of shared capitalist compensation in affecting employee outcomes**

Dependent variables	Shared capitalism base effect (1)	High performance policies: Base effect (2)	High performance policies: Shared cap. Interaction (3)	Closely supervised: Base effect (4)	Closely supervised: Shared cap. interaction (5)
Participation in decisions					
Part. in job decisions (1–4 scale)(ordered probit)	0.056***	0.212***	0.009***	–0.037***	–0.015***
	(0.008)	(0.013)	(0.003)	(0.004)	(0.001)
Part. in group/dept. goals (1–4 scale)(ordered probit)	0.017**	0.238***	0.013***	0.008*	–0.011***
	(0.007)	(0.013)	(0.003)	(0.004)	(0.001)
Part. in company decisions (1–4 scale)(ordered probit)	–0.020**	0.211***	0.021***	0.030***	–0.007***
	(0.008)	(0.013)	(0.003)	(0.004)	(0.001)
In employee involvement team (0–1)(linear prob.)	0.011***	0.070***	0.006***	0.002	–0.001
	(0.003)	(0.007)	(0.002)	(0.002)	(0.000)
Satisfaction with participation (1–4 scale)(ordered probit)	–0.010	0.251***	0.024***	0.019***	–0.010***
	(0.007)	(0.013)	(0.003)	(0.004)	(0.001)
Company treatment of employees					
When co. does well, ees. share benefits (1–7 scale)(OLS)	0.187***	0.396***	–0.031***	0.013**	–0.008***
	(0.011)	(0.018)	(0.004)	(0.006)	(0.001)
Co. is fair to ees. (1–7 scale)(OLS)	0.090***	0.422***	–0.010***	0.017***	–0.010***
	(0.010)	(0.017)	(0.004)	(0.006)	(0.001)
Grade of co. on sharing info (0–4 scale)(OLS)	0.043***	0.272***	–0.002	0.029***	–0.010***
	(0.007)	(0.012)	(0.003)	(0.004)	(0.001)
Grade of co. on trustworthiness (0–4 scale)(OLS)	0.050***	0.287***	–0.004	0.028***	–0.010***
	(0.007)	(0.012)	(0.003)	(0.004)	(0.001)
Grade of co. on employee relations (0–4 scale)(OLS)	0.043***	0.257***	0.000	0.029***	–0.011***
	(0.007)	(0.011)	(0.002)	(0.004)	(0.001)
Supervision					
Freedom from close supervision (0–10 scale)(OLS)	0.017	0.031	0.012		
	(0.014)	(0.027)	(0.006)		

Training					
Formal job training in past 12 mos. (0–1)(OLS)	0.015***	0.092***	0.001	0.005***	0.000
	(0.003)	(0.007)	(0.002)	(0.002)	(0.000)
Hours of training in past 12 mos. (Tobit)	2.047***	11.048***	0.076	0.344	–0.106*
	(0.398)	(1.002)	(0.209)	(0.239)	(0.055)
Informal job training from co-workers (1–4 scale)(ordered probit)	0.005	0.188***	0.008***	0.030***	–0.004***
	(0.007)	(0.012)	(0.003)	(0.004)	(0.001)
Pay and benefits					
Fixed pay (natural logarithm)(OLS)	0.028***	0.017***	–0.001	–0.009***	–0.001*
	(0.003)	(0.005)	(0.001)	(0.002)	(0.000)
Fixed pay % diff. from market (OLS)	0.249**	0.870***	0.012	0.297***	–0.073***
	(0.124)	(0.218)	(0.047)	(0.071)	(0.016)
Total compensation % diff. from market (OLS)	0.558***	0.771***	0.094*	0.184**	–0.084***
	(0.134)	(0.239)	(0.050)	(0.078)	(0.018)
Grade of co. on wages (0–4 scale)(OLS)	0.041***	0.141***	–0.002	0.007**	–0.006***
	(0.007)	(0.011)	(0.003)	(0.004)	(0.001)
Grade of co. on benefits (0–4 scale)(OLS)	0.057***	0.187***	–0.008***	0.007*	–0.006***
	(0.007)	(0.011)	(0.002)	(0.004)	(0.001)
Job security					
Job security (1–4 scale)(ordered probit)	0.065***	0.098***	0.002	–0.029***	–0.005***
	(0.006)	(0.015)	(0.003)	(0.004)	(0.001)
Job satisfaction					
Job satisfaction (1–7 scale)(OLS)	–0.007	0.264***	0.019***	0.001	–0.009***
	(0.008)	(0.014)	(0.003)	(0.004)	(0.001)

Notes: Each row represents results of a separate regression, with standard errors in parentheses underneath. See appendix A for variable definitions and descriptive statistics. Based on NBER company data. Job and demographic controls include age, sex, race, tenure, occupation, earnings, full-time status, management level, supervisory status, disability status, closeness of supervision, ease of seeing workers, payment on an hourly rate, and company fixed effects.

***Significant at the 1 percent level.

**Significant at the 5 percent level.

*Significant at the 10 percent level.

8A.1, the most consistent result is that profit-sharing intensity (measured using the most recent bonus as a percent of pay) is linked to greater participation in decisions and greater satisfaction with participation (columns [1] through [5]). The small negative coefficients on profit sharing eligibility (columns [2], [3], and [5]) indicate that very low profit sharing bonuses are associated with lower participation and satisfaction—an effect that is erased as the bonus size increases. In addition, employee ownership is linked to greater participation in decisions (columns [1] through [4]) but satisfaction with participation is linked to employee-owned stock as a percent of pay (column [5]).

Examining the different types of employee ownership, the data show some significant associations but no strong patterns. The 401(k) stock intensity is associated with greater involvement in job and department decisions (columns [1] and [2]), while involvement in company decisions is highest among those with any 401(k) employer stock or those who retain stock from exercised options (column [3]). These latter two groups are also more likely to be in employee involvement (EI) teams (column [4]), while satisfaction with participation is highest among those holding open market stock or with large ESOP or 401(k) stakes (column [5]). As noted earlier, given the ERISA rules about coverage within a company, it is more sensible to make inferences about the effects of ESOPs by comparing workers between companies with and without ESOPs, which requires elimination of company fixed effects in the calculations. When this is done at the bottom of table 8A.1, the estimates show that ESOP participants are more likely to be involved in job, department, and company decisions (columns [1] through [3]), but are much *less* likely to be satisfied with their participation (column [5]). This latter result, which is consistent with the within-company comparison, suggests that the simple membership in ESOPs in these companies may have raised the desire for participation more than they raised actual participation (or alternatively, that the additional participation itself raised desires for more participation in ESOP companies) so that one must examine the incentive intensity of the ESOP. The impact of an ESOP on satisfaction with participation is more closely tied to the ESOP value as a percent of pay—that is, ownership intensity in relationship to one's economic situation—than to simple membership in an ESOP plan.

8.3.2 Company Treatment of Employees

Both the GSS and the NBER company survey asked a variety of quality of work life questions. Item 2 in table 8.1 contains results for ten of those measures.[3]

The national survey data give generally positive results. Shared capital-

3. The GSS contains other quality of work life measures that we also analyzed. The results (available on request) were broadly similar across these measures, generally showing positive relationships to profit sharing but not to the other shared capitalism measures.

ism employees are more likely to say that they are treated with respect, management-employee relations are good, promotions are handled fairly, and worker safety is a high priority with management. A measure that reflects directly on the "management by stress" theories is the employee's perception of stress at work, which is not significantly related to the shared capitalism index. In additional calculations not presented here, we examined the positive worker safety result using breakdowns by type of shared capitalism program. In contrast to studies that found no consistent relationship between employee ownership and worker safety (Rooney 1992; Rhodes and Steers 1981), our data show that employee-owners as well as profit-sharers are more likely to report that worker safety is a high priority with management.

The NBER data, in contrast, show consistently positive results for shared capitalism and company treatment. Shared capitalism is positively linked to perceptions that the company shares success with employees and is fair to employees, and to grades workers give to the company on sharing information, trustworthiness, and employee relations. These positive associations become smaller in magnitude but remain positive and highly significant when controlling for several human resource policies (being in an EI team, training, and job security). Disaggregating by type of shared capitalism program in table 8A.2, profit sharing and gain sharing eligibility are strongly linked to perceptions that the company shares and is fair to employees (columns [1] and [2]), while profit-sharing intensity is strongly associated with all three of the grades (columns [3] through [5]). Employee-owners are also more likely to say the company shares with employees (column [1]), while the size of the ownership stake is a strong predictor of each of the five measures.

Comparisons among employee ownership types show an interesting disparity. Having more employer stock in a 401(k) plan is positively linked to each of the measures, while ESOP membership and stake are positively associated with perceptions that the company shares with employees, but ESOP membership is negatively associated with the other four perceptions of company treatment both with and without company fixed effects. This is consistent with the finding that ESOP members are less likely to be satisfied with their participation in decisions.

8.3.3 Supervision

Since incentive programs are one way to reduce the principal-agent problem when supervision is difficult or costly, we expect less supervision in shared capitalist environments. In addition, we expect supervisors to be more concerned with maintaining a cooperative atmosphere that helps solve the free rider problem than with watching workers work.

The GSS asked respondents for views of their supervisors, while the NBER survey asked about the degree of supervision. As seen in item 3 of table 8.1, shared capitalism employees are more likely to see their supervisors as helpful and caring, while they are less likely to report that they are closely supervised both before and after controlling for other HR policies. When broken out by type of shared capitalism program in table 8A.3, the strongly significant result is that ESOP members have greater freedom from supervision (column [1]). Most of the coefficients on other programs are positive, which indicates that each program contributes to the strongly positive shared capitalism coefficient in table 8.2.

8.3.4 Training

The national GSS data in table 8.2 show that shared capitalism employees are more likely to say they have the training opportunities they need. The NBER data show that they report a higher likelihood of formal job training in the past year, greater hours of training, and higher levels of informal job training from fellow workers, with and without controls for participation in an EI team and job security. The breakdowns by plan in table 8A.3 show that both training and hours of training are higher among workers with profit sharing and employee owners, and are also positively linked to size of gain-sharing bonus and employee ownership stake. But training is negatively related to the size of stock option value from future potential profits (columns [2] and [3]). Among the types of employee ownership, training and training hours are highest among ESOP participants and those with 401(k) employer stock.

The pattern of coefficients is quite different for informal job training from co-workers, which suggests that informal job training often substitutes for formal training. Both stock option holding and the size of the stake are positively linked to informal training (table 8A.3, column [4]). Also, while ESOP members are more likely to get formal training, they are less likely to get informal training. Gain sharing is positively associated with informal training, as is the size of a workers' higher profit-sharing stake. The broad range of associations between shared capitalism and formal and informal training suggest that training is complementary with shared capitalism.

8.3.5 Pay and Benefits

Table 8.1 shows that pay tends to be higher among employees with greater shared capitalist forms of pay in both the national GSS and NBER company data. Employees in the NBER company data set with greater shared capitalism are more likely to say that their fixed pay is at least equal to market and their compensation is higher than market. Shared capitalism employees in the national survey are more likely to feel they are paid what they deserve. Employees with greater shared capitalism in both data sets rate their companies as better on fringe benefits. The NBER results are not affected by the inclusion of several human resource policies. When the shared capitalism programs are broken out in table 8A.4, most of the shared capitalism types are associated with higher fixed pay, though the gain-sharing bonus intensity and employee ownership stake are inversely related to pay. There are few associations with the employee's rating of fixed pay relative to market (column [2]), but total compensation relative to market is higher among gain sharers and those who have bigger profit-sharing bonuses and are employee-owners through Employee Stock Purchase Plans (ESPPs) and 401(k) plans (columns [4] and [5]). The pay and benefit results indicate that shared capitalism does not generally substitute for fixed pay or other benefits. This rejects a simple compensating differences story of shared capitalist modes of pay, although the higher pay may help compensate for greater effort or other forms of costly behavior.

8.3.6 Co-Worker Relations

Does shared capitalism help or hurt relations with fellow workers? Employees with greater shared capitalism in the GSS data set are more likely to report that their co-workers can be relied on for help when needed, and that their co-workers take a personal interest in them. Such helpfulness and interest presumably make work more pleasant and increase employee welfare directly, but may also lay the foundation for cooperation among employees that can increase workplace performance (explored in chapters 2 and 4).

8.3.7 Job Security

Shared capitalism is associated with greater job security. Employees higher in the shared capitalist index report a lower likelihood of losing their jobs, and in the national GSS data they report a lower likelihood of being laid off in the past year. The NBER results are maintained when controlling for participation in an EI team and receipt of training. When broken out by shared capitalism policy, both profit-sharing eligibility and the size of the profit share are linked to greater job security (table 8A.5, column [1]). Owning employer stock, and the size of the ownership stake and stock option value, are also positively associated with job security. The breakdowns by type of employee ownership indicate that job security is highest among ESOP participants and those holding 401(k) employer stock, and those with greater holdings in both of those plans. The findings that job security is greater for employee-owners than for other workers is consistent with prior research on the employment stability and company survival of employee ownership firms (Blair, Kruse, and Blasi 2000; Park, Kruse, and Sesil 2004).

8.3.8 Job Satisfaction

Job satisfaction is positively linked to the shared capitalism index in both the national GSS and NBER company data, but the result is statistically significant only in the NBER data. This NBER result disappears, however, when controlling for the human resource policies. The strong association between shared capitalism and these human resource policies indicates that there may be important complementarities, which we explore in table 8.2.

When the policies are broken out in table 8A.5, job satisfaction is positively associated with the size of the profit-sharing and gain-sharing bonuses, and with participation in an ESOP when company fixed effects are removed (column [2]). The positive ESOP result on job satisfaction presumably reflects the positive effects of ESOP membership on training, freedom from supervision, rating of benefits, and job security overpowering ESOP participants' lower satisfaction with participation in decisions (table 8A.1) and their lower ratings for the company on several measures (table 8A.2).

8.3.9 Complementarities

Both theory and evidence support the idea that there may be important complementarities among human resource policies in affecting workplace performance (e.g., Levine and Tyson 1990; Huselid 1995; Ichniowski et al. 1996). These complementarities may also affect employee outcomes: for example, job satisfaction may be increased more by combining shared capitalism with employee involvement and training than by the sum of the policies in isolation.

Measurement of high-performance human resource policies varies among studies. One analysis divides them into seven broad categories: group incentive pay, teamwork/employee involvement, training, employment security, information sharing, flexible job assignment, and recruitment and selection (Ichniowski, Shaw, and Prennushi 1997). The NBER surveys contain measures of each of these, but not for every company.[4] For our investigation of complementarities, we created a human resource policy index that gives one point each for being in an employee involvement team, receiving formal training in the past twelve months, and having high job security, and we then interact this index with the shared capitalism index.[5]

Shared capitalism may also interact with supervision in affecting employee outcomes. Shared capitalist policies may, as noted, help substitute for close supervision of workers by providing greater incentives for workers to work hard and monitor their co-workers. The finding that shared capitalism is associated with greater freedom from supervision lends support to this idea (table 8.1). When shared capitalist policies are combined with close supervision, however, the results may be negative. If workers are not given much latitude in how they do their work, shared capitalist policies may serve mainly to shift financial risk to workers, resulting in more negative worker behavior and attitudes. At a minimum, combining shared capitalism with

4. Flexible job assignment was measured as job rotation at six companies, and rigorous selection was measured at one large company.

5. We also experimented with indices using measures of information sharing, job rotation, and rigorous selection, producing a similar pattern of results. Here we use the index based only on employee involvement, training, and job security since the sample sizes are smaller for job rotation and rigorous selection, and the grade of the company on sharing information reflects an employee evaluation of the policy's success (highly correlated with evaluations of the company on other dimensions), rather than the existence of a policy.

close supervision sends a mixed message to employees: "We want you to work harder and be more committed to the company because of your (profit share/employer stock/stock options), but we're still going to keep a close eye on you." Workers may not respond well to this mixed message.

Table 8.2 assesses interactions between the shared capitalism index and other workplace policies to assess possible complementarities in effects on employee attitudes. The statistical analysis shows that shared capitalism interacts with high performance policies and supervision in affecting a number of employee outcomes.[6] The interaction with high performance policies shows that employees are especially likely to have high participation, and to be satisfied with their participation, when they are covered by both shared capitalist and high performance policies (column [3]). The interaction is also positive with informal training and overall job satisfaction. The interaction is negative, however, on perceptions of company sharing, fairness, and benefits; the coefficients indicate that shared capitalism has a positive effect both for those with and without high performance policies, but has a more positive effect for those who are not also covered by high performance policies.

The pattern is more straightforward with respect to supervision: the combination of shared capitalism with close supervision produces a more negative outcome in almost every case (column [5]). The main effect of close supervision is generally positive (column [4]), indicating that in the absence of shared capitalism, having close supervision may often be a good thing (e.g., giving workers a better sense of what they are supposed to do). But the main effect is counteracted in most cases, however, by the negative shared capitalism interaction—for example, the predicted overall effect of increased supervision on perceptions of company fairness is negative whenever the shared capitalism index is 2 or greater.

The contingent effects of shared capitalism on job satisfaction are illustrated in figure 8.1, which uses the regression results from table 8.2. When workers are covered by high performance policies and have low or average levels of supervision, the effects of increased shared capitalism are positive (top two lines). When they are not covered by high-performance policies, and/or are very closely supervised, the effects of shared capitalism are slightly or very negative (bottom four lines). While the overall relationship between shared capitalism and job satisfaction is close to zero after controlling for other policies (table 8.1), these results illustrate that the other policies can greatly condition the effects of shared capitalism.

The same caveats issued in the "Studying Shared Capitalism" section of the introduction and in chapter 4 apply here. The GSS findings may reflect

6. When the high performance index included the outcome being predicted, that item was deleted from the high performance index (e.g., employee involvement was deleted from the high performance index in predicting participation in an employee involvement team).

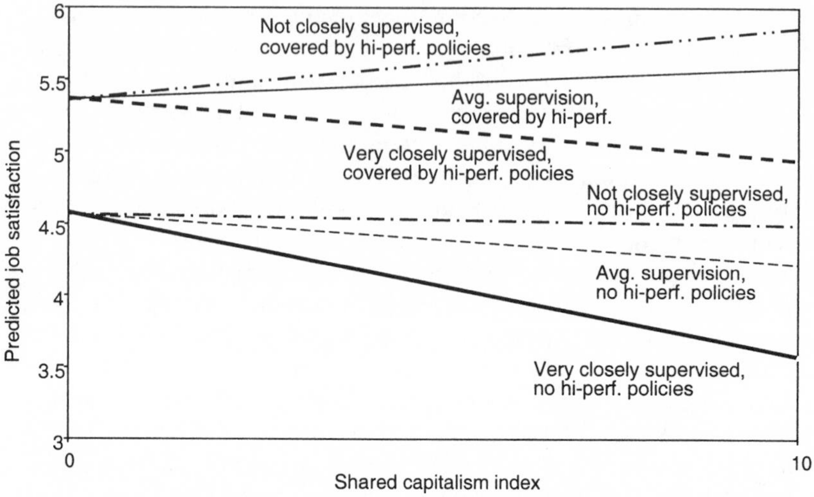

Fig. 8.1 The contingent effects of shared capitalism on job satisfaction

selectivity of shared capitalist firms, or of workers into shared capitalism firms, and the NBER findings may reflect selectivity of workers into shared capitalism plans within the firms. Such selectivity makes causal interpretations open to criticism. As described in the "Studying Shared Capitalism" section, we experimented with specifications to reduce endogeneity but had little luck in finding suitable exogenous variables that would predict the endogenous variables but not directly affect the outcome variables of interest. Even if there is substantial selectivity among workers or firms, however, such selectivity may operate primarily to lead workers and firms into shared capitalism arrangements where it is most likely to have benefits. If this is the case, the shared capitalism is having good effects even in the presence of selectivity, although we are not able to confidently infer what would happen if other workers and firms adopted shared capitalism.

8.4 Conclusion

Do workers gain by sharing? The evidence generally supports an answer of "yes," with some caveats. Both the national GSS and NBER company data indicate that shared capitalism is positively linked to participation in decisions, evaluations of company climate and employee treatment, perceptions of helpfulness by supervisors, lower levels of supervision, and higher levels of training, pay and benefits, job security, and job satisfaction. Almost all of these relationships remain strong when controlling for other human resource policies. This rejects the "management by stress" theories of work innovation.

When broken out by type of shared capitalist program, profit sharing was most consistently linked to the positive outcomes, although gainsharing, stock options, and employee ownership also affect some outcomes positively. In many cases the positive effect was tied to simply being covered by a policy (e.g., being eligible for profit sharing, or being an employee-owner), but there were also many cases in which the effect was tied to the size of the financial stake involved (size of most recent bonus, or value of employer stock or stock options).

Estimated negative relations between some aspects of shared capitalism and some outcomes are also informative about how this form of financial sharing operates. In particular, while being a member of an ESOP was linked to a number of positive outcomes (participation in decisions, perception that the company shares, freedom from supervision, formal training, pay and benefit levels, job security, and job satisfaction), in the NBER data set ESOP members also had lower satisfaction with participation in decisions and lower ratings of the company on fairness, trustworthiness, and employee relations. One possible reason is that employee-owners may be frustrated by unfulfilled desires for greater participation in decisions (above the higher levels they already have). Another possible reason is that some ESOP accounts have too little stock to be meaningful and some employees may have negative attitudes when they are called owners but have very little ownership so the size of the ownership stake is important. The importance of the size of the ownership stake is highlighted by the finding that satisfaction with participation rises with the value of employee-owned stock as a percent of pay. The dynamics of employee ownership may work differently for ESOPs than for other forms of ownership: it is the only form where all eligible workers are automatically enrolled and called owners even with miniscule accounts.

Finally, our data reveals potentially important complementarities of shared capitalism with other workplace policies, particularly with high performance work policies and closeness of supervision. Those who are covered by the combination of high-performance policies with shared capitalism are most likely to report high participation in decisions, satisfaction with participation, and overall job satisfaction. The combination of close supervision with shared capitalism, however, has negative effects on almost every outcome.

Overall, our findings are consistent with theories that stress the linkage between group incentive pay systems and other labor and personnel relations policies. Taken as a package, a high performance work system involves greater participation, higher quality of supervision, more formal training, better wages and benefits, higher job satisfaction, and better job security. Employers who are concerned about company performance, and workers who are concerned about the quality of their working life, have reasons to be interested in this package. Our findings that shared capitalist programs are often associated with these policies and outcomes indicate that there is good potential for workers to gain through sharing.

Appendix

Table 8A.1 Participation in decisions by type of shared capitalism plan

Dependent variable	Involved in job decs. (1–4 scale) oprobit (1)	Involved in dept. goals (1–4 scale) oprobit (2)	Involved in co. decs. (1–4 scale) oprobit (3)	In EI team (0–1 dummy) OLS (4)	Satisfied w/ participation (1–4 scale) oprobit (5)
Bonuses					
Profit sharing	0.016 (0.022)	–0.067 (0.021)***	–0.101 (0.022)***	0.046 (0.008)***	–0.048 (0.021)**
Profit sharing bonus as % of base pay	0.269 (0.115)**	0.547 (0.098)***	0.389 (0.097)***	0.087 (0.039)**	0.321 (0.096)***
Gain sharing	–0.052 (0.030)*	–0.071 (0.027)***	–0.002 (0.028)	0.013 (0.011)	0.028 (0.026)
Gain sharing bonus as % of base pay	0.188 (0.133)	0.149 (0.111)	0.129 (0.107)	0.074 (0.043)*	0.040 (0.106)
Individual bonus	0.096 (0.028)***	0.123 (0.025)***	0.093 (0.027)***	0.005 (0.010)	0.040 (0.025)
Individual bonus as % of base pay	0.280 (0.135)**	–0.044 (0.112)	–0.174 (0.111)	–0.036 (0.044)	0.207 (0.110)*
Stock options					
Stock option holding	–0.002 (0.045)	0.052 (0.039)	0.033 (0.038)	–0.052 (0.015)***	–0.054 (0.037)
Stock option value as % of base pay	0.007 (0.007)	0.017 (0.006)***	0.011 (0.005)**	0.008 (0.002)***	0.015 (0.005)***
Employee ownership					
Any employee ownership	0.043 (0.020)**	0.039 (0.019)**	0.043 (0.021)**	0.032 (0.008)***	–0.016 (0.019)
Employee-owned stock as % of pay	0.018 (0.010)*	0.016 (0.009)*	0.007 (0.009)	0.002 (0.004)	0.026 (0.009)***
n	34,439	34,347	34,309	34,671	34,337
(pseudo) R^2	0.125	0.117	0.086	0.123	0.074
Cut point 1	0.149 (0.292)	1.958 (0.256)	2.617 (0.262)		0.132 (0.252)
Cut point 2	0.937 (0.292)	2.709 (0.256)	3.541 (0.262)		1.194 (0.252)
Cut point 3	2.026 (0.292)	3.911 (0.256)	4.631 (0.263)		2.743 (0.252)

Breakdowns by type of employee ownership					
ESOP	0.071 (0.056)	–0.008 (0.054)	–0.040 (0.056)	0.055 (0.022)**	–0.253 (0.053)***
ESOP stock as % of pay	0.029 (0.022)	0.048 (0.021)**	0.029 (0.020)	0.002 (0.008)	0.052 (0.020)***
ESPP	0.027 (0.044)	0.065 (0.039)*	0.038 (0.040)	–0.006 (0.016)	0.057 (0.038)
ESPP stock as % of pay	–0.031 (0.036)	–0.032 (0.031)	–0.003 (0.030)	0.003 (0.012)	–0.035 (0.030)
401(k) stock	0.031 (0.018)	0.016 (0.018)	0.032 (0.019)*	0.042 (0.007)***	0.021 (0.018)
401(k) stock as % of pay	0.046 (0.017)***	0.030 (0.015)**	0.011 (0.016)	–0.007 (0.006)	0.028 (0.015)*
Stock from options	–0.067 (0.043)	0.044 (0.038)	0.089 (0.037)**	0.039 (0.015)***	–0.009 (0.037)
Stock from options as % of pay	0.029 (0.025)	–0.012 (0.021)	–0.030 (0.020)	–0.009 (0.008)	0.025 (0.020)
Open mkt. stock	–0.046 (0.032)	0.014 (0.028)	0.027 (0.029)	0.002 (0.011)	0.069 (0.028)***
Open mkt. stock as % of pay	–0.072 (0.053)	–0.046 (0.045)	0.000 (0.044)	0.061 (0.018)***	–0.044 (0.045)
ESOP coefficients without fixed effects					
ESOP	0.126 (0.035)***	0.227 (0.033)***	0.252 (0.034)***	0.014 (0.013)	–0.103 (0.032)***
ESOP stock as % of pay	0.007 (0.021)	0.047 (0.019)***	0.003 (0.018)	–0.001 (0.007)	0.015 (0.018)

Notes: All regressions include the control variables from table 8.2. Standard error in parentheses. Oprobit = ordered probit

***Significant at the 1 percent level.

**Significant at the 5 percent level.

*Significant at the 10 percent level.

Table 8A.2 **Company treatment of employees by type of shared capitalism plan**

Dependent variable	Ees. share when co. does well (1–7 scale) OLS (1)	Co. fair to ees. (1–7 scale) OLS (2)	Co. grade: sharing info (0–4 scale) OLS (3)	Co. grade: trustworthy (0–4 scale) OLS (4)	Co. grade: ee. relations (0–4 scale) OLS (5)
Bonuses					
Profit sharing	0.481 (0.030)***	0.126 (0.029)***	–0.003 (0.019)	–0.018 (0.019)	–0.031 (0.018)*
Profit-sharing bonus as % of base pay	0.089 (0.136)	0.188 (0.131)	0.258 (0.087)***	0.261 (0.089)***	0.397 (0.083)***
Gain sharing	0.106 (0.038)***	0.136 (0.037)***	0.021 (0.024)	0.037 (0.025)	0.021 (0.023)
Gain sharing bonus as % of base pay	–0.079 (0.151)	–0.167 (0.146)	0.074 (0.097)	0.005 (0.099)	0.107 (0.092)
Individual bonus	0.047 (0.036)	0.023 (0.035)	0.074 (0.023)***	0.105 (0.024)***	0.082 (0.022)***
Individual bonus as % of base pay	0.475 (0.156)***	0.398 (0.151)***	0.030 (0.100)	0.142 (0.102)	–0.022 (0.095)
Stock options					
Stock option holding	–0.078 (0.054)	–0.061 (0.052)	0.033 (0.034)	0.059 (0.035)*	0.035 (0.033)
Stock option value as % of base pay	0.006 (0.008)	0.004 (0.007)	0.003 (0.005)	0.000 (0.005)	0.003 (0.005)
Employee ownership					
Any employee ownership	0.116 (0.028)***	0.005 (0.027)	–0.016 (0.018)	–0.008 (0.018)	–0.013 (0.017)
Employee-owned stock as % of pay	0.041 (0.013)***	0.027 (0.012)**	0.027 (0.008)***	0.022 (0.008)***	0.016 (0.008)**
n	34,433	34,395	34,303	34,242	34,271
(Pseudo) R^2	0.196	0.203	0.164	0.205	0.179

Breakdowns by type of employee ownership					
ESOP	–0.021 (0.077)	–0.207 (0.074)***	–0.242 (0.049)***	–0.158 (0.050)***	–0.197 (0.047)***
ESOP stock as % of pay	0.027 (0.028)	0.026 (0.027)	0.035 (0.018)*	0.027 (0.018)	0.023 (0.017)
ESPP	0.120 (0.055)**	0.075 (0.053)	–0.009 (0.035)	0.028 (0.036)	0.006 (0.034)
ESPP stock as % of pay	0.006 (0.042)	–0.001 (0.041)	–0.016 (0.027)	0.010 (0.028)	0.002 (0.026)
401(k) stock	0.161 (0.025)***	0.037 (0.025)	0.019 (0.016)	0.024 (0.017)	0.020 (0.016)
401(k) stock as % of pay	0.065 (0.022)***	0.066 (0.021)***	0.067 (0.014)***	0.048 (0.014)***	0.042 (0.013)***
Stock from options	0.042 (0.053)	0.001 (0.051)	–0.088 (0.034)***	–0.068 (0.034)**	–0.050 (0.032)
Stock from options as % of pay	0.008 (0.028)	0.031 (0.027)	0.024 (0.018)	0.027 (0.019)	0.016 (0.017)
Open mkt. stock	0.010 (0.040)	0.055 (0.039)	0.056 (0.026)**	0.062 (0.026)**	0.030 (0.024)
Open mkt. stock as % of pay	0.013 (0.064)	–0.010 (0.062)	–0.029 (0.041)	–0.071 (0.041)*	–0.025 (0.039)
ESOP coefficients without fixed effects					
ESOP	0.231 (0.047)***	–0.119 (0.045)***	–0.042 (0.030)	–0.103 (0.030)***	–0.047 (0.028)*
ESOP stock as % of pay	0.102 (0.026)***	0.033 (0.025)	0.050 (0.017)***	0.024 (0.017)	0.017 (0.016)

Notes: All regressions include the control variables from table 8.2. ees. = employees; OLS = ordinary least squares. Standard error in parentheses.

***Significant at the 1 percent level.

**Significant at the 5 percent level.

*Significant at the 10 percent level.

Table 8A.3 Supervision and training by type of shared capitalism plan

Dependent variable:	Free from supervision (0–10 scale) OLS (1)	Formal training (0–1 scale) OLS (2)	Training hours Tobit (3)	Informal training (1–4 scale) oprobit (4)
Bonuses				
Profit sharing	0.068 (0.044)	0.021 (0.009)**	2.487 (1.192)**	–0.014 (0.021)
Profit-sharing bonus as % of base pay	0.175 (0.203)	0.067 (0.039)*	6.948 (5.084)	0.190 (0.095)**
Gainsharing	–0.106 (0.057)*	–0.010 (0.011)	–0.081 (1.470)	0.081 (0.026)***
Gain-sharing bonus as % of base pay	0.174 (0.225)	0.125 (0.044)***	24.545 (5.652)***	0.036 (0.105)
Individual bonus	0.029 (0.054)	0.050 (0.011)***	3.718 (1.403)***	0.035 (0.025)
Individual bonus as % of base pay	0.344 (0.233)	–0.138 (0.045)***	–20.235 (5.823)***	–0.023 (0.109)
Stock options				
Stock option holding	–0.014 (0.080)	0.006 (0.016)	–1.398 (2.053)	0.096 (0.037)***
Stock option value as % of base pay	0.017 (0.011)	–0.009 (0.002)***	–1.010 (0.280)***	0.016 (0.005)***
Employee ownership				
Any employee ownership	0.034 (0.041)	0.045 (0.008)***	5.437 (1.133)***	–0.047 (0.019)**
Employee-owned stock as % of pay	0.025 (0.019)	0.011 (0.004)***	1.041 (0.493)**	–0.005 (0.009)
n	34,671	34,671	33,834	34,437
(Pseudo) R^2	0.177	0.148	0.024	0.031
Cut point 1				–1.497 (0.252)
Cut point 2				–0.598 (0.252)
Cut point 3				0.786 (0.252)

Breakdowns by type of employee ownership				
ESOP	0.402 (0.114)***	0.054 (0.022)**	7.987 (3.198)**	–0.099 (0.054)*
ESOP stock as % of pay	0.056 (0.042)	–0.002 (0.008)	0.205 (1.090)	–0.019 (0.019)
ESPP	0.051 (0.082)	0.011 (0.016)	2.352 (2.120)	0.024 (0.038)
ESPP stock as % of pay	–0.005 (0.063)	0.015 (0.012)	0.986 (1.595)	–0.012 (0.030)
401(k) stock	0.057 (0.038)	0.050 (0.007)***	6.971 (1.056)***	–0.007 (0.018)
401(k) stock as % of pay	0.016 (0.032)	0.022 (0.006)***	1.973 (0.835)**	0.012 (0.015)
Stock from options	–0.006 (0.078)	0.028 (0.015)*	1.093 (1.974)	–0.015 (0.037)
Stock from options as % of pay	–0.018 (0.042)	–0.007 (0.008)	–0.086 (1.068)	–0.003 (0.020)
Open mkt. stock	–0.027 (0.060)	–0.004 (0.012)	0.584 (1.507)	–0.028 (0.028)
Open mkt. stock as % of pay	0.046 (0.095)	0.003 (0.018)	–0.268 (2.357)	–0.012 (0.044)
ESOP coefficients without fixed effects				
ESOP	0.403 (0.067)***	0.169 (0.014)***	15.145 (1.857)***	–0.087 (0.032)***
ESOP stock as % of pay	0.121 (0.040)***	0.018 (0.008)***	2.043 (1.000)**	–0.012 (0.018)

Notes: All regressions include the control variables from table 8.2. Standard error in parentheses.

***Significant at the 1 percent level.

**Significant at the 5 percent level.

*Significant at the 10 percent level.

Table 8A.4 **Pay and benefits by type of shared capitalism plan**

Dependent variable:	Fixed pay (natural log) OLS (1)	Fixed pay (% diff. from mkt.) OLS (2)	Total comp. (% diff. from mkt.) OLS (3)	Grade of co. on wages (0–4 scale) OLS (4)	Benefits (0–4 scale) OLS (5)
Bonuses					
Profit sharing	0.015 (0.007)**	0.222 (0.340)	–0.051 (0.362)	0.069 (0.018)***	0.068 (0.018)***
Profit-sharing bonus as % of base pay	0.168 (0.032)***	1.057 (1.490)	8.130 (1.587)***	0.194 (0.085)**	0.329 (0.084)***
Gainsharing	0.028 (0.009)***	0.374 (0.439)	1.544 (0.456)***	0.033 (0.024)	0.026 (0.024)
Gain-sharing bonus as % of base pay	–0.079 (0.035)**	–0.664 (1.668)	–3.522 (1.765)*	0.059 (0.095)	0.021 (0.094)
Individual bonus	0.007 (0.008)	–0.725 (0.423)*	–0.607 (0.444)	0.023 (0.023)	0.089 (0.022)***
Individual bonus as % of base pay	0.039 (0.036)	4.148 (1.712)**	12.875 (1.832)***	0.193 (0.098)**	–0.119 (0.097)
Stock options					
Stock option holding	0.160 (0.013)***	0.594 (0.629)	1.013 (0.666)	–0.002 (0.033)	0.024 (0.033)
Stock option value as % of base pay	0.012 (0.002)***	0.282 (0.081)***	0.601 (0.088)***	0.007 (0.005)	0.002 (0.005)
Employee ownership					
Any employee ownership	0.066 (0.007)***	0.012 (0.308)	0.251 (0.331)	–0.008 (0.016)	0.040 (0.016)**
Employee-owned stock as % of pay	–0.009 (0.003)***	–0.127 (0.158)	0.244 (0.158)	0.000 (0.008)	0.002 (0.008)
n	27,359	27,320	26,401	34,408	34,363
(Pseudo) R^2	0.765	0.063	0.137	0.108	0.164

Breakdowns by type of employee ownership					
ESOP	0.144 (0.020)***	–0.168 (1.020)	0.751 (1.331)	–0.051 (0.048)	0.031 (0.047)
ESOP stock as % of pay	–0.006 (0.007)	–0.414 (0.360)	0.949 (0.401)**	–0.008 (0.018)	0.018 (0.017)
ESPP	0.051 (0.013)***	0.943 (0.651)	1.629 (0.698)**	0.037 (0.034)	0.060 (0.034)*
ESPP stock as % of pay	–0.086 (0.010)***	0.079 (0.488)	–0.041 (0.532)	0.002 (0.027)	–0.008 (0.026)
401(k) stock	0.042 (0.007)***	–0.188 (0.307)	0.219 (0.323)	–0.004 (0.016)	0.029 (0.016)*
401(k) stock as % of pay	–0.006 (0.005)	–0.270 (0.309)	–0.079 (0.252)	0.011 (0.014)	–0.008 (0.013)
Stock from options	0.012 (0.012)	1.354 (0.580)**	1.503 (0.620)**	–0.003 (0.033)	–0.035 (0.033)
Stock from options as % of pay	0.005 (0.007)	–0.233 (0.306)	–0.126 (0.332)	0.007 (0.018)	0.017 (0.018)
Open mkt. stock	0.072 (0.010)***	0.833 (0.434)*	0.956 (0.463)**	0.003 (0.025)	0.011 (0.025)
Open mkt. stock as % of pay	–0.018 (0.015)	–1.548 (0.684)**	–1.006 (0.743)	–0.058 (0.040)	–0.034 (0.039)
ESOP coefficients without fixed effects					
ESOP	0.193 (0.017)***	0.834 (0.555)	–0.674 (0.665)	0.006 (0.028)	0.299 (0.027)***
ESOP stock as % of pay	0.037 (0.010)***	–0.766 (0.388)**	1.643 (0.379)***	–0.063 (0.017)***	–0.010 (0.016)

Notes: All regressions include the control variables from table 8.2. Standard error in parentheses.

***Significant at the 1 percent level.

**Significant at the 5 percent level.

*Significant at the 10 percent level.

Table 8A.5 Job security and satisfaction by type of shared capitalism plan

Dependent variable:	Job security (1–4 scale) oprobit (1)	Job satisfaction (1–7 scale) OLS (2)
Bonuses		
Profit sharing	0.102 (0.021)***	–0.063 (0.023)***
Profit-sharing bonus as % of base pay	0.486 (0.098)***	0.255 (0.105)**
Gain sharing	0.068 (0.027)***	0.025 (0.029)
Gain-sharing bonus as % of base pay	–0.021 (0.109)	0.270 (0.117)**
Individual bonus	0.057 (0.026)**	0.023 (0.028)
Individual bonus as % of base pay	–0.046 (0.112)	0.168 (0.121)
Stock options		
Stock option holding	0.040 (0.039)	–0.008 (0.041)
Stock option value as % of base pay	0.011 (0.005)**	0.007 (0.006)
Employee ownership		
Any employee ownership	0.082 (0.020)***	–0.006 (0.021)
Employee-owned stock as % of pay	0.018 (0.009)**	0.001 (0.010)
n	34,671	34,525
(Pseudo) R^2	0.042	0.107
Cut point 1	–1.917 (0.259)	
Cut point 2	–1.175 (0.259)	
Cut point 3	0.476 (0.259)	
Breakdowns by type of employee ownership		
ESOP	–0.001 (0.056)	–0.038 (0.059)
ESOP stock as % of pay	0.042 (0.021)**	–0.002 (0.022)
ESPP	–0.058 (0.040)	–0.027 (0.042)
ESPP stock as % of pay	–0.005 (0.031)	–0.001 (0.033)
401(k) stock	0.096 (0.018)***	–0.001 (0.020)
401(k) stock as % of pay	0.054 (0.015)***	0.018 (0.017)
Stock from options	–0.089 (0.038)**	–0.006 (0.041)
Stock from options as % of pay	0.013 (0.020)	–0.003 (0.022)
Open mkt. stock as % of pay	0.038 (0.046)	–0.033 (0.049)
Open mkt. stock	0.008 (0.029)	0.005 (0.031)
ESOP coefficients without fixed effects		
ESOP	0.299 (0.034)***	0.090 (0.036)***
ESOP stock as % of pay	0.043 (0.020)**	–0.029 (0.020)

Notes: All regressions include the control variables from table 8.2. Standard error in parentheses.

***Significant at the 1 percent level.

**Significant at the 5 percent level.

*Significant at the 10 percent level.

References

Akerlof, G. 1982. Labor contracts as partial gift exchange. *Quarterly Journal of Economics* 97 (4): 543–69.

Azfar, O., and S. Danninger. 2001. Profit-sharing, employment stability, and wage growth. *Industrial and Labor Relations Review* 54 (3): 619–30.

Bakan, I., Y. Suseno, A. Pinnington, and A. Money. 2004. The influence of financial participation and participation in decision-making on employee job attitudes. *International Journal of Human Resource Management* 15 (3): 587–616.

Blair, M., D. Kruse, and J. Blasi. 2000. Is employee ownership an unstable form? Or a stabilizing force? In *The new relationship: Human capital in the American corporation,* ed. T. Kochan and M. Blair, 571–87. Washington, DC: The Brookings Institution.

Black, S., L. Lynch, and A. Krivelyova. 2004. How workers fare when employers innovate. *Industrial Relations* 43 (1): 44–66.

Blasi, J., M. Conte, and D. Kruse. 1996. Employee ownership and corporate performance among public corporations. *Industrial and Labor Relations Review* 50 (1): 60–79.

Blasi, J., D. Kruse, and A. Bernstein. 2003. *In the company of owners: The truth about stock options (and why every employee should have them).* New York: Basic Books.

Bonin, J. P., and L. Putterman. 1987. *Economics of cooperation and the labor-managed economy.* New York: Harwood Academic Publishers.

Brown, S., and J. G. Sessions. 2003. Attitudes, expectations, and sharing. *Labour* 17 (4): 543–69.

Cappelli, P., and D. Neumark. 2004. External churning and internal flexibility: Evidence on the functional flexibility and core-periphery hypotheses. *Industrial Relations* 43 (1): 148–82.

Conyon, M., and R. Freeman. 2004. Shared modes of compensation and firm performance: UK evidence. In *Seeking a premiere league economy,* ed. R. Blundell, D. Card, and R. Freeman, 109–46. Chicago: University of Chicago Press.

Craig, B., and J. Pencavel. 1992. The behavior of worker cooperatives: The plywood companies of the Pacific Northwest. *American Economic Review* 82 (5): 1083–1105.

———. 1993. The objectives of worker cooperatives. *Journal of Comparative Economics* 17 (2): 288–308.

Cramton, P., H. Mehran, and J. Tracy. 2008. ESOP fables: The impact of Employee Stock Ownership Plans on labor disputes. *Federal Reserve Bank of New York Staff Reports,* no. 347, September.

Dube, A., and R. Freeman. 2001. Shared compensation systems and decision-making in the US job market. Incomes and Productivity in North America, Papers from the 2000 Seminar. Washington, DC: Secretariat of the Commission for Labor Cooperation.

Estrin, S., and D.C. Jones. 1992. The viability of employee-owned firms: Evidence from France. *Industrial and Labor Relations Review* 45 (2): 323–38.

Freeman, R., and J. Rogers. 2006. *What workers want, 2nd ed.* Ithaca, NY: ILR Press Books.

Handel, M., and M. Gittleman. 2004. Is there a wage payoff to innovative practices? *Industrial Relations* 43 (1): 67–97.

Handel, M., and D. Levine. 2004. Editors' introduction: The effects of new work practices on workers. *Industrial Relations* 43 (1): 1–43.

Heywood, J., U. Jirjahn, and G. Tsertsvadze. 2005a. Does profit sharing reduce conflict with the boss? Evidence from Germany. *International Economic Journal* 19 (2): 235–50.

———. 2005b. Getting along with colleagues—Does profit sharing help or hurt? *Kyklos* 58 (4): 557–73.

Huselid, M. 1995. The impact of human resource management practices on the turnover, productivity, and corporate financial performance. *Academy of Management Journal* 38: 635–72.

Ichniowski, C., T. Kochan, D. Levine, C. Olson, and G. Strauss. 1996. What works at work: Overview and assessment. *Industrial Relations* 35 (3): 299–333.

Ichniowski, C., K. Shaw, and G. Prennushi. 1997. The effects of human resource practices on productivity: A study of steel finishing lines. *American Economic Review* 87 (3): 291–313.

Kardas, P., A. L. Scharf, and J. Keogh. 1998. Wealth and income consequences of ESOPs and employee ownership: A comparative study from Washington state. *Journal of Employee Ownership Law and Finance* 10 (4): 3–52.

Keef, S. P. 1998. The causal association between employee share ownership and attitudes: A study based on the long framework. *British Journal of Industrial Relations* 36 (1): 73–82.

Kim, E. H., and P. Ouimet. 2008. Employee capitalism or corporate socialism? Broad-based employee stock ownership. Working Paper. Ross School of Business, University of Michigan, October.

Kroumova, M. 2000. Investment in employer stock through 401(k) plans: Is there reason for concern? PhD dissertation. New Brunswick, NJ: Rutgers University.

Kruse, D. 1984. *Employee ownership and employee attitudes: Two case studies.* Norwood, PA: Norwood Editions.

———. 1993. *Profit sharing: Does it make a difference?* Kalamazoo, MI: W. E. Upjohn Institute for Employment Research.

———. 1998. Profit sharing and the demand for low-skill workers. In *Generating jobs: Increasing the demand for low-skill workers,* ed. R. Freeman and P. Gottschalk, 105–53. New York: Russell Sage Foundation.

Kruse, D., and J. Blasi. 1997. Employee ownership, employee attitudes, and firm performance: A review of the evidence. In *The human resources management handbook, part 1,* ed. D. Lewin, D. J. B. Mitchell, and M. A. Zaidi, 113–51. Greenwich, CT: JAI Press.

Levine, D., and L. D'Andrea Tyson. 1990. Participation, productivity, and the firm's environment. In *Paying for productivity: A look at the evidence,* ed. A. Blinder, 183–237. Washington, DC: Brookings Institution.

Long, R. J. 1981. The effects of formal employee participation in ownership and decision making on perceived and desired patterns of organizational influence: A longitudinal study. *Human Relations* 34 (10): 847–76.

———. 1982. Worker ownership and job attitudes: A field study. *Industrial Relations* 21 (2): 196–215.

Park, R., D. Kruse, and J. Sesil. 2004. Does employee ownership enhance firm survival? In *Advances in the economic analysis of participatory and labor-managed firms,* vol. 8, ed. V. Perotin and A. Robinson, 3–33. New York: Elsevier Science, JAI.

Pendleton, A. 2006. Incentives, monitoring, and employee stock ownership plans: New evidence and interpretations. *Industrial Relations* 45 (4): 753–77.

Pendleton, A., N. Wilson, and M. Wright. 1998. The perception and effects of share ownership: Empirical evidence from employee buy-outs. *British Journal of Industrial Relations* 36 (1): 99–123.

Quarrey, M., and C. Rosen. 1993. *Employee ownership and corporate performance.* Oakland, CA: National Center for Employee Ownership.

Renaud, S., S. St-Onge, and M. Magnan. 2004. The impact of stock purchase plan participation on workers' individual cash compensation. *Industrial Relations* 43 (1): 120–47.

Rhodes, S. R., and R. M. Steers. 1981. Conventional vs. worker-owned organizations. *Human Relations* 34 (12): 1013–35.

Robinson, A., and H. Zhang. 2005. Employee share ownership: Safeguarding investments in human capital. *British Journal of Industrial Relations* 43 (3): 469–88.

Rooney, P. Employee ownership and worker participation: Effects on health and safety. *Economic Letters* 39 (3): 323–28.

Scharf, A., and C. Mackin. 2000. *Census of Massachusetts companies with employee stock ownership plans (ESOPs).* Boston: Commonwealth Corporation.

Ugarkovi, M. 2007. Profit sharing and company performance. Dissertation. Universitat Dortmund, Deutscher Universitats Verlag, Wiesbaden. Available at: www.duv.de.

Weitzman, M. L. 1984. *The share economy.* Cambridge, MA: Harvard University Press.

Winther, G., and R. Marens. 1997. Participatory democracy may go A long way: Comparative growth performance of employee ownership firms in New York and Washington states. *Economic and Industrial Democracy* 18 (3): 393–422.

9

Does Employee Ignorance Undermine Shared Capitalism?

John W. Budd

Since the birth of the modern employment relationship a few centuries ago, employers have struggled with how to reward and motivate employees. Contemporary information technologies, global competitive pressures, and demographic changes have heightened these struggles as the employment relationship is increasingly characterized by contingencies rather than stability (Cappelli 1999). Against this backdrop, shared capitalism compensation plans seek to motivate employees by tying their pay to various measures of organizational and employee performance (Freeman 2001; Conyon and Freeman 2004). But shared capitalism will likely only be successful in motivating employees if employees know about and understand such plans, especially the extent to which they are individually covered by forms of shared capitalism. In other words, incentives that are unknown to employees are unlikely to affect their behavior.

We know that in general, knowledge is often imperfect. Various Gallup polls leave little doubt of this fact.[1] In a 2005 poll, 29 percent of Americans indicated that they believe that both evolution and creationism are probably true, in spite of the contradictory nature of these two theories. On the 60th anniversary of D-Day, 35 percent could not identify Germany as the Allied

John W. Budd is the Industrial Relations Land Grant Chair and a professor of Human Resources and Industrial Relations at the Carlson School of Management, University of Minnesota.

I am grateful to Richard Freeman, Doug Kruse, and Joseph Blasi for giving me the opportunity to write this chapter, to Doug for his help with the data, and to Doug, Joseph, Brigitte Madrian, and seminar participants at the University of Minnesota and Iowa State University for helpful comments. An earlier version of this chapter was presented at the NBER Shared Capitalism Research Conference in October 2006.

1. The polls cited here are dated August 5–7, 2005; May 21–23, 2004; August 28–September 15, 2003; and June 25–27, 1999.

forces' D-Day enemy. More than 50 percent of Americans cannot identify the first ten amendments to the Constitution as the "Bill of Rights." A large majority of Americans admit that they know very little about the European Union, including 80 percent who do not know that it has a larger population than the United States. And 18 percent incorrectly believe the sun revolves around the earth. With respect to economic knowledge, only 34 percent of adults managed to get an "A" or "B" on a basic economics quiz done by the National Council on Economic Education in 2005 (Markow and Bagnaschi 2005).

As will be shown in the next section, previous research has also uncovered significant amounts of ignorance in the employment relationship, specifically pertaining to employees' imperfect understanding of privately- and publicly-provided benefits. As such, it is reasonable to hypothesize that some employees are ignorant about shared capitalism compensation programs. To test this hypothesis, this chapter analyzes over 20,000 employee surveys linked to employer-provided shared capitalism coverage information from ten to fourteen private sector companies collected under the NBER Shared Capitalism research project. Consistent with the literature on other aspects of the employment relationship, significant levels of misunderstanding and inaccuracy are uncovered. Employee ignorance might very well undermine shared capitalism, though this ignorance might stem from ineffective corporate communications and uneven implementation in addition to employee inattentiveness.

9.1 Research on Employee Ignorance

Previous research shows that employee ignorance of privately- and publicly-provided employee benefits is not a trivial concern. For example, the 1998 British Workplace Employee Relations Survey (WERS 98) contains manager-provided indications regarding whether several family-friendly benefits are available in the workplace along with individual-provided responses on whether the employee thinks these benefits are available to him or her. Among workplaces with a family-friendly benefit (according to the manager), large fractions of employees do not indicate that this benefit is personally available to them. For example, even after trying to control for imperfect workplace coverage, only one-quarter of employees in workplaces with parental leave benefits correctly perceive that they are entitled to parental leave. The analogous fractions for job sharing arrangements and employer-subsidized child care benefits are one-quarter and one-fifth, respectively. In other words, there appears to be a significant discrepancy between availability and awareness (Budd and Mumford 2004, 2006).

Several studies of retirement benefits provide additional documentation of employee ignorance of privately-provided benefits. Mitchell (1988, 35) matched survey responses for over 600 workers to administrative pension plan data and found that "pension misinformation and missing information are quite widespread." Luchak and Gunderson (2000) surveyed employees of a large public utility and found moderate levels of pension knowledge—employees responded correctly to seven questions about their pensions about half of the time. Only 28 percent of the employees accurately knew the formula used to calculate benefit amounts and only 36 percent could identify one of the eligibility requirements for retiring early. Analyses of individuals in the University of Michigan Health and Retirement Study also uncover significant levels of pension ignorance (Chan and Stevens 2008, Gustman and Steinmeier 2005). For example, one-third of the respondents are not able to provide enough information to construct any estimate of their pension's present value; among those providing enough information, only half estimate their pension's present value within a factor of two (Chan and Stevens 2008). An imperfect understanding of how 401(k) retirement plans work is illustrated by Choi, Laibson, and Madrian's (2005) finding that half of vested employees aged 59.5 years and older at seven firms with employer matching policies fail to take advantage of this match even though this is essentially giving up free income because there are no tax penalties for these workers to immediately cash out these contributions. With respect to health insurance, Reschovsky, Hargraves, and Smith (2002) find that 25 percent of respondents cannot correctly identify whether they are covered by an HMO or non-HMO plan.

Turning to publicly-provided benefits, a phone survey in 1995 and another in 2000 revealed that 40 percent of US workers had not heard of the Family and Medical Leave Act (FMLA), which was enacted by the US Congress in 1993; moreover, among those who had heard of the law, 50 percent were unsure as to whether they were personally eligible to use it (Budd and Brey 2003; Waldfogel 2001). Though not a publicly-provided benefit per se, there are also serious shortcomings in workers' knowledge of the employment-at-will legal doctrine. For example, in the United States it is legal to fire someone to make room for another employee to do the same job at a lower wage, and also to fire someone who is mistakenly believed to have stolen money. But Kim (1997) documents that less than 20 percent of surveyed employees can correctly identify these scenarios as being legal. In separate surveys, Rudy (2002) and Freeman and Rogers (2006) similarly document extensive employee ignorance about the general lack of legal restrictions on firing workers. In two surveys of low-income workers in New York City, less than 20 percent could correctly identify the value of the minimum wage (Brennan Center for Justice 2006).

The imperfect use of publicly-provided social insurance programs is also partially attributed to imperfect knowledge of these programs. Twenty-five to 40 percent of unemployed individuals eligible for unemployment insurance do not receive it (McCall 1995). Budd and McCall (1997, 2004) find a significantly higher take-up rate among blue-collar unionized workers relative to comparable nonunion workers and ascribe this, in part, to the role that unions provide in providing information and combating uncertainty and ignorance. Hirsch, Macpherson, and DuMond (1997) similarly attribute greater levels of workers' compensation receipt among unionized workers, compared to similar nonunion individuals, at least partially to union-provided information on workers' compensation systems. That unions can play such a role indicates that employees are not fully aware of these types of employee benefits.

In fact, issues of employee knowledge, ignorance, and usage of privately- and publicly-provided benefits are important enough for Budd (2007) and Budd and Mumford (2004) to add a union facilitation face to Freeman and Medoff's (1984) famous monopoly and voice faces of labor unions and for others to devote significant attention to how to make labor policies effective (e.g., Weil 1996, 2005). A lack of perfect knowledge is also consistent with theories of bounded rationality in which time constraints and cognitive limitations prevent individuals from gathering and processing complete information (March and Simon 1958; Simon 1982). So employee ignorance of privately- and publicly-provided employee benefits is a meaningful concern and it is reasonable to hypothesize that similar issues apply to shared capitalism compensation plans.

With that said, an important issue in much of this research is measuring employee coverage or eligibility. Typically, researchers have only an imperfect indicator of this key variable. Studies of publicly-provided benefits typically must impute eligibility from administrative eligibility criteria. Budd and Mumford's (2004, 2006) studies of privately-provided family-friendly benefits rely on matching employer information about whether a specific benefit is available for any employees in a workplace to employee responses about whether they personally could use this benefit. Similar issues are present in the following analyses in that the employer-provided information on coverage of shared capitalism programs might not be perfectly accurate for each individual employee. So while the previous literature supports the need to empirically examine the extent of employee ignorance of shared capitalism programs, it also reminds us to be careful as to how ignorance is measured.

9.2 Measuring Ignorance of Shared Capitalism Programs

To analyze employees' accurate knowledge or ignorance of their employers' policies and programs requires two levels of data: company-provided reports pertaining to coverage or applicability and employee indications of awareness. As summarized in figure 9.1, with these two sources of information, four outcomes are possible: the employee accurately responds that they are not covered by a policy, the employee accurately responds that they are covered by a policy, the employee indicates that they are not covered by or aware of a policy for which the company indicated that they are (employee

		Coverage (Company Reported)	
		No	Yes
Perceived Coverage (Employee Reported)	No	Accurate No	Employee Ignorance
	Yes	False Positive	Accurate Yes

Fig. 9.1 Measuring employee knowledge and ignorance

ignorance), and the employee indicates that they are covered by a policy for which the company indicated that the policy is not offered by the employer generally or to that employee specifically (false positive). Frequently-analyzed surveys like the Current Population Survey that only contain individual-level data can only be used to measure employee awareness, while organizational surveys only capture coverage rates. Linked employer-employee data are required to assess employee accuracy and ignorance.

The NBER Shared Capitalism data set contains linked employer-employee information on several shared capitalism programs and can therefore be used to analyze the accuracy and shortfalls of employees' understanding of these programs. The NBER data set is described in the "Studying Shared Capitalism" section of the introduction to this volume. The companies are not representative of the entire population of US companies, but this is not a major concern for the following analyses because the focus here is on measuring employee ignorance in shared capitalism firms rather than on estimating coverage rates across the population. If anything, the results might be biased against employee ignorance to the extent that information about the plans of interest might be disseminated more widely in firms in which shared capitalism programs are prominent (as in the sampled firms) compared to companies in which they are not.

The employee surveys ask questions pertaining to the respondent employee's job, supervision, relations with co-workers, attitudes, and demographic characteristics. Of particular interest for this analysis are a number of questions pertaining to participation in, and sometimes awareness of, various shared capitalism programs—performance-related pay, employee stock ownership, 401(k)s, deferred profit sharing, stock options, and employee stock purchase plans. The applicability of these programs to sets of employees was determined by the data collection team through interviews with managers and from the companies' Form 5500 filings with the Internal

Revenue Service. In a majority of cases, the shared capitalism programs include or exclude all employees uniformly, but the performance-related pay plans sometimes vary across different groups of workers. For example, one company reports that a profit-sharing plan only applies to managerial employees while another company reports that an individual bonus program excludes unionized employees. These types of variations in coverage are matched to the employee surveys using the employees' self-reported job characteristics. Four of the smaller companies are omitted from some of the following analyses because employees were not directly asked about their perceived eligibility for performance-related pay.

As shown in figure 9.1, whenever an individual's response to whether or not a specific shared capitalism program applies to them personally does not match the company-provided information for that employee, it is characterized here as an employee inaccuracy—either in the form of ignorance or a false positive. This assumes that the company-provided information is accurate for each individual employee. While the company responses are matched to each employee based on any job characteristics that the managers indicate determine coverage, it is useful to explicitly note that this falls short of the ideal situation in which employee-by-employee administrative data are available. As such, one cannot rule out the possibility that some employees have better information on the applicability of specific programs than are contained in these data. For example, a relatively new employee might be excluded from a program until after completing a probationary period. The multivariate analyses will try to control for some of these possibilities by using job and demographic characteristics as control variables (see appendix table 9A.1 for variable definitions and summary statistics), but ultimately the measures of employee inaccuracy may overstate the true extent of inaccuracy.

9.3 Aggregate Shared Capitalism Ignorance Rates

Table 9.1 presents aggregate coverage, perceived coverage, and ignorance rates for several shared capitalism programs. Profit-sharing plans are those in which pay or bonuses depend on company profits or performance. Seven of the companies indicate that a profit-sharing plan applies to all employees, six have plans that apply to some employees, and one reported no such plan.[2] As shown in column (1) of table 9.1, this means that according to their employer, 85 percent of employees are covered by a profit-sharing

2. Three of the companies with universal applicability and the one company with no coverage are dropped from the analyses because employee-level coverage was imputed rather than asked directly. The next three measures in table 9.1 were also imputed at the employee level for these same four companies so they are again dropped from the analyses. For gain-sharing plans, all four reported no coverage. For individual-level performance pay, one reported uniform coverage, one no coverage, and two partial coverage. For all forms of performance pay, three of the dropped organizations have uniform coverage and one has no coverage.

Table 9.1 **Employee-level coverage, perceived coverage, and ignorance rates of shared capitalism programs**[a]

Shared capitalism plan	Coverage (company reported) (1)	Perceived coverage (employee reported) (2)	Mismatches: Overall (3)	Mismatches: Ignorance[b] (4)	Mismatches: False positive[c] (5)
Profit-sharing plan (company-based performance pay)	0.849	0.703	0.246	0.231	0.071
	[45,759]	[45,759]	[45,759]	[38,829]	[32,164]
Gain-sharing plans (work group or departmental-based performance pay)	0.170	0.270	0.264	0.484	0.674
	[7,406]	[7,406]	[7,406]	[1,261]	[1,998]
Individual-based performance pay	0.291	0.282	0.209	0.374	0.354
	[45,759]	[45,759]	[45,759]	[13,319]	[12,908]
Employee Stock Ownership Plan (ESOP)[d]	1.000	0.817	0.183	0.183	—
	[4,362]	[4,362]	[4,362]	[4,362]	
Stock option grants[e]	1.000[e]	0.912	0.088	0.088	—
	[6,347]	[6,347]	[6,347]	[6,347]	

Source: NBER Shared Capitalism data set.

[a]Sample sizes are in brackets.

[b]Employees who do not perceive that they are covered when their employer says they are; sample limited to covered employees.

[c]Employees who perceive that they are covered when their employer says they are not; sample limited to employees reporting that they are covered.

[d]The results in this row are limited to ESOP companies because individual-level questions were only asked in these companies.

[e]The results in this row are limited to four companies that granted stock options to all employees in the previous year. Employees with less than a year of tenure are excluded from the sample.

plan. Employees were separately asked if they were eligible for performance-related pay in which the size of the payments depended on company profits or performance; 70 percent of the employees perceived that they are covered by such a plan. Comparing this to the company-reported 85 percent coverage rate reveals a significant discrepancy. Moreover, this aggregate comparison understates the extent of mismatch because false positives can be offsetting ignorance (recall figure 9.1). In fact, for profit-sharing plans, 25 percent of the employee responses fail to match the company-reported response (see column [3] of table 9.1).

Columns (4) and (5) decompose these mismatches. Among the 38,829 employees that the companies say are covered by profit-sharing plans, 8,960 employees (23 percent) report that they are not covered. This is labeled here as employee ignorance, though such misunderstandings might, in some cases, be rooted in a lack of clear corporate communication rather than employee inattentiveness. With complex organizational structures, companies might not effectively communicate whether rewards track work group, department, plant, division, or corporate performance. Taken literally, column (4) implies that the remaining 77 percent of employees are correctly aware that they are covered by a profit-sharing plan; a more nuanced interpretation is that of the employees that companies say are covered by a profit-sharing plan, 77 percent have a similar perception. Turning to column (5), among the 32,164 employees who perceive that they are covered by a profit-sharing plan, 2,295 of them are not covered according to their employer. In other words, 7 percent of perceived coverage stems from false positives.

The remaining rows of table 9.1 repeat this exercise for other measures of shared capitalism. Only 17 percent of the employees are covered by gain-sharing plans (pay-for-performance based on team or group performance) according to the companies, but 27 percent of the employees believe their pay depends on team or group performance. Only half of the employees covered by such plans accurately report this coverage, and more than 60 percent of the employees' affirmative responses are inconsistent with their company's description of their plan.[3] Again, this may reflect a combination of employee errors, imperfect corporate communication, and uneven implementation.

A similar qualitative pattern is apparent for individual-based performance pay. Twenty percent of the observations are mismatched while more than one-third of individuals covered by an individual-based performance pay plan are unaware of this and one-third of the affirmative responses are false positives. These levels of misunderstanding might stem from explicit versus

3. The two largest companies are excluded from the gain-sharing analyses throughout this chapter because they both have gain-sharing-type plans for some employees, but it is not possible to identify these employee groups in the NBER Shared Capitalism data set. It is therefore impossible to identify whether individual employee responses pertaining to gain sharing are accurate or inaccurate in these two companies.

Table 9.2 Employees that do not know about shared capitalism programs

	Fraction of negative responses that are "Don't Know"
Eligible for performance-based pay	19.77% (1,838 / 9,295)
Received performance-based bonuses last year	7.83% (1,219 / 15,560)
Participate in the ESOP	32.33% (258 / 798)
Ever received stock options	14.02% (89 / 635)
Ever exercised stock options, currently hold stock options, participate in an Employee Stock Purchase Plan, or bought company stock on the open market	All < 1%
Participate in a 401(k) plan	17.55% (1,506 / 8,583)

Source: NBER Shared Capitalism data set.

implicit views of performance-based pay such that companies report a lack of formal gain sharing or individual-based programs, while employees nonetheless believe that their pay ultimately reflects team, group, or individual performance even in the absence of a formal, formulaic incentive program. The first two rows of table 9.2 reveal other dimensions of employee ignorance about pay-for-performance programs. Twenty percent of the 9,295 employees who did not indicate that they are eligible for performance-based pay actually do not know if they are eligible. Of those who did not state that they earned performance-based pay last year, 8 percent do not know if they did so.

Returning to table 9.1, the fourth row presents the summary results for eight of the companies that have employee stock ownership plans (ESOPs).[4] As shown in column (1), these ESOPs apply uniformly to all employees in these organizations. Among the employees in these eight companies, 82 percent indicate that they participate in the ESOP while 18 percent indicate that they do not. Even though the question is worded as participation rather than coverage or eligibility, this 18 percent nonparticipation rate likely reflects a significant amount of ignorance. The ESOPs rarely exclude large groups of employees except, in some cases, unionized employees and probationary employees. So setting these exclusions aside momentarily, lack of reported participation equates to lack of awareness. But what about these potential exclusions? None of the companies indicated that unionized employees are

4. A ninth ESOP company is excluded from the analyses because employees in this company were not asked if they participate in the ESOP.

excluded and recalculating the statistics in row 4 of table 9.1 for nonunion employees only reduces the mismatch rate by less than one percentage point. Turning to probationary exclusions, the mismatch rate falls to 16 percent when employees with less than six months of tenure are excluded, and to 13 percent when those with less than one year of tenure are omitted. So perhaps the rate of ignorance for ESOPs is around 15 percent (roughly). Also, row 3 of table 9.2 shows that of the 798 self-reported nonparticipants, 32 percent indicate that they do not know if they participate in the ESOP.

In the Shared Capitalism data set, four companies report that they provided stock option grants to all of their employees within the past year. The last row of table 9.1 shows that among employees with at least one year of tenure at these four companies, 91 percent indicated receiving stock option grants. This translates to an ignorance rate of 9 percent. Of those who did not indicate that they have ever received stock options, 14 percent responded that they do not know if they have ever received such options (see table 9.2). Uncertainty about exercising stock options, currently holding stock options, and buying company stock, however, is negligible.

Other measures of shared capitalism programs are available in the data, but an analysis as in table 9.1 is not appropriate because participation is voluntary and employees were generally not asked about eligibility in the surveys. In particular, of the employees eligible for 401(k) plans according to their employer, 16 percent indicate that they do not participate in a 401(k) plan. But this might reflect a choice not to participate rather than ignorance. Nevertheless, among employees who fail to say that they participate in a 401(k) plan, 18 percent of them indicate that they do not know if they participate (see table 9.2). This suggests that employees have imperfect information about this form of shared capitalism, just as the other results in tables 9.1 and 9.2 demonstrate that employees have imperfect understandings of pay-for-performance, ESOP, and stock option programs.

9.4 Predicting and Explaining Employee Ignorance

Multivariate estimation can be used to assess the extent to which demographic, job, and company characteristics predict mismatches between employer and employee beliefs about the coverage of shared capitalism pay programs. Characteristics that are strong predictors of these mismatches might hold important clues to explaining the sources of inaccuracy and mismatch. To this end, tables 9.3, 9.4, and 9.6 present probit results in which the indicators from columns (3) through (5) of table 9.1 are the dependent variables: overall mismatches, employee ignorance, and false positives for each of the shared capitalism plans. The estimates reported in these tables are marginal effects, rather than probit coefficients, calculated using the standard algorithm: all of the variables are set to their sample mean values, and the marginal effects for continuous independent variables are calculated as the change in probability for a small change in the variable, while the marginal effects for dummy variables are calculated as the change in probability associated with changing the dummy variable from zero to one. The standard errors are robust to arbitrary forms of heteroskedasticity. The sample sizes are smaller than in table 9.1 because of missing observations for the independent variables, especially educational attainment. Sample means of the independent variables are reported in appendix table 9A.1.

Table 9.3 reports probit results for overall mismatches.[5] More specifically, the sample for each model includes all nonmissing observations and the dependent variable equals one if the employer and employee responses for the particular shared capitalism do not agree. In terms of figure 9.1, all four interior cells are used and the dependent variable indicates observations that fall into the two inaccurate cells. These models, therefore, pool both ignorance and false positives. Column (1) reports the results for profit-sharing plans. Recall from table 9.1 that 24.6 percent of the responses are mismatches. Compared to high school dropouts, employees who graduated from high school or attended college are significantly less likely to erroneously report profit-sharing coverage. Women, married individuals, higher-paid employees, employees who expect to work at the employer for a long time, and US employees are also less likely to be mismatched. Age and tenure both exhibit a quadratic relationship with the probability of mismatch; increases in each of these measures reduces the predicted probability of a mismatch up to thirty-three years of age and nineteen years of tenure. Sales employees are much more likely to erroneously report whether they are covered by a profit-sharing plan as are unionized employees.

Turning to gain-sharing plans (column [2]), women are again less likely to have a mismatch with their employers' responses and tenure has a similar quadratic relationship. Higher-paid employees, those not paid by the hour, sales occupations, and unionized employees are predicted to have a higher likelihood of an erroneous response; as will be shown in table 9.6, these results apparently stem from these employees overstating the frequency of gain-sharing plans. With respect to individually-based performance pay plans (column [3]), those who are estimated as being associated with a lower probability of a mismatched report are nonwhite, higher-paid, US employees, and those who work in larger companies. In contrast to the other types of performance-based plans, increases in tenure are associated with a greater likelihood of a mismatched response.

The results for company size and unionization merit a special note. These two variables are included in the results here because one would expect that unionization and company size can affect the quality and quantity of

5. Tables 9.3 and 9.6 do not include results for ESOPs or stock option grants because the companies analyzed have universal ESOP or stock option grant programs that rules out the possibility of false positives; as such, the overall mismatch results reduce to the employee ignorance results reported in table 9.4.

Table 9.3 Probit analyses of employer-employee mismatches[a]

	Profit sharing (1)	Gain sharing (2)	Individual-based incentives (3)
High school graduate[b]	–0.047**	0.042	0.010
	(0.014)	(0.055)	(0.021)
Attended college[b]	–0.034**	–0.002	0.038
	(0.017)	(0.053)	(0.019)
Employee age (years ÷ 10)	–0.037**	0.024	0.020
	(0.019)	(0.053)	(0.022)
Age squared (÷ 1,000)	0.056**	–0.030	–0.021
	(0.022)	(0.063)	(0.026)
Female	–0.029**	–0.035**	0.001
	(0.005)	(0.014)	(0.006)
Nonwhite	0.011	–0.034	–0.021**
	(0.006)	(0.020)	(0.007)
Currently married	–0.012**	–0.009	0.006
	(0.006)	(0.016)	(0.007)
Number of children under age 18	0.008**	–0.008	0.004
	(0.002)	(0.006)	(0.003)
Tenure at current employer (years ÷ 10)	–0.074**	–0.038	0.059**
	(0.009)	(0.025)	(0.010)
Tenure squared (÷ 1,000)	0.195**	0.188**	–0.046
	(0.027)	(0.081)	(0.030)
Expects to work for employer for a long time	–0.021**	0.005	0.015**
	(0.007)	(0.019)	(0.007)
Last year's total noncontingent pay (log)	–0.066**	0.076**	–0.017**
	(0.005)	(0.017)	(0.005)
Paid by the hour	0.010	–0.166**	–0.108**
	(0.007)	(0.019)	(0.007)
Sales occupation	0.377**	0.112**	0.015
	(0.013)	(0.031)	(0.011)
Unionized	0.073**	0.120**	0.004
	(0.013)	(0.029)	(0.013)
Works in the United States	–0.106**	–0.073	–0.048**
	(0.010)	(0.053)	(0.010)
Total company employees (÷ 100,000)	0.022	–0.200	0.332**
	(0.016)	(0.184)	(0.017)
Dependent variable mean	0.171	0.271	0.220
Model χ^2 test p-value	< 0.0001	< 0.0001	< 0.0001
Sample size	23,478	4,753	23,478

Source: NBER Shared Capitalism data set.

[a]Each entry contains the marginal effect and robust standard error (in parentheses) from a probit model where the dependent variable indicates employer-employee mismatches about the shared capitalism plan denoted in each column heading.

[b]High school dropout is the omitted category for the two educational attainment variables.

**Significant at the 5 percent level.

employee information. But recall that the NBER Shared Capitalism data set consists of employees from fourteen companies, and four of these are not used here because the eligibility questions for performance-related pay were imputed. As such, the results are based on only ten companies. All of the unionized employees are concentrated in three of these companies. And the variable on total employment only takes on ten distinct values (one value for each company). As such, it is difficult to distinguish these variables from company-specific effects and unlike for the other variables in these models, the results for unionization and company size are not robust to the inclusion of company-specific effects. So the results for these two variables are presented here with caution.

Table 9.4 presents the probit results for employee ignorance. In these models, the samples are restricted to individuals for which the company indicates they are covered by the relevant shared capitalism program. The dependent variable equals one if the employee does not perceive him or herself as being covered. In other words, the dependent variable indicates those individuals I am labeling as ignorant or unaware. In terms of figure 9.1, these models are limited to the second column and estimate the probability of being in the top cell (employee ignorance) in this column. Negative coefficients indicate a reduced likelihood of ignorance or lack of awareness. None of the predictors are consistent across all of the shared capitalism plans, but some patterns appear to hold across two or three plans. Greater educational attainment generally reduces employee ignorance, as do higher earnings and expectations of working at the employer for a long time. Hourly employees are more likely to fail to recognize coverage by a performance-based pay plan relative to salaried employees, as are unionized employees, except for the case of gain-sharing plans. Sales employees are more likely to be unaware of company-level profit-sharing plans but, not surprisingly, are less likely to be ignorant of individual-based incentives. Age and tenure exhibit quadratic relationships with the probability of ignorance, though increasing the quantities increases rather than decreases ignorance pertaining to individual-level performance pay plans. The overall results for ignorance about ESOPs and stock option grants appear generally similar as for the performance-based pay plans.

As the results for each variable tend to vary from program to program, an alternative way to approach these results is to ask what each model as a whole implies for the predicted probability of employee ignorance across different profiles of employees. For example, the results in column (1) of table 9.4 predict that the probability of being ignorant about the existence of a profit-sharing plan is 62 percent for a single, twenty-one-year-old, nonwhite, high-school dropout father of two making $25,000 per year with no expectation of working for a long time for his 200 employee company of one year in a union-represented, nonsales, hourly job in the United States. In contrast to this less-educated, low-paid, young worker profile, consider a

Table 9.4 **Probit analyses of employee ignorance[a]**

	Profit sharing (1)	Gain sharing (2)	Individual-based incentives (3)	ESOPs (4)	Stock option grants (5)
High school graduate[b]	–0.058**	—	–0.031	0.042	0.001
	(0.013)		(0.055)	(0.036)	(0.021)
Attended college[b]	–0.066**	–0.034	–0.097	0.030	–0.013
	(0.018)	(0.045)	(0.057)	(0.030)	(0.026)
Employee age (years ÷ 10)	–0.043**	0.169	0.157**	–0.038	0.027
	(0.019)	(0.212)	(0.051)	(0.037)	(0.019)
Age squared (÷ 1,000)	0.067**	–0.174	–0.146**	0.042	–0.024
	(0.022)	(0.248)	(0.060)	(0.045)	(0.022)
Female	–0.029**	0.090*	0.011	–0.033**	–0.017**
	(0.006)	(0.045)	(0.013)	(0.012)	(0.005)
Nonwhite	0.023**	0.117	–0.085**	0.003	–0.003
	(0.007)	(0.098)	(0.012)	(0.017)	(0.006)
Currently married	–0.016**	0.061	–0.008	–0.023	–0.001
	(0.006)	(0.054)	(0.014)	(0.013)	(0.006)
Number of children under age 18	0.009**	–0.024	0.007	0.006	–0.001
	(0.002)	(0.018)	(0.005)	(0.005)	(0.002)
Tenure at current employer (years ÷ 10)	–0.087**	–0.082	0.115**	–0.402**	–0.038**
	(0.009)	(0.073)	(0.018)	(0.027)	(0.012)
Tenure squared (÷ 1,000)	0.228**	0.203	–0.015	1.160**	0.109**
	(0.027)	(0.202)	(0.062)	(0.095)	(0.050)
Expects to work for employer for a long time	–0.025**	–0.012	–0.037**	–0.006	–0.001
	(0.007)	(0.051)	(0.016)	(0.015)	(0.008)
Last year's total noncontingent pay (log)	–0.074**	–0.126**	–0.213**	–0.080**	–0.012**
	(0.005)	(0.053)	(0.013)	(0.017)	(0.006)
Paid by the hour	–0.004	0.101	0.256**	0.022	0.027**
	(0.007)	(0.091)	(0.032)	(0.015)	(0.011)
Sales occupation	0.412**	–0.296	–0.117**	–0.046	0.011
	(0.014)	(0.187)	(0.013)	(0.019)	(0.008)
Unionized	0.207**	–0.259**	0.204**	0.223**	—
	(0.032)	(0.090)	(0.080)	(0.085)	
Works in the United States	–0.069**	–0.014	0.015	—	–0.014
	(0.010)	(0.329)	(0.015)		(0.011)
Total company employees (÷ 100,000)	0.066**	–8.738**	0.530**	–1.309**	–0.386**
	(0.019)	(3.389)	(0.044)	(0.412)	(0.027)
Dependent variable mean	0.164	0.495	0.312	0.151	0.078
Model χ^2 test p-value	< 0.0001	< 0.0001	< 0.0001	< 0.0001	< 0.0001
Sample size	21,325	827	9,435	2,827	5,331

Source: NBER Shared Capitalism data set.

[a]Each entry contains the marginal effect and robust standard error (in parentheses) from a probit model where the dependent variable indicates employee ignorance about the shared capitalism plan denoted in each column heading.

[b]High school dropout is the omitted category for the two educational attainment variables, except in column (2).

**Significant at the 5 percent level.

better-educated, salaried, experienced worker profile: a married, forty-five-year-old, white, college-educated, childless woman making $75,000 per year with expectations of working for a long time in her 200 person company of fifteen years in a nonunion, nonsales, salaried job in the United States only has a 4 percent chance of failing to correctly realize that she is covered by a profit-sharing plan. Table 9.5 summarizes these predictions for the various shared capitalism plans. The pattern of results are quite similar with the exception of the gain-sharing results—younger, inexperienced, low-educated, and low-paid employees are significantly more likely to be unaware of shared capitalism programs than their middle-aged, higher paid, better educated, salaried counterparts.

Besides ignorance or lack of awareness, the second dimension of employer-employee mismatches consists of false positive responses—situations in which employees' perception that they are covered by a shared capitalism program contradicts their employers' statements that they are not. Table 9.6 presents the probit results for false positives. In these models, the samples are restricted to individuals who indicated that they are covered by the relevant shared capitalism program and the dependent variable equals one if the company did not indicate that this employee was covered. In terms of figure 9.1, these models are limited to the second row and estimate the probability of being in the left-most cell (false positives) in this row. The results

Table 9.5 **Predicted ignorance rates for different employee profiles**

Employee profile	Profit sharing (1)	Gain sharing (2)	Individual-based incentives (3)	ESOPs (4)	Stock option grants[a] (5)
A single, 21-year-old, non-white, high school dropout father of two making $25,000 per year with no expectation of working for this company for a long time and one year of tenure working in a union-represented, nonsales, hourly job in the United States for a company with 200 employees.	0.624 (0.117)	0.719 (0.458)	0.697 (0.274)	0.809 (0.266)	0.377 (0.177)
Average over the relevant estimation sample	0.164 (0.129)	0.495 (0.127)	0.313 (0.176)	0.152 (0.150)	0.078 (0.111)
A married, 45-year-old, white, college-educated, childless woman making $75,000 per year with expectations of working for this company for a long time with 15 years of tenure in a nonunion, nonsales, salaried job in the United States for a company with 200 employees.	0.040 (0.043)	0.813 (0.262)	0.261 (0.055)	0.003 (0.121)	0.045 (0.087)

Source: Calculated from table 9.4.
Note: Standard deviations in parentheses.
[a]Excludes unionization and total company employees.

Table 9.6 **Probit analyses of false positives[a]**

	Profit sharing (1)	Gain sharing (2)	Individual-Based Incentives (3)
High school graduate[b]	0.004	—	–0.162**
	(0.006)		(0.053)
Attended college[b]	0.007**	0.112**	–0.193**
	(0.002)	(0.052)	(0.097)
Employee age (years ÷ 10)	–0.008**	–0.168	–0.042
	(0.003)	(0.178)	(0.067)
Age squared (÷ 1,000)	0.009**	0.256	0.118
	(0.003)	(0.210)	(0.078)
Female	0.003**	0.060	–0.054**
	(0.001)	(0.032)	(0.015)
Nonwhite	–0.001	0.157**	–0.108**
	(0.001)	(0.046)	(0.014)
Currently married	–0.002	–0.020	–0.033
	(0.001)	(0.038)	(0.018)
Number of children under age 18	0.001	–0.038**	0.0001
	(0.0003)	(0.015)	(0.006)
Tenure at current employer (years ÷ 10)	0.001	–0.267**	0.135**
	(0.002)	(0.057)	(0.025)
Tenure squared (÷ 1,000)	–0.013**	0.205	–0.142
	(0.005)	(0.183)	(0.085)
Expects to work for employer for a long time	–0.001	0.092**	0.012
	(0.001)	(0.045)	(0.020)
Last year's total noncontingent pay (log)	–0.004**	0.0001	–0.356**
	(0.001)	(0.042)	(0.020)
Paid by the hour	0.002**	0.384**	0.582**
	(0.001)	(0.052)	(0.024)
Sales occupation	0.009**	0.176**	—
	(0.003)	(0.041)	
Unionized	0.253**	–0.838**	0.519**
	(0.026)	(0.026)	(0.069)
Works in the United States	–0.023**	–0.075	0.167**
	(0.003)	(0.092)	(0.017)
Total company employees (÷ 100,000)	–0.036**	—	–0.109**
	(0.003)		(0.048)
Dependent variable mean	0.028	0.675	0.297
Model χ^2 test *p*-value	< 0.0001	< 0.0001	< 0.0001
Sample size	18,343	1,287	7,470

Source: NBER Shared Capitalism data set.

[a]Each entry contains the marginal effect and robust standard error (in parentheses) from a probit model where the dependent variable indicates an employee-reported false positive about the shared capitalism plan denoted in each column heading.

[b]High school dropout is the omitted category for the two educational attainment variables, except in column (2), where high school dropouts are excluded from the sample.

**Significant at the 5 percent level.

Table 9.7 **Predicted false positive rates for different employee profiles**

Employee profile	Profit sharing (1)	Gain sharing (2)	Individual-based incentives (3)
A single, 21-year-old, nonwhite, high school dropout father of two making $25,000 per year with no expectation of working for this company for a long time and one year of tenure working in a union-represented, nonsales, hourly job in the United States for a company with 200 employees.	0.660 (0.342)	0.090 (0.469)	0.999 (0.419)
Average over the relevant estimation sample	0.028 (0.094)	0.676 (0.378)	0.294 (0.335)
A married, 45-year-old, white, college-educated, childless woman making $75,000 per year with expectations of working for this company for a long time with 15 years of tenure in a nonunion, nonsales, salaried job in the United States for a company with 200 employees.	0.038 (0.083)	0.121 (0.181)	0.265 (0.066)

Source: Calculated from table 9.6.
Note: Standard deviations in parentheses.

are mixed and job characteristics seem more consistently important than demographic characteristics for explaining false positives. This suggests that variations in false positive responses stem more from variations in employer offerings of shared capitalism plans than from variations in employee beliefs about their prevalence. In other words, employees in jobs that are less likely to have a pay-for-performance plan are more likely to make a false positive error. Except for the case of gain-sharing programs, higher paid employees are less likely to make a false positive error whereas hourly and unionized employees are more likely to make this mistake. Table 9.7 repeats the exercise of table 9.5 in presenting the predicted probabilities of a false positive for two different employee profiles. Younger, inexperienced, low-educated, and low-paid employees are significantly more likely to misunderstand the applicability of company and individual-based performance pay plans than their middle-aged, higher paid, better educated, salaried co-workers.

9.5 Other Measures of Shared Capitalism Ignorance

The primary focus of this chapter is trying to assess the extent of employee ignorance about shared capitalism programs by analyzing mismatches between employer and employee statements pertaining to the applicability of three pay-for-performance plans plus ESOP and stock option plans. However, there are several other questions in the NBER Shared Capitalism data set that can be used to examine the importance of employee ignorance for potentially undermining employee involvement in decision making. The

Table 9.8 Other measures of employee ignorance

Question [survey pool]	Response categories of interest (1)	Frequency of response (2)
How frequently do you feel that the Company is reaching out to you to inform you (through meetings, newsletters, e-mail, or Internet) about the goals of the company, overall workplace performance, changes to workplace organization, or implementation of new technology? [3 companies]	Occasionally or never	28.54% (735 / 2,575)
How frequently do you reach out to inform yourself (through meetings you set up or conversations that you initiate or material you read, or use of the Internet or other means) about the goals of the company, overall workplace performance, changes to workplace organization, or implementation of new technology? [2 companies]	Occasionally or never	43.97% (747 / 1,699)
I get the information I need to do my job. [1 company]	Strongly disagree, disagree, or do not know	26.94% (7,999 / 29,689)
We are kept informed of important issues in the organization. [1 company]	Strongly disagree, disagree, or do not know	45.46% (13,528 / 29,757)
I am kept informed about changes affecting my work. [1 company]	Strongly disagree, disagree, or do not know	43.40% (12,881 / 29,678)
To what extent do you understand your company's overall plan for being successful? [7 companies]	Not at all or very little	14.76% (4,981 / 33,747)

Source: NBER Shared Capitalism data set.

responses to six relevant questions are summarized in table 9.8. Nearly 30 percent of employees at three companies believe that their company only occasionally or never reaches out to them to provide information about company goals and workplace changes; nearly 45 percent at two companies report that they personally seek out such information on their own only occasionally or never. A quarter of employees at one large company failed to agreed with the statement that they have the information needed to do their job; around 40 percent failed to agree with the statements that they are kept abreast of important issues in the organization and in their jobs. And 15 percent of employees across seven companies believe that they understand their company's plan for being successful only a little or not at all.

To the extent that shared capitalism programs aim to provide workers with incentives for making better decisions, these questions are relevant to the understanding of such programs. More specifically, the responses to these six questions reveal nontrivial numbers of employees who believe that they have insufficient information and are not kept up-to-date on important changes. As nearly all of these questions were asked in only one or two companies, additional research needs to assess generalizability of the responses, but the pattern of results is suggestive of employee ignorance that can undermine shared capitalism programs by creating roadblocks to informed decision making. This is another dimension of employee ignorance that should not be overlooked.

9.6 The Impact of Ignorance

Space considerations prevent a comprehensive analysis in this chapter of the effect of ignorance on the operation of shared capitalism programs. But the employee mismatches documented here are a form of a measurement error that can affect econometric estimates of the effect of shared capitalism on various outcomes. The NBER Shared Capitalism data do not contain performance measures per se, but consider two questions that are perhaps related to individual employee performance: willingness to work hard and loyalty. For the former, employees were asked to respond on a 1 = strongly disagree to 5 = strongly agree scale to the statement, "I am willing to work harder than I have to in order to help the company I work for succeed." There is widespread agreement with this statement with a mean response of 4.02 and a standard deviation of 0.899. For the latter, employees were asked, "How much loyalty would you say you feel toward the company you work for as a whole?" with response choices of 1 = no loyalty at all, 2 = only a little, 3 = some, 4 = a lot.[6] The average response to this question is 3.33 with a standard deviation of 0.798.

One might expect that if shared capitalism programs are effective that they would improve workers' willingness to work hard and their loyalty toward their employers. Columns (1) and (3) of table 9.9 show that in regressions with and without additional control variables similar to those in the probit models, employees who believe they are covered by an individual or company-based performance-based pay plan have higher levels of willingness to work hard and loyalty. These are the type of regression models that one might estimate in these data, ignoring issues of mismatch and ignorance. But again, these effects might be biased because of measurement error associated with mismatch and ignorance. Columns (2) and (4), therefore, include separate indicators for three cells of figure 9.1: accurate yes', employee ignorance, and false positives; accurate no's are the omitted reference category. With the exception of the loyalty model with control variables, the effect size for accurate yes is always larger than the estimates in columns (1) and (2). In most of the cases, the employee ignorance estimate is smaller than

6. In actuality, the response scales of both of these questions in the original data collection were the opposite of what are presented here, but I have reverse-coded them so that higher numerical responses indicate higher levels of willingness to work hard and loyalty.

Table 9.9 Regression analysis of the effect of performance-based pay on work attitudes

	(1)	(2)	(3)	(4)
Dependent variable: Willingness to work hard[a]				
Employee believes covered by an individual or company-level performance-based pay plan	0.142**	—	0.058**	—
	(0.010)		(0.016)	
Employer-employee matched responses for an individual or company-level performance-based pay plan (accurate no is omitted category)				
Accurate yes	—	0.263**	—	0.135**
		(0.015)		(0.029)
Employee ignorance	—	0.175**	—	0.116**
		(0.018)		(0.032)
False positive	—	0.154**	—	0.206**
		(0.023)		(0.042)
Additional controls[b]	No	No	Yes	Yes
Adjusted R^2	0.005	0.007	0.058	0.059
Sample size	44,799	44,799	23,507	23,507
Dependent variable: Loyalty[c]				
Employee believes covered by an individual or company-level performance-based pay plan	0.175**	—	0.057**	—
	(0.010)		(0.014)	
Employer-employee matched responses for an individual or company-level performance-based pay plan (accurate no is omitted category)				
Accurate yes	—	0.234**	—	0.031
		(0.014)		(0.025)
Employee ignorance	—	0.097**	—	–0.010
		(0.017)		(0.029)
False positive	—	0.219**	—	0.276**
		(0.021)		(0.037)
Additional controls[b]	No	No	Yes	Yes
Adjusted R^2	0.009	0.009	0.077	0.079
Sample size	41,278	41,278	23,197	23,197

Source: NBER Shared Capitalism data set.

[a]To what extent do you agree or disagree with this statement? "I am willing to work harder than I have to in order to help the company I work for succeed." 1 = strongly disagree, 5 = strongly agree (mean = 4.02, standard deviation = 0.899).

[b]Controls for education, age, gender, marital status, children, tenure, fixed pay, hourly occupation, sales occupation, union status, and US employee.

[c]How much loyalty would you say you feel toward the company you work for as a whole? 1 = no loyalty at all, 2 = only a little, 3 = some, 4 = a lot (mean = 3.33, standard deviation = 0.798).

**Significant at the 5 percent level.

the accurate yes estimate, though surprisingly individuals who are labeled as ignorant about performance-based pay are estimated to have higher levels of willingness to work hard and loyalty than individuals in the accurate no category. The false positive employees have the largest effects in many cases, which is consistent with them acting as if they were covered by performance-based pay plans even though they may or may not be in reality. In sum, the overall pattern of results in table 9.9 is consistent with information being important, including the existence of measurement error in the econometric models and also with the potential for shared capitalism programs to be more effective when employees and employers have good information.

9.7 Conclusions

An analysis of the NBER Shared Capitalism data set of thousands of employee responses linked to company-provided information from fourteen private-sector organizations reveals significant fractions of employees whose perceptions of whether or not they are covered by various shared capitalism programs do not match their employers' policies. In fact, between 18 and 25 percent of the employee responses on the perceived coverage of company, group, and individual-level incentive pay plans and of ESOPs disagree with the employer-provided coverage information. There is a particularly large discrepancy between employee and employer understandings of group or team-level gain-sharing plans, but nontrivial levels of ignorance and false positive responses are observed for all of the plans. Probit analyses allow a comparison of middle-aged, highly-paid, well-educated, salaried workers to those that are younger, inexperienced, low-educated, and low-paid; the latter are significantly more likely to be unaware of or misunderstand the coverage of company and individual-based performance pay plans.

Such shared capitalism programs seek to tie employee pay to performance. If this is intended simply as a risk-sharing mechanism between employers and their employees, then ignorance of shared capitalism plans is detrimental to employees, but is probably not a significant concern with respect to corporate performance. In contrast, if a goal of shared capitalism programs is to provide incentives for employee performance, then employee ignorance has the potential to undermine this goal. Put simply, how can incentives work if employees are not aware of their existence? For example, 37 percent of employees that their employers say are covered by individual-based incentives fail to perceive that they are in fact covered by such an incentive plan. Other research shows that employees act upon their own imperfect information—Chan and Stevens (2008) found that misinformed individuals based their retirement decisions on their own, misinformed views of their pension wealth. These regression results for employee attitudes regarding their willingness to work hard and their loyalty to their employer are consistent with other research and further suggest that ignorance can undermine both the practice of shared capitalism programs, and the econometric estimation of their effects.

With that said, the previous literature on employee ignorance reminds us that some caution is warranted. The figures reported here assume that the company-reported information is completely accurate for each individual employee even though the company-reported coverage measures are for groups of employees rather than individuals. As such, some employees might correctly report that they are not covered, but this appears here as ignorance if they are part of a larger covered group. However, if individual employees are excluded from various compensation programs, this is most likely on the basis of tenure (if probationary employees are excluded) and job characteristics (such as certain occupations or unionized workers being excluded). But the probit results show that inaccuracies are also correlated with demographic characteristics and with whether an employee expects to work for the organization for a long time. The possibility exists that these characteristics are substituting for incomplete job-level controls in the econometric models, but to the extent that this is only partially true, these multivariate results suggest that at least some of the observed inaccuracies are due to misunderstandings and ignorance. This is not to say that employees are always to blame. Companies might not effectively communicate whether pay-for-performance plans are based on individual, group, plant, division, or corporate performance, or individual managers might not implement a plan in the manner expected by higher-level corporate policymakers.

In addition to employee ignorance, the analyses document significant numbers of false positive responses—that is, employees that believe they are covered by a shared capitalism program when their employer states that they are not. This aspect of overall inaccuracy might not undermine the incentive intentions of shared capitalism if perception becomes reality: workers that believe they are covered by an incentive-based plan might act as if there are incentives, at least until they find out they were wrong. In fact, the results on false positives suggests that rhetoric has perhaps outpaced reality. False positive responses occur when employees overestimate the presence of pay-for-performance plans. The probit results show that workers who are lower paid, paid hourly, or unionized are particularly likely to overestimate the presence of pay-for-performance plans. In other words, these workers believe that they are covered by an incentive-based plan—perhaps based on contemporary rhetoric on the contingent employment relationship—even when they are not (at least not formally according to their employers). As such, there might be an opening for companies to increase the presence or formalization of pay-for-performance plans among these workers.

On the other hand, the false positive results are similar to the results on the lack of awareness of shared capitalism programs in revealing the complexity of informational issues for shared capitalism programs—significant numbers of employees differ from their employers in their understandings of critical issues pertaining to pay determination and, especially in the case of gain-sharing plans, are covered by programs administered by local managers that the corporate-level human resources staff has difficulty monitoring.

In general then, the shared capitalism plans that are more difficult for employees to explicitly observe, such as pay-for-performance plans, have high levels of informational mismatch, whereas plans that include explicit or tangible markers, such as stock grants or stock options, have low levels of informational problems. Employees may have difficulty understanding whether their pay is based on individual or group performance, but they know when they have received 100 shares of stock.

The results of these analyses strongly suggest that corporations with shared capitalism programs might consider improving their employee communications programs. Shared capitalism programs are not free—they involve cash and/or stock outlays to employees as well as administrative costs. These costs are presumably only justified if they generate returns for the corporation through enhanced employee performance. Without effective communications programs, the benefits of shared capitalism will likely be dampened by employee ignorance, and the expenses of shared capitalism programs might not be justified. Since spreading information about a program is generally not costly, these findings suggest that firms may be ignorant about the extent of employee ignorance and the corresponding need for better communications about shared capitalism programs.

The results of this chapter are also important for researchers. The mismatches between employer and employee reports of shared capitalism programs represent a form of measurement error that can have the usual econometric problem: regression estimates of the effects of these programs on, for example, organizational performance, are likely biased toward zero and therefore underestimate the true potential of shared capitalism programs with perfect information. Finally, not only can employee ignorance undermine both research on and the practice of shared capitalism, but it should also give pause to economists and others that continue to assume that workers have perfect information. Contemporary theories as well as private and public policies must reflect the complexities of imperfect labor markets with information gaps.

Appendix

Table 9A.1 Independent variable definitions and summary statistics

	Mean (standard deviation)
1 if employee is a high school graduate but did not attend any college	0.193 (0.394)
1 if employee attended college (includes college graduates and nongraduates)	0.785 (0.411)
Age of employee (years)	41.451 (9.980)
1 if employee is female	0.296 (0.456)
1 if employee's race is nonwhite	0.189 (0.392)
1 if employee is currently married or living as married	0.746 (0.435)
Number of children under age 18	0.987 (1.167)
Years worked for current employer	9.226 (8.661)
1 if employee expects to work at the current employer for a long time	0.844 (0.363)
Log of last year's total noncontingent pay (base pay and overtime)	10.838 (0.646)
1 if employee is paid by the hour	0.411 (0.492)
1 if employee is in a sales occupation	0.072 (0.259)
1 if employee is unionized	0.053 (0.223)
1 if employee works in the United States	0.890 (0.312)
Total number of employees for the company	35,848.998 (16,345.097)

Source: NBER Shared Capitalism data set.

Note: The sample statistics presented here are for the 23,478 observations that have complete information for the probit models in columns (1) and (3) of table 8.3.

References

Brennan Center for Justice. 2006. Do New Yorkers know the minimum results from a spot survey of employers and workers in New York City. Economic Policy Brief no. 4, NYU School of Law. Available at: http://www.brennancenter.org.

Budd, J. W. 2007. The effect of Unions on employee benefits and non-wage compensation: Monopoly power, collective voice, and facilitation. In *What do unions do?*

A twenty-year perspective, ed. T. Bennett and B. E. Kaufman, 160–92. New Brunswick, NJ: Transaction Publishers.
Budd, J. W., and A. Brey. 2003. Unions and family leave: Early experience under the Family and Medical Act. *Labor Studies Journal* 28 (Fall): 85–105.
Budd, J. W., and B. P. McCall. 1997. The effect of unions on the receipt of unemployment insurance benefits. *Industrial and Labor Relations Review* 50 (3): 478–92.
———. 2004. Unions and unemployment insurance benefits receipt: Evidence from the CPS. *Industrial Relations* 43 (April): 339–55.
Budd, J. W., and K. Mumford. 2004. Trade unions and family-friendly policies in Britain. *Industrial and Labor Relations Review* 57 (2): 204–22.
———. 2006. Family-friendly work practices in Britain: Availability and perceived accessibility. *Human Resource Management Journal* 45:23–42.
Cappelli, P. 1999. *The new deal at work: Managing the market-driven workforce.* Boston: Harvard Business School Press.
Chan, S., and A. H. Stevens. 2008. What you don't know can't help you: Pension knowledge and retirement decision making. *Review of Economics and Statistics* 90 (2): 253–66.
Choi, J. J., D. Laibson, and B. C. Madrian. 2005. $100 bills on the sidewalk: Suboptimal saving in 401(k) plans. NBER Working Paper no. 11554. Cambridge, MA: National Bureau of Economic Research, August.
Conyon, M. J., and R. B. Freeman. 2004. Shared modes of compensation and firm performance: UK evidence. In *Seeking a premier economy: The economic effects of British economic reforms, 1980–2000,* ed. D. Card, R. Blundell, and R. B. Freeman, 109–46. Chicago: University of Chicago Press.
Freeman, R. B. 2001. The shared Capitalist model of work and compensation. *Reflets et Perspectives de la vie Economique* 40:169–81.
Freeman, R. B., and J. L. Medoff. 1984. *What do Unions do?* New York: Basic Books.
Freeman, R. B., and J. Rogers. 2006. *What workers want,* updated ed. Ithaca, NY: Cornell University Press.
Gustman, A. L., and T. L. Steinmeier. 2005. Imperfect knowledge of social security and pensions. *Industrial Relations* 44 (2): 373–95.
Hirsch, B. T., D. A. Macpherson, and J. M. DuMond. 1997. Workers' compensation recipiency in union and nonunion workplaces. *Industrial and Labor Relations Review* 50 (2): 213–36.
Kim, P. T. 1997. Bargaining with imperfect information: A study of worker perceptions of legal protection in an at-will world. *Cornell Law Review* 83: 105–60.
Luchak, A. A., and M. Gunderson. 2000. What do employees know about their pension plan? *Industrial Relations* 39 (4): 646–70.
March, J. G., and H. A. Simon. 1958. *Organizations.* New York: Wiley.
Markow, D., and K. Bagnaschi. 2005. What American teens and adults know about economics. Rochester, NY: Harris Interactive. Available at: http://www.ncee.net/cel/.
McCall, B. P. 1995. The impact of unemployment insurance benefit levels on recipiency. *Journal of Business and Economic Statistics* 13 (2): 189–98.
Mitchell, O. S. 1988. Worker knowledge of pension provisions. *Journal of Labor Economics* 6 (1): 21–39.
Reschovsky, J. D., J. L. Hargraves, and A. F. Smith. 2002. Consumer beliefs and health plan performance: It's not whether you are in an HMO but whether you think you are. *Journal of Health Policy, Politics and Law* 27 (3): 353–77.
Rudy, J. 2002. What they don't know won't hurt them: Defending employment-at-will in light of findings that employees believe they possess just cause protection. *Berkeley Journal of Employment and Labor Law* 23:307–67.

Simon, H. A. 1982. *Models of bounded rationality.* Cambridge, MA: MIT Press.
Waldfogel, J. 2001. Family and medical leave: Evidence from the 2000 surveys. *Monthly Labor Review* 124 (9): 17–23.
Weil, D. 1996. Regulating the workplace: The vexing problem of implementation. In *Advances in industrial and labor relations, vol. 7,* ed. D. Lewin, B. E. Kaufman, and D. Sockell, 247–86. Greenwich, CT: JAI Press.
———. 2005. Individual rights and collective agents: The role of old and new workplace institutions in the regulation of labor markets. In *Emerging labor market institutions for the twenty-first century,* ed. R. B. Freeman, J. Hersch, and L. Mishel, 13–44. Chicago: University of Chicago Press.

10

Who Benefits from Shared Capitalism? The Social Stratification of Wealth and Power in Companies with Employee Ownership

Edward J. Carberry

10.1 Introduction

The spread of various forms of shared capitalism in the last three decades raises a number of interesting questions relating to the persistence of broader patterns of inequality in the United States. Since shared capitalism programs broaden corporate ownership and how financial returns of this ownership are distributed, as more employees gain access to these programs, what happens to existing patterns of stratification? Do shared capitalism programs mitigate or exacerbate existing patterns of income and wealth inequality? How do women and nonwhites, groups that traditionally experience these inequalities most powerfully, fare with respect to shared capitalism? Finally, do companies with these programs open up access to other forms of participation within organizations, such as access to positions of power, authority, and influence?

Such questions are important for corporate managers in companies with shared capitalism and companies considering these plans. If certain groups of employees experience inequities in terms of participating in these plans and the financial value they receive from these plans, these realities may detract from the potential that these plans offer for aligning employee behaviors with long-term corporate strategy and for creating organizational cultures of fairness. These questions are also relevant for organizational and management theory, and for our understanding of social inequality in the twenty-first century economy. Few studies have made connections between the vast literature on the causes, characteristics, and consequences of shared capitalism and the large body of sociological research that has examined the

Edward J. Carberry is an assistant professor at the Rotterdam School of Management, Erasmus University.

impact of gender, race, and ethnicity on such outcomes as income, wealth, and power in the workplace. This chapter takes a modest first step toward better understanding the connections between shared capitalism and social stratification.

More specifically, this chapter will examine how access to shared capitalism, returns from shared capitalism programs, and organizational power and authority within companies with shared capitalism are stratified by gender, race, ethnicity, and disability. The analysis is based on the NBER data set of over 40,000 employees in fourteen US companies with at least one type of shared capitalism program. This data set provides rich individual level information on participation in different shared capitalist programs, financial returns, and assets held in shared capitalist programs, and access to and perceptions of various types of power and authority.

Our knowledge of how different groups do with respect to these outcomes is severely limited, as existing research on shared capitalism has largely ignored these issues. Gaining a better understanding of these outcomes will provide a richer perspective on how the returns of shared capitalism are distributed and the potential effects of this distribution on the effectiveness of shared capitalism. A central motivation of this chapter is to take seriously the effect of social inequality on employee outcomes, and the possibility that social inequality can mitigate the relationship between shared capitalism and corporate performance. This chapter will not examine the causes of stratification within the sample companies, nor will it provide an in-depth analysis of the consequences of shared capitalist programs for long-term trends in inequality. Rather, the analysis will examine the concrete outcomes for different demographic groups and thus provide a detailed picture of the contours of stratification within shared capitalist companies. This chapter will also examine relationships between social stratification and employee attitudes toward their jobs, their employers, and shared capitalism itself. Ultimately, another goal of this chapter is to open up a research and theoretical space on which future studies of stratification and shared capitalism can build, both to better understand the long-term impacts of shared capitalism on broader patterns of social inequality and to expand the existing theoretical frameworks on social stratification to incorporate new forms of compensation and wealth generation in the twenty-first century economy.

After reviewing the existing literature on income inequality generally, this chapter will turn to the empirical analysis, which will first examine whether women and different minority groups face barriers to accessing shared capitalist programs. Next, the analysis will examine the effect of gender, race, ethnicity, and disability on the value of assets that employees acquire through shared capitalist programs. This chapter will then analyze how power and authority are distributed among different demographic groups within companies with shared capitalism. Finally, I will consider the impacts of social stratification on employee attitudes and conclude with a discussion of some implications for management theory and practice.

Overall, the results reveal substantial disparities between the outcomes of women and men, nonwhite and whites, and employees with and without disabilities in terms of access to shared capitalism and the financial value provided by this participation. Although many of these effects appear to stem from existing mechanisms of occupational segregation, women and African Americans have lower plan values, even accounting for differences in education, occupation, and salary. This suggests that the structure and operation of certain forms of shared capitalism generates disparities beyond those created by extant mechanisms of stratification. The analysis provides a more mixed view of barriers to power and authority because formal structures of employee involvement appear to open up access to workplace power for some groups. The findings also reveal that, despite these disparities, access to shared capitalism and participation in employee involvement practices have positive effects on employee attitudes among all of the demographic groups.

10.2 The Persisting Significance of Gender, Race, and Ethnicity

Analyzing gaps in the economic and organizational outcomes for groups with different ascriptive statuses has been a central focus of a vast literature on social stratification in the last three decades (Morris and Western 1999). These analyses have focused primarily on gaps in earnings, but also on gaps in wealth, socioeconomic status, and power and authority within organizations. A common story emerges from this literature: in the United States, the postwar prosperity of the 1950s and 1960s reduced or held constant inequality levels within all demographic groups. Since the early 1970s, however, median earnings have declined for most groups, and in the 1980s, inequality accelerated rapidly, with the trend continuing through today (Morris and Western 1999). The lone exception is that since 1973, the real value of wages for women has increased across all income levels, while the real value of wages for most men has declined or remained constant. Women, however, continue to earn less than men. A recent analysis from the Economic Policy Institute (2006) indicates that college-educated women earn 24 percent less than college-educated men, that women are disproportionately represented in minimum wage jobs, and that women are less likely to earn high wages (10.1 percent of women versus 17.6 percent of men earn at least three times the poverty level wage).

Similarly, although African Americans experienced increases in the real value of their wages in the postwar period, this trend for the most part stopped in the mid-1970s, and earnings inequality has increased among African Americans in the last two decades (Morris and Western 1999). In addition, the median income for African Americans is only 55.6 percent that of whites, and 29.4 percent of African American households, as compared to 13 percent of white households, have zero or negative net worth (Economic Policy Institute 2006). Other racial and ethnic groups have not been the subject of as much attention as women and African Americans, but the overall trends reflect similarly negative outcomes. In their analysis of census data from 1970, 1980, and 1990, Hirschman and Snipp (1999) found similarly negative effects of race/ethnicity on the socioeconomic status (a measure of occupational attainment) among African Americans, Hispanics, and Native Americans. However, the outcomes for Asian Americans were equal to or greater than that of whites. In terms of earnings, all racial and ethnic groups, except for Japanese Americans, earned less than whites, and the gaps were the largest for African Americans, Hispanics, and Native Americans.

Explaining the differential outcomes of men and women, and of whites and nonwhites, has been the topic of a large body of literature on social stratification. Reviewing this literature is beyond the scope of this chapter, but the evidence provides strong empirical support for the explanation that inequality is the result of women and minorities being consistently segregated into different labor markets than men and whites, and that these labor markets consist of primarily different (and lower-paying) occupations (Grusky 2001). The literature has also revealed that occupational segregation itself has been driven primarily by mechanisms of social closure that emanate from social conflict for jobs and access to jobs, differential access to educational opportunities that are crucial for occupational attainment, and cultural views that devalue female and nonwhite labor (Grusky 2001). In addition, women and African Americans have each faced their own unique set of barriers. For the former, the legacy of slavery, geographic segregation, and the decimation of the domestic manufacturing sector have cut many African Americans off from educational opportunities, social networks, and formal labor markets (Massey and Denton 1993; Wilson 1980). Although women have recently faced fewer barriers to education, they have been uniquely affected by the devaluation of their paid labor market skills and abilities and relegated to a primary role as unpaid, domestic labor (Grusky 2001).

Morris and Western (1999) have argued that despite the importance of these specific forces shaping access to economic opportunities for different groups, all groups have been significantly and similarly affected by some common recent trends. In the last two decades demographic forces, such as the rise of the baby boomers, the increase in the number of women entering the workforce, and an increase in the number of unskilled immigrants, have all increased the supply of available workers. These demographic changes have coincided with deindustrialization, globalization, the decline of unions, the rise of market-based employment relations (e.g., contract work, subcontracting, temporary employment), and the expansion of the service sector, which provides lower paying jobs with fewer benefits for unskilled workers than the manufacturing jobs that they replaced.

The empirical evidence on inequality in the United States, therefore, presents a sobering account of the reality of equal access to economic opportunity. The persistence of inequality produces a range of negative economic and social consequences for all demographic groups, but serious solutions remain politically anathema at this stage. In the absence of new legislation to both mitigate these outcomes and address root causes, as well as large-scale cultural shifts in attitudes about the legitimacy and function of inequality, these patterns are likely to continue. In the last three decades, however, the diffusion of shared capitalism programs has opened up new avenues of economic opportunity since these programs provide a way for employees to access a source of income and wealth beyond their fixed pay; that is, through the ownership of stock and direct sharing of profits of their employing companies. Broadening capital ownership and profit sharing to groups earning less in the labor market may, therefore, help reduce income and wealth inequality. However, since access to these plans and the value that employees receive are often a direct function of income and occupation, shared capitalism may also exacerbate existing patterns of income inequality even as it increases the wealth of lower paid employees. Although the shared capitalism data analyzed in the chapter does not allow us to test these claims directly, it does allow us to gain a better understanding of inequality relating to participation in, and the value generated by, shared capitalism. I now turn to the evidence presented by the NBER data set of companies with shared capitalism.

10.3 Data and Methodology

This chapter uses the NBER data set of employees in fourteen firms with shared capitalism plans, described in the "Studying Shared Capitalism" section of the introduction to this volume. The focus of the statistical analyses is on examining the effect of being in one of six demographic categories (female, African American, Hispanic, Asian American, Native American, and having a disability) on a number of outcomes relating to access to shared capitalism, the financial value of shared capitalism, and access to organizational power. The analyses compare outcomes of women to men, each nonwhite group to whites, and employees with disabilities to those without disabilities. For example, when compared to men, are women more or less likely to participate in shared capitalism? Statistically, such comparisons are accomplished through the use of general linear regression models, and more specifically, logit and ordered logit models. In terms of reporting, the results for the logit and ordered logit models report coefficients rather than odds ratios. The only exception to the logit and ordered logit approach is in the analysis for financial value of shared capitalism, which uses ordinary least squares (OLS) regression. For this analysis, all outcomes were coded so that higher values represent more positive outcomes. For example, the answers for the question, "*how much influence do you have in deciding how you do your job and organize your work?*" were "*1 = a lot, 2 = some, 3 = only a little, 4 = none.*" These responses were reversed coded for the analysis.

For all outcomes relating to shared capitalism and workplace power, I report results for two models. The first includes the demographic variables of interest and controls for firm level effects. The second also includes controls (coefficients unreported) for occupation, education, organizational tenure, fixed pay, wealth, and individual firms, all of which may have an impact on the outcomes. Of particular interest is modeling the effects of occupation. A large body of a sociological research has demonstrated that an important driver of income inequality is the consistent segregation of women and racial and ethnic minorities into different labor markets than men and whites, labor markets that consist of primarily different (and lower-paying) occupations (Grusky 2001). Such segregation may be important for shared capitalism outcomes if women and nonwhites are more likely to be in occupations that are less likely to participate in shared capitalism. For example, if the results indicate that women are less likely to participate in shared capitalism, but the models do not control for occupation, this effect may be due to the fact that women could be segregated into occupations that have restricted access to shared capitalism, rather than due to something unique about how organizations structure shared capitalism plans.

In fact, confirming the evidence from past research, there is strong evidence of occupational segregation by gender, race, ethnicity, and disability status among employees in the sample. Appendix table 10A.1 shows results from logit models predicting the effect of demographic characteristics on the likelihood of being in different occupations, controlling for firm level differences, among employees in the sample. All groups are less likely to be in management positions, which have better access to shared capitalism and workplace power. The same is true for professional/technical positions, with the exception of Asian Americans. Therefore, controlling for occupation will permit a more nuanced understanding of the potential sources of disparities between different groups; that is, do disparities stem from occupational segregation and/or the specific ways in which shared capitalism plans are structured? In considering the results that account for occupational segregation, however, it is important to recognize that the occupational categories are broad. Although more fine grained occupational categories would have permitted a more detailed analysis of the role of occupational segregation, the survey did not collect data on more detailed occupational categories. In addition to the aforementioned controls, for all outcomes, I examined the impact of these demographic statuses for younger employees (under forty). I also ran models that included interaction terms to examine the effect of gender and race/ethnicity together. I do not report results for these models in the tables, but highlight the notable findings in the discussion. Finally, the results highlighted in the subsequent discussion focus on those effects that were statistically significant at least at the $p < .05$ level. The discussion of the results, to which this chapter now turns, is intended to illuminate overall trends and patterns and not discuss every finding in detail.

10.4 Descriptive Statistics

Before exploring the influence of gender, race, ethnicity, and disability on access to and returns from shared capitalism, table 10.1 provides summary information about the demographic characteristics of the sample, including participation rates in shared capitalism plans, values of shared capitalism assets, salary, and wealth.[1]

On all measures, men do better than women. Men have a higher rate of participation in employee ownership, profit sharing, and gain sharing, as well as higher average values for employee ownership assets, salary, and wealth. In terms of race and ethnicity, whites have the best outcomes on most measures, with the exception of Asian Americans, who have the highest average values for shared capitalism assets and salary, and the highest participation rates in gain-sharing plans. African Americans have the lowest value of shared capitalist assets and wealth, while Hispanics have the lowest average participation in shared capitalism and lowest average salaries. To gain a better understanding of the significance and magnitude of these differences, this chapter now turns to a deeper analysis of shared capitalism outcomes for various demographic groups.

In the discussion that follows, I focus on those results that are statistically significant. However, it is important to note that the number of employees within each demographic group may influence the statistical significance of some of the findings. For example, there are only 460 Native Americans in the sample, compared to almost 12,000 women. These sample sizes mean that the standard errors for women are lower, and this makes it easy to establish statistical significance. This also means that there will be little discussion of the outcomes of Native Americans. This does not necessarily mean that Native Americans do not experience disparities in various outcomes, but that statistically, it is difficult to establish relationships between being Native American and the outcomes of primary interest. Also, the sample sizes for African Americans, Hispanics, Asian Americans, and employees with disabilities are similar, so making comparisons of significant differences among these groups are relatively easy. Making comparisons between these groups and women, however, should be made with some caution.

1. Wealth is defined as total assets minus debts. More specifically, respondents were asked to report their wealth by including the "value of their house minus the mortgage, plus their vehicles, stocks and mutual funds, cash, checking accounts, retirement accounts including 401(k) and pension assets, and so forth."

Table 10.1 **Descriptive statistics on demography and shared capitalism**

Demographic group	Percent participating in any form of employee ownership	Mean value of stock held in all employee ownership plans	Percent eligible for profit sharing	Percent eligible for gain sharing	Mean salary	Mean wealth	Number of respondents
Women	62	$40,957	69	16	$45,895	$229,794	11,942
Men	67	$69,834	72	24	$62,805	$318,327	26,383
White	71	$62,006	77	21	$60,251	$322,965	28,698
African Americans	58	$20,735	55	13	$41,462	$118,580	1,739
Hispanics	39	$32,647	56	17	$37,983	$139,319	2,745
Asian Americans	61	$85,137	66	30	$63,634	$310,826	2,989
Native Americans	58	$41,784	56	13	$42,251	$197,618	460
Employees with disabilities	60	$54,820	66	17	$46,258	$220,727	2,256

10.5 Access to Shared Capitalist Programs

Do rates of participation in shared capitalism programs vary between different demographic groups? If rates do vary, to what extent and why? Table 10.2 shows the results of logit regression models that predict the effect of gender, race, ethnicity, and disability status on participation in the six primary types of shared capitalist programs that were measured by the NBER survey. The models examined participation rates only among those employees who were eligible for specific plans, not for the entire sample. For example, the models that examine participation rates for broad-based stock option plans only include employees in companies that had such plans, rather than for the entire sample. For each plan, the table reports the results from two models: the first includes only the demographic variables and controls for firm effects, and the second includes these variables along with additional controls for occupation, education, tenure, income, and wealth. Interpreting the logit coefficients requires a mathematical transformation known as exponentiation. This transformation yields a new number known as an odds ratio, which compares the odds that a woman will participate in an Employee Stock Ownership Plan (ESOP) to the odds that a man will participate in an ESOP. For example, the coefficient for women participating in ESOPs (without controls) is –.157, which when transformed yields an odds ratio of .85. Hence, women are 15 percent less likely to participate in ESOPs. Table 10.4 reports the results from table 10.2 in this more digestible form.

When examining the results for plan participation, it is essential to keep in mind the rules governing different forms of shared capitalism. ESOPs are governed by federal legislation that requires that most employees participate. For other types of shared capitalism plans, such as broad-based employee stock option plans (BBSOPs), profit sharing, and gain sharing, management decides who will participate among employees who are eligible. For still other forms of shared capitalism, such as employee stock purchase plans (ESPPs) and 401(k) plans, employees themselves decide whether or not they will participate. For these last two types of plans, the law requires that most employees are eligible (for example, ESPPs must be available to all full-time employees with two years of service), but employees ultimately have the choice of whether or not they will participate.

Table 10.2 indicates that women, African Americans, and employees with disabilities are less likely to participate in ESOPs. However, these effects all become statistically insignificant with controls of occupation, education, tenure, and fixed pay, indicating that the effects in these first models are likely the result of existing patterns of occupational segregation. Two other significant findings, unreported in table 10.2, are that both African American men and men with disabilities are less likely to participate in ESOPs. Any findings that reveal barriers to ESOP participation, however, are notable because of the strict legal requirements of ESOPs. Companies can, however, exclude

Table 10.2 **Predicting participation in shared capitalism**

	ESOP		BBSOP		ESPP		401(k)		Profit sharing		Gain sharing	
Female	–0.157	0.016	–0.125	0.236	–0.076	0.089	0.229	0.401	–0.111	0.028	–0.105	0.028
	(0.093)**	(0.142)	(0.109)	(0.140)**	(0.069)	(0.079)	(0.028)***	(0.045)***	(0.046)***	(0.068)	(0.092)	(0.137)
African American	–0.668	–0.297	–0.585	–0.300	–0.407	–0.142	–0.438	–0.338	–0.829	–0.556	–0.688	0.082
	(0.165)***	(0.253)	(0.273)**	(0.319)	(0.182)**	(0.198)	(0.058)***	(0.085)***	(0.092)***	(0.136)***	(0.190)***	(0.321)
Hispanic	–0.622	–0.236	–0.399	0.255	–0.147	0.188	–1.435	–0.008	–0.647	–0.407	–0.969	–0.340
	(0.224)***	(0.338)	(0.284)	(0.350)	(0.167)	(0.187)	(0.045)***	(0.092)	(0.079)***	(0.130)***	(0.132)***	(0.260)
Asian	0.221	0.309	–0.271	0.041	0.309	0.466	–1.011	0.077	–0.785	–0.420	–0.697	–0.418
	(0.391)	(0.498)	(0.236)	(0.295)	(0.111)***	(0.123)***	(0.044)***	(0.076)	(0.083)***	(0.127)***	(0.135)***	(0.197)**
Native American	–0.395	–0.551	–0.704	–0.307	–0.689	–0.697	–0.561	–0.004	0.071	0.094	–0.679	–0.187
	(0.454)	(0.619)	(0.454)	(0.484)	(0.359)**	(0.396)**	(0.106)***	(0.183)	(0.231)	(0.315)	(0.343)**	(0.681)
Disability	–0.271	–0.428	–0.309	–0.224	–0.113	0.039	–0.226	–0.184	0.135	0.080	0.148	0.229
	(0.176)	(0.266)	(0.239)	(0.281)	(0.156)	(0.176)	(0.053)***	(0.081)**	(0.099)	(0.144)	(0.189)	(0.281)
Fixed pay (log)		0.915		1.165		0.465		1.038		0.308		–0.032
		(0.178)***		(0.179)***		(0.092)***		(0.055)***		(0.087)***		(0.156)
Wealth (log)		0.198		0.113		0.184		0.181		0.097		0.195
		(0.045)***		(0.047)***		(0.027)***		(0.015)***		(0.023)***		(0.046)***
Firm effects	Yes	Yes	Yes	Yes	Yes	Yes	Yes	Yes	Yes	Yes	Yes	Yes
Occupation, education, and tenure controls		Yes		Yes		Yes		Yes		Yes		Yes
Constant	0.905	–12.339	1.305	–11.425	–0.379	–8.005	0.761	–11.885	2.230	–2.805	1.956	–0.356
	(0.193)***	(1.997)***	(0.131)***	(1.945)***	(0.170)**	(1.006)***	(0.018)***	(0.578)***	(0.032)***	(0.924)***	(0.068)***	(1.640)
Observations	3,678	2,743	8,637	8,002	8,633	8,002	33,919	22,687	25,239	18,170	7,584	5,854

Note: Standard errors in parentheses.

***Significant at the 1 percent level.

**Significant at the 5 percent level.

those employees who work part time, and these groups may be more likely to work part time.

The results for BBSOPs and ESPPs reveal few group disparities in participation rates. In fact, Asian Americans are more likely to participate in ESPPs, and women are more likely to receive stock options, even with controls for occupation, education, and tenure. In terms of the groups that do face barriers, although African Americans are less likely to receive stock options and participate in ESPPs, these effects disappear when controls are included. Men with disabilities, however, are less likely to receive stock options. For 401(k) plans, all groups except women are less likely to participate, but the effects for African Americans and employees with disabilities are the only ones that remain with controls for occupation and education. The results show that access is most restricted for profit-sharing plans, as African Americans, Hispanics, and Asian Americans are less likely to participate, even with controls. Although these same groups, plus Native Americans, are less likely to participate in gain-sharing plans, only the effects for Asian Americans remain with controls.

We can view the results according to which groups have the worst outcomes and how access to specific plans varies. Overall, African Americans and Asian Americans have the worst outcomes. In terms of specific plans, the most notable difference is that while there are disparities in participation rates for all plans, for ESOPs, stock options, and ESPPs, most of these appear to be due to existing patterns of occupational segregation. For participation in 401(k), profit-sharing, and gain-sharing plans, while there are similar disparities resulting from occupational segregation, the results also show that the ways in which companies structure and operate these plans generate additional disparities. One possible explanation lies in the ways in which decisions regarding participation are made. In profit-sharing and gain-sharing plans, for example, management decides who will participate. The disparities for virtually all nonwhites in the former may reflect subtle mechanisms of discrimination, social closure, or work devaluation in the decision-making process. However, the decisions regarding stock option plan participation are also with management, and only one group, men with disabilities, face restricted access, so this issue requires further research. In addition, African Americans and employees with disabilities are less likely to participate in 401(k) plans, but women are more likely to participate. With this form of shared capitalism, employees choose whether to participate. The lower levels of participation for these two groups may be related to their lower levels of pay and wealth; that is, employees in these two groups may be less willing and able to financially invest for the future given their lower current pay levels. However, other groups that face similar constraints, such as women and other minority groups, do not have similarly restricted access. The lower levels of participation in 401(k) plans for these groups may also reflect different knowledge levels about these plans or different attitudes toward retirement saving. Future research is necessary to determine the types of specific mechanisms that shape stratification patterns in access. Whether participation is determined by management or employees may be one important factor, but may not be the only one.

In considering the results for participation in shared capitalist plans, stratification in participation rates appears to be shaped primarily by existing mechanisms of stratification, which place women and minorities into occupational and income groups for which access to shared capitalism is restricted. For example, employees in production jobs are less likely to participate in ESPPs and African Americans are more likely to be in production jobs. The exceptions to this are 401(k) plans, profit sharing, and gain sharing, in which some minorities face additional barriers beyond occupational status, education, and income level. Moreover, the results indicate that those employees that have higher incomes are more likely to participate in shared capitalism. To take a closer look at the wealth employees receive through these plans, I now turn to an analysis of the financial value that different groups receive through shared capitalism plans.

10.6 Financial Value of Shared Capitalism

Of those employees who participate in shared capitalist programs, do different groups receive different levels of returns? To answer this question, I examined the effect of being in different demographic groups on the value of shared capitalism. Table 10.3 shows the results of ordinary least squares (OLS) models that predict the natural logarithm of plan assets. I only included those employees who participated in these plans. To the extent that certain groups are less likely to participate in certain plans, therefore, the effects for all employees within these groups who work in these companies is likely understated. For example, African Americans are less likely to participate in profit-sharing plans. If those who participate in these plans have significantly negative values for profit sharing, the overall difference in value of profit sharing for African Americans—combining lower participation and lower values for those who do participate—would be large. Similar to the results for plan participation, the table reports results from two sets of models. The first includes just the demographic variables and firm-level dummies. The second include controls for occupation, education, fixed pay, and wealth and individual firms.

The models in table 10.3 regress the independent variables on the natural logarithm of the financial value held or received from the various forms of shared capitalism. I used log transformations to control for the effects of outliers. The specific dependent variables for which I used the logged transformation include:

- *ESOP:* approximate total value of company stock that employees hold in their ESOPs.

Table 10.3 **Predicting financial value of shared capitalism**

	ESOP		BBSOP		ESPP		401(k)		Profit sharing		Gain sharing	
Female	–0.368	–0.203	–0.298	–0.135	–0.206	–0.079	–0.990	–0.261	–0.537	–0.124	–0.586	–0.162
	(0.074)***	(0.066)***	(0.036)***	(0.031)***	(0.030)***	(0.029)***	(0.048)***	(0.045)***	(0.020)***	(0.016)***	(0.042)***	(0.030)***
African American	–0.544	–0.040	–0.466	–0.076	–0.361	–0.019	–1.568	–0.675	–0.549	–0.099	–0.789	–0.254
	(0.161)***	(0.144)	(0.111)***	(0.091)	(0.104)***	(0.094)	(0.114)***	(0.100)***	(0.053)***	(0.042)**	(0.117)***	(0.085)***
Hispanic	–0.526	–0.027	–0.318	–0.083	–0.208	–0.055	–0.893	–0.258	–0.672	0.026	–0.799	–0.090
	(0.243)**	(0.202)	(0.083)***	(0.068)	(0.070)***	(0.062)	(0.115)***	(0.099)***	(0.041)***	(0.037)	(0.081)***	(0.065)
Asian	–0.428	–0.178	–0.356	–0.049	–0.076	0.171	–0.607	–0.316	–0.291	0.032	–0.502	–0.047
	(0.296)	(0.258)	(0.043)***	(0.037)	(0.035)**	(0.033)***	(0.122)***	(0.107)***	(0.035)***	(0.027)	(0.055)***	(0.039)
Native American	–0.537	–0.192	–0.380	–0.336	0.040	0.188	–0.502	0.040	–0.526	–0.066	–0.285	–0.066
	(0.407)	(0.309)	(0.226)	(0.182)	(0.227)	(0.208)	(0.202)**	(0.167)	(0.097)***	(0.073)	(0.228)	(0.177)
Disability	0.211	0.170	–0.031	0.062	–0.143	–0.066	–0.287	–0.083	–0.298	–0.020	–0.457	–0.079
	(0.147)	(0.121)	(0.085)	(0.070)	(0.075)	(0.068)	(0.096)***	(0.081)	(0.042)***	(0.032)	(0.083)***	(0.059)
Fixed pay (log)		0.835		0.804		0.364		1.027		1.249		1.046
		(0.088)***		(0.036)***		(0.034)***		(0.057)***		(0.021)***		(0.034)***
Wealth (log)		0.204		0.365		0.269		0.316		0.100		0.132
		(0.024)***		(0.011)***		(0.010)***		(0.017)***		(0.006)***		(0.011)***
Firm effects		Yes		Yes		Yes		Yes		Yes		Yes
Occupation, education, and tenure controls		Yes		Yes		Yes		Yes		Yes		Yes
Constant	10.225	–2.402	10.845	–3.896	8.234	1.049	9.162	–6.682	7.521	–6.488	7.845	–4.328
	(0.205)***	(1.001)**	(0.055)***	(0.378)***	(0.078)***	(0.354)***	(0.028)***	(0.614)***	(0.014)***	(0.220)***	(0.034)***	(0.350)***
Observations	2,100	1,806	8,170	7,617	6,816	6,430	10,816	9,062	20,847	16,088	6,455	5,335
R^2	0.29	0.59	0.35	0.59	0.35	0.50	0.12	0.45	0.48	0.75	0.49	0.74

Notes: Results are based on ordinary least squares (OLS) regressions. The dependent variables are measured as logarithms. Standard errors in parentheses.

***Significant at the 1 percent level.

**Significant at the 5 percent level.

- *BBSOP:* total stock option value, or, the sum of the money an employee would receive if they exercised all vested and unvested stock options at the time of the survey (net of purchase price) plus the value of the stock currently held by employees from exercising any stock options, plus the amount of money an employee has made from exercising any stock options, from the company in the past and selling the shares.
- *ESPPs:* total value of company stock an employee owns from purchases of stock made through an ESPP.
- *401(k):* total value of company stock an employee holds through a 401(k) plan.
- *Profit sharing:* value of payments an employee received in the previous year from a profit-sharing plan.
- *Gain sharing:* value of payments an employee received in the previous year based on work group or department performance.

The value of stock acquired in most shared capitalist plans is linked directly to salary, so we should find that stratification in these values reflects existing patterns of income stratification shown in table 10.1.

Since the results in table 10.3 are for ordinary least squares regressions, the coefficients are interpreted differently than the logit coefficients for plan participation reported in table 10.2. Table 10.4 shows the results of table 10.3 with the statistically significant coefficients transformed to percentage differentials, providing an easier way to assess the magnitudes of the disparities in the financial value of shared capitalism for different groups.

In comparison to the findings regarding access to shared capitalism, the results for financial value reveal more negative outcomes for women, nonwhites, and employees with disabilities. For ESOPs, women, African Americans, and Hispanics receive less value than their comparison groups (men and whites). For BBSOPs and ESPPs, these groups plus Asian Americans receive less value. For these three plans, once controls are added for occupation, education, tenure, fixed pay, and wealth, many of the significant effects drop out. This suggests that the lower plan values for these plans are mostly due to existing patterns of occupational segregation and educational attainment, as well as lower levels of fixed pay. A notable exception is women, who have significantly lower plan values than men, even when controlling for these variables. For 401(k) plans, profit sharing, and gain sharing, all groups have lower plan values in the models without controls for occupation, education, and income, and more of these effects remain with controls, relative to the three plans discussed first. For example, these effects remain for 401(k) plans for all groups except Native Americans and employees with disabilities. These effects also remain for women and African Americans for both profit-sharing and gain-sharing plans. Overall, women have the worst outcomes, followed by African Americans. Women receive lower financial values through all type of plans, even after controlling for occupation, education, and income.

Table 10.4 **Magnitudes of significant differences in shared capitalism**

	Basic differences (no controls)						Adjusted differences (w/controls)					
	ESOP	BBSOP	ESPP	401(k)	Profit sharing	Gain sharing	ESOP	BBSOP	ESPP	401(k)	Profit sharing	Gain sharing
Likelihood of participation												
Female	–15%			+25%						+49%		
African American	–51%	–57%	–43%	–35%						–29%		
Hispanic	–54%			–76%								
Asian	+25%		+36%	–64%					+60%			
Native American				–43%								
Disability				–20%						–17%		
Financial values if one participates												
Female	–31%	–26%	–19%	–63%	–42%	–44%	–18%	–13%	–8%	–23%	–12%	–15%
African American	–42%	–37%	–30%	–80%	–42%	–55%				–49%	–9%	–22%
Hispanic	–41%	–27%	–19%	–59%	–49%	–55%				–23%		
Asian		–30%	–7%	–46%	–25%	–39%			+19%	–27%		
Native American					–41%							
Disability					–26%	–37%						

Note: Based on coefficient estimates in tables 10.2 and 10.3.

What accounts for these findings? For some plans, the disparities in the financial value of shared capitalism for certain demographic groups are primarily due to the existing mechanisms of stratification, such as occupational segregation that leads to certain groups earning less income. For other plans, the way in which companies structure and operate them creates additional disparities. What specifically in the plan design and operation of 401(k), profit-sharing, and gain-sharing plans leads to these disparities? For plans in which management decides how much employees receive, these disparities could be the results of subtle forms of work devaluation and discrimination. For 401(k) plans, the disparities could stem from certain groups of employees having lower levels of discretionary income for investing in these plans. On the whole, the results suggest that shared capitalism plans may not be altering existing patterns of income and wealth stratification and could be exacerbating these gaps, since those employees with higher salaries are more likely to participate and receive more financial value through shared capitalism. This is not surprising given that the way in which these plans allocate value is based on some formula of pay. Testing the long-term impact of shared capitalism on existing patterns of income and wealth stratification more completely, however, will require comparing outcomes within a group of similar employees in similar organizations without shared capitalism, which is beyond the more modest scope of this chapter.

10.7 Access to Power and Authority

In addition to access to income and wealth, access to power and authority in the workplace are important dimensions of social stratification. Power and authority at the job, work group, department, and company level can be a source of status, prestige, and well-being, as well as a source of occupational and income attainment (Smith 2002). Brass (2002) defines power in the workplace as the opposite of dependency, deriving from control of critical resources on which others are dependent, along with the ability to recognize this position and act upon it. Power can be formal—residing in the hierarchy of positions—and informal, emanating from the myriad ways in which employees can control access to resources through structural positions in social networks and personality traits. In addition, over the last three decades, a number of companies have implemented various practices that broaden decision-making authority by providing employees with structured ways to have input into company, department, work group, and job level decisions (Osterman 2001).

In reviewing the research on racial and gender differences in the attainment of workplace authority, Smith (2002, 534) found that "men are more likely than women to have authority, and employer behaviors and organizational policies are more important than women's attitudes and behaviors in explaining the gender gap in authority." For race and ethnicity, Smith (2002, 528–29) concludes that:

> "The literature documents important racial differences in the authority attainment of the two groups most studied—blacks and whites. Major conclusions point to systematic discriminatory practices in the processes that lead to authority and in the amount of financial returns that blacks receive for occupying positions of authority similar to those of whites."

Hence, the research on the stratification of power within the workplace has found similar outcomes and explanations for the outcomes of women and African Americans as the literature on income inequality. Do women, different racial and ethnic groups, and employees with disabilities face barriers to accessing power and authority in companies with shared capitalism, or do these groups fare better within these companies? These questions become more salient in light of numerous studies (NCEO 2006) that have found that shared capitalism has the most significant effect on corporate performance when it is combined with significant levels of employee involvement through practices such as work teams, offline employee committees that make decisions on such issues as quality and safety, and formal training programs. This suggests that shared capitalism companies may have a high incidence of power-sharing practices relating to employee involvement.

The NBER survey collected data on a number of measures of power and authority in the workplace, and hence provides a way to begin examining some of these issues. In this chapter, I focus on two sets of measures. The first set includes what might be called traditional measures of power: access to management and supervisory positions, intensity of supervision, promotions, and job security. The second set of measures incorporates the effects of practices associated with employee involvement: perceptions of influence on job, department, and company level decisions; access to self-directed work teams and offline employee committees; different forms of training; and job rotation. In the last two decades, there has been a gradual increase in the number of companies using these practices (Osterman 2001), and they represent alternative ways in which employees can exercise power and influence over decisions, co-workers, and the control of resources. Taken together, the results from both sets of measures of power and authority reveal some similar patterns of stratification as those relating to access to and the value of shared capitalism programs, but there are also some important differences.

10.8 Power and Authority: Management, Supervision, Promotions, and Job Security

Table 10.5 shows results for models that predict the effect of demographic characteristics on the likelihood of employees being managers. These models

Table 10.5 **Predicting access to management, freedom from supervision, number of promotions, and job security**

	Upper management	Middle management	Supervisor	Freedom from close supervision		Promotions		Job security	
Female	–0.388	–0.385	–0.402	0.021	0.034	–0.147	–0.084	0.006	0.016
	(0.111)***	(0.057)***	(0.033)***	(0.021)	(0.024)	(0.022)***	(0.026)***	(0.024)	(0.043)
African American	0.383	–0.211	–0.096	–0.597	–0.501	–0.417	–0.246	–0.670	–0.510
	(0.233)	(0.151)	(0.077)	(0.049)***	(0.053)***	(0.050)***	(0.056)***	(0.054)***	(0.087)***
Hispanic	0.318	–0.127	0.036	–1.036	–0.532	–0.286	0.187	–0.271	0.118
	(0.210)	(0.129)	(0.074)	(0.039)***	(0.055)***	(0.039)***	(0.056)***	(0.043)***	(0.085)
Asian	–1.048	–0.549	–0.466	–0.681	–0.590	–0.613	–0.081	–0.291	–0.198
	(0.242)***	(0.090)***	(0.060)***	(0.036)***	(0.046)***	(0.037)***	(0.046)**	(0.040)***	(0.068)***
Native American	0.134	0.047	–0.205	–0.159	0.166	–0.112	0.246	–0.234	–0.258
	(0.474)	(0.270)	(0.157)	(0.095)**	(0.107)	(0.093)	(0.111)**	(0.106)**	(0.228)
Disability	–0.313	–0.077	–0.328	–0.183	–0.152	–0.110	–0.159	–0.452	–0.206
	(0.236)	(0.119)	(0.071)***	(0.043)***	(0.048)***	(0.044)***	(0.051)***	(0.050)***	(0.104)**
Firm effects	Yes	Yes	Yes	Yes	Yes	Yes	Yes	Yes	Yes
Occupation controls	No	No	No	No	Yes	No	Yes	No	Yes
Education and tenure controls	Yes	Yes	Yes	No	Yes	No	Yes	No	Yes
Constant	–2.746	–1.879	–0.327	n.a.	n.a.	n.a.	n.a.	n.a.	n.a.
	(0.111)***	(0.070)***	(0.047)***	n.a.	n.a.	n.a.	n.a.	n.a.	n.a.
Observations	28,470	27,729	28,603	34,180	28,204	34,030	28,198	32,383	11,319

Notes: Models for upper management, middle management, and supervisor are logit models. Models for intensity of supervision, promotions, and job security are ordered logit models. Standard errors in parentheses.

***Significant at the 1 percent level.

**Significant at the 5 percent level.

include controls for education, tenure, and firm effects. Table 10.5 also shows results for models predicting employee perceptions of supervision, promotions, and job security. For each of the last three outcomes, table 10.5 shows the results from two models. The first includes controls for firm level effects, while the second adds controls for occupation, education, and tenure.

I used logit models to predict the likelihood of employees being in different managerial positions because the dependent variable was binary ("yes" or "no" response). I used ordered logit models to predict the likelihood of different responses on the questions regarding supervision, promotion, and job security because these dependent variables had more than two possible outcomes. Interpreting these coefficients requires a similar process as interpreting the logit coefficients in table 10.2. For example, the coefficient for African Americans and closeness of supervision is .501. Exponentiating this yields an odds ratio of 0.55, indicating that African Americans are 45 percent less likely, on average, to report higher scores on this question; that is, they are less likely to report freedom from close supervision.

The results from table 10.5 reveal that women and Asian Americans are less likely to be in management roles, and that nonwhite employees and employees with disabilities are more likely to report close supervision, fewer promotions, and less job security. For the last three findings, most of the results remain with controls for occupation, education, and tenure. Women, Asian Americans, and employees with disabilities have the worst outcomes. Women, for example, are less likely to be represented in all levels of management and are less likely to be promoted. Asian Americans are less likely to be in all levels of management, are more likely to be closely supervised, less likely to be promoted, and report lower job security. Employees with disabilities are less likely to be supervisors and have negative outcomes on all other measures. All groups except Hispanics are less likely to be promoted, and although all groups except women report less job security, this effect drops for Hispanics and Native Americans once controls for occupation, education, and tenure are included.

Overall, the results on this first set of measures of power and authority suggest that women, nonwhites, and employees with disabilities face significant barriers to accessing workplace power. These findings are not surprising because they reflect broader patterns in the stratification of workplace power and authority (Smith 2002). The results show that the mechanisms that lead to these outcomes also operate within shared capitalism companies. The findings raise some interesting questions. Why do women and Asian Americans face similar barriers to entering management, while other groups appear not to? Why do nonwhite employees and employees with disabilities have similarly negative outcomes regarding close supervision and job security? Why do women and most nonwhite employees receive fewer promotions? How do these groups fare with respect to other forms of power and authority? This chapter now turns to examining this last question.

10.9 Power and Authority: Employee Involvement in Decision Making and Training

The NBER survey also included a number of questions relating to other dimensions of power, including perceptions about the level of influence over different types of decisions, access to different types of teams and employee committees, access to different types of training, and participation in job rotation. These outcomes reflect different dimensions of power than those discussed in the previous section. Do women and minorities face similar barriers to power and authority through these practices and are employee involvement practices opening up new avenues of power for these groups? Table 10.6 reports results from models predicting the effect of gender, race, ethnicity, and disability on the likelihood of employees participating in these practices.

The first three models examine the likelihood that employees in different demographic groups reported having influence on, respectively, decisions at the company level, setting goals for their department or work group, and decisions about how to do their jobs. For each of these questions, respondents were asked how much involvement they had over decisions at these three different levels using a scale of 1 to 4, coded here as 1 = "none" and 4 = "a lot." I used ordered logit models to predict the effects of different demographic characteristics on different responses. The next three models examine the likelihood that employees in these different groups will be involved in, respectively, employee committees, self-directed teams, and efforts to develop innovative products or services. These dependent variables for these models were binary, and I therefore used logit models. Positive coefficients mean more involvement. The last three models examine the likelihood that employees in different demographic groups will receive formal training (yes or no), receive informal job training from peers (scale of 1 to 4, with 1 being "not at all" and 4 being "to a great extent"), and participate in job rotation efforts (scale of 1 to 3, with 1 being "never" and 3 being "frequently"). Hence, for the last three outcomes, positive coefficients mean that employees are more likely to be involved in these practices.

For each of the employee involvement outcomes, table 10.6 reports results from two models, the first with only firm level controls, and the second with controls for occupation, education, tenure, and individual firms. In the models without controls, women, African Americans, and employees with disabilities have the lowest levels of involvement. Women for example, are less likely to be involved in all practices, except for informal training and job rotation. African Americans are less likely to be involved in all practices except for company level decisions and job rotation. Employees with disabilities are less likely to be involved in all practices, except for job rotation. Some of the negative outcomes for these three groups disappear with controls for occupation, education, and tenure. Interestingly, with controls,

Table 10.6 **Predicting access to employee involvement practices**

	A							
	Involved in company level decisions		Involved in setting goals for department or work group		Involved in deciding how to organize work or do job		Involved in offline employee committees	
Female	–0.357	–0.207	–0.137	0.077	–0.046	0.054	–0.266	–0.115
	(0.023)***	(0.027)***	(0.022)***	(0.026)***	(0.023)**	(0.028)**	(0.026)***	(0.031)***
African American	–0.019	0.185	–0.243	0.012	–0.446	–0.169	–0.167	–0.017
	(0.053)	(0.059)***	(0.049)***	(0.055)	(0.050)***	(0.056)***	(0.059)***	(0.066)
Hispanic	0.199	0.484	0.167	0.307	–0.222	–0.032	–0.081	0.009
	(0.042)***	(0.059)***	(0.039)***	(0.057)***	(0.040)***	(0.060)	(0.046)**	(0.067)
Asian	0.286	0.237	–0.027	–0.114	–0.262	–0.467	–0.100	–0.130
	(0.039)***	(0.050)***	(0.037)	(0.048)***	(0.040)***	(0.052)***	(0.043)**	(0.056)**
Native American	0.056	0.092	–0.038	0.041	–0.253	0.039	–0.082	–0.043
	(0.100)	(0.120)	(0.094)	(0.111)	(0.095)***	(0.114)	(0.111)	(0.134)
Disability	–0.161	–0.067	–0.403	–0.220	–0.556	–0.330	–0.134	–0.050
	(0.047)***	(0.055)	(0.043)***	(0.050)***	(0.045)***	(0.052)***	(0.052)***	(0.060)
Firm effects	Yes	Yes	Yes	Yes	Yes	Yes	Yes	Yes
Occupation, education, and tenure controls	No	Yes	No	Yes	No	Yes	No	Yes
Observations	34,034	28,103	34,062	28,119	34,154	28,161	33,822	27,943

(*continued*)

Table 10.6 (continued)

	B									
	Involved in self-directed work team		Involved in innovation efforts		Formal training		Informal training		Job rotation	
Female	–0.115	–0.065	–0.857	–0.629	–0.249	–0.123	0.120	0.127	0.481	0.395
	(0.030)***	(0.037)**	(0.041)***	(0.051)***	(0.025)***	(0.030)***	(0.023)***	(0.026)***	(0.027)***	(0.033)***
African American	–0.118	–0.128	–0.194	0.146	–0.104	0.173	–0.301	–0.302	0.572	0.264
	(0.064)**	(0.071)**	(0.082)***	(0.097)	(0.055)**	(0.062)***	(0.051)***	(0.055)***	(0.055)***	(0.062)***
Hispanic	0.134	0.289	–0.219	0.144	0.150	0.120	–0.088	–0.240	0.060	0.287
	(0.048)***	(0.077)***	(0.060)***	(0.098)	(0.044)***	(0.066)**	(0.040)**	(0.057)***	(0.045)	(0.070)***
Asian	0.296	0.756	0.110	0.271	0.203	–0.041	–0.359	–0.408	0.182	0.664
	(0.057)***	(0.095)***	(0.064)**	(0.109)***	(0.046)***	(0.059)	(0.038)***	(0.048)***	(0.052)***	(0.081)***
Native American	–0.027	0.008	–0.303	0.072	–0.192	–0.039	–0.225	–0.195	0.262	0.089
	(0.114)	(0.139)	(0.147)**	(0.185)	(0.105)**	(0.126)	(0.095)***	(0.111)**	(0.104)***	(0.127)
Disability	–0.152	–0.177	–0.323	–0.134	–0.307	–0.121	–0.343	–0.243	0.151	–0.050
	(0.057)***	(0.068)***	(0.073)***	(0.092)	(0.049)***	(0.058)**	(0.045)***	(0.051)***	(0.051)***	(0.061)
Firm effects	Yes	Yes	Yes	Yes	Yes	Yes	Yes	Yes	Yes	Yes
Occupation, education, and tenure controls	No	Yes	No	Yes	No	Yes	No	Yes	No	Yes
Observations	21,161	15,773	20,945	15,492	34,008	28,049	34,116	28,130	24,228	18,543

Notes: Panel A: models for involvement in company decisions, setting goals for department, and how to organize work are ordered logit models. Models for offline committees are logit models. Standard errors in parentheses. Panel B: models for self-directed teams, innovation efforts, and formal training are logit models. Models for informal training and job rotation are ordered logit models.

***Significant at the 1 percent level.

**Significant at the 5 percent level.

women are more likely to participate in department and job level decisions. This suggests that women are more likely to be in jobs that are not involved in such efforts, but that once this is controlled for, women are actually more likely to be involved. Similarly, once controls are added, African Americans are more likely to participate in company level decisions and formal training efforts. Also, the negative effects for department level decisions, offline committees, and innovation efforts disappear (but do not become positive) for African Americans with controls. For employees with disabilities, the negative effects disappear for involvement in company level decisions, employee committees, and innovation efforts.

Hispanics appear to have the best access to employee involvement practices. In the models with controls, they are more likely to participate in company and department level decisions, self-directed work teams, formal training, and job rotation. They are only less likely to participate in informal training efforts. Asian Americans, however, have mixed outcomes. For models with controls, they are more likely to participate in company level decisions, self-directed work teams, innovation efforts, and job rotation. They are, however, less likely to participate in departmental and job level decisions, employee committees, and informal training. For both Hispanics and Asian Americans, there are similar patterns for the models with and without controls for occupation, education, and tenure.

In terms of specific practices (with controls), there are some interesting patterns. Nonwhite employees are more likely to participate in company level decisions, but all nonwhite groups are also less likely to participate in job level decisions. For self-directed work teams, the results are mixed, as women, African Americans, and employees with disabilities are less likely to be involved, while Hispanics and Asians are more likely. Asian Americans are the only group more likely to participate in innovation efforts, and all groups except women are less likely to participate in informal training. Finally, all groups are more likely to participate in job rotation.

Overall, the results for the second set of power outcomes reveal that workplace practices relating to employee involvement appear to open up at least some avenues of power for women, nonwhites, and employees with disabilities. There are fewer disparities, in comparison to the first set of power measures, and all groups, except employees with disabilities, are actually more likely to participate in at least some practices. These findings raise a number of questions for future research. Why are certain groups less likely to participate in job level decisions and self-directed teams? Why are certain groups more likely to participate in company level decisions? Why do Hispanics have the best outcomes? Why do women and African Americans do the worst? Why are most groups less likely to receive informal training opportunities? Why are all groups more likely to participate in job rotation programs? One possible explanation for some of the findings discussed here is that formalized practices, such as self-directed teams, may require equal access. In contrast, less formal practices, such as informal on-the-job training, may create opportunities for certain types of employees to be excluded. Only future research will be able to test the validity of these types of explanations. Gaining a better understanding of the workplace level mechanisms through which certain groups are excluded from different involvement practices is essential to understanding how access to power and authority within these companies is stratified. The results presented here provide a strong case that such mechanisms are in operation, but also that access to employee involvement practices appears to be open for more diverse types of employees.

10.10 Putting the Pieces Together

What do the overall patterns of stratification look like in shared capitalist companies? Table 10.7 summarizes the outcomes for different demographic groups. The percentages in each cell represent the percentages of statistically significant negative coefficients for all outcomes within each of the four sets of variables discussed before: access to shared capitalism, value of assets in shared capitalism, and the two sets of power measures. Negative coefficients represent disparities in outcomes between specific demographic groups and their comparison groups (men for women, whites for each nonwhite group, and employees without disabilities for employees with disabilities). The qualitative assessment is based on the following broad categories: few disparities (0 to 33 percent negative outcomes), some disparities (34 percent to 66 percent), and many disparities (67 percent to 100 percent). The table shows the overall patterns for all outcomes both with and without controls for occupation, education, and tenure.

This table provides a concise way to assess overall outcomes for women, racial and ethnic minorities, and employees with disabilities. For participation in shared capitalism plans, although all groups experience at least some disparities in participation rates, many of these attenuate in the models that include controls for education, occupation, fixed pay, and tenure. African Americans have the highest percentage of disparities both with and without controls. In terms of the financial value held in shared capitalism plans, most groups experience many disparities in outcomes, but these effects attenuate with controls, with the exception of women and African Americans. Hence, many of the disparities that employees in these groups experience, with respect to participating in shared capitalism and the financial value of shared capitalism, are the result of existing processes of occupational segregation and income inequality. African Americans and women, however, still have relatively high percentages of disparities, even with controls.

For the first set of power and authority outcomes (access to management, level of supervision, promotions, and job security), most groups experience a high percentage of disparities in the models without controls. The

Table 10.7 **Summary of disparities in shared capitalism and access to power**

	Disparities in participation in shared capitalism		Disparities in financial value of shared capitalism		Disparities in access to power: Management positions, supervision, promotions, job security		Disparities in access to power: Participation in employee involvement practices		Summary: Percentage of all outcomes with disparities	
	Without controls	With controls	Without controls	With controls	Without controls	With controls	Without controls	With controls	Without controls	With controls
Women	Some (40%)	None	Many (100%)	Many (100%)	Few (33%)	Many (67%)	Many (78%)	Some (56%)	Many (67%)	Some (56%)
African Americans	Many (100%)	Some (40%)	Many (100%)	Some (57%)	Many (100%)	Some (50%)	Many (78%)	Few (33%)	Many (92%)	Some (41%)
Hispanics	Some (60%)	Few (20%)	Many (100%)	Few (14%)	Many (100%)	Few (17%)	Some (44%)	Few (11%)	Many (71%)	Few (15%)
Asian Americans	Some (40%)	Few (20%)	Many (86%)	Few (14%)	Many (100%)	Many (100%)	Few (33%)	Some (44%)	Some (58%)	Some (48%)
Native Americans	Some (40%)	Few (20%)	Few (29%)	None	None	None	Some (44%)	Few (11%)	Some (42%)	Few (4%)
Employees with disability	Few (20%)	Few (20%)	Some (57%)	None	Many (100%)	Many (67%)	Many (89%)	Some (56%)	Some (63%)	Few (33%)

Note: Coding scheme: Few (0–33%), some (33%–66%), many (66%–100%).

presence of controls mitigates these disparities somewhat for African Americans and greatly for Hispanics, but they remain relatively high for women, Asian Americans, and employees with disabilities. Out of all the four sets of measures, this set of power and authority measures has the highest overall percentages of disparate outcomes. For access to power and authority via employee involvement practices, the percentages of disparities are lower, suggesting that these practices are opening up avenues of power for many demographic groups. There are, however, many disparities for women, African Americans, and employees with disabilities in the first sets of models. Some of the percentages drop when controls are added, suggesting that these disparities are the result of these groups being segregated into occupations that have lower levels of participation in these plans. Moreover, as previously noted, most groups have at least some positive outcomes on this second set of power measures. Women, Asian Americans, and employees with disabilities all have some disparities when controls are added.

The last column provides a summary measure for each group by listing the percentage of disparities for all twenty-seven measures. For models without controls, African Americans have the highest percentage of negative outcomes overall, followed by Hispanics, women, and employees with disabilities. For the models with controls, women have the highest percentage of disparities, followed by Asian Americans and African Americans. Although Asian Americans have few disparities for shared capitalist outcomes, they have a higher percentage of disparities with respect to workplace power, particularly with respect to the first set of measures. The pattern for employees with disabilities is similar. Hispanics have a low percentage of negative outcomes across all outcomes. Hence, women and African Americans experience the most disparities in outcomes relating to shared capitalism and access to power, followed by Asian Americans and employees with disabilities.

Overall, the number of disparities is lowest with respect to accessing shared capitalism and accessing power through employee involvement practices. However, the data reveal clear disparities in how shared capitalism plans allocate stock, profits, and other financial returns between different groups. The data also suggest that women, nonwhites, and employees with disabilities face more barriers to accessing traditional measures of power than new forms of power through employee involvement practices. Finally, although the results provide strong evidence that these disparities are importantly shaped by occupational segregation, the specific ways in which shared capitalism and workplace power are structured also have important effects on the stratification of outcomes for different demographic groups, independent of existing patterns of occupational segregation.

The results of this analysis provide a strong case that, with respect to access to shared capitalism and the value of assets held in these plans, the outcomes are very similar to existing patterns of inequality. To the extent that the value of assets provided by shared capitalism is linked to existing compensation systems, which themselves are stratified by gender, race, ethnicity, and disability, this is not surprising. In addition, the ways in which companies structure certain types of plans leads to additional disparities. For 401(k) plans, for example, these disparities may stem from the fact that lower income groups, in which women and minorities are overrepresented, have relatively low levels of discretionary income to invest. The barriers that African Americans, Hispanics, and Asian Americans face to accessing profit sharing and gain sharing, however, is a pattern that needs to be researched in more detail, as it is the only form of nonvoluntary shared capitalism and management choosing who participates that seems to be shaped by mechanisms not operating at the occupational or income level. It is clear that the unequal access to these plans and the lower value of the assets held in these plans by women and African Americans serves as a reminder that these groups still face strong barriers to accessing economic opportunities relative to men and whites.

In terms of the stratification of organizational power in shared capitalist companies, the evidence is more mixed. Overall, the stratification of outcomes relating to organizational power reflects the generally restricted access to these forms of power that past research has found in samples of companies without shared capitalism (Smith 2002). Hence, companies with shared capitalism do not appear to be opening up access to these forms of power, and the mechanisms that create these inequalities are likely deeply entrenched. Women and all minority groups on the whole have restricted access to formal power through management positions and are more closely supervised. However, the evidence on access to influence over decision making, self-directed work teams, employee committees, training opportunities, and job rotation in these companies reveals that these practices appear to open up power for most groups.

Future research on stratification of organizational power, therefore, needs to closely examine the actual processes through which workplace innovations are implemented and become institutionalized, and how these interact with existing stratification mechanisms. A reasonable conjecture is that since employee involvement practices are usually implemented at a specific point in time, they are more visible, and hence the ability of management and other groups to exclude certain types of people may be more difficult. The social forces shaping access to power through management positions, individual autonomy, promotions, and job security are more complex and subtle, and hence may be more resilient to significant changes in the short term. Finally, an important question is whether participation rates in employee involvement practices within shared capitalism companies differs from rates in companies without shared capitalism. Our understanding of these anomalies and the overall trends will benefit greatly from future research that examines more deeply the direct ways in which existing mechanisms of stratification shape shared capitalist outcomes, and how employee involvement practices alter the distribution of power and authority in the workplace and other levels of organizational decision making.

10.11 Employee Attitudes and Social Stratification

One could argue that the patterns of stratification discussed previously are not surprising, since they reflect similar stratification patterns in the wider economy and society. This certainly appears to be the case, and the question of whether or not such stratification is good, bad, or meaningless is beyond both the scope and intention of this chapter. More practically, what do these stratification outcomes mean for the effectiveness of shared capitalist programs, the quality of work life, and corporate performance? This question is important because companies spend significant resources designing, implementing, and maintaining different forms of shared capitalist programs and employee involvement practices. Often, companies adopt such practices with the hope that these innovations will help motivate employees to work harder and smarter, stay with the company longer, and align more closely with a company's strategy, things that will help the company perform better in the long term. Although this analysis is not intended to examine the effects of stratification, shared capitalism, or employee involvement on corporate economic performance, the NBER survey collected data on the attitudes of employees toward their jobs, their companies, and shared capitalism, outcomes that can have important effects on employee and corporate performance. This provides a unique opportunity to examine how shared capitalism and employee involvement practices influence workplace attitudes for different groups.

Other chapters in this book show that shared capitalism appears to affect important attitudes of employees in general. For example, chapter 4 finds that shared capitalism is positively related to perceived employee-management relations and other measures of company treatment of employees, while chapter 7 finds a positive relationship to performance-related attitudes such as intention to stay with the company, loyalty, willingness to work hard, and perceived job effort. It is possible, however, that these positive results across employees in general mask important variation among demographic groups. It is, therefore, valuable to explore such variation also as a way of testing the role of diversity in shared capitalism and the importance of extending shared capitalism to all employee groups.

Table 10.8 shows the results from models examining the impact of shared capitalism and employee involvement on three important workplace attitudes for men, women, whites, African Americans, Hispanics, Asian Americans, Native Americans, and employees with disabilities. The Shared Capitalism Index simply adds up the number of shared capitalism programs in which employees participate. The Participation Index adds up employee

Table 10.8 **Results from ordered logit models examining the effect of gender, race, ethnicity, and disability on attitudes**

	Men	Women	White	African American	Hispanic	Asian American	Native American	Disability
				Stay at job				
Shared capitalism index	0.084	0.072	0.06	0.111	0.047	0.125	0.218	0.149
	(0.010)***	(0.016)***	(0.009)***	(0.038)***	–0.04	(0.031)***	(0.081)***	(0.034)***
Participation index	0.253	0.25	0.279	0.204	0.177	0.166	0.165	0.215
	(0.008)***	(0.013)***	(0.008)***	(0.028)***	(0.031)***	(0.024)***	(0.061)***	(0.027)***
Observations	17,734	7,894	21,140	1,122	1,024	1,669	259	1,355
				Willingness to work hard				
Shared capitalism index	0.058	0.038	0.057	0.062	0.014	0.087	0.009	0.107
	(0.009)***	(0.014)***	(0.008)***	(0.036)**	–0.037	(0.031)***	–0.074	(0.031)***
Participation index	0.259	0.214	0.246	0.225	0.228	0.192	0.204	0.261
	(0.008)***	(0.011)***	(0.007)***	(0.027)***	(0.029)***	(0.025)***	(0.056)***	(0.025)***
Observations	17,759	7,904	21,161	1,126	1,026	1,673	261	1,359
				Loyalty to company				
Shared capitalism index	0.095	0.099	0.074	0.096	0.123	0.134	0.246	0.213
	(0.010)***	(0.015)***	(0.009)***	(0.038)***	(0.041)***	(0.033)***	(0.079)***	(0.033)***
Participation index	0.372	0.307	0.367	0.267	0.363	0.33	0.302	0.304
	(0.008)***	(0.012)***	(0.008)***	(0.028)***	(0.033)***	(0.027)***	(0.060)***	(0.026)***
Observations	17,494	7,787	20,863	1,100	1,002	1,651	258	1,332

Note: Standard errors in parentheses.
***Significant at the 1 percent level.
**Significant at the 5 percent level.

responses on three measures of employee participation: the level of involvement in company level decisions, department or group level decisions, and job level decisions. The higher the value of this variable, the higher the level of overall involvement. The models also include controls (unreported) for occupation, education, tenure with the organization, and firm level effects. The models presented use ordered logit specifications, and positive coefficients represent more positive outcomes.

What is most striking about these results is their consistency. Both participation in shared capitalism and participation in decision making have a positive and statistically significant effect on all three attitudes for all groups. There are three exceptions to this pattern. Shared capitalism does not have a positive effect on the likelihood of Hispanics staying at their jobs or on their willingness to work harder, or on the willingness of Native Americans to work harder. In no cases, however, does either shared capitalism or participation in decision making have a negative impact on attitudes. Both shared capitalism and employee involvement have the strongest effects, in terms of the magnitude of the coefficients, on employees' loyalty to the company. The Employee Involvement Index also has stronger effects on all attitudes than the Shared Capitalism Index. Overall, the results provide strong evidence that both participation in shared capitalism and in various levels of decision making lead to improvements in attitudes for all groups, despite the fact that many of these groups do not do as well as others in terms of accessing shared capitalism and power.

10.12 Conclusion: Implications for Management

Although these results should be very interesting to social scientists, they also have important implications for management. First, since the value of assets acquired through shared capitalism is usually directly related to pay, it is not possible to assume that implementing shared capitalism creates instant equity and fairness. The reality is that the implementation and operation of these plans occurs within broader structures of stratification, and this reality may have negative consequences for the effectiveness of these plans if employees perceive their implementation and operation as unfair. Substantial disparities may be particularly important if certain demographic groups are concentrated in crucial occupational roles and experience disparities in access to and the benefits of shared capitalism. Ittner, Lambert, and Larcker (2003), for example, found that the performance effects of employee stock option grants were influenced by larger grants to certain key employees, such as technical employees, managers, and individual contributors who were nonexempt.

Furthermore, the results show that, beyond the traditional mechanisms of stratification, the ways in which certain types of shared capitalism (401(k) plans, profit sharing, and gain sharing) are designed and operated can create further disparities in access and financial value for different groups. Hence, to the extent that the structures of specific forms of shared capitalism are flexible in terms of who gets access and the value of the financial benefits that flow from these plans, management has the leverage to design plans to address the disparities uncovered in this analysis. The bottom line is that these disparities most likely produce outcomes that individuals in diverse categories would experience as unfortunate. However, the results from the analysis of employee attitudes provides very strong evidence that higher levels of participation in shared capitalism and involvement in decision making can lead to better employee attitudes for all groups.

This chapter has revealed that the access that different demographic groups have to shared capitalism and the wealth these groups receive through shared capitalism is sometimes unequal. Future research is necessary to understand the long-term effects of shared capitalism on broader patterns of inequality in the United States. However, the results reveal that when offered to diverse groups, shared capitalism and progressive human resource policies, such as employee involvement in decision making, are associated with better attitudes. This suggests that companies with diverse employee populations can benefit from paying attention to traditional inequalities, and how shared capitalism is shaped by and, in turn, influences these inequalities. This type of inequality, if left unaddressed, can siphon off the potential positive effects of shared capitalism for individual employees and for the firm.

Appendix

Table 10A.1 **Results from logit models examining the effect of gender, race, ethnicity, and disability on the likelihood of being in particular occupations**

	Management	Professional/ technical	Sales	Administrative support	Production	Customer service
Women	–0.717	–0.283	–0.673	2.165	–0.021	1.153
	(0.042)***	(0.030)***	(0.061)***	(0.059)***	(0.028)	(0.072)***
African American	–0.848	–0.705	–0.474	–0.293	1.080	–0.319
	(0.118)***	(0.079)***	(0.157)***	(0.112)***	(0.068)***	(0.178)**
Hispanic	–0.363	–0.410	–0.156	–0.155	0.507	0.337
	(0.074)***	(0.057)***	(0.104)	(0.101)	(0.049)***	(0.109)***
Asian	–0.508	0.624	–0.653	–0.780	–0.106	0.188
	(0.068)***	(0.046)***	(0.092)***	(0.138)***	(0.054)**	(0.137)
Native American	–0.719	–0.765	–0.112	–0.113	0.897	–0.002
	(0.209)***	(0.156)***	(0.253)	(0.246)	(0.122)***	(0.312)
Disability	–0.730	–0.465	–0.577	–0.006	0.810	–0.167
	(0.098)***	(0.065)***	(0.142)***	(0.103)	(0.058)***	(0.156)
Constant	–1.796	–1.243	–2.917	–4.029	0.102	–3.697
	(0.025)***	(0.020)***	(0.038)***	(0.056)***	(0.018)***	(0.056)***
Observations	33,913	33,913	32,720	33,913	33,571	21,275

Note: Standard errors in parentheses.

***Significant at the 1 percent level.

**Significant at the 5 percent level.

References

Brass, D. 2002. Intraorganizational power and dependence. In *The Blackwell companion to organizations,* ed. J. A. C. Baum, 138–57. Malden, MA: Blackwell Publishers, Ltd.

Economic Policy Institute. 2006. *The state of working America 2006/2007.* Washington, DC: Economic Policy Institute.

Grusky, D. 2001. The past, present, and future of social inequality. In *Social stratification: Class, race, and gender in sociological perspective, 2nd ed.,* ed. D. B. Grusky, 3–51. Boulder, CO: Westview Press.

Hirschman, C., and M. Snipp. 1999. The state of the American dream: Race and ethnic socioeconomic inequality in the United States, 1970–1990. In *Social stratification: Class, race, and gender in sociological perspective, 2nd ed.* ed. D. B. Grusky, 623–36. Boulder, CO: Westview Press.

Ittner, C., R. Lambert, and D. Larcker. 2003. The structure and performance consequences of equity grants to employees of new economy firms. *Journal of Accounting and Economics* 34 (1–3): 89–127.

Massey, D., and M. Dention. 1993. *American apartheid.* Cambridge, MA: Harvard University Press.

Morris, M., and B. Western. 1999. US earnings inequality at the close of the 20th century. *Annual Review of Sociology* 25:623–57.

National Center for Employee Ownership (NCEO). 2006. Employee ownership and corporate performance. Available at: http://www.nceo.org/library/corpperf.html.

Osterman, P. 2001. *Working in America: A blueprint for the new labor market.* Cambridge, MA and London: MIT Press.

Smith, R. 2002. Race, gender, and authority in the workplace: Theory and research. *Annual Review of Sociology* 28:509–42.

Wilson, W. J. 1980. *The declining significance of race.* Chicago: University of Chicago Press.

11

Show Me the Money
Does Shared Capitalism Share the Wealth?

Robert Buchele, Douglas L. Kruse, Loren Rodgers, and Adria Scharf

Cheerleaders for the "ownership society" tout the growing share of US households owning stock—up from 31.7 percent in 1989 to 51.9 percent in 2001.[1] What is less often advertised is that stock ownership remains highly concentrated. The bottom 90 percent of households owns only 23 percent of all stock and just 12 percent of all directly held stock (which confers direct control or voting rights on stockholders).[2] Only 27 percent of households in the bottom 90 percent of the wealth distribution own (directly or indirectly) more than $10,000 of stock (calculated from Wolff [2004, table 13a]). If own-

Robert Buchele is a professor of economics at Smith College. Douglas L. Kruse is a professor of human resource management and labor studies and employment relations at the Rutgers School of Management and Labor Relations, and a research associate of the National Bureau of Economic Research. Loren Rodgers is Project Director at the National Center for Employee Ownership. Adria Scharf is director of the Richmond Peace Education Center, and an associate of Ownership Associates, Inc.

Earlier drafts of this chapter were presented at the Russell Sage/NBER conference in New York City, October 6–7, 2006 and at the Labor and Employment Relations conference, Boston, Massachusetts, January 5–8, 2006. We have benefited from comments on these drafts by Mark Aldrich, Joseph Blasi, Eric Kaarsemaker, Jeff Keefe, and Chris Mackin. This research is supported by a grant from the Russell Sage Foundation and the Rockefeller Foundation. The National Opinion Research Center at the University of Chicago provided valuable assistance with the US General Social Survey that provides a national sample comparison group in our analysis.

1. This figure includes both directly held stock and indirect holdings in mutual funds and retirement accounts. See Wolff (2004, table 12b). An important reason why the incidence of stock ownership has risen in recent decades is the replacement of defined benefit with defined contribution pension plans. Nevertheless, 34 percent of households have no (defined benefit or defined contribution) pension plan (Wolff 2005, table 5), and "more than one-fifth of all households nearing retirement (those between the ages of 56 and 64) had no retirement savings other than Social Security" (Weller and Wolff 2005, 2).

2. These statistics are from Wolff (2004, table 13a) and Kennickell (2003, table 10), respectively. All statistics in this section are for 2001.

ership is measured by households' ownership stake in the corporate sector of the US economy, a large majority of American households have little or no meaningful claim to membership in the ownership society.

This concentration of stock ownership implies a corresponding concentration of income from capital, which contributes to growing income inequality since dividends and capital gains have been a growing share of market-based income in the past thirty years, and capital income disproportionately goes to high-income households (Mishel, Bernstein, and Allegretto 2007, 79, 81). Employee stock ownership may help reduce this growing inequality by contributing to broad-based wealth building and income growth across the economic spectrum.

This chapter addresses four sets of questions surrounding employee stock ownership as a wealth-sharing tool, going beyond previous studies in the scope of the inquiry and the use of new data sources. First, how much on average do employee owners own in "shared capitalist" firms (those with broad-based employee ownership, profit sharing, gain sharing, and/or stock options), and more generally? Second, how is company stock distributed among employee-owners, which ownership structures distribute wealth most equitably, and how does the distribution of employee stock ownership wealth compare to the distribution of wealth among US households? Third, to what extent does employer stock substitute for other forms of compensation (higher pay and benefits) and for other forms of wealth? And fourth, what effect might universal employee ownership of employer stock have on the overall distribution of stock ownership and pension wealth in the United States?

11.1 History and Review of Employee Ownership

Employee ownership has a long history in the United States. Various progressive employers and labor unions worked at setting up a variety of profit-sharing and employee ownership plans in the 1800s. These attempts became more common in the early 1900s and culminated in some well-known attempts in the 1920s before the market collapse in 1929. Immediately after the market collapse, employee stock ownership was less popular but it increased in popularity as the government and employers supported a number of retirement savings plans that offered a role for employer stock and a number of tax benefits that made it possible for employees to buy stock on their own (Blasi, Kruse, and Bernstein 2003)

Employee stock ownership plans (ESOPs) were first promoted as a matter of public policy by a provision in the Employee Retirement and Security Act of 1974 (ERISA), authored by Senator Russell Long, allowing for tax deductible contributions of company stock to a workers' trust. Unlike forms of employee stock ownership in the 1920s, which were based on the investment of worker savings by working-class and middle-class workers, the ESOP offered employers tax incentives to distribute shares to workers without workers buying the stock with their savings. The idea was to limit worker risk. Long was influenced by Louis Kelso, a San Francisco investment banker and lawyer who set up the first ESOP at a California newspaper in 1956 and published *The Capitalist Manifesto* (with Mortimer Adler) in 1958. Kelso advocated employee ownership as a means of counteracting (in his view) a declining share of labor income inevitably resulting from labor-saving technical change (Kelso and Adler 1958, chapter 4). Long advocated employee ownership on other grounds as well—including promoting labor peace, securing workers' allegiance to the capitalist system, and improving workers' motivation and productivity. But Long and Kelso's chief interest in ESOPs was as a vehicle for building workers' wealth and increasing their share of capital and income from capital.[3] And a chief interest of this chapter is to determine the extent to which companies with shared capitalism plans do this.

The stock of companies with ESOPs can be publicly traded or privately held and can be minority-owned or 100 percent owned by the employees. But in any case, according to the participation guidelines of ERISA, the ownership must be *broad-based.* With few exceptions, ESOPs are required by law to cover all employees age twenty-one and over who work more than 1,000 hours per year and have at least a year of service with the company.

Several recent studies have estimated the size of employees' ownership stakes in employee stock ownership plans. A census of Washington state ESOPs (Kardas, Scharf, and Keogh 1998) found median pension assets per participant of $31,600 (versus $5,400 for a matching sample of non-ESOP control companies). A 2005 study of Ohio companies found median ESOP account balances of $30,000 (cited in Rosen [2005, 4]), and two surveys of Massachusetts ESOPs found average assets to range from $39,900 per participant (Scharf and Mackin 2000) to $56,200 per participant (Mackin 2005). Finally, a survey of sixteen S corporation ESOPs found median employee account balances of $75,000 to $100,000 (Rosen 2005).

In addition to ESOPs, there are a number of other popular employee ownership mechanisms: employee stock purchase plans (ESPPs), company stock in 401(k) plans, and broad-based stock option plans. Each of these plans—like ESOPs—has implications for retirement savings and employee risk.

ESPPs emerged gradually in the late 1800s and early 1900s as various industrialists sought ways to encourage workers to buy company stock in order to secure loyalty and create a common bond between labor and management. These plans spread rapidly in the context of welfare capitalism

3. Paraphrasing Mill, Kelso and Adler (1958, 85) wrote that "no man's ownership of (capital) should be so extensive as to exclude others from an economically significant participation in the production of wealth."

before the crash of 1929. They grew again in popularity after World War II, encouraged by a variety of tax incentives created by changes in the federal Internal Revenue Code.

Today, ESPPs constitute one of the "quiet" mechanisms of employee ownership in many major American corporations. In recent times, companies have typically allowed workers to buy stock through a payroll deduction at 85 percent of the market price. Many workers have come to see ESPPs as a supplement to their retirement savings; however long-term employees can accumulate substantial ESPP investments that dominate their retirement savings and raise serious issues of diversification.

Another form of employee ownership is the 401(k) retirement plan. While the US Congress worked intentionally to expand employee ownership through ESOPs, other models of employee ownership emerged with little governmental guidance. In the late seventies, the Internal Revenue Code was amended to allow for company contributions to tax-sheltered individual retirement trusts. The idea was that both company and worker contributions to these plans would be invested in stocks, bonds, and other assets, and this accumulated wealth would provide a supplement to the worker's main retirement fund—a defined benefit pension plan. These 401(k) defined contribution plans (called that because only the initial employer contribution, and not the final benefit, was defined) were originally intended for top management. But many companies have replaced their workers' defined benefit pension plans with defined contribution plans, shifting the risk associated with retirement income planning from employers to employees.

Increasingly, workers came to see these plans as useful supplements to their retirement. As the plans grew in number and popularity in the late 1980s and early 1990s, companies began matching employee contributions in company stock, and 401(k) plans emerged as vehicles for employee ownership. Companies next added company stock as an investment choice whereby workers could direct their own contributions to be used to buy company stock. Many companies found that employee ownership often grew rapidly under such plans. Although this has raised concerns about diversification when retirement plans are excessively invested in company stock, most observers agree that matching contributions of company stock to 401(k) retirement plans—within reason—has a useful role to play in expanding employee ownership.

The most recent development in the world of employee ownership is the "broad-based" stock option plan. These gained currency in the 1980s when high-tech firms began offering them to workers involved in developing computer and information systems hardware and software, often broadly to all employees in these firms (see Blasi, Kruse and Bernstein [2003]). Unlike ESPPs and employee purchases of company stock in 401(k) plans, employee stock options often require no investment of employees' savings. Employees are awarded options to buy company stock (after a vesting period), typically at the price it is trading on the day the options are awarded, for a ten-year period. If employees exercise their options and hold the stock, broad-based stock options become a way to finance ongoing employee ownership. If employees exercise their stock options and immediately sell the stock (which is much more usually the case), they can pocket the profit on the stock price's increase. In this case, the stock options serve as a form of cash profit sharing, based on company performance as measured by its stock price.

Broad-based stock option plans have become more common in a variety of manufacturing and service businesses. Stock options for employees, like ESOPs, involve lower risk for workers because they do not require the investment of workers' savings. However, when stock options are used in lieu of higher base pay or conventional retirement plans—as was sometimes the case in the tech sector start-ups of the 1980s and early 1990s—they are, in effect, risking employees' savings. Mature high-tech companies today, however, typically use broad-based stock options in combination with market level base pay and benefits.

Today, employee stock ownership is well established in the US economy. Blasi, Kruse, and Bernstein (2003, appendix C) calculate that in 2002 there were 24.1 million participants in 11,561 pension plans that held company stock.[4] About 8.2 million (34 percent) of these participants were in employee stock ownership plans (including ESOPs and similar plans called KSOPs),[5] and these held 59 percent of all company stock in employee pension plans. The ESOPs are "by far the most common form of employee ownership in the US" (Rosen 2005, 5). Another 13.6 million employees held company stock in 401(k) plans and 1.4 million in ESPPs. In addition, 10.6 million employees held stock options in the companies they work for.

Employee-owners bear two distinct types of risk. First, employees who have their own "skin in the game," having purchased company stock with their own funds, bear the risk of potential investment loss. This risk is minimized in ESOPs because the company stock allocated to workers' ESOP accounts is almost always contributed by the employer with no out-of-pocket cost to the employee.[6] At the other extreme, company stock acquired

4. As Kruse (2002) points out, these figures double count companies and employees who have more than one plan. His calculations (for 1998) suggest a lower-bound estimate of around 20 million employees (or 18 percent of all private sector workers) holding stock in their companies through various defined contribution pension plans (ESOPs, KSOPs, and 401(k)s that hold employer stock) and profit-sharing and employee stock purchase plans in 2002. The individual respondent-based General Social Survey data discussed in chapter 1 avoids such double-counting.

5. A KSOP is a combination ESOP and 401(k) plan in which employees' 401(k) contributions are matched by employer contributions of company stock to their ESOP accounts.

6. In one company the initial purchase of company stock at the founding of the KSOP was financed by a rollover from employees' existing 401(k) accounts. Employees of this company are an exception to the "no skin in the game" depiction of ESOP participants. Subsequent stock allocations to the KSOP have been provided by the employer.

through employee stock purchase plans is financed primarily by employee savings.

Second, employees who have concentrations of assets invested in a single company bear risk associated with inadequate diversification. This problem is exacerbated by a firm-specific risk for employee-owners whose jobs (and incomes), as well as a substantial portion of their savings, depend on the fortunes of the company they work for. This is an inevitable feature of any form of employee ownership, but it is likely to be greatest for ESOP employees who accumulate company shares in retirement accounts with limited opportunities for diversification. Federal law now allows workers close to retirement to diversify holdings in their ESOP accounts. The risk, however, appears generally to be manageable: portfolio theory suggests that a moderate amount of employee ownership can be part of a prudent portfolio depending on how other assets are diversified (chapter 3, this volume).

The inadequate diversification issue has come up most frequently with respect to ESOPs because of their retirement-plan structure. Although ESOPs are legally organized as retirement plans, scholars caution that they should not be thought of as a substitute for a diversified retirement plan (e.g., see Kruse [2002]), and indeed, all but one of the fourteen companies (including nine ESOPs) in the NBER study also have regular diversified 401(k) retirement plans. One plan in a large publicly-traded corporation, which is based mainly on broad-based stock options and profit sharing, actually prohibits its employees from holding its company stock in their diversified 401(k) plan. Among the subset of nine ESOPs, surveyed employees at three companies had less than half of their pension assets in the employer's stock, while employees at three other companies had between half and three-quarters, and employees at another three companies had over three-quarters of pension assets invested in their employer's stock. Clearly, many of these plans should be more diversified, but we need to bear in mind that employee-owners inevitably face greater ownership risk. To the extent that employee ownership increases wealth as well as risk, the question becomes whether this wealth-risk trade-off leaves employee-owners better off or not.[7]

It should also be kept in mind that there are millions of small business owners and farmers who have their wealth and livelihood tied up in their business, and it is commonly thought that such an undiversified concentration of wealth can provide very high incentives that motivate high levels of effort and productivity (as told in many rags-to-riches stories). High concentrations of employee-owned stock in some employees' portfolios may similarly promote strong incentives and economic success in some cases,

7. We thank Jeff Keefe for this point and for pointing out that the US system of employment-based health insurance, life insurance, savings plans, and so forth, exposes American workers in general to high levels of firm-specific risk. Employee-ownership further increases this risk. The better these benefits (including ownership) are, the greater the firm-specific risks are. But this does not mean that employees would be better off without them.

even if such employees are violating norms of diversification in the same way as many small business owners and farmers.

11.2 Profile of the NBER Companies

The NBER and GSS data sets used in this chapter are described in the "Studying Shared Capitalism" section of the introduction. Table 11.1 provides more detail on the stock sharing programs that the fourteen NBER companies have in place, which include nine ESOP-type plans (eight ESOPs and one KSOP), three 401(k) plans that invest in the employer's stock as well as other assets, five employee stock purchase plans (ESPPs), and six stock option plans (SOPs). Nine of these companies (identified with bold company numbers in table 11.1) are majority employee-owned ESOP-type

Table 11.1 **NBER company plans and disposition of company stock**

Company[a]	Plans	Stock is Publicly Traded/ Privately Held	Percent of Stock Held by Employees	Participation Rate (% holding co. stock)[d]	Value per Employee-Owner[d,e]
1	ESOP	Private	100%	88.5%	$239,139
2	ESOP	Private	100	81.9	23,827
3	ESPP, SOP	Public	n.a.	97.1	138,430
4	ESOP	Private	77	64.1	26,155
5	ESOP	Private	33[b]	39.1	7,877
6	401(k), ESPP, SOP	Private	100	88.5	36,623
7	ESOP, ESPP, SOP	Public	5[c]	88.1	15,865
8	KSOP	Private	100	77.5	166,713
9	ESOP	Private	100	69.3	38,411
10	ESOP	Private	75	52.0	40,407
11	401(k), ESPP, SOP	Public	n.a.	82.0	39,547
12	ESOP	Private	100	87.1	99,000
13	ESPP, SOP	Public	n.a.	60.3	175,687
14	401(k), SOP	Public	n.a.	67.7	27,952

Notes: ESOP = Employee Stock Ownership Plan; KSOP = A 401(k) plan with matching contributions of company stock to a companion ESOP. 401(k) = A 401(k) plan that holds company stock, as well as other assets. (All but one of these companies has a regular 401(k) plan.) ESPP = Employee Stock Purchase Plan; SOP = Company grants stock options (broad based in all but one case). n.a. = not available.

[a]Bold numbers indicate a subset of nine ESOPs (or near-ESOPs) that are broken out in some subsequent analyses.

[b]33 percent at the time of the survey, soon after increased to 67 percent.

[c]15 percent, including unexercised stock options.

[d]Includes only US-based, full-time employees (thirty-five or more hours per week), age 18 and over, with at least one year of service. Employees who did not know if they owned their employer's stock (about 15 percent of this subsample) are assumed not to. In the case of stock option plans, employees who have ever received stock options are counted, even if they do not currently hold company stock.

[e]Average value of employer stock for employees owning company stock.

plans (including one KSOP and one set up as a 401(k)).[8] In some of the following tables, we report results for this subset of majority-owned ESOP companies.

All of the privately held ESOP companies in the NBER study are majority owned; most are 100 percent employee owned. Overall participation rates of eligible employees (the percent of employees participating in at least one plan) are high, especially in the ESOPs.[9] The average value of company stock holdings (for employees with any stock) varies widely across companies—from just under $8,000 to over $239,000.

11.3 Ownership Stakes

In this section we examine the extent of participation in employee stock ownership, the size of employees' ownership stakes, the importance of ownership relative to base pay, and the value of company stock in relation to employees' total wealth. These measures are reported for all fourteen companies in the NBER study, a subsample of the nine ESOP companies in the NBER study, and for the combined 2002 and 2006 General Social Surveys (GSS). The measures are also broken down by position: management versus nonmanagement.

Table 11.2 presents various measures of employee stock ownership in the NBER shared capitalism companies and the GSS national samples.[10] Panel A confirms a very high participation rate, for managers and nonmanagers alike, in the NBER companies, with nearly 87 percent of surveyed employees in these firms reporting that they own employer stock—far higher than the 29 percent incidence of employee ownership in the national sample of private-sector employees.[11]

8. One of the companies included in this group holds its company stock in a 401(k) rather than an ESOP. One became majority owned shortly after its employee survey was conducted.

9. As noted in table 11.1, overall about 15 percent of the employees surveyed responded that they did not know if they held any employer stock. Here these employees are counted as nonparticipants (rather than dropped from the sample), significantly reducing reported participation rates for some companies. In the remaining tables they are excluded from the calculation of participation rates and company stock values.

10. All stock ownership and pay estimates presented here and following are reported in 2006 dollars.

11. The GSS asked respondents: "Do you own any shares of stock in the company where you now work, either directly or through some type of retirement or stock plan?" Those who answered affirmatively were asked for "a general estimate of how much cash you would get if all this stock were sold today." They were not asked how they acquired their company stock, but it is likely that the majority of the GSS employee-owners did so through an employer-sponsored program (rather than simply through open market purchases). Freeman (2007, 2) indicates that the great majority of private sector employees who own shares in their company do so via either ESOPs or 401(k) plans.

The incidence of company stock ownership among GSS respondents may itself seem surprisingly high. Note that this estimate is based on a sample of permanent, full-time, private sector employees, who are eighteen or over and have been in their current job for at least one year, and excludes respondents who did not know if they owned company stock—all conditions favoring a high participation rate.

Table 11.2 Employee stock ownership by employee position

	NBER Full Data set	NBER ESOP companies[a]	GSS national sample 2002 and 06
A. Percent owning employer stock			
All employees	86.8%	88.6%	29.3%
Managers	96.5	97.1	33.9
Others	85.6	87.4	28.5
(Sample size)	(24,918)	(3,889)	(1370)
B. Value per employee[b]			
All employees	$52,759	$76,041	$10,590
Managers	126,948	202,078	17,814
Others	41,745	55,756	9,576
(Sample size)	(24,202)	(4,314)	(1,245)
C. Value per employee-owner[c]			
All employees	$61,059	$85,926	$47,961
Managers	131,654	208,190	63,281
Others	49,030	63,874	45,109
All employees (median)	15,484	22,767	15,000
Managers (median)	46,452	70,560	28,016
Others (median)	13,340	20,645	11,206
(Sample size)	(20,912)	(3,423)	(276)
D. Value of employer stock as a percentage of annual base pay (NBER) or earnings (GSS)[c]			
All employees	65.4%	118.5%	75.8%
Managers	95.5	179.8	62.0
Others	60.0	107.3	78.3
(Sample size)	(18,796)	(2,527)	(269)
E. Value of employer stock as a percentage of total wealth[c]			
All employees	19.5%	28.0%	
Managers	21.9	34.1	
Others	19.0	26.7	
(Sample size)	(18,789)	(2,419)	

Notes: All measures are based on a sample of US-based, full-time (thirty-five or more hours per week) employees of for-profit companies, who are age 18 and over and have at least one year of service. Employees who reported that they did not know if they owned their employer's stock are dropped from these calculations.

[a]This is a subset of nine majority-owned, privately-held ESOP companies identified in table 11.1

[b]Includes employees who own no employer stock.

[c]Includes only employees who own employer stock.

The two most important sources of company stock ownership in the NBER study are (a) ESOPs (including KSOPs and 401(k) plans that hold company stock), in which stock accumulates in employees' retirement accounts; and (b) stock option plans, where employees are free to (and usually do) sell their shares immediately upon exercising their options. Consequently, we expect company stock ownership to be higher for employees in the subset of nine ESOP companies than for employees of all of the companies in the NBER study, and indeed this is the case (see panel B of table 11.2). Company stock holdings per employee (including those with no stock) are about $52,800 in the NBER full data set, and $76,000 for the nine NBER ESOPs. Based on the General Social Surveys, employees nationwide own on average $10,600 worth of their employers' stock.

We see in panel C that the average stake of *employee-owners* (i.e., employees who own some company stock) is $61,000 for all NBER companies and $85,900 for the NBER ESOPs. The average ownership stake of employee-owners in the GSS national sample is $48,000. For the NBER shared capitalist firms, nonmanagers ("Others") own roughly one-third as much company stock as managers, and the median holdings of the employee-owners is only about a quarter of the mean.[12] Although skewed toward the top, the distribution of employee-owned stock is considerably less skewed than is the distribution of wealth in general.

Company stock contributions to ESOP accounts are governed by ERISA and generally vary in proportion to participants' taxable earnings (with a cap of $220,000 in 2006). But the longer an employee has been in the plan, the more stock he or she can potentially accrue, so differences in ownership stakes among employees can be due to differences in length of service as well as differences in pay levels. In the case of the NBER ESOPs, controlling for job tenure reduces the manager versus nonmanager gap in average company stock holdings in panel C by just 9 percent, because in fact, there is little difference between managers and others in average job tenure.[13] But it reduces the mean-median gap for all employees by 50 percent.[14] The ESOP account balances increase, on average, by about $8,400 per year of service. As a result, a large part of the variation in account balances among ESOP participants at any point in time is not due to unequal stock allocations to ESOP accounts, but simply to differences in each employee's time-in-plan.

Panel D shows the value of employer stock holdings relative to base pay. In all cases employee-owners own stock worth two-thirds or more of their annual base pay, with a higher ratio for managers than for others in the NBER companies but a higher ratio for others than for managers in the GSS. This reversal—with stock being more important (relative to pay) for nonmanagement employees than for managers—is due more to their relatively low pay than to large company stock holdings.

12. The ratio of mean to the median employer stock holdings is a rough measure of the degree to which the distribution of company stock ownership is skewed to the right, with a relatively small number of employee-owners holding much more stock than the bulk of more typical owners. For perspective, Wolff (2004, table 1) reports a 13:1 ratio of mean to median household financial net worth in 2001 ($298,500 versus $23,200).

13. Tenure-adjusted stock values for nonmanagerial employees are obtained by regressing stock value on job tenure for these employees and using this regression equation to find the expected stock value for nonmanagerial employees who have the mean job tenure of managerial employees.

14. Tenure-adjusted stock values are obtained by adjusting each employee's stock value by the expected difference in value for someone with that employee's job tenure versus the mean job tenure for the sample.

Finally, panel E reports employees' estimates of the value of their company stock relative to their total wealth. While company stock represents somewhat over half of pension assets, on average, for the full sample of NBER employees (not shown in tables), it represents only about 20 percent, on average, of their total wealth.

Table 11.3 (panel A) reports the value of stock options held by employees in the NBER and the 2006 GSS data sets. Just 22 percent of employees in

Table 11.3 Stock options by employee position

	NBER full data set	NBER broad-based stock option cos.a	GSS national sample 2002 and 06
A. Percent holding stock options			
All employees	22.1%	93.2%	17.1%
Managers	44.1	97.1	18.4
Others	19.4	92.4	16.9
(Sample size)	(27,952)	(5,896)	(1,359)
B. Value per employee[b]			
All employees	$55,592	$262,931	
Managers	183,935	566,146	
Others	38,730	196,498	
(Sample size)	(27,711)	(5,711)	
C. Value per stock option holder[c]			
All employees	$259,740	$282,841	
Managers	428,614	583,424	
Others	205,995	213,264	
All employees (median)	80,042	93,383	
Managers (median)	112,805	213,446	
Others (median)	80,042	80,042	
(Sample size)	(5,931)	(5,309)	
D. Value of stock options as a percentage of annual base pay[c]			
All employees	175.6%	189.6%	
Managers	219.7	287.7	
Others	161.9	167.2	
(Sample size)	(5,769)	(5,185)	
E. Value of stock options as a percentage of total wealth[c]			
All employees	54.5%	58.9%	
Managers	45.2	57.5	
Others	57.4	59.3	
(Sample size)	(5,617)	(5,102)	

Notes: All measures are based on a sample of US-based, full-time (35 or more hours per week) employees of for-profit companies, who are age 18 and over and have at least one year of service. Employees who reported that they did not know if they hold stock options are dropped from these calculations.

[a]This is a subset of five SOP companies (excluding company fourteen which is not broad-based) identified in table 11.1.

[b]Total value of vested and unvested options. Includes employees who hold no stock options.

[c]Total value of vested and unvested options. Includes only employees who hold stock options.

the NBER companies and 17 percent of employees in the GSS hold stock options, but among the five broad-based stock option companies in the NBER study, 93 percent hold options to purchase their employers' stock. The average value of these options if exercised on the day the employee took the survey was $262,000 per employee (panel B) or $283,000 per option holder (panel C).[15]

Focusing on the broad-based stock options companies, we see that on average management holds options worth about 2.5 times more than other employees' options ($583,400 versus $213,300). On average, employees in these companies hold options worth almost two years' pay (panel D), and in the case of managers, almost three years' pay. On average, over half of their wealth is held in these stock options (panel E).

11.4 Do Employee-Owners Pay with Lower Wages?

Skeptics of employee ownership suggest that (for equivalent workers and working conditions) whatever value ownership confers on employees must be offset by correspondingly lower wages, since the market insures that total (risk-adjusted) compensation must be the same everywhere. And there are reasons, besides competitive theory, to suppose that employees receiving company stock might pay for it with lower wages. Unionized workers in airlines and trucking—industries under pressure of deregulation in the late 1970s and 1980s—made large wage concessions in return for ownership shares to save their companies and their jobs, usually through concessionary employee ownership plans. But these concessionary plans represent a very small percentage of all plans (Blasi 1988, 94; Russell 1985, 200). Some high-tech startups, such as Amazon, acknowledged a compensation strategy of luring talent on the cheap with stock options and below-market pay.[16]

The preponderance of empirical evidence, however, goes the other way. In a pre/post study of ESOPs adopted by public companies between 1980 and 2004, Kim and Ouimet (2008) find significant increases in employee compensation following the adoption of ESOPs, particularly for ESOPs owning more than 5 percent of a company where the long-term increase in compensation is 4.5 percent.[17] A study of 490 firms with broad-based stock options found that these companies paid their employees 8 percent

15. The values reported here are the net gain the employee would realize if his/her stock options were exercised and the stock sold.

16. Statistical evidence for wage substitution is harder to come by than anecdotal evidence. One tangentially related study of Italian producer co-ops by Pencavel, Pistaferri, and Schivardi (2006) finds that "a worker in a co-op earned 15–16% less than a worker in a capitalist enterprise," controlling for age, gender, region, establishment size, industry, and occupation.

17. A similar method used on German firms adopting profit-sharing plans also concluded that profit sharing supplemented rather than substituted for standard compensation (Ugarkovi 2007).

more than all other public companies when most of them introduced their stock-option plans in the mid-1980s, and continued to pay 8 percent more a decade later (Sesil et al. 2007). Blasi, Conte, and Kruse (1996) found that compensation per employee was 23 percent higher in publicly-traded companies with more than 5 percent of their stock held in broad-based employee stock ownership plans than it was in other firms. Kardas, Scharf, and Keogh (1998) found mean and median wages of ESOP companies in Washington State to be higher than a matched set of control companies. And Kruse and Blasi (2001), matching 1,176 pairs of ESOP and non-ESOP companies, found that the ESOP companies were over four times more likely to have traditional defined benefit plans and over five times more likely to have 401(k) plans—in addition to their ESOPs.

What do our data say on this issue? Employees in the NBER companies receive higher pay than employees in the GSS, but this simple comparison does not account for the select nature of the NBER firms. For a more finely tuned examination of the relationship between employee ownership and pay levels, we compare wages (and perceptions about them) of employee-owners and nonowners *within* data sets. First we consider employees' views about their base pay relative to the base pay of similarly qualified employees in similar jobs at other companies. Responses to this question are reported in table 11.4. Differences in the pattern of responses between owners and nonowners in the NBER data are consistent with the substitution hypothesis, and they are statistically significant. However, they are very small. In particular, the percentage of employee-owners who felt that they were paid below market was only one percentage point more than the percentage of nonowners who felt that they were paid below market (39.5 percent versus 38.5 percent). Responses of GSS employee-owners and nonowners do not

Table 11.4 **Perceptions of base pay relative to market for employee-owners and nonowners**

	NBER full data set		GSS 2006 national sample	
	Employee-owners	Nonowners	Employee-owners	Nonowners
1 Below market	14.2%	17.8%	15.5%	18.5%
2	25.3	20.7	14.3	11.0
3 At market	42.5	41.8	41.1	49.1
4	15.1	15.0	15.5	10.6
5 Above market	2.9	4.7	13.7	10.8
	$\chi^2 = 72.9$ ($p = .000$)		$\chi^2 = 6.90$ ($p = .141$)	
Sample size	19,093	2,836	168	464

Notes: All subsamples are restricted to US-based employees of for-profit, private sector companies, who are 18 or over, usually work at least 35 hours per week, and have at least one year of service with their employer. Respondents were asked "Do you believe your fixed annual wages last year were higher or lower than those of employees with similar experience and job descriptions in other companies in your region?"

differ significantly (due in part to the much smaller sample size) and are not consistent with substitution. In fact, a substantially higher percentage of employee-owners felt that they were paid *above* market (29.2 percent versus 21.4 percent).

Next we consider the relationship between employees' pay and their ownership stakes (more specifically, the annual *increase* in their ownership stake). The key independent variable in this analysis is the ratio of the value of the employee's accrued company stock *per year of service* (indicating the annual growth of his/her ownership stake) to his or her annual base pay. A negative relationship between this variable and pay suggests that the more important ownership growth is relative to pay, the lower pay will be—in other words, ownership substitutes for pay. A positive relationship is inconsistent with the substitution hypothesis.[18]

In table 11.5, panel A, seven different measures of pay are regressed on this independent variable (i.e., the annual increase in stock ownership relative to annual pay), controlling for an extensive list of personal and job-related determinants of pay. The first two dependent variables in panel A are the log of base pay and of total pay. The next four are employees' assessments of their pay (fixed and total) relative to the pay of employees in similar jobs at other companies in their region. The last dependent variable indicates respondents' assessment of how hard would it be to find another job with pay and benefits comparable to what they now have. In twelve of the fourteen regressions, the coefficient of the key ownership share variable is positive; in six of these it is statistically significant (at better than a 5 percent level of significance), and in every case where the relationship is statistically significant, it is positive. These results suggest that if there is any relationship between company stock ownership and pay, it is a complementary one.

Panel B of table 11.5 presents similar regressions based on the GSS data. Here the five dependent variables are log earnings, perceptions of pay relative to market, assessments of pay and fringe benefits, and the difficulty of finding another job with comparable pay and benefits. In four of these five regressions the signs of the key coefficient are positive, and in two the statistically significant estimates the coefficients are positive.

The main finding here is that there is no evidence that employee ownership substitutes for wages or benefits. On the contrary, it appears on average to be an add-on, with employees' ownership stake growing without sacrificing pay.[19]

18. We use the average annual increase in ownership stake since the level of stock ownership depends heavily on years of service, which obscures the relationship between pay and ownership.

19. These relationships were also estimated for samples restricted to nonmanagers and for the five NBER companies with the lowest pay, all with similar results. In no case was there statistically significant evidence of substitution of ownership for pay or benefits.

Table 11.5 **Does employer stock substitute for pay?**

A NBER data set		
	Ratio of annual ownership stake to base pay	
Dependent variable	Full data set	Nine ESOPs
1. Log base pay	.006	.000
	(.012)	(.042)
2. Log total pay	.114***	.068
	(.013)	(.043)
3. Base pay relative to market	.073**	.016
(5 point scale: 1. below, . . . 5. above)	(.040)	(.175)
4. Base pay percent of market	.765	–.294
(percent below/above market)	(.585)	(3.05)
5. Total pay relative to market	.218***	.431***
(5 point scale: 1. below, . . . 5. above)	(.041)	(.159)
6. Total pay percent of market	3.313***	7.155***
(percent below/above market)	(.690)	(2.925)
7. Difficulty replacing pay and benefits	–.002	.088
(3 point scale: 1. easy, . . . 3. not at all easy)	(.024)	(.090)

B GSS national sample 2002 and 06	
	Ratio of annual ownership stake to earnings
1. Log earnings	.238
	(.109)
2. Base pay relative to market	.682
(5 point scale: 1. below, . . . 5. above)	(1.017)
3. Paid what you deserve	–.107
(5 point scale: 1. much less, . . . 5. much more)	(.173)
4. Fringe benefits are good	.798**
(4 point scale: 1. not true, . . . 4. very true)	(.378)
5. Difficulty replacing pay and benefits	1.657**
(3 point scale: 1. easy, . . . 3. not at all easy)	(.694)

Notes: Each entry involves a separate regression. The key independent variable is the ratio of the value of employer stock (divided by years of tenure) to annual earnings. All regressions include controls for sex, age, education, job tenure, hours worked, management, hourly, union membership, and company fixed effects. Equations A. 3, 5, and 7 and B. 2, 3, 4, and 5 are ordered probits; others are OLS. Samples are restricted as indicated in table 11.4. Standard errors are in parentheses.

***Significant at the 1 percent level.

**Significant at the 5 percent level.

11.5 Does Employee Ownership Build Wealth?

Here we turn to the question of whether employee ownership actually adds to wealth or just changes the composition of wealth, substituting company stock for other forms of wealth (e.g., assets in a 401(k) account or an IRA). Do employees, for example, buy company stock through an employee stock purchase plan *instead* of buying other stock or *in addition to* other stock? In the former case, employee ownership would just be a substitute for other forms of wealth, rather than an addition to them.

Of course, we cannot know what the wealth levels of employee-owners would have been in the absence of employee ownership, but we can see whether employee ownership is associated with higher levels of overall wealth or not. If it is, that is prima facie evidence that employee ownership does not fully substitute for other forms of wealth and thus increases total wealth.[20]

Table 11.6 presents some evidence on this question. Two regressions are reported for the NBER full data set and two for the nine NBER ESOP companies. In each regression the dependent variable is the employee's wealth. Because wealth is a categorical variable in this data set, interval regressions are used to assess the relationship of employee ownership to overall wealth.[21] The key independent variable in the first regression on each data set is the value of company stock held in *all* plans. In the second regression this variable is replaced by the value of company stock in *each* plan. All regressions also include a set of controls for other potential determinants of wealth that might be correlated with the level of company stock holdings (see table notes).

The first and most general result is the coefficient of 0.942 on company stock in all plans in the first regression, which implies that each additional dollar of employer stock is associated with 94.2 cents of higher wealth. That is, there appears to be very little reduction in other wealth associated with increasing employee ownership (only about 6 cents less other wealth as employee ownership increases by one dollar). For nine NBER ESOPs the corresponding coefficient is 0.801, which indicates that wealth rises 80.1 cents as employee ownership increases by one dollar, so other wealth is decreasing by only 20 cents. While we cannot know what the wealth of employees would have been in the absence of employee ownership, these results cast doubt on a simple story of dollar-for-dollar substitution.

The regressions that include all plan types indicate the effect on total wealth of increases in the value of company stock in each of the various methods of stock ownership—ESOPs, 401(k)s, Employee stock purchase plans (ESPPs), exercised stock options, and open market purchases. In these regressions, all of the coefficients are positive and statistically signifi-

20. Moreover, as Joseph Blasi has pointed out to us, even if employee ownership is substituting for other wealth dollar for dollar, that does not mean there is no net gain for the employee. It still allows for a higher level of consumption at the same level of wealth. This is especially relevant for stock options, where options are usually exercised and the stock immediately sold. The proceeds can be reinvested (increasing wealth) or spent (increasing consumption), but in either case there is a welfare gain.

21. The NBER surveys asked employees to put their wealth into one of between nine and sixteen categories (depending on the survey). The regressions were run using Stata's intreg command, with dollar values adjusted for inflation to represent 2006 values.

Table 11.6 **Does employer stock displace other wealth?**

	Dependent variable: Wealth			
	NBER full data set		Nine NBER ESOPs	
Independent variables	(1)	(2)	(3)	(4)
Value of employer stock from				
All plans	0.942***		0.801***	
	(.023)		(.034)	
ESOP		1.007***		0.880***
		(.098)		(.045)
401(k)		1.280***		0.661***
		(.100)		(.051)
ESPP		3.590***		3.062***
		(.106)		(0.725)
Open market purchases		2.179***		
		(.148)		
Exercised stock options		0.646***		
		(.020)		

Notes: All regressions run as interval regressions due to categorical coding of wealth. Controls include earnings, sex, age, marital status, family size, number of children, education, job tenure, hours worked, management, paid hourly, union membership, and company fixed effects. Samples are restricted as indicated in table 11.4. Standard errors in parentheses.
***Significant at the 1 percent level.

cant, indicating that employee ownership is associated with higher wealth. The ESOP coefficient in the full data set is not significantly different from one, inconsistent with no substitution of ESOP stock with other wealth, while the coefficient of 0.880 in the ESOP-only regression indicates only minimal substitution for other wealth. The coefficients on open market purchases and stock purchased through ESPPs are much larger than one, which probably indicates that increases in (other) wealth lead to increased investment in the employer's stock.[22] Exercised stock options have a coefficient of 0.646, suggesting that an extra dollar of stock from stock options is associated with 64.6 cents of greater wealth, and the remainder of the extra dollar (35.4 cents) may be substituting for other wealth as employees save less as this form of wealth increases. A similar story may apply to the 401(k) coefficient in the ESOP-only regression. While these estimates are necessarily rough, they are generally inconsistent with the idea that employee ownership is substituting for other wealth, and more consistent with the idea that

22. The large ESPP coefficient might also be partly due to the fact that company stock in ESPPs is typically bought at a 20 percent discount, so every dollar of stock purchased automatically raises wealth by $1.25. Also, employees are most likely to buy company stock when its price is rising, and if the price does rise the value of their wealth will rise more than their dollar investment.

increasing employee stock ownership by a dollar tends to raise employee wealth by almost a dollar.

Another way to examine the wealth impact of employee ownership across the economic spectrum is to compare the distribution of wealth classes with and without employee ownership. Figures 11.1 and 11.2 provide such a comparison for the full NBER sample and ESOP sample. Within each sample, the distribution of employees by wealth class was predicted using

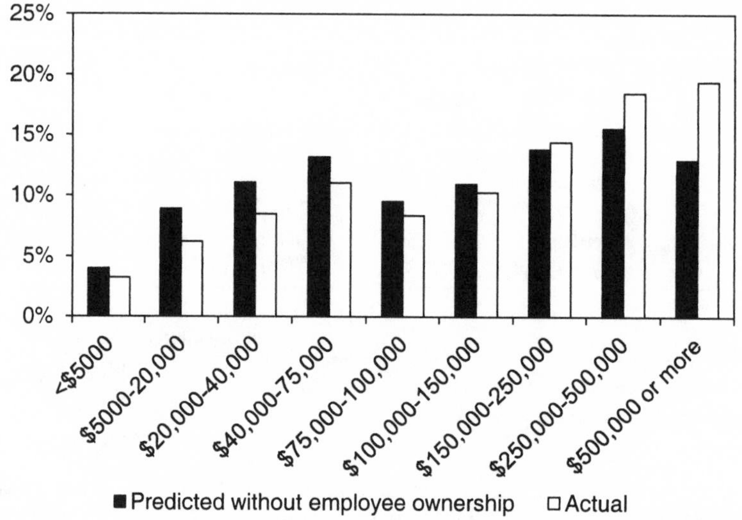

Fig. 11.1 **Wealth class distribution for employees in shared capitalism companies**

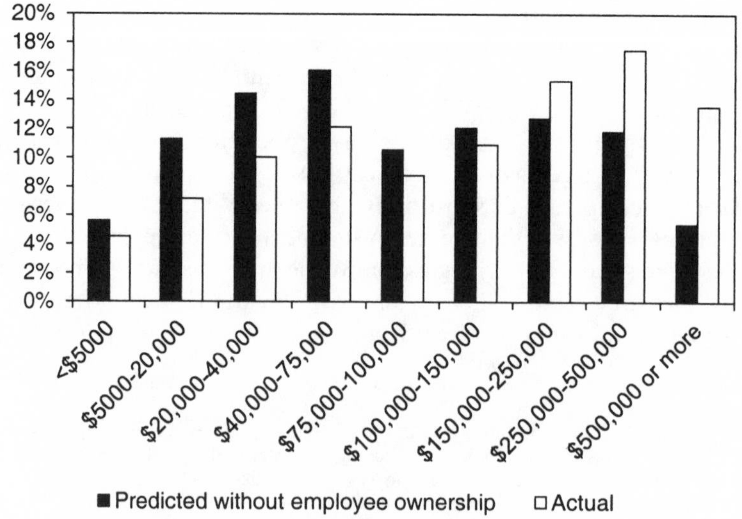

Fig. 11.2 **Wealth class distribution for ESOP employees**

multinomial logits, and the probabilities of membership in each class were then predicted with the value of employer stock set to zero.[23] If employee ownership makes no difference in the levels or distribution of wealth (that is, if it fully substitutes for other wealth), then these predicted and actual distributions will be identical.

As seen in figure 11.1, employee ownership among the NBER shared capitalism employees appears to decrease membership in the six lowest wealth classes (< \$150,000) and increase membership in the classes above that, particularly in the > \$500,000 class. Figure 11.2 finds the same pattern among employees in ESOP companies, but with more dramatic differences. Combined membership in the four lowest wealth categories (< \$75,000) is 47 percent without employee ownership, and 34 percent with employee ownership. These figures are consistent with the idea that employee ownership is enhancing wealth, not substituting for other forms of wealth.

11.6 The Distribution of Employee Stock Ownership and the Distribution of Wealth

Finally, we assess the distribution of company stock ownership and of all wealth (net worth). Table 11.7, panel A, shows the distribution of employer stock across employees (for the NBER companies and GSS employees) and compares it with Edward Wolff's estimates of the distribution of all stock across households. In both the NBER full sample and the ESOP subsample the top 10 percent of employees hold 64 percent of employer stock and the next 50 percent hold almost all the rest. In the GSS the top 10 percent hold an estimated 73 percent of the company stock (which is likely to be a lower bound estimate[24]), and the next 50 percent hold the remaining 27 percent. By way of a rough comparison, Wolff (2004) finds that the top 10 percent

23. The predictors used in the multinomial logits were gender, age, married, BA degree, graduate degree, black, Hispanic, household size, number of children, tenure, natural logarithm of annual earnings, and dollar value of employer stock held. The predicted likelihoods were averaged within each wealth class for an estimate of the percent of employees who would be in each wealth class.

24. A problem with estimating the distribution of company stock ownership in the GSS sample is that 30 percent of the respondents who reported that they owned company stock did not report the value of that stock (usually because they did not know, rather than refused to say). Omitting these respondents from the calculation lends an upward bias to the distribution, resulting in an estimate that 91 percent of the company stock is held by the top 10 percent. We have no way of knowing the actual stock holdings of those who did not respond to the question. The GSS estimates in table 11.7 are based on imputing stock values for employees who said they owned company stock but did not report how much. This imputation was done by regressing stock value on pay, sex, age, education, tenure, and position (management versus other) for the portion of the sample of employees who report stock value and using the resulting equation to estimate stock values for those who did not report. This procedure relies on the assumption that employee-owners who are statistically alike in their personal characteristics will have similar company stock holdings. Since it is likely that employee-owners who do not know the value of their company stock do not hold as much of it as their statistically similar counterparts who do know, we take 73.3 percent as a rough "lower bound" estimate of the share of company stock held by the top 10 percent of GSS employees.

Table 11.7 Distribution of stock ownership and wealth

Wealth class	NBER employees full sample	NBER employees ESOPs	GSS employees national sample 2002 and 2006	Wolff 2001 (households)
		A. Share of stock[a]		
Top 10%	64.0%	64.0%	73.3%[b]	76.9%[c]
Next 50%	34.9	34.5	26.7	22.4
Bottom 40%	1.1	1.6	0.0	0.7
		B. Share of all wealth (net worth)		
Top 10%	56.3%	58.5%		71.5%[d]
Next 50%	39.5	37.4		28.2
Bottom 40%	4.2	4.0		0.3
		C. Share of all wealth excluding employer stock		
Top 10%	57.0%	61.0%		
Next 50%	39.2	36.0		
Bottom 40%	3.8	3.0		

Notes: NBER and GSS samples are restricted as indicated in table 11.4. NBER sample employees who reported that they did not know if they owned employer stock are excluded.

[a]NBER and GSS samples show share of employer stock. Wolff 2001 includes all stock.

[b]Imputes the value of employer's stock for employee-owners who did not report it (see footnote 24).

[c]Wolff (2004, table 13a).

[d]Wolff (2004, table 2).

of households hold 77 percent of all stock.[25] It is not surprising to find a more equal distribution of company stock among employees of the shared capitalism companies in the NBER study (with over a third of company stock held by those between the fortieth and ninetieth percentile). Many fewer GSS respondents are employee-owners and even fewer of them are likely to be employed in companies with a broad-based employee ownership plan.

Turning to panel B of table 11.7, we find that in the NBER full sample, the top 10 percent of employees' households hold 56.3 percent of all wealth, compared to 58.5 percent for the ESOP sample.[26] The nationally-representative

25. Comparisons in panel A of this table are confounded by inconsistencies in the unit of observation between the NBER/GSS data (company stock value per employee) and Wolff's data (stock value per household). This observation does not apply to panel B, where the unit of observation is the household in the NBER/GSS data, as well as Wolff's data.

26. Because the NBER wealth data are based on categorical variables rather than exact dollar values, the figures in table 11.7, panel B, are approximations. The calculation of the wealth distribution is based on assigning mean dollar values to each category using data from the 2004 Survey of Consumer Finances (SCF). When the ninetieth and fortieth percentiles fell within a wealth category, the distribution of wealth within that category in the SCF was used in order to estimate the total wealth of those above and below those percentiles. For example, if those in the $500,000 to 1,000,000 wealth category covered the eighty-fifth to ninety-fifth percentiles

Survey of Consumer Finances (SCF) data analyzed by Wolff show 71.5 percent of wealth held by the top 10 percent of households, pointing toward a more equal distribution of wealth among the NBER employees. While this is consistent with the idea that employee ownership can broaden the wealth distribution, it must be noted that wealth was measured in different ways in the two data sets, which muddies the comparison.[27] In addition, comparison between these samples may be affected by demographic differences (e.g., age, marital status, and household size) that are related to wealth levels. A straightforward way to examine the influence of employee ownership on wealth distribution while controlling for demographic differences is to calculate the distribution for employees both with and without employer stock (assuming that employer stock is not substituting for other forms of wealth, as is strongly suggested by the earlier results). Panel C of table 11.7 shows that when employee ownership is subtracted from estimated wealth holdings, the share of wealth held by the top 10 percent is 57.0 percent among NBER employees, just slightly higher than the 56.3 percent figure that includes employer stock (panel B). Both the middle and lower groups see slightly increased shares of wealth from adding employee ownership. The difference is larger in the ESOP sample, where 61.0 percent of the wealth excluding employer stock is held by the top 10 percent, and adding employer stock decreases that share to 58.5 percent, with increases in the shares of both the middle and bottom wealth holders. This indicates that ESOPs may play a stronger role than other forms of employee ownership in broadening ownership of wealth.

Examination of employee ownership by wealth class can also shed light on how employee ownership affects the wealth distribution. Table 11.8 shows

of the NBER distribution, the median of the $500,000 to 1,000,000 category was identified in the SCF distribution, and the mean wealth was calculated above that median and multiplied by the number of NBER employees in the ninetieth to ninety-fifth percentiles for an estimate of total wealth among employees in that part of the distribution. That figure was then added to an estimate of total wealth for those in the ninety-fifth to one-hundredth percentiles, using mean SCF wealth for each category multiplied by the number of employees in that category, to determine the total held by the top 10 percent. This procedure assumes that wealth is distributed similarly within each category for the NBER and SCF samples. While only an approximation, it is unlikely to lead to any systematic bias.

27. The SCF includes detailed measures of many forms of wealth, with exact dollar values, which are added to arrive at a total wealth figure. The NBER surveys, in contrast, included a single question asking employees to put their total wealth in one of nine to thirteen categories. The question was: "People have various assets that constitute their wealth. These include the value of their house minus the mortgage, plus their vehicles, stocks and mutual funds, cash, checking accounts, retirement accounts including 401(k) and pension assets, and so forth. Taking account of all of these things would you say that the WEALTH of you and your spouse is. . . ." As described in the previous note, the NBER figures are based on assigning mean dollar values to each response category using data from the 2004 SCF, in order to make the NBER and Wolff/SCF measures as comparable as possible. An earlier version of this study used a wealth measure from the 2006 GSS that was based on the NBER measure, but subsequently the National Opinion Research Corporation determined that there were problems in the administration of this GSS question so we have not included those data here.

Table 11.8 **Employee ownership distribution by wealth class**

	Percent of employee's wealth in			
	Employee ownership		All stocks	
Wealth class	NBER full sample	NBER ESOPs	SCF[a]	NBER
< $5,000	16.3	26.8	1.4	19.6
$5,000–20,000	16.7	18.7	8.9	23.0
$20,000–40,000	16.4	19.1	13.7	23.3
$40,000–75,000	17.7	22.4	12.9	26.2
$75,000–100,000	18.0	24.8	13.6	28.2
$100,000–150,000	17.2	24.7	14.4	29.0
$150,000–250,000	17.8	26.6	16.9	31.9
$250,000–500,000	17.3	27.9	19.4	34.3
$500,000 or more	19.5	35.3	26.8	39.4

[a]Survey of Consumer Finances.

that average employee ownership, as a percent of wealth, is very similar across the wealth categories for the NBER sample, with only a slightly higher figure (19.5 percent) for the richest class compared to the poorest class (16.3 percent). There is a similar pattern for ESOPs, with fairly uniform percentages across the wealth classes, although a higher percentage in the richest class. This indicates that while employee ownership may increase wealth, it appears unlikely to have much effect on the shape of the distribution among employee-owners since everyone's wealth is going up by a similar percentage (assuming a similar rate of substitution of employee ownership for other wealth across the categories). The NBER-SCF comparison in table 11.8 clearly shows that employee ownership increases stock ownership as a percentage of wealth across all of the wealth categories. This reinforces the finding at the top of table 11.7 that stock ownership is greater amid middle and lower employees in the NBER companies than in the national samples.

The data in tables 11.6 to 11.8 point toward a wealth-enhancing effect of employee ownership but suggest that the shape of the wealth distribution (reflecting the relative amounts held by those at the top, middle, and bottom) within the group of employee-owners may not be greatly affected by employee ownership. This is not surprising when one considers that employee ownership plans often distribute company stock in proportion to salary, and salary is also distributed unequally. Some simple calculations illustrate this point. If each person in the NBER data set were simply given an amount of company stock equal to 10 percent of their yearly pay, we estimate that the percent of wealth held by the top 10 percent would fall from 56.3 percent (table 11.7) to 55.7 percent. If a similar total were distributed in equal dollar amounts ($5,989) to each employee, that figure would fall only to 55.5 percent. The fact that employee ownership is only a small portion of most

Table 11.9 **Pension wealth: NBER employees and all households**

	All NBER companies assets in all pensions[a]		NBER ESOPs assets in all pensions[a]		Wolff 2001 estimates of household pension wealth[b]	
	Mean	Median	Mean	Median	Mean	Median
Age 18 and over	$67,035	$34,006	$102,589	$31,738	$94,800	$10,900
Percent in employer stock	31.2%		71.5%			
Sample size	22,558		3,076			
Ages 47–64	$100,802	$49,875	$165,469	$54,409	$170,800	$50,000
Percent in employer stock	33.9%		73.7%			
Sample size	7,709		925			

Note: Sample is restricted as indicated in table 11.7.

[a]There are nine companies with majority-owned ESOPs. Assets include employer and other stock in ESOPs and 401(k) plans. Dollar values have been adjusted to 2001 levels for comparison with Wolff's figures.

[b]Value of employees' Defined Benefit and Defined Contribution pension plans. Wolff (2005, table 11).

workers' wealth, and is often distributed in proportion to pay that is itself unequal, indicates that employee ownership as currently practiced is likely to make only a modest difference in the distribution of wealth.

Finally, table 11.9 compares the mean and median pension wealth of employees in the NBER (full and ESOP sample) with Wolff's estimates of mean and median household pension wealth. Here again we run into the problem of inconsistent units of observation, and the comparison likely favors Wolff's measure because households may have more than one member with a pension plan and therefore more pension assets.

We expect pension values to be higher for the NBER ESOP companies than for all NBER companies because ESOPs operate as retirement plans, with stock accumulating in them until the employee retires (or otherwise leaves the company). The mean pension wealth for the ESOPs is just a little higher than the mean in Wolff's Survey of Consumer Finances data, but the *median* is almost three times higher ($32,000 versus $11,000), suggesting that companies with broad-based employee ownership do benefit mid-level or median employees in their effect on the distribution of pension assets. Turning to the "pre-retirement," forty-seven to sixty-four age group, however, we find no practical difference between the median pension assets of employees of these ESOPs versus Wolff's households.

11.7 Conclusion

These results indicate that shared ownership builds wealth for employees. The average value of company stock held by employee owners in the nine majority-owned ESOP companies is almost $86,000, and the average value of stock options held by option holders (if exercised on the day of their survey) in the five broad-based stock option companies is almost $283,000. Median holdings are considerably lower ($22,800 and $93,400, respectively), and nonmanagers' holdings are only about one-third those of managers, on average. Nonetheless, comparison of the NBER and GSS data sets shows that if all employees worked for companies with broad-based employee-ownership plans like the NBER firms, a lot more employees would own a lot more company stock.

There is no evidence that employees' ownership gains are offset by lower wages or benefits. While increases in company stock ownership appear to be partially offset by decreases in other wealth, there is a substantial net gain in total wealth resulting from increases in employee ownership—with a one dollar increase in ownership associated with almost a one dollar increase in total wealth. We find some evidence here that the general pattern of capital ownership and income going almost exclusively to the top 10 percent is partly reversed by employee ownership, with expanded stock ownership among those at the middle and bottom of the wealth distribution.

While employee-ownership inevitably increases employees' firm specific risks in proportion to the value of company stock owned, the risk-reward trade-off appears to be manageable (chapter 3, this volume). Since employee ownership does not cause a substantial decrease in ownership of other assets, this increased risk applies only to assets that employees would not have if they worked at a non-employee-ownership company. In addition, employee ownership is only a small portion of wealth for most employee owners, consistent with the bounds suggested by portfolio theory (assuming other assets are properly diversified). These results indicate that broad-based employee ownership may be raising wealth for many workers without unduly increasing worker risk.

References

Blasi, J. 1988. *Employee ownership: Revolution or ripoff?* New York: HarperBusiness.

Blasi, J., M. Conte, and D. Kruse. 1996. Employee stock ownership and corporate performance among public companies. *Industrial and Labor Relations Review* 50 (1): 60–79.

Blasi, J., D. Kruse, and A. Bernstein. 2003. *In the company of owners: The truth about stock options (and why every employee should have them).* New York: Basic Books.

Freeman, S. F. 2007. Effects of ESOP adoption and employee ownership: Thirty years of research and experience. Organizational Dynamics Working Paper no. 07-01, University of Pennsylvania.

Kardas, P., A. Scharf and J. Keogh. 1998. Wealth and income consequences of ESOPs and employee ownership: A comparative study from Washington state. *Journal of Employee Ownership Law and Finance* 10 (4): 3–52.

Kelso, L. O., and M. Adler. 1958. *The capitalist manifesto.* New York: Random House.
Kennickell, A. B. 2003. A rolling tide: Changes in the distribution of wealth in the US, 1989–2001. Working Paper, Board of Governors of the Federal Reserve System.
Kim, E. H., and P. Ouimet. 2008. Employee capitalism or corporate socialism? Broad-based employee stock ownership. Draft, Ross School of Business, University of Michigan, October.
Kruse, D. 2002. Research evidence on prevalence and effects of employee ownership. *Journal of Employee Ownership Law and Finance* 14 (4): 65–90.
Kruse, D., and J. Blasi. 2001. *A population study of the performance of ESOP and non-ESOP privately-held companies.* School of Management and Labor Relations, Rutgers University, New Brunswick, NJ, May.
Mackin, C. 2005. *2005 Census of Massachusetts companies with Employee Stock Ownership Plans (ESOPs).* Boston: Commonwealth Corporation.
Mishel, L., J. Bernstein, and S. Allegretto. 2007. *The state of working America 2006/2007.* Ithaca, NY: Cornell University Press.
Pencavel, J., L. Pistaferri, and F. Schivardi. 2006. Wages, employment and capital in capitalist and worker-owned firms. *Industrial and Labor Relations Review* 60 (1): 23–44.
Rosen, C. 2005. *Retirement security and wealth accumulation in S ESOP companies.* Oakland: The National Center for Employee Ownership.
Russell, R. 1985. *Sharing ownership in the workplace.* New York: State University of New York Press.
Scharf, A., and C. Mackin. 2000. *Census of Massachusetts companies with Employee Stock Ownership Plans (ESOPs).* Boston: Commonwealth Corporation.
Sesil, J., M. Kroumova, D. Kruse, and J. Blasi. 2007. Broad-based employee stock options in the United States: Company performance and characteristics. *Management Revue* 18 (2): 5–22.
Ugarkovi, M. 2007. Profit sharing and company performance. PhD dissertation. Universitat Dortmund, Deutscher Universitats Verlag, Wiesbaden. Available at: www.duv.de.
Weller, C., and E. N. Wolff. 2005. Retirement income: The crucial role of Social Security. Washington, DC: Economics Policy Institute.
Wolff, E. N. 2004. Changes in household wealth in the 1980s and 1990s in the US. The Levy Institute of Bard College, Working Paper no. 407.
———. 2005. Is the equalizing effect of retirement wealth wearing off? The Levy Institute of Bard College, Working Paper no. 420.

Epilogue (and Prologue)

Joseph R. Blasi, Douglas L. Kruse, and
Richard B. Freeman

At this writing the US model of capitalism faces great problems. The implosion of Wall Street due to excessive leverage, inadequate regulations, and poor incentives and financial contracts that induced many at the top of the financial hierarchy to undertake highly risky investments, has produced the greatest economic decline since the Great Depression. Many see the US economic model as driven by Wall Street finance that has failed to deliver the goods. This book has studied a different part of the American model—one that has received less attention but has proven far more successful. Shared capitalism has long been of interest for its potential to affect workplace productivity, employee-management relations, quality of work life, job security, worker pay, the distribution of wealth, and broader participation in the economic system. In exhibit 1 in the introduction we listed six key "take-away" findings from our research:

1. Shared capitalism is a significant part of the US economic model.
2. Worker co-monitoring helps shared capitalist firms overcome incentives to free ride.
3. The risk of shared capitalist investments in one's employer is manageable.
4. Shared capitalism improves the performance of firms.
5. Shared capitalism improves worker well-being.
6. Shared capitalism complements other labor policies and practices.

Hopefully the preceding chapters have convinced the reader that these are reasonable conclusions to reach from the evidence, despite the limitations inherent in nonexperimental science.

Taken together, these findings create a picture of shared capitalism that is at odds with some common complaints about it. Economists have two major criticisms of shared capitalism: that free riding will undo any positive effects of group incentives on effort and performance, and that workers are generally risk-averse and will be harmed by the financial risk in shared capitalism plans.

Both free riding and financial risk are real concerns. Free riding clearly exists: profit sharing and gain sharing appear to work best in small groups where the incentive to be a free rider is reduced, and some workers admit free riding off the efforts of others in response to shirking co-workers (saying "some other employee will probably take action")(chapter 2, this volume). And financial risk is obviously a concern: some workers express a desire for lower fixed pay over higher average pay that varies, and some prefer their next pay increase to be all fixed pay with no profit sharing, stock, or options (chapters 1 and 3).

The picture of shared capitalism in the book shows that free riding and financial risk are surmountable concerns, and that broad-based financial participation can create a framework for cooperative corporate culture even in large groups or firms. The combination with a more cooperative corporate culture is what helps overcome free riding and create the performance benefits.

Our overall interpretation builds on the ideas of reciprocity and gift exchange, and the body of theory and research on bundles of high performance work practices. There is increasing evidence that reciprocity plays a strong role in a wide range of economic and social relationships, helping encourage norms of cooperation (Axelrod 1984; Fehr and Gachter 2000; Gintis et al. 2005). Formal economic models also show how employment relationships can be built on reciprocity and gift exchange (Akerlof 1982).

A key element in our overall interpretation is that shared capitalism pay and wealth appears to generally come on top of standard pay and benefits—that is, it represents "gravy" for the worker rather than substituting for other pay and benefits. This is consistent with the other studies on this question, several of which use administrative data and pre/post designs on firms and individuals (Kim and Ouimet [2008]; Sesil et al. [2007]; Blasi, Conte, and Kruse [1996]; Kardas, Scharf, and Keogh [1998]; Kruse [1998]; Renaud, St-Onge, and Magnan [2004]; and others reviewed in Handel and Gittleman [2004], and Kruse [1993, 113–14]). If this is true, in the long run shared capitalism firms must be getting productivity increases, because there is no other way for a competitive firm to pay for the "gravy" aspects of the compensation package. The evidence presented here shows a number of performance benefits, such as decreased turnover, increased loyalty, increased monitoring of shirkers, increased willingness to work harder for the firm, and increased investments in formal and informal training. This is consistent with efficiency wage theory in which higher compensation levels can essentially pay for themselves through higher productivity. In particular, the gift exchange version of efficiency wage theory shows how firms can provide a "gift" of high compensation that raises worker morale, and workers reciprocate with a "gift" of greater productivity (Akerlof 1982). The message sent by a "gift" of profit sharing, stock, or options on top of regular pay and benefits may be especially good for creating and reinforcing a sense of common interest and the value of a reciprocal relationship. In addition, the increased performance benefits are consistent with known evidence about the role of high performance work practices, which complement and strengthen the gift exchange. The lower supervision that is optimal under shared capitalism and such work practices may create an opportunity to save on supervisory costs, which itself increases productivity.

The higher compensation associated with shared capitalism helps address financial risk concerns. Risk is obviously an important issue when variable pay (of any sort) is substituting for fixed pay, and risk-averse people will require a risk premium (higher average pay) to compensate for the added risk. We find that the shared capitalism package generally includes more than enough compensation for the added risk associated with variable pay—it provides gravy even after taking the extra risk into account, as shown by the reduced turnover intentions. Some firms combine lower risk forms of shared capitalism—such as profit sharing and gain sharing and stock options—with higher risk forms of shared capitalism—such as those based on buying company stock with worker savings. Even when shared capitalism is not gravy, portfolio theory suggests that shared capitalism can be part of a prudently-diversified portfolio if properly managed (chapter 3, this volume). Having a separate diversified retirement plan in addition to an employee ownership plan, being paid above market wages, and not funding employee stock ownership using worker savings, can all play a role in minimizing risk. So concerns over financial risk can be overcome: it is striking that even the most risk-averse workers are likely to prefer some shared capitalism in their pay (chapter 1, this volume).

The higher compensation may also help address the free rider problem. Workers may reciprocate the extra compensation from shared capitalism by wanting to "keep work standards high," which was one of the most common reasons cited by shared capitalism employees for taking action against shirkers. Keeping standards high is part of the "gift" that workers give to firms in return for higher compensation, helping substitute for close supervision. Unlike a simple increase in fixed pay, shared capitalism can also create norms for reciprocity among workers, since workers collectively will benefit from higher performance (another common reason for taking action against shirkers is "poor performance will cost me and other employees in bonus or stock value"). The finding that close supervision is counterproductive when combined with shared capitalism is consistent with this interpretation—close supervision may send a mixed message that undermines the gift exchange understanding of the employment relationship.

The complementarity between shared capitalism and other human resource policies is an important part of our story. Overall these results show that shared capitalism can have positive effects on workplace performance and worker outcomes, but one does not automatically get these effects by simply installing a shared capitalism plan. The context matters greatly. The effects are more likely and more pronounced when shared capitalism is extended to workers who are not closely supervised and who are covered by high performance policies like employee involvement and training. This makes sense: shared capitalism provides some financial motivation, but this motivation will make little difference if workers do not have the opportunities and skills to improve workplace performance. High performance policies can provide these opportunities and skills, and help to create a more cooperative gift-exchange culture in which workers share information and discourage free riding. One implication is that the benefits from adopting a high performance policy like employee involvement or training will depend on what other policies are already in place, or are being adopted at the same time.

Such complementarity is strongly supported by recent research on how bundles of high performance work practices can reduce turnover, increase, productivity, and improve the stock market performance of firms. The idea is that the human resource policies and practices of the firm work better when they form a coherent whole; namely, when selection and recruitment, training, work organization, performance management, and reward systems are all pulling in the same direction and are integrated with the strategy of the firm. A significant body of evidence and thought laying out this effect now exists (see Huselid [1995]; Ichniowski, Shaw, and Prennushi [1997], Jackson and Schuler [1995]; Appelbaum et al. [2000]; and the meta-analysis in Combs et al. [2006]). This fits with a major theme of this book: that employees should not simply be provided shared capitalist incentives without a supporting group of firm policies and practices to engage them in taking greater responsibility for the welfare of the firm. Throughout the studies included in this volume, we consistently see that bundles of human resource policies that support high performance play a strong complementary role together with shared capitalist practices. This finding cuts across the different data sets, countries, and outcomes under study.

The broad spread of shared capitalism across industries and different types of jobs is consistent with a gift-exchange/reciprocity and supportive corporate culture interpretation. If shared capitalism were implemented primarily for one narrow purpose, such as to reduce turnover or to motivate creative activity that is hard to monitor, then its effects would likely show up only in particular industries, firms, or jobs where it serves that purpose best. As shown in chapter 1, however, while the prevalence of shared capitalism varies by industry, with the highest level in the computer services industry, shared capitalism is well-represented throughout the economy. This is not consistent with the notion that shared rewards will only work in particular niches or for particular groups. Rather, it indicates that shared capitalism can be useful wherever workers have some discretion in how they do their jobs. Such discretion appears to be widespread—in fact, close to 85 percent of employees in the General Social Survey (GSS) report that it is very or somewhat true that they have a lot of freedom to decide how to do their work. This figure varies little by major industry or occupation, and is above 80 percent even for blue-collar workers. If one takes this at face value, 85 percent of employees have a "gift" they can give to the company, by using their discretion in ways that can help the company. This gift can be given in reciprocal exchange for the higher compensation, training, employee participation in decisions, job security, and other worker benefits that we have found to be part of the shared capitalism package. As long as employees have some discretion in how they do their jobs, such a gift exchange is a possibility. Viewed in this way, it is not surprising that firms across the economy have implemented shared capitalism, and that nearly half of all workers participate in some form of shared capitalism.

The ideas of gift exchange and reciprocity may also help to explain the high prevalence of shared capitalism plans in large firms. Viewed strictly from the perspective of the free rider problem, the higher prevalence of shared capitalism in large firms is a puzzle, since theory and evidence indicate that the free rider problem is worse there than in small firms. The puzzle might be partly explained by the fixed costs of setting up plans, which can be spread across a larger number of participants in large firms. But if the free rider problem is overwhelming in large firms, why set up shared capitalism plans at all? What good are they, even if the fixed costs can be spread around? The answer seems to be that shared capitalism plans can help performance even in very large companies. For example, a pre/post comparison using productivity data and matched pairs of similar firms found significant productivity increases among firms adopting profit-sharing plans that had more than 12,000 employees as well as among smaller firms (Kruse 1993). Such a result makes no sense from the perspective of the free rider problem (each worker gets only 1/12,000th of the profits from his or her increased effort), but can make sense if the workers are responding with reciprocity to a new plan that is perceived to be generous to workers. In effect, it appears that shared capitalism and a complementary culture may allow large firms to function like smaller firms.

The idea of bundles of high performance work practices may also help to explain why employee perceptions of greater influence, lower levels of supervision, the presence of teams, and employer-sponsored training are more common with some types of shared capitalism. (chapter 1). It would appear that some managers have found the right way to imbed shared capitalist practices into their organizational culture, or conversely, to alter that culture to complement shared capitalist modes of pay. When managers combine various forms of shared capitalism, as is common, they are also combining the work practices that are usual with each type of reward sharing. (It is nonetheless the case that simply observing what firms do does not necessarily tell us what may be optimal.)

In sum, we think gift exchange/reciprocity and high performance work practices play a large part in explaining the positive effects of shared capitalism for both employers and workers. Workers seem to generally respond well to shared capitalism when it is perceived as coming on top of standard pay and benefits, and is connected to high performance policies such as employee involvement, training, and job security that gives workers extra skills, opportunities, and incentives for higher work standards. Close supervision, however, sends a contrary message that undercuts norms of reciprocity and the potential for better performance.

Two Scenarios of Shared Capitalism

Taken as a whole, the empirical results of this research suggests two scenarios of shared capitalism, one that is more likely to optimize its advantages for firms and workers and one that is less likely to do so.

One can characterize the more optimal shared capitalism as having these characteristics:

- Fixed wages at or above the market rate.
- Combinations of shared capitalism that balance more and less risky approaches and reduce wage substitution by avoiding financing shared capitalism with worker savings.
- Training, employee involvement in decision making, job security, and other complementary high performance work practices.
- Low supervision of workers.
- Prudent diversification of worker wealth.
- Retirement plans in addition to shared capitalism to protect workers' futures.
- Higher than average grades on employee-management relations and trust in management.

One can characterize the less optimal shared capitalism as having these characteristics:

- Pay below the market rate.
- Combinations of shared capitalism that shift risk to workers by financing shared capitalism with lower wages and out of worker savings.
- Lack of complementary high performance work practices.
- Close supervision of workers.
- Imprudent diversification of worker wealth.
- Lack of retirement plans in addition to shared capitalism to protect workers' futures.
- Lower than average grades on employee-management relations and trust in management.

Implications for Social Science Analysis of Economic Behavior

As these studies show, shared capitalism directly engages several fundamental issues in economic theory. Many if not most economists will be surprised by the current wide prevalence of shared capitalism documented in the recent GSS surveys. The broad prevalence and variety in shared capitalism arrangements make it a promising area of study for testing and elaborating existing theories, and developing new ones. Some of the fundamental issues involved in shared capitalism are:

- *Theory of the firm and principal-agent theory:* Under what conditions is it efficient for all profits to go to a central monitor (Alchian and Demsetz 1972)? How does this depend on the informational content of monitoring done by workers versus supervisors (Nalbantian 1987; Putterman and Skillman 1988)? In what ways might shared capitalism plans mitigate the myriad of principal-agent problems that exist throughout every organization? Can these plans work well only in companies where workers have homogeneous interests (Hansmann 1996)? How do these plans affect a range of investment, employment, and other issues debated in the traditional labor-managed firm literature (Dow 2003)?
- *Residual control and residual returns:* What does shared capitalism teach us about the broader issue of the benefits of matching residual control to residual returns, and how this should be done (Milgrom and Roberts 1992)? Employee involvement without any gain sharing may be efficiency-destroying—for example, employees in employee involvement plans may just make their jobs more comfortable (residual control without residual returns). Shared capitalism plans give some of the residual returns to a broad group of employees, which may be efficiency-enhancing only if these employees have significant discretion (residual control) in how they do their jobs.
- *Risk aversion and portfolio theory:* How can we learn from shared capitalism about how workers decide about alternatives involving risk and why and how this can aid or hurt their economic well-being? While behavioral finance is being applied to people's investments and other financial decisions, shared capitalism provides an interesting setting in which to examine millions of workers who confront decisions about and experience reactions to employee stock ownership, profit sharing, gain sharing, and broad-based stock options in the American workplace. The broad implications of behavioral decision theory for economics has been addressed by Kahneman (2003). We have only begun to explore the many questions raised by this important literature. The wealth portfolios of these millions of shared capitalist workers also involve important issues of portfolio theory (Markowitz 1959). How does the financial risk of shared capitalism fit into portfolio theory, and how can and do workers respond to and manage that risk? How does the

increased employment security with shared capitalism affect the financial risk? How do combinations of low risk and high risk shared capitalism programs help employees and employers manage such risk? What is the role of forms of employee stock ownership that are not funded by employee savings (such as ESOPs and company stock matches) in reducing the high risk of company stock ownership? How can shared capitalist programs be better structured for workers who have high economic insecurity?

- *Game theory and the free rider problem:* How can cooperative solutions to the "Prisoner's Dilemma" in game theory be established and maintained in market settings? What types of policies and relationships are needed?
- *Compensation theories:* How and when is shared capitalism a substitute or complement to other compensation methods such as efficiency wages, implicit contracts, tournaments, bonding, and deferred wages, particularly when information about workers and the work process is imperfect and supervision is costly?
- *Strategic human resource management:* Is the shared capitalism/complementary work culture scenario an optimal combination for most firms? Or does this depend on the strategy that each firm has for satisfying customers and creating profit? Are there firms where the potential positive effects of the complementary scenario are outweighed simply by concentrating most of the rewards in a very small group of special employees? Or is there a role for shared capitalism that broadly includes all employees yet also differentially and richly rewards top performers? That is, can the benefits of shared capitalism and a complementary corporate culture be obtained where there is broad shared capitalism and large differentiation of rewards at the same time?

Shared capitalism also raises issues central to social sciences other than economics. In the field of psychology, study of shared capitalism can also yield insights into the psychological contract between employees and employers, determining if and how employee attitudes and behavior are affected (Rousseau and Shperling 2003). For sociologists, shared capitalism can provide lessons about the functioning and effects of corporate culture, the effects of differential versus shared rewards on the position of social groups within organizations and society, and whether the distribution of power, prestige, and rewards in social organizations are amenable to change that maintains efficiency of performance while reducing inequality. For political scientists, shared capitalism involves issues of social capital (Putnam 2000) and the spillover effects of workplace decision making on broader political participation and engagement (Pateman 1970; Mason 1982; Dahl 1985). It raises questions of political economy and the design of public policy. For example, are there governmental and legislative levers that can advance shared capitalism in a way that maximize its advantages to society while minimizing its disadvantages, if that were a political goal of a society?

In sum, shared capitalism provides a rich opportunity for social scientists to address these and many other questions that touch on basic theories about how people live and work together. Our findings and those of others working in this area show that shared capitalism has met the market test of surviving and prospering in a competitive economy that J. B. Clark posed for it over a century ago. There still remains much to be learned about this fascinating and important part of the capitalist world. We look forward to seeing future analyses of the shared capitalist story, using better data, more sophisticated econometrics, field and lab experiments, and stronger theoretical models than those we have employed. We also look forward to learning more from firms about their experiences with this innovative form of arranging work and pay.

References

Akerlof, G. 1982. Labor contracts as partial gift exchange. *Quarterly Journal of Economics* 97 (4): 543–69.

Alchian, A. A., and H. Demsetz. 1972. Production, information costs, and economic organization. *American Economic Review* 62 (5): 777–95.

Appelbaum, E., T. Bailey, P. Berg, and A. Kalleberg. 2000. *Manufacturing advantage: Why high-performance work systems pay off.* Ithaca, NY: Cornell University Press.

Axelrod, R. 1984. *The evolution of cooperation.* New York: Basic Books.

Blasi, J., M. Conte and D. Kruse. 1996. Employee stock ownership and corporate performance among public companies. *Industrial and Labor Relations Review* 50 (1): 60–80.

Combs, J., Y. Liu, A. A. Hall, and D. Ketchen. 2006. How much do high-performance work practices matter? A meta-analysis of their effects on organizational performance. *Personnel Psychology* 59 (October): 501–28.

Dahl, R. 1985. *A preface to economic democracy.* Berkeley, CA: University of California Press.

Dow, G. 2003. *Governing the firm: Workers' control in theory and practice.* Cambridge: Cambridge University Press.

Fehr, E., and S. Gachter. 2000. Fairness and retaliation: The economics of reciprocity. *Journal of Economic Perspectives* 14 (3): 159–81.

Gintis, H., S. Bowles, R. Boyd, and E. Fehr, eds. 2005. *Moral sentiments and material interests: The foundation of cooperation in economic life.* Cambridge, MA: MIT Press.

Handel, M., and M. Gittleman. 2004. Is there a wage payoff to innovative practices? *Industrial Relations* 43 (1): 67–97.

Hansmann, H. 1996. *The ownership of enterprise.* Cambridge, MA: Harvard University Press.

Huselid, M. 1995. The impact of human resource management practices on the turnover, productivity, and corporate financial performance. *Academy of Management Journal* 38:635–72.

Ichniowski, C., K. Shaw, and G. Prennushi. 1997. The effects of human resource management practices on productivity: A study of steel finishing lines. *American Economic Review* 87 (3): 291–313.

Jackson, S., and R. S. Schuler. 1995. Understanding human resource management in the context of organizations and their environments. *Annual Review of Psychology* 46 (January): 237–64.

Kahneman, D. 2003. A psychological perspective on economics. *American Economic Review* 92 (2): 161–68.

Kardas, P., A. Scharf, and J. Keogh. 1998. Wealth and income consequences of ESOPs and employee ownership: A comparative study from Washington state. *Journal of Employee Ownership Law and Finance* 10 (4): 3–52.

Kim, E. H., and P. Ouimet. 2008. Employee capitalism or corporate socialism? Broad-based employee stock ownership. Working Paper. Ross School of Business, University of Michigan, October.

Kruse, D. 1993. *Profit sharing: Does it make a difference?* Kalamazoo, MI: W. E. Upjohn Institute for Employment Research.

———. 1998. Profit sharing and the demand for low-skill workers. In *Generating jobs: Increasing the demand for low-skill workers,* ed. R. Freeman and P. Gottschalk, 105–53. New York: Russell Sage Foundation.

Markowitz, H. M. 1959. *Portfolio selection: Efficient diversification of investments.* New York: Wiley.

Mason, R. 1982. *Participatory and workplace democracy: A theoretical development in critique of liberalism.* Carbondale and Edwardsville, IL: Southern Illinois University Press.

Milgrom, P., and J. Roberts. 1992. *Economics, organization, and management.* Englewood Cliffs, NJ: Prentice Hall.

Nalbantian, H. 1987. Incentive compensation in perspective. In *Incentives, cooperation, and risk sharing,* ed. H. Nalbantian, 3–46. Totowa, NJ: Rowman and Littlefield.

Pateman, C. 1970. *Participation and democratic theory.* New York: Cambridge University Press.

Putnam, R. 2000. *Bowling alone: The collapse and revival of American community.* New York: Simon and Schuster.

Putterman, L., and G. Skillman, Jr. 1988. The incentive effects of monitoring under alternative compensation schemes. *International Journal of Industrial Organization* 6 (1): 109–19.

Renaud, S., S. St-Onge, and M. Magnan. 2004. The impact of stock purchase plan participation on workers' individual cash compensation. *Industrial Relations* 43 (1): 120–47.

Rousseau, D. M., and Z. Shperling. 2003. Pieces of the action: Ownership and the changing employment relationship. *Academy of Management Review* 28 (4): 115–34.

Sesil, J., M. Kroumova, D. Kruse, and J. Blasi. 2007. Broad-based employee stock options in the United States: Company performance and characteristics. *Management Revue* 18 (2): 5–22.

Appendix A
Variable Definitions and Descriptive Statistics (All Chapters)

Categories of Variables

Compensation

1. Shared capitalism
2. Pay and benefits

Work Organization

3. Employee participation in decisions
4. Training
5. Supervision
6. High performance work practices
7. Other work organization measures

Worker Attitudes and Behavior

8. Job satisfaction and company treatment of employees
9. Co-worker relations
10. Job security and expectations
11. Responding to shirking
12. Innovation outcomes
13. Other performance-related attitudes and behavior
14. Risk aversion and preferences over pay

1. Shared Capitalism

Shared capitalism index (GSS): Eight-point index with one point each for profit-sharing eligibility, gain-sharing eligibility, owning any company stock, holding any stock options, receiving a profit-sharing bonus in the past year, receiving a gain-sharing bonus in the past year, having an above-median profit- and gain-sharing bonus as a percent of pay, and having an above-median company stock holding as a percent of pay. Mean = 1.48, s.d. = 2.14, n = 1,919.

Shared capitalism index (NBER): Ten-point index with all items in GS index, plus one point each for receiving a stock option grant in the past year, and having above-median stock option holdings as a percent of pay. Mean = 3.60, s.d. = 2.65, n = 40,522. Chapter 7's mean for company with innovation data = 2.59, s.d. = 1.85, n = 27,507.

Profit sharing (GSS and NBER): "In your job are you eligible for any type of performance-based pay, such as individual or group bonuses, or any type of profit sharing? What does the size of these performance-based payments depend on? Company profits or performance?" (0 = no, 1 = yes), GSS mean = .372, n = 2,184, NBER mean = 713, n = 41,018.

Profit sharing as percent of pay (GSS and NBER): If "yes" to profit sharing, answer to "What was the approximate total dollar value of the payment(s) you received [in the most recent year of bonuses]?" divided by basepay + overtime, otherwise 0. GSS mean = .024, s.d. = .066, n = 1,944, NBER mean = .068, s.d. = .124, n = 40,485.

Gain sharing (GSS and NBER): "In your job are you eligible for any type of performance-based pay, such as individual or group bonuses, or any type of profit sharing? What does the size of these performance-based payments depend on? Work group or department performance?" (0 = no, 1 = yes), GSS mean = .257, n = 2,184, NBER mean = .207, n = 41,023.

Gain sharing as percent of pay (GSS and NBER): If "yes" to gain sharing, answer to "What was the approximate total dollar value of the payment(s) you received [in the most recent year of bonuses]?" divided by basepay + overtime, otherwise 0. GSS mean = .017, s.d. = .061, n = 2,013, NBER mean = .033, s.d. = .106, n = 40,767.

Profit/gain sharing (NBER company with innovation data in chapter 7): If "yes" to receives profits based on "company profits or performance" and/or "Workgroup or department performance" (0 = no, 1 = yes). Mean = .74, s.d. = .441, n = 27,676.

Profit/gain sharing as percent of base pay (NBER company with innovation data in chapter 7): If "yes" to receive profits based on "company profits or performance" and/or "Work group or department performance," answer to "What was the approximate total dollar value of the payment(s) you received [in the most recent year of bonuses]?" divided by basepay + overtime, otherwise 0. Mean = .043, s.d. = .090, n = 27,420.

Individual bonus (GSS and NBER): "In your job are you eligible for any type of performance-based pay, such as individual or group bonuses, or any type of profit sharing? What does the size of these performance-based payments depend on? Individual performance?" (0 = no, 1 = yes). GSS mean = .290, n = 2,184, NBER mean = .290, n = 41,019. Chapter 7's mean for company with innovation data = .140, s.d. = .343, n = 27,676.

Individual bonus as percent of pay (NBER): If "yes" to individual bonus, answer to "What was the approximate total dollar value of the payment(s) you received [in the most recent year of bonuses]?" divided by basepay + overtime, otherwise 0. Mean = .050, s.d. = .125, n = 40,547. Chapter 11's mean for company with innovation data = .013, s.d. = .064, n = 27,609.

Hold employer stock (GSS): "Do you own any shares of stock in the company where you now work, either directly or through some type of retirement or stock plan?" (0 = no, 1 = yes), mean = .212, n = 2,202.

Employer stock as percent of pay (GSS): If "yes" to "hold employer stock," answer to "Please give a general estimate of how much cash you would get if all this stock were sold today?" divided by annual earnings, otherwise 0, mean = .111, s.d. = .977, n = 2,186.

Hold employer stock (NBER): Any employer stock held through ESOP, Employee Stock Purchase Plan, 401(k), exercised stock options, or open market purchases (0 = no, 1 = yes), mean = .640, n = 41,206. Chapter 7's mean for company with innovation data = .53, s.d. = .499, n = 27,825.

Employer stock as percent of pay (NBER): If "yes" to "Hold employer stock," the sum of answers to questions about value of stock held in different plans, divided by basepay + overtime, otherwise 0. NBER mean = .398, s.d. = .808, n = 40,367. Chapter 7's mean for company with innovation data = .227, s.d. = .476, n = 27,469.

Hold stock options (GSS and NBER): "Do you currently hold any stock options in your company (vested or unvested)?" (0 = no, 1 = yes), GSS mean = .123, n = 2,188, NBER mean = .219, n = 41,166. Chapter 7's mean for company with innovation data = .03, s.d. = .179, n = 27,816.

Stock options as percent of pay (NBER): If "yes" to "Hold stock options," the sum of answers to questions about value of vested and unvested stock, divided by basepay + overtime, otherwise 0. NBER mean = .395, s.d. = 1.490, n = 40,922. Chapter 7's mean for company with innovation data = .018, s.d. = .225, n = 27,716.

ESOP (NBER): Participant in ESOP (0 = no, 1 = yes), mean = .081, n = 41,109.

ESOP stock as percent of pay (NBER): Employer stock held in ESOP, divided by basepay + overtime, otherwise 0, mean = .067, s.d. = .417, n = 41,002.

ESPP (NBER): Hold stock purchased through Employee Stock Purchase Plan (0 = no, 1 = yes), mean = .176, n = 41,169.

ESPP stock as percent of pay (NBER): Employer stock held in Employee Stock Purchase Plan, divided by basepay + overtime, otherwise 0, mean = .078, s.d. = .304, n = 41,168.

401(k) stock (NBER): Hold employer stock in 401(k) plan (0 = no, 1 = yes), mean = .335, n = 40,885.

401(k) stock as percent of pay (NBER): Employer stock held in 401(k) plan, divided by basepay + overtime, otherwise 0, mean = .189, s.d. = .525, n = 40,730.

Stock from exercised options as percent of pay (NBER): Employer stock held from exercised options, divided by basepay + overtime, otherwise 0, mean = .052, s.d. = .396, n = 40,956.

Stock from exercised options (NBER): Hold employer stock from exercised options (0 = no, 1 = yes), mean = .050, n = 41,032.

Open mkt. stock as percent of pay (NBER): Employer stock purchased on open market, divided by basepay + overtime, otherwise 0, mean = .019, s.d. = .165, n = 41,144.

Open market stock (NBER): Hold stock purchased on open market (0 = no, 1 = yes), mean = .073, n = 41,145.

2. Pay and Benefits

Yearly earnings (GSS): Total yearly earnings from main job (natural log), mean = 10.12, s.d. = 1.05, n = 1,888.

Paid what you deserve (GSS): "How fair is what you earn on your job in comparison to others doing the same type of work you do?" (1–5 scale, 1 = much less than what you deserve, 5 = much more than you deserve), mean = 3.43, s.d. = .86, n = 2,171.

Fringe benefits good (GSS): "My fringe benefits are good." (1–4 scale, 1 = not at all true, 4 = very true), mean = 2.87, s.d. = 1.09, n = 2,198.

Fixed pay (NBER): Yearly base pay + overtime (natural log), mean = 10.710, s.d. = .783, n = 31,162.

Fixed pay difference from market (NBER): "Do you believe your fixed annual wages are higher or lower than those of employees with similar experience and job descriptions in other companies in your region? By what percent is it higher or lower?" mean = –4.76, s.d. = 17.10, *n* = 31,793.

Fixed pay at or above market (NBER): "Do you believe your fixed annual wages are higher or lower than those of employees with similar experience and job descriptions in other companies in your region?" (rated on scale of 1 = lower to 5 = higher, recoded for this variable as 0 = less than 3, 1 = 3 or greater), mean = 594, *n* = 35,860.

Total compensation difference from market (NBER): "Do you believe your total compensation is higher or lower than those of employees with similar experience and job descriptions in other companies in your region? By what percent is it higher or lower?" mean = –2.07, s.d. = 18.81, *n* = 30,440.

Grade of company on wages (NBER): "If you were to rate how well this company takes care of workers on a scale similar to school grades, what grade would you give in these areas? Paying good wages." (0–4 scale, 0 = *F*, 4 = *A*), mean = 2.54, s.d. = 1.06, *n* = 40,679.

Grade of company on benefits (NBER): "If you were to rate how well this company takes care of workers on a scale similar to school grades, what grade would you give in these areas? Giving fair benefits to workers" (0–4 scale, 0 = *F*, 4 = *A*), mean = 2.64, s.d. = 1.08, *n* = 40,611.

3. Employee Participation in Decisions

Lot of say on job (GSS): "I have a lot of say about what happens on my job" (1–4 scale, 1 = strongly disagree, 4 = strongly agree), mean = 2.83, s.d. = .88, *n* = 2,204. (In chapter 1, "*Lot of say on job*" is coded 1 for "strongly agree" and 0 otherwise.)

Make decisions with others (GSS): "In your job, how often do you take part with others in making decisions that affect you?" (1–4 scale, 1 = never, 4 = often), mean = 3.08, s.d. = .93, *n* = 2,211. (In chapter 1, "*Often make decisions with others*" is coded 1 for "often" and 0 otherwise.)

Help set way things done on job (GSS): "How often do you participate with others in helping set the way things are done on your job?" (1–4 scale, 1 = never, 4 = often), mean = 3.14, s.d. = .92, *n* = 2,210. (In chapter 1, "*Often help set way things done on job*" is coded 1 for "often" and 0 otherwise.)

High participation in decision (GSS): This measure has a score of 1 if the sum of scales of the previous two items is 7 or 8, and 0 otherwise. Mean = .466, *n* = 2,226.

Participation index (GSS): Average of "Often help set way things done on job," "Often make decisions with others," and binary measure of "Lot of say on job" (alpha = .737).

Freedom in doing work (GSS): "I am given a lot of freedom to decide how to do my own work." (1–4 scale, 1 = not at all true, 4 = very true), mean = 3.31, s.d. = .85, *n* = 2,208.

In EI team (NBER): "Some companies have organized workplace decision-making in ways to get more employee input and involvement. Are you personally involved in any team, committee, or task force that addresses issues such as product quality, cost cutting, productivity, health and safety, or other workplace issues?" (0 = no, 1 = yes), mean = .35, *n* = 40,122.

Involved in job decisions (NBER): "How much involvement and direct influence do YOU have in: Deciding HOW to do your job and organize the work?" (1–4 scale, 1 = none, 4 = a lot), mean = 3.27, s.d. = .87, *n* = 40,750. (In chapter 1, "*Lot of involvement in job decisions*" is coded 1 for "a lot" and 0 otherwise.)

Involved in department goals (NBER): "How much involvement and direct influence do YOU have in: Setting GOALS for your work group or department" (1–4 scale, 1 = none, 4 = a lot), mean = 2.59, s.d. = 1.04, *n* = 40,594. (In chapter 1, "*Lot of involvement in setting department goals*" is coded 1 for "a lot" and 0 otherwise.)

Involved in company decisions (NBER): "How much involvement and direct influence do YOU have in: Overall company decisions?" (1–4 scale, 1 = none, 4 = a lot), mean = 1.71, s.d. = .86, *n* = 40,520. (In chapter 1, "*Lot of involvement in company decisions*" is coded 1 for "a lot" and 0 otherwise.)

Satisfied with participation (NBER): "Overall, how satisfied are you with the influence you have in company decisions that affect your job and work life?" (1–4 scale, 1 = not at all satisfied, 4 = very satisfied), mean = 2.61, s.d. = .85, *n* = 40,545.

4. Training

Training opportunities (GSS): "I have the training opportunities I need to perform my job safely and competently." (1–4 scale, 1 = not at all true, 4 = very true), mean = 3.48, s.d. = .74, *n* = 2,204.

Formal training (NBER): "In the last twelve months have you received any formal training from your current employer, such as in classes or seminars sponsored by the employer?" (0 = no, 1 = yes), mean = .564, *n* = 40,460.

Training hours (NBER): If "yes" to formal training, answer to "About how many hours of formal training have you received in the last twelve months? If "no" to formal training, coded as 0. Mean = 17.80, s.d. = 40.38, *n* = 39,426.

Informal training (NBER): "To what extent have fellow employees taught you job skills, problem solving, short cuts, or other ways to improve your work, on an informal basis?" (1–4 scale, 1 = not at all, 4 = to a great extent), mean = 2.89, s.d. = .85, n = 40,651.

5. Supervision

Supervisor helpful (GSS): "My supervisor is helpful to me in getting the job done." (1–4 scale, 1 = not at all true, 4 = very true), mean = 3.26, s.d. = .88, n = 2,197.

Supervisor cares (GSS): "My supervisor is concerned about the welfare of those under him or her." (1–4 scale, 1 = not at all true, 4 = very true), mean = 3.26, s.d. = .88, n = 2,185.

Closeness of supervision (NBER): "Are you closely supervised, or do you work fairly independently of close supervision?" (0–10 scale, 0 = independent of close supervision, 10 = closely supervised), mean = 3.35, s.d. = 2.63, n = 40,845 (reverse-scored for chapter 1 measure, "*Free from supervision*").

6. High Performance Work Practices

High performance policy index (NBER)(index mean = 1.77, s.d. = .86, n = 37,125):

Additive index of:

a) Employee involvement team: "Some companies have organized workplace decision-making in ways to get more employee input and involvement. Are you personally involved in any team, committee, or task force that addresses issues such as product quality, cost cutting, productivity, health and safety, or other workplace issues?" (0 = no, 1 = yes), mean = .347, n = 40,122.

b) Formal training: "In the last twelve months have you received any formal training from your current employer, such as in classes or seminars sponsored by the employer?" (0 = no, 1 = yes), mean = .564, n = 40,460.

c) Job security: "Thinking about the next twelve months, how likely do you think it is that you will lose your job or be laid off?" (coded for scale as 0 = very likely or fairly likely, 1 = not too likely or not at all likely), mean = .843, n = 38,510.

High performance work system (HPWS) (NBER company with innovation data, chapter 7): Mean of following six binary items:

a) "Are you personally involved in any team, committee, or task force that addresses issues such as product quality, cost cutting, productivity, health and safety, or other workplace issues?" (0 = no, 1 = yes).

b) "In the last twelve months have you received any formal training from your current employer, such as in classes or seminars sponsored by the employer?" (0 = no, 1 = yes).

c) "How frequently do you participate in a job rotation or cross-training program where you work or are trained on a job with different duties than your regular job?" (0 = never or occasionally, 1 = frequently).

d) "How effective is your work area or team at selecting the very best people to be part of our team/area?" (based on 1–7 scale, item coded as 0 = ineffective or neutral [1 to 4], 1 = effective [5 to 7]).

e) "Thinking about the next twelve months, how likely do you think it is that you will lose your job or be laid off?" (0 = very or somewhat likely, 1 = not very or not at all likely).

f) "How effective is your work area or team at sharing information and ideas with each other?" (based on 1–7 scale, item coded as 0 = ineffective or neutral [1 to 4]), 1 = effective [5 to 7]).

Index mean = .46, s.d. = .240, n = 27,801, alpha = .46.

High performance work system team (HPWST) (NBER company with innovation data, chapter 7): Mean of following items, all measured on a 1–7 scale (1 = very ineffective, 4 = neutral, 7 = very ineffective).

a) "How effective is your work area or team at selecting the very best people to be part of our team/area?"

b) "How effective is your work area or team at setting clear performance goals?"

c) "How effective is your work area or team at getting training on skills we need to solve customer problems?"

d) "How effective is your work area or team at sharing information and ideas with each other?"

e) "How effective is your work area or team at meeting our customers either in our facilities or theirs?"

f) "How effective is your work area or team at rewarding members of the group for excellent work?"

Index mean = 4.36, s.d. = 1.32, n = 27,251, alpha = .88.

7. Other Work Organization Measures

Work as part of team (GSS and NBER): "In your job, do you normally work as part of a team or group, or do you work mostly on your own?" (coded 1 if part of team, 0 otherwise), GSS mean = .58, n = 2,206, n = NBER mean = .59, n = 32,301.

Ease of observing co-worker performance (GSS and NBER): "In your job how easy is it for you to see whether your co-workers are working well or poorly? Please rate on a scale of 0 to 10." (0 = not at all easy, 10 = very easy), GSS mean = 7.71, s.d. = 3.18, n = 2,394; NBER mean = 6.81, s.d. = 2.73, n = 40,791.

Frequently participate in job rotation (NBER): "How frequently do you participate in a job rotation or cross-training program where you work or are trained on a job with different duties than your regular job?" (coded 1 if worker responded "frequently," and 0 otherwise), NBER mean = .112, n = 30,262.

Alignment: Mean of following items, all measured on a 1–4 scale (1 = not at all, 2 = very little, 3 = to some extent, 4 = to a great extent):

a) "To what extent do you understand your company's overall plan for being successful?"

b) "To what extent do you personally agree with this plan?"

c) "To what extent do you feel that the company is providing you with the information, training, and resources necessary to help achieve the goals of this plan?"

d) "To what extent do you feel that your company's culture encourages you to share your ideas about how to achieve the goals of this plan?"

Index mean = 2.87, s.d. = .686, n = 27,492, alpha = .83.

8. Job Satisfaction and Company Treatment of Employees

Job satisfaction (GSS): "All in all, how satisfied would you say you are with your job?" (1–4 scale, 1 = not at all satisfied, 4 = very satisfied), mean = 3.27, s.d. = .80, n = 1,656.

Job satisfaction (NBER): "How satisfied are you in your job?" (1–7 scale, 1 = completely dissatisfied, 7 = completely satisfied), mean = 5.04, s.d. = 1.29, n = 40,842.

Treated with respect (GSS): "At the place where I work, I am treated with respect" (1–4 scale, 1 = strongly disagree, 4 = strongly agree), mean = 3.27, s.d. = .68, n = 2,209.

Management-employee relations (GSS): "In general, how would you describe relations in your work place between management and employees?" (1–5 scale, 1 = very bad, 5 = very good), mean = 3.95, s.d. = .99, n = 2,205.

Management is trustworthy (GSS): "I trust the management at the place where I work." (1–4 scale, 1 = strongly disagree, 4 = strongly agree), mean = 2.97, s.d. = 0.85, n = 2,201.

Promotions handled fairly (GSS): "Promotions are handled fairly." (1–4 scale, 1 = not at all true, 4 = very true), mean = 2.84, s.d. = .98, n = 2,083.

Worker safety is high priority (GSS): "The safety of workers is a high priority with management where I work." (1–4 scale, 1 = not at all true, 4 = very true), mean = 3.31, s.d. = .70, *n* = 2,194.

Stress (GSS): "How often do you find your work stressful?" (1–5 scale, 1 = always, 5 = never), mean = 3.08, s.d. = 1.03, *n* = 2,209.

Employees share when company does well (NBER): "When the company does well, employees share the benefits." (1–7 scale, 1 = strongly disagree, 7 = strongly agree), mean = 5.00, s.d. = 1.78, *n* = 40,676.

Company fair to employees (NBER): "Overall, this company is fair to its employees." (1–7 scale, 1 = strongly disagree, 7 = strongly agree), mean = 4.75, s.d. = 1.71, *n* = 40,632.

Company grade on employee relations (NBER): "If you were to rate how well this company takes care of workers on a scale similar to school grades, what grade would you give in these areas? Overall relations with employees." (0–4 scale, 0 = *F*, 4 = *A*), mean = 2.45, s.d. = 1.07, *n* = 40,464.

Company grade on sharing info (NBER): "If you were to rate how well this company takes care of workers on a scale similar to school grades, what grade would you give in these areas? Sharing information with employees." (0–4 scale, 0 = *F*, 4 = *A*), mean = 2.44, s.d. = 1.11, *n* = 40,523.

Company grade on trustworthy (NBER): "If you were to rate how well this company takes care of workers on a scale similar to school grades, what grade would you give in these areas? Trustworthiness in keeping its promises." (0–4 scale, 0 = *F*, 4 = *A*), mean = 2.33, s.d. = 1.15, *n* = 40,385.

9. Co-Worker Relations

Co-workers can be relied on for help (GSS): "The people I work with can be relied on when I need help." (1–4 scale, 1 = not at all true, 4 = very true), mean = 3.37, s.d. = .75, *n* = 2,207.

Co-workers take personal interest in me (GSS): "The people I work with take a personal interest in me." (1–4 scale, 1 = not at all true, 4 = very true), mean = 3.21, s.d. = .82, *n* = 2,197.

10. Job Security and Expectations

Job security (GSS and NBER): "Thinking about the next twelve months, how likely do you think it is that you will lose your job or be laid off?" (1–4 scale, 1 = not at all likely, 4 = very likely), GSS mean = 3.27, s.d. = .87, *n* = 2,198, NBER mean = 3.09, s.d. = .76, *n* = 38,510.

High job security (GSS and NBER): "Thinking about the next twelve months, how likely do you think it is that you will lose your job or be laid off?" (coded 1 if "not at all likely" or "not very likely", and 0 otherwise), GSS mean = .883, n = 1,190; NBER mean = .843, n = 38,510.

Not laid off in past year (GSS): "Were you laid off your main job at any time in the last year?" (0 = yes, 1 = no), mean = .920, n = 2,212.

See myself working here a long time (NBER): "Which ONE of the following statements best describes how you think of your current employer? 1 = I see myself working here for the foreseeable future (a long time), 0 = I do not see myself working here very long." Mean = .817, n = 40,589.

Current job is part of long-time career (NBER): "Thinking about your current job (rather than your employer), do you look upon it as part of your long term career, or a position that is not part of your long term career?" (1 = yes, 0 = no) Mean = .762, n = 40,575.

11. Responding to Shirking

Potential employee actions against shirkers (GSS and NBER): "If you were to see a fellow employee not working as hard or well as he or she should, how likely would you be to:

a) Talk directly to the employee
b) Speak to your supervisor or manager
c) Talk about it in a work group or team
d) Do nothing"

See distribution of answers in chapter 2, table 2.1.

Anti-shirking index: Answers to previous questions were coded on a 1–4 scale (1 = not at all likely, 4 = very likely), and scales were added for "talk directly to the employee," "speak to your supervisor or manager," and "do nothing" (reverse-scored)(3–12 scale). GSS alpha = .795, mean = 7.81, s.d. = 2.94, n = 2,115, NBER alpha = .69, mean = 7.57, s.d. = 2.49, n = 35,869.

Past employee actions against shirkers (NBER):
"Have you ever seen one of your fellow employees not working as hard or well as he or she should over an extended time period?" (0 = no, 1 = yes), Mean = .586, n = 32,010. If responded "yes," then "What action, if any, did you take?

a) Talk directly to the employee
b) Speak to your supervisor or manager
c) Talk about it in a work group or team
d) Do nothing"

See distribution of answers in chapter 2, table 2.2.

"What was the outcome of your actions?

Employee not working well resented it
Other employees appreciated it
Supervisor appreciated it
Employee not working well improved
Other"

See distribution of answers in chapter 2, table 2.10.

Why people do or do not act against shirkers (NBER):
"Why might you be *likely to do something* when a fellow employee is not working as hard or well as he or she should? (Mark all that apply)

I like helping others
Employee might help me in the future
Poor performance will cost me and other employees in bonus or stock value
Other employees appreciate it when someone steps forward
Want to keep work standards high
Employee's poor performance could affect my own job
Other (What?)

Why might you be *likely to do nothing* when a fellow employee is not working as hard or well as he or she should? (Mark all that apply)

Employee not working well would resent it
Other employees would react poorly
It's the supervisor's job, not mine
Some other employee will probably take action
Some other employee could take care of it
There's no financial benefit for me
Nothing in it for me personally
Other (What?)

See distribution of answers in chapter 2, table 2.9.

12. Innovation Outcomes

Culture for Innovation: Mean of following items, all measured on a 1–4 scale (1 = never or almost never, 2 = sometimes, 3 = often, 4 = always or almost always).
"How often do the following things occur in your facility?"
a) "Ideas for developing innovative products and services are put forward."
b) "Meaningful time is invested in testing good ideas for innovative products and services."

c) "Innovative ideas are carefully considered and fairly evaluated."
d) "Resources are made available to support and develop a good idea that could lead to an innovative product or service."
e) "People who have an innovative idea receive recognition for it."
f) "People who have an innovative idea receive financial rewards for it."
g) "My ideas for innovative products and services have been taken seriously." Index mean = 2.87, s.d. = .626, *n* = 27,067, alpha = .86

Innovative Ideas: Mean of following items, all measured on a 1–4 scale (1 = not at all, 2 = very little, 3 = to some extent, 4 = to a great extent).
a) "I would be willing to be more involved in efforts to develop innovative products and services."
b) "I have good ideas for innovative products or services."
c) "I have good ideas for improvements in existing products and services."
Index mean = 2.74, s.d. = .731, *n* = 26,939, alpha = .83

13. Other Performance-Related Attitudes and Behavior

Not likely to search for new job (GSS): "How likely is it that you will decide to look hard for a job with another organization within the next twelve months?" (1–3 scale, Very likely/Somewhat likely/Not at all likely), mean = 2.37, s.d. = .79, *n* = 2,400.

Not likely to search for new job (NBER): "How likely is it that you will decide to look hard for a job with another organization within the next twelve months?" (1–4 scale, Already looking/Very likely/Somewhat likely/Not at all likely), mean = 3.42, s.d. = .83, *n* = 40,722.

Would turn down another job for more pay to stay with this company (NBER): "To what extent do you agree or disagree with this statement? 'I would turn down another job for more pay in order to stay with this company.'" (1–5 scale, 1 = strongly disagree, 5 = strongly agree), mean = 1.75, s.d. = 1.14, *n* = 1,175.

Absenteeism (NBER): "About how many days have you been absent from work in the last six months (not counting vacation)?" mean = 1.77, s.d. = 7.66, *n* = 39,582.

Co-worker effort (GSS and NBER): "At your workplace, how hard would you say that people work?" (0–10 scale, 0 = not at all hard, 10 = very hard), GSS mean = 6.93, s.d. = 2.42, *n* = 2,386, NBER mean = 7.07, s.d. = 2.10, *n* = 40,738.

Proud to be working for employer (GSS): "I am proud to be working for my employer." (1–4 scale, 1 = strongly disagree, 4 = strongly agree), mean = 3.19, s.d. = .69, *n* = 2,401.

Co-workers have enough interest in company issues to get involved (NBER): "People at [company] have too little interest in company-wide issues to get involved in them." (1–7 scale, 1 = strongly agree, 7 = strongly disagree), mean = 4.22, s.d. = 1.60, *n* = 40,563.

Co-workers generally encourage each other to make extra effort (NBER): "At your workplace, would you say employees generally ENCOURAGE each other to make an extra effort on the job, DISCOURAGE each other from making an extra effort, or would you say they DON'T CARE how hard other employees work?" (–1 = discourage, 0 = don't care, 1 = encourage), mean = .74, s.d. = .48, *n* = 13,314.

Loyalty to company (NBER): "How much loyalty would you say you feel toward the company you work for as a whole?" (1–4 scale, No loyalty at all/Only a little/Some/A lot), mean = 3.34, s.d. = .80, *n* = 40,091.

Willing to work harder to help company (NBER): "To what extent do you agree or disagree with this statement? 'I am willing to work harder than I have to in order to help the company I work for succeed?'" (1–5 scale, 1 = strongly disagree, 5 = strongly agree), mean = 4.02, s.d. = .90, *n* = 40,712.

Frequency of suggestions (NBER): "How often have you taken such ideas [for making your department or company more effective] to someone in the company in the past?" (1 = never, 2 = occasionally, 3 = monthly, 4 = weekly, 5 = daily), mean = 2.21, s.d. = .83, *n* = 31,141.

Summative outcomes variable (NBER): Additive index of "not likely to search for new job," "loyalty to company," "willing to work harder to help company," "see myself working here a long time," and "current job is part of long-time career," minus 3 so scale = 0–12 (used in chapter 3 on risk). Mean = 9.49, s.d. = 2.26, *n* = 33,467.

14. Risk Aversion and Preferences Over Pay

Risk loving (NBER): "Some people like to take risks and others dislike taking risks. Where would you place yourself on a scale of how much you like or dislike taking risks, where 0 is hating to take any kind of risk and 10 is loving to take risks?" (In chapter 1, High risk aversion = 0 to 3 on this scale, medium risk aversion = 4 to 6, and low risk aversion = 7 to 10.) Mean = 5.62, s.d. = 2.43, *n* = 40,326.

Highest price paid for a bet (NBER): "You are offered a bet. You have a 10 percent chance of winning $1,000. Would you take the bet if it cost you: (mark highest price you would pay: $0, $1, $10, $20, $50, $100, $150)." Mean = $23.37, s.d. = 32.40, *n* = 34,751.

Type of pay preferred (NBER): "If it was your choice and yours alone, would you prefer that you be paid: 0 = All fixed wage or salary, with no profit-sharing, company stock, or stock options; 1 = Paid in part with a variable amount dependent on company performance, through profit sharing, company stock, or stock options." Mean = .784, n = 13,199.

Preference for new bonus plan (NBER): "If your employer announced a new compensation plan that would give up to 10 percent of pay in the form of bonuses, would you like this pay to be based on (mark all that apply): Your individual performance (mean = .769, n = 13,379), Your work group performance (mean = .371, n = 13,379), Company profits or performance. (Mean = .585, n = 13,379.)

Would vote to sell company (NBER): "If you owned stock in a company where you worked and an outside investor offered to buy the company for 50 percent more than the market value of the stock, would you vote to sell the company?" Mean = .409, n = 13,188.

Lower pay accepted for company-based bonus (NBER): "Imagine that you work for a company that offers you the opportunity to participate in a bonus program. Over time, the bonus will pay you on average 10 percent of your regular pay, but it could be higher or lower in any given year depending on the company's performance that year. How much less regular pay would you be willing to accept in order to get the possible performance bonus?" Mean = 3.31, s.d. = 3.56, n = 29,246.

Preference for next pay increase (NBER): "For your next pay increase, would you prefer that it come in the form of: 1 = All fixed wages, with no profit sharing, company stock, or stock options; 2 = Split between fixed wages and profit sharing, company stock, or stock options; 3 = All in the form of profit sharing, company stock, or stock options." Mean = 1.86, s.d. = .62, n = 25,869.

Appendix B
The Shared Capitalist Thermometer Index

As a first step in assessing the relation of shared capitalism to employee outcomes, we constructed a thermometer-style index of shared capitalism. This index assigns one point each when the worker was covered by any of the shared capitalist forms of compensation about which the survey asked, with additional points for recent bonuses or grants, and for large bonuses or stock holdings. For questions with a continuous numeric answer, we gave the item a value of 1 if the respondent had a value greater than the median value. Because there is no natural ordering of shared capitalist systems in the sense that a firm first introduces profit sharing, then adds employee ownership, and then gain sharing, the index is not a Guttman scale. It is a simple summated rating (Bartholomew et al. 2002; Bartholomew 1996), using dichotomous scoring.

In the GSS, there are eight variables in the index: profit-sharing eligibility, gain-sharing eligibility, owning any company stock, holding stock options, receiving a profit-sharing bonus in the past year, receiving a gain-sharing bonus in the past year, having an above-median profit- and gain-sharing bonus as a percent of pay, and having an above-median company stock holding as a percent of pay. In the NBER data there are ten variables in the index: all of the aforementioned items plus one point each for receiving a stock option grant in the past year, and having above-median stock option holdings (including unvested options if they could be exercised today) as a percent of pay.

Indices of this style have both advantages and disadvantages. On the plus side, they provide a quick and ready measure of the extent of shared capitalist arrangements that makes it easy to compare results across surveys and to summarize the broad thrust of findings. Since our firm surveys covered

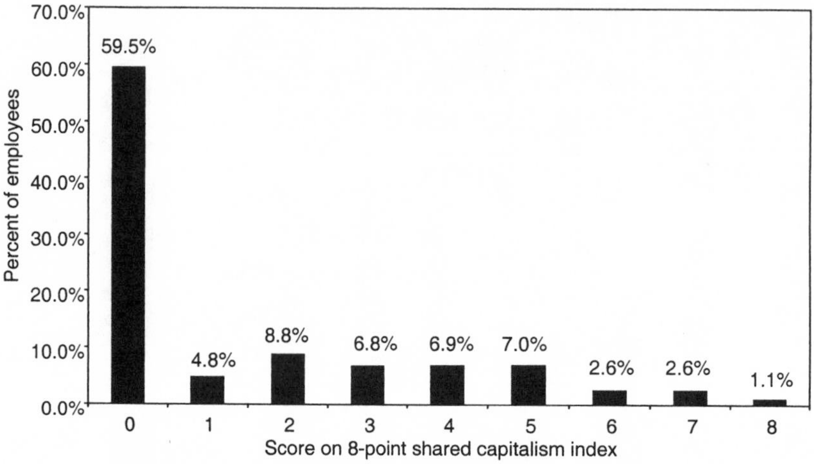

Fig. B1 Distribution of shared capitalism index in GSS

only firms with some shared capitalist arrangements, the index allows us to differentiate workers with differing degrees of incentive to their firm's programs. On the negative side, the index treats different programs the same even though they potentially have different effects on particular outcomes. It postulates a single scale with equal weights rather than using factor analysis or other statistical modelling to obtain weights for given factors. To deal with these problems, we also estimate the relationship of the outcomes to the different types of shared capitalism, introduced as dummy or continuous variables in regressions.[1] By comparing the results using the shared capitalism index to the results using the disaggregated measures, we can assess the loss of information due to the amalgamation of the measures into a single index.

Figure B1 shows the distribution of our shared capitalism index in the GSS. This survey estimates that 40 percent of US workers have some form of shared capitalist program. This estimate is close to that obtained by Dube and Freeman in the WRPS. The mean score of the index is 1.48—a figure greatly affected by the substantial number of workers without shared capitalism systems. Conditional on having a program, most workers report scores in the range of 2 to 5, with 6 percent reporting scores of 6 or greater. Figure B2 gives the distribution of the index in the NBER survey data. It also shows a nonnormal distribution, with the most common scores as 2 to 4 but a sizable number of workers scoring 7 or above. There is sufficient varia-

1. There are statistical techniques to deal with the formation of latent variable indices from questions of the sort that we are amalgamating into a single summated rating. See Bartholomew et al. (2002) and Spector (1992).

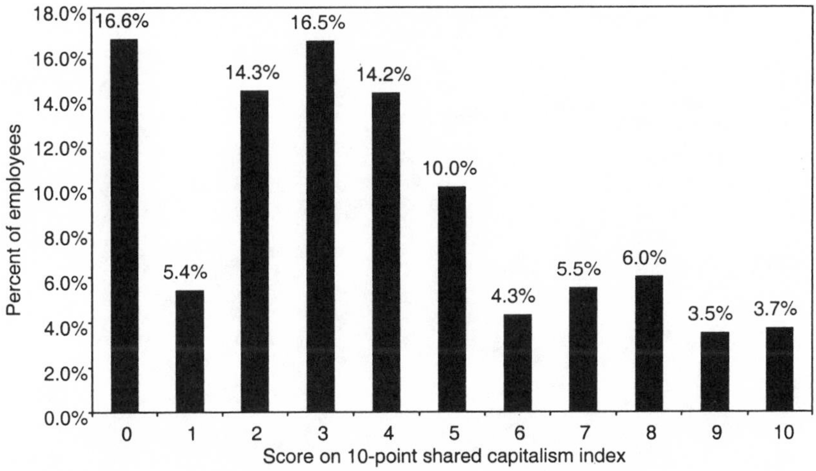

Fig. B2 Distribution of shared capitalism index in NBER companies

tion in the index to differentiate the extent of the shared capitalist "treatment" on workers.

References

Bartholomew, D. 1996. *The statistical approach to social measurement.* New York: Academic Press.

Bartholomew, D., J. Galbraith, I. Moustkaki, and F. Steele. 2002. *The analysis and interpretation of multivariate data for social scientists.* Chapman and Hall/CRC.

Spector, P. E. 1992. *Summated rating scale construction: An introduction (Quantitative Applications in Social Sciences, 82).* London: Sage.

Contributors

Joseph R. Blasi
Rutgers University
School of Management and Labor Relations
200 B Levin Building
94 Rockafeller Road
New Brunswick, NJ 08903

Alex Bryson
National Institute of Economic and Social Research
2 Dean Trench Street
Smith Square
London SW1P 3HE England

Robert Buchele
Department of Economics
Smith College
10 Prospect Street, # 103
Northampton, MA 01063

John W. Budd
Center for Human Resources and Labor Studies
University of Minnesota
3-300 Carlson School of Management
321 19th Avenue South
Minneapolis, MN 55455-0438

Edward J. Carberry
Department of Business-Society Management
Rotterdam School of Management
Erasmus University
Burgemeester Oudlaan 50, Room T07-15
3062PA Rotterdam, The Netherlands

Arindrajit Dube
Center on Wage and Employment Dynamics
Institute for Research on Labor and Employment
University of California, Berkeley
2521 Channing Way #5555
Berkeley, CA 94720-5555

Richard B. Freeman
Herbert A. Ascherman Chair
Department of Economics
Harvard University
National Bureau of Economic Research
1050 Massachusetts Avenue
Cambridge, MA 02138

Erika E. Harden
Rutgers University
School of Management and Labor Relations
94 Rockafeller Road
New Brunswick, NJ 08903

Douglas L. Kruse
School of Management and Labor Relations
Rutgers University
94 Rockafeller Road
Piscataway, NJ 08854

Harry M. Markowitz
Rady School of Management
University of California, San Diego
9500 Gilman Drive
La Jolla, CA 92093-0553

Christopher Mackin
Ownership Associates, Inc.
122 Mount Auburn Street
Cambridge, MA 02138

Rhokeun Park
College of Business Administration
Kwangwoon University
26 Kwangwoon-gil, Nowon-gu
Seoul, Korea 139-701

Loren Rodgers
The National Center for Employee Ownership (NCEO)
1736 Franklin Street, 8th Floor
Oakland, CA 94612

Adria Scharf
The Richmond Peace Education Center
400 W. 32nd Street
Richmond, VA 23225

Author Index

Subject Index

Page numbers followed by f *or* t *refer to figures or tables, respectively.*